The Global Virtual University

What will universities be like in the knowledge society of the future?

'Lalita Rajasingham and John Tiffin have brilliantly sketched a philosophical foundation for the future of the university in an era of rapid technological change and globalisation ... This book is essential reading for students and faculty within existing universities, and for policy makers whose major challenge will be to enable the learning society on a global scale.'

Professor Donald E. Hanna, University of Winconsin

This book is about the shift from the contemporary university of the nation state to the global virtual university of the future. The authors launched their idea of virtual universities on the Internet with the publication of *In Search of the Virtual Class: Education in an Information Society* in 1995. Since then, virtual universities have multiplied worldwide.

This book, based on material gathered from research projects carried out in Japan, Brazil, USA, Australia and New Zealand, describes key aspects of the global university and presents a paradigm from which it might be constructed.

As leading figures in this field, the authors argue that the universities of the future will be virtual, global and student centred, taking advantage of such technological advances as broadband telecommunications, artifical intelligence and HyperReality.

This unique visionary text will be critical reading for academics, postgraduate students, and for anyone involved in policy making and planning within the university community and administration.

John Tiffin is Emeritus Professor of Communications at Victoria University of Wellington, New Zealand. **Dr Lalita Rajasingham** is Senior Lecturer and Director of Graduate Programmes in Communications in the School of Information Management, Victoria University of Wellington, New Zealand.

The Global Virtual University

John Tiffin and
Lalita Rajasingham

RoutledgeFalmer
Taylor & Francis Group

LONDON AND NEW YORK

Learning Resources
Centre

12545201

First published 2003
by RoutledgeFalmer
11 New Fetter Lane, London EC4P 4EE

Simultaneously published in the USA and Canada
by RoutledgeFalmer
29 West 35th Street, New York, NY 10001

RoutledgeFalmer is an imprint of the Taylor & Francis Group

© 2003 John Tiffin and Lalita Rajasingham

Typeset in Times by
HWA Text and Data Management, Tunbridge Wells
Printed and bound in Great Britain by
Biddles Ltd, Guildford and King's Lynn

British Library Cataloguing in Publication Data
A catalogue record for this book is available from the British Library

Library of Congress Cataloging in Publication Data
Tiffin, John.
 The global virtual university / John Tiffin and Lalita Rajasingham.
  p. cm.
 Includes bibiographical references and index.
 1. Universities and colleges–Computer networks–Cross-cultural
 studies. 2. Virtual reality in higher education–Cross-cultural studies.
 3. University extension–Cross-cultural studies.
 I. Rajasingham, Lalita. II. Title.

LB2395.73T54 2003
378'.00285'4678–DC21

ISBN 0–415–28701–4 (hbk)
ISBN 0–415–28702–2 (pbk)

Contents

Illustrations

Figures

Tables

Foreword

This book, *The Global Virtual University* by John Tiffin and Lalita Rajasingham offers a magnificent virtual vision. But the vision is not utopian. It is armed with the marvels of the new communication and information technologies (CIT). It is also adorned with the rich regalia of an institution that has for centuries survived the vicissitudes of time and space. The vision contains breadth, depth, erudition, and realism. Engagingly, it also provides us with many staged virtual examples.

Tiffin and Rajasingham offer us a vision that responds to a desperate global need. That need has been dramatically demonstrated by the recent raging events and debates. Beginning with Samuel Huntington's *Clash of Civilisations* thesis (1993, 1996), the world has been intently focused on the North-South rather than the East-West conflicts of the Cold War era. It is also contemplating a possible bloody war of civilisations.

A burning international debate has ensued. Voices countering the Huntington thesis have been raised. Benjamin Barber (1995) has characterised the conflict as 'Jihad vs. McWorld'. I had called the same phenomenon a conflict between two current world pathologies: 'Identity vs. Commodity Fetishism' (Tehranian 1981). Edward Said (2001) has called Huntington's thesis 'a clash of ignorance', Tariq Ali (2002) has called it a clash of market and religious fundamentalisms. In 1996, the Toda Institute for Global Peace and Policy Research chose 'Dialogue of Civilisations for Global Citizenship' for its motto. Four years later, in 2000, the Institute brought together peace scholars from eight civilisations to engage each other in a serious dialogue. The results were later published in *Dialogue of Civilisations: A New Peace Agenda for the New Millennium*, including perspectives from Shamanism, Hinduism, Buddhism, Confucianism, Judaism, Christianity, Islam, and Secular Humanism. At the initiative of President Mohammad Khatami of Iran, the United Nations designated 2001 as the Year of Dialogue among Civilisations.

Ironically, however, 2001 coincided with the terrorist September 11 attack on the United States. That tragedy has ushered in a new era that threatens to pitch the world's rich against the world's poor in a global civil war. The clash could be, as Huntington has put it, 'between the West and the rest'. In a *New York Times* article, on November 27, 2002, Thomas Friedman dramatised 'the clash' with an imaginary letter from President George W. Bush to the Muslim world warning it of the dire consequences of its belligerence. In the meantime, a parallel war is being waged on all sides to match the war of words.

Are we facing a conflict of unabashed material interests such as the control of Middle East oil, irreconcilable confrontation of fanaticisms, or an unembellished clash of civilisations? All three factors are probably at work in a complex bundle to camouflage human greed and ignorance. 'Civilisation is a race between education and catastrophe', as H.G. Wells has so aptly put it. The challenge facing the world now is how to educate the globe's 6.2 billion people in avoiding future catastrophes. Such an education calls for a revival of the core values of compassion and enlightenment embedded in all great civilisations – East or West. But it also demands the development of the cognitive and professional skills needed for survival in a technologically driven world.

Tiffin and Rajasingham respond to this daunting challenge by calling for three concurrent transformations: in higher education, knowledge modalities, and civilisational boundaries.

Under the impact of CIT, the transformation in higher education has already begun. The explosion of virtual universities is threatening to overtake the functions of traditional universities. Eli Noam (1995) has argued that the end is near. According to this view, conventional universities have already lost much of their functions of knowledge production (to transnational corporations and think tanks), knowledge distribution (to virtual universities), and knowledge storage (to data banks, electronic libraries, Internet, and World Wide Web). Some conventional universities, however, have responded to the challenge. Many universities have already launched or are experimenting with a complex variety of distance education programmes.

Universities are not, however, knowledge factories. They are vital and interactive social institutions. Along with other cultural and scientific institutions (religious, artistic, literary, and scientific establishments), they act as the moral and intellectual guardians of their societies. They are important conduits for socialisation, recruitment, innovation, reflection, service, and empowerment (Tehranian 1996). Tiffin and Rajasingham acknowledge all of this. But they persuasively argue that a more universal higher education is now made technologically possible by liberating learning from time and space.

The new virtual universities are globalising, democratising, and transforming knowledge. Conventional universities in the Hindu-Buddhist, Confucian, Judaic, Christian, and Islamic worlds imposed certain boundaries on knowledge. Those boundaries were closely associated with metaphysical worldviews. Modern universities imposed a different set of boundaries on knowledge closely tied to the new positivism and empiricism of modern science. The parameters of knowledge could expand only with paradigm shifts from Newtonian to Darwinian and Einsteinian worldviews. String and chaos theories have further expanded those parameters. But virtual universities are further expanding the boundaries by globalising, democratising, and relativising all knowledge. Those who claim to have arrived at the Truth, whether metaphysical or scientific, are increasingly under the suspicion that they have lost it.

Truth is increasingly considered to be the search for the truths. Two prominent theologians, one Jewish and another Muslim, have called for tolerance, nay celebration, of differences (Sacks 2002; Soroush 1378/1999). That means dialogue with other peoples, cultures, and civilisations. In this fashion, the concept of civilisation itself is undergoing a profound transformation. Civilisation is no longer to be considered as a definite destination. Rather, it must be viewed as a journey, a process of becoming. No nation can therefore claim to have arrived at a civilised state. Clash of civilisations is thus a bloody game only for the fanatics. Dialogue among civilisations is therefore the only path for negotiating problems and solutions. Such new perspectives fostered by conventional as well as virtual universities can perhaps save humanity from the follies and catastrophes of its own making.

That is the good news. However, the same information and communication technologies that have immensely enhanced educational opportunities have also enabled Al-Qaide to plan globally for terror in a communication, financial, and political network. The same technologies also have placed us in a global fishbowl. To pacify the revolutionary poor hungering for bread, Marie Antoinette today would not have been able to suggest, 'Let them eat cake'. She would have been chastised in the face of images of famine in Africa and elsewhere as portrayed by the global television networks. Such utter ignorance of the world by the affluent would have been unthinkable.

On the other hand, the same CI technologies have enabled the world's poor and marginalised populations to witness the lifestyle of the rich on television. Exposure to global advertising has whetted their appetite for consumer goods that are effectively out of their reach. Rising expectations and frustrations among the poor are displaying themselves in rising alienation, regression, and aggression. The human insecurities of the marginalised are in turn mirrored in the human insecurities of the entrenched. Ghettoes of the poor in urban slums thus find their mirror image in the ghettoes of the rich in the gated communities defended by electronic surveillance.

To build a more peaceful and prosperous world for all, can virtual learning transform the human energies mobilised for violence into human efforts for peace and development? For an eloquent response to this critical question, dear reader, I cannot offer you a better source than the last two concluding paragraphs of this splendid book.

Majid Tehranian
University of Hawaii at Manoa
Toda Institute for Global Peace and Policy Research
Honolulu, Hawaii
27 November 2002

References

Ali, T. (2002) *The Clash of Fundamentalisms: Crusades, Jihads, and Modernity*, London: Verso.

Barber, Benjamin (1995) *McWorld vs. Jihad*. New York: Random House.

Friedman, Thomas (2002) 'Op-ed', *The New York Times*, 27 November.

Huntington, S.P. (1993) 'The Clash of Civilisations', *Foreign Affairs*, Summer.

Huntington, S.P. (1996) *The Clash of Civilisations and the Remaking of World Order*, New York: Simon and Schuster.

Noam, E. (1995) 'Electronics and the dim future of the university', *Science*, 270, October 13: 247–9.

Sacks, J. (2002) *The Dignity of Difference*, London and New York: Continuum.

Said, E. (2001) 'The Clash of Ignorance', *The Nation*, October 12.

Soroush, Abdol-Karim (1378/1999) *Sarathaye mostaghim* (The Straight Paths). Tehran: Sarat Cultural Foundation.

Tehranian, M. (1981) 'The fetish of identity: communications revolution and fundamentalist Revivals', *Media Asia*, 8: 1.

Tehranian, M. (1996) 'The end of university?', *The Information Society*, 12: 441–7.

Tehranian, M. and Chappell, D.W. (eds) (2002) *Dialogue of Civilisations: A New Peace Agenda for the New Millennium*, London: I.B. Tauris.

Preface

The information society is becoming a knowledge society. An education system is needed to match. Industrial societies became possible with universal primary and secondary education. A knowledge society needs tertiary education that is available to anyone throughout their adult life.

Tertiary education is primarily provided by universities whose traditional role has been to prepare the managerial and professional elites of nations. Now they need to become a service that caters to everyone. And if globalisation is to mean anything more than exploitation of the wretched of the earth by the powerful and privileged, it must mean making university education available to everyone everywhere who wants it regardless of nation, culture or creed. A quite extra-ordinary demand for university education and change in the civilising mission of universities is in the making. What kind of university can meet it?

The modern university was set up to respond to the needs of the society that sustains and legitimises it. It is not designed or equipped to respond to the new global demands. Dependence on traditional transport and building technologies and classroom-based teaching restricts its hinterland and makes rapid expansion impossible without lowering standards.

There has to be a better way to respond to the global demand for university education and to manage how this is done without turning universities into corporate boot camps. There has to be a way that is more economic and therefore possible, more matched to the times we live in and the technology we work with, more open to people with languages other than English and more concerned with the curricular needs and cultural concerns of globalisation itself.

In 1995 we published *In Search of the Virtual Class: Education in an Information Society*, in which we outlined the idea of a virtual university based on the Internet that could be available to anyone anywhere. The following year the Open University of Catalonia (Universitat Oberta de Catalunya) was operating entirely on the Internet. Since then virtual universities have proliferated. However, not all have been as successful or as concerned with standards as the UOC. It is the economic advantages of the Internet that attract rather than the opportunity to develop a new kind of university that redresses the problems of the old and addresses the needs of a new age.

Our interest has been with the potential of a virtual university that is uncoupled from the accrediting structures of nations and operating from a global broadband telecommunications platform where the norm of personal computing power makes possible distributed virtual reality with artificial intelligence. Such a technological environment will, like television and guns, become global and if, like television and guns, it is perceived as the means for pleasure and survival, even the poor will find some way of accessing the technology. Instead of providing bare bones degrees, it will be possible for virtual universities to offer the full flavour of academic life that has until now been available only to those who attend 'real' universities.

In 'The Idea of a University', published in 1873, Cardinal John Newman defined the modern university as we know it (Newman 1996). Newman (1902) also coined the term 'virtual university'. When we first used this term in the 1980s we had in mind the concept of 'virtual networks' in telecommunications, the exciting new idea of 'virtual reality' introduced by Jaron Lanier and our own experiments with 'virtual classes' using a 'computaphone' as we explored how a university could be a function of computer and communications technologies. Newman (1902: 4), however, applied the term 'virtual university' to the great metropolises of the industrial revolution, because their bringing together of people and ideas placed them at the heart of the dynamic changes that were taking place in society. It is a rich idea. If living in nineteenth-century Manchester was to be at the very heart of the industrial revolution, then being on the Internet in the twenty-first century means being part of the knowledge revolution.

Coming from different cultures ourselves, we recognise the dangers of ethno-centricity that Timothy Reagan raises in his work on *Non-Western Educational Traditions*. In seeking the common principles that underlie all education he uses the linguistic concepts of 'relative universals' for properties that are generally held in common and 'absolute universals' for properties for which there are no exceptions (Reagan 2000: 15). In turn we look for the universals in universities that make them universities and should, therefore, be incorporated in any university of the future.

Universities are nothing if not communication systems and, therefore, the idea of a university in the abstract is a paradigm. The universals of a university can then be seen as the key elements of the university paradigm and individual universities as syntagmatic expressions of this paradigm.

We write of the university paradigm not from a statistical basis, nor solely from the Anglophone literature, but from meetings at conferences and communications on the Internet with academics from around the world who already embrace global collegiality. We also write from our experience of the universities where we have taught and studied in different countries. We have often been struck by the remarkable similarity between universities. Looking at the idea of the university as a paradigm helps us to understand why this is the case and fills us with hope that no matter where students and teachers are from, they would find themselves at home in a global virtual university that conforms to the age-old paradigm of the university. This book describes the kind of radical changes universities need if there is to be a better way for them in the age of globalisation, but it also argues that universities must stay within the universals that have seen them survive for as long as civilisation itself.

The relationship between universities and civilisation is close. This book was written in the shadow of the events of 11 September 2001, amid talk of crusades, growing paranoia and the emergence of atavistic fears of other cultures. It carries the suggestion that a global virtual university could be a step towards sanity, towards wisdom, towards finding the knowledge we need to deal with global problems in a global way.

Acknowledgements

We are indebted to a large number of academics who gave generously of their views of the problems facing today's universities and on the idea of a global virtual university. In particular, we would like to express our gratitude to those who acted as a founding faculty for the idea of a global virtual university: Dr Barry Brown, University of Saskatchewan, Gajaraj Dhanarajan, Vice-Chancellor and CEO of the Commonwealth of Learning, Dr Anne Hill-Duin, Iowa State University, Dr Meheroo Jussawallah, Emeritus Fellow East West Centre, Dr Fred Litto, President of the School of the Future at the University of Sao Paulo, Dr Roy Lundin, Queensland University of Technology, Dr Madanmohan Rao of Microland, Ing. Horacio Reggini, Dean of the Engineering Faculty of the Catholic University of Argentina, Dr Alexander Romiszowski, Syracuse University, Dr Majid Tehranian, University of Hawaii, Dr Nadia Magnenat von Thalmann, Director MIRALab University of Geneva, Prof. Armando Rocha Trindade, Rector of the Open University of Portugal, Prof. Emeritus John Sinclair, University of Birmingham, Dr Nobuyoshi Terashima, Dean of Global Information and Telecommunications Studies at Waseda University, Dr Georgette Wang, Dean of Communications at Hong Kong Baptist University, and Dr Esa Saarinen, Helsinki University of Technology.

We would also like to acknowledge those who were associated with us in our virtual reality experiments and in seeking to make syntagms from our paradigm of a global virtual university. They include: Dr Margaret Allan, Scott Allan, Dr David Ashworth, Dr Gordon Boyce, Dr Noel Bridgeman, Sue Chard, Gowan Duff, Prof. Chris Kissling, Matthew and Karen Lloyd, Simon Lonsdale, Liz Mirams, Dr Minako O'Hagan and Alan Strawbridge.

We also thank Prof. Stuart McCutcheon Vice-Chancellor, Victoria University of Wellington and Prof. Emeritus of Mathematics John Harper and Prof. Anuar Zaini Md Zain Vice-Chancellor, University of Malaya for taking time to express their thoughts on the university of the future.

Research was assisted by a fellowship from the Telecommunications Advancement Organisation of Japan and a New Zealand/Japan Exchange Programme Grant. We also look back with gratitude to the influences that came from playing the roles of student, teacher, fellow and associate in the universities of: Addis Ababa (when it was Haile Selassie), Bologna, Cambridge, Catalonia, Chulalongkorn, De LaSalle (Philippines), Florida State, Ghana, Hawaii, James Cook, Leeds, Liverpool, Los Banos (Philippines), Melbourne, National Chung Cheng, Pernambuco, Simon Fraser, Victoria, Waseda and Wisconsin.

We recognise a special debt of gratitude to:

The Rector of the University of Bologna, the oldest university in the world, for inaugurating the idea of the 'newest university in the world'.

Dr Nobuyoshi Terashima for linking us into HyperReality, collaborating with us on the HyperClass research project and reviewing those parts of the book that relate to HyperReality; Dr Don Hanna for reading the idea; Anne Gooley for hosting our experiments at the Queensland Open Learning Network; Prof. Somasundram Puvi-Rajasingham for his inimical epistemological contributions; Sara Hudson for helping us in our researches; Simon Lonsdale for making the technology possible; our postgraduate students for entering into the spirit of a global virtual university; Dr Annette Patterson and her colleagues at James Cook University for considering what would be involved in accrediting a global virtual university; Alison Foyle our editor at RoutledgeFalmer for good guidance; and to Dr Margaret Allan a very special thanks for endless editing, subtle and unsubtle suggestions and inexhaustible patience with paradigms on top of paradigms.

Finally we want to thank Victoria University of Wellington which in the very highest academic tradition unstintingly supported our research over seventeen years, even though it did not necessarily agree with its subject.

Chapter 1

The universals of a university

The purpose of a university is to address the great issues of its time.

(Wang 1999: verbal personal communication)

… the university was no longer a place of learning, but a commercial enterprise, a degree shop run by soulless administrators who cut costs ruthlessly and over-worked the shrinking numbers of their academic staff.

(Hewett 1999: 155)

… a bureaucratic institution for sifting, sorting and credentialing the otherwise undifferentiated masses.

(Miller 1998: 22)

A Northern Territory University Professor has been threatened with decapitation if students fail an English language exam this week.

(*The Australian* 2002)

… the knowledge factory, as it were, at the centre of the knowledge economy.

(*The Economist* 1997)

Introduction

The Chancellor of the University was required to give his final address stark naked then to lie on his belly while his head was chopped off. His body was then placed in an open grave without shroud or coffin and his head was stuck on a pole for a fortnight, after which it was thrown in the river to make room for the head of the University's High Steward (Richards 1995).

This is not an undergraduate fantasy. The university was Cambridge, the year was 1535, the Chancellor was John Fisher and the High Steward was Sir Thomas More. Their problem was that they held to the monolithic authority of the pope to reveal God's meaning for the world and decide such issues as whether a king could divorce a queen. Papal authority was the keystone in the structure of logic that universities taught and the mindset that held the medieval world together. But

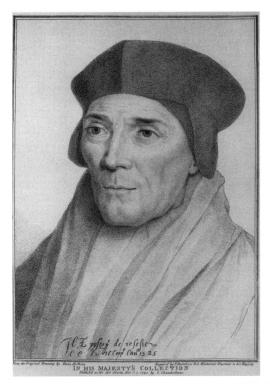

Figure 1.1   John Fisher Chancellor of Cambridge University (1514–35). (Permission of the Master and Fellows of St John's College, Cambridge.) Heading up a university has been a risky occupation since the days of Socrates

the Reformation had begun. Papal infallibility was under question. North of the European Alps powerful renaissance princes like Henry VIII were asserting the sovereignty of the state. In the edifice of the medieval university were appearing the first cracks that would ultimately open the way for the modern university. University academics that failed to adjust what they taught and researched accordingly suffered similar fates to More and Fisher.

Since the 1960s it seems as though all the world could see that once again 'the times they are a-changing', except for those who managed the modern university. They continued to operate as though by some divine right, while the world they were supposed to prepare people for changed about them. Not anymore. Once again the heads of chancellors and vice-chancellors roll, albeit virtually. Is this 'the end of university?' as Majid Tehranian (1996) asks.

Universities are still focused on the receding national issues of the countries they serve at a time when globalisation is becoming the burning issue, not globalisation in the sense of a neoliberal economic environment for free trade, but in the fuller sense that Marshall McLuhan envisaged when he wrote of a global village

(McLuhan and Fiore 1967). We are all inextricably interconnected in a global information environment that brings global awareness and with it global responsibility for sustainable development, for seeking solutions for pollution, poverty, pandemics and climatic change, and for learning to live together. No country, not even the USA, can think of itself anymore as 'an island, entire of itself'. The challenge is to develop a university that rises above partisanship to cultivate cadres of professionals who deal with global issues.

This book is about the idea of a global virtual university. Who should teach what to whom and how in the future? Who will academics serve when universities are global, how will they be paid and by whom, how will they and their students be assessed? What rules, procedures and philosophies will hold them together? To address these questions we consider the university as a paradigm.

The university paradigm

If one were to name a single text as a starting point for thinking about the idea of a university as a paradigm it would have to be Thomas Kuhn's *The Structure of Scientific Revolutions* (Kuhn 1962). By casting doubt on the objectivity of the scientific method, it brought into question the philosophical grounds on which the modern university stands.

Kuhn used paradigm to mean 'what the members of a scientific community, and they alone, share' (Kuhn 1977: 294) and explained that such

> communities are characterised by the relative fullness of communication within the group and by the relative unanimity of the group's judgement in professional matters. To a remarkable extent the members of a given community will have absorbed the same literature and drawn similar lessons from it.
>
> (Ibid.: 296)

The history of science according to Kuhn is not a logical progression toward revealing the nature of the world we live in. Rather, science develops in stages of well defined norm paradigms separated by scientific revolutions. In a norm paradigm research results complement each other. New knowledge fills in missing pieces in the jigsaw puzzle of the norm paradigm. Practitioners are trained to solve problems according to the norm paradigm and have a vested interest in its preservation. When research findings do not fit the norm paradigm, a paradox is created. If the research and the researcher are discredited, the norm paradigm is reinforced, but if the problem proves to lie with the paradigm, the resulting scientific revolution involves competition between new paradigms until a new norm paradigm emerges to resolve the paradox. Science seen like this is more a self-maintaining cultural communication system than an objective search for truth.

Kuhn's concept of paradigms has been widely applied in other fields. Heinich (1970) talks of educational paradigms and Carlotta Perez (1983) of technological paradigms. The way Kuhn applies the concept of a paradigm to science can be applied to any university discipline. Indeed it fits any socially established system of knowledge.

A hundred years after Fisher and More of Cambridge were executed for upholding the primacy of the papacy in resolving any paradoxes that might present themselves to a university, Galileo Galilei of the University of Padua was accused of heresy by the Inquisition for arguing the heliocentric case that the earth orbited the sun. Galileo, however, was on the southern side of the Alps where the counter-Reformation was in full swing and the pope still ruled on paradoxical issues according to the norm paradigm as defined by the Bible. Galileo was only saved from torture and execution by recanting. Yes, the earth was the centre of the universe, as of course it had to be because God located the Garden of Eden there.

Dava Sobel (1999) links the life of Galileo with that of his daughter who was a nun in a closed order. Their correspondence shows how the philosopher and the seminarist were both locked into a world where everything was explained and justified in terms of God's intention as interpreted by the Roman Catholic Church. The dominance of such a mindset can only be understood by comparing it to the scientific rationalism in which the developed world and its universities are immersed today. Michel Foucault calls such *zeitgeist* an episteme by which he means an all-encompassing body of unconscious knowledge peculiar to a particular time and place.

There is similarity between Foucault's idea of an episteme and Kuhn's concept of a paradigm (Major-Poetzl 1983: 86). Kuhn's idea that 'when paradigms change, the world itself changes with them' (1962: 110) reflects Foucault's view of an episteme as a worldview that is so comprehensive it is not possible for people in one episteme to comprehend the way people in another episteme think (Foucault 1970). We could think of an episteme as a metaparadigm of all the paradigms by which people live as they eat, dress, work, fight, play, talk (and go to university). The difference between an episteme and other paradigms, such as those of the university, science and clothes, is in its comprehensiveness. We can walk away from a game of tennis or a lecture on political science and recognise that other people play different games and take different subjects, but we cannot as readily exit from the episteme we live in or comprehend epistemes we do not live in. We are conscious of our use of the paradigms within an episteme. We seek to acquire knowledge of paradigms so that we 'know' how to do things in ways of which our society approves. We go to university to learn advanced complex paradigms and to critique them so that we can improve them, but we do not lightly shift paradigms. To do so is to invite discord in the harmony of the intermeshed paradigms that make an episteme.

Galileo looked outside his episteme when he saw the mountains of the moon through his new telescope and worked out that Venus orbited the sun and that the heavens were not immutable. Galileo wrote about his discoveries from scientific and mathematical, not biblical, premises and in Italian not Latin, so that the reader could follow the reasoning instead of having to accept it. The issue with Fisher was who should decide what God intended marriage to be. The issue at the centre of Galileo's trial was the source of knowledge: who explained the world, God or humans? This was the key philosophical issue that would ultimately distinguish the medieval from the modern episteme and consequently, the medieval from the modern university.

In the medieval university knowledge was based on God's will as it was revealed in the Latin version of the Bible. In the modern university, knowledge is based on the texts of authoritative, widely-referenced authors who rationalise along accepted logical grounds and intertextualise with a community of peers to develop agreed bodies of knowledge preferably in the language of the state that supports the university. These constitute the national norm paradigms of the subjects that, in sum, make up the curriculum of a national education system. Students sit exams that test their comprehension of what the textbook writers intended them to understand. Then they go forth to teach, manage and practise in the professional community for which their study of the knowledge paradigm has prepared them, bringing scientific rationalism to bear on the problems of industrial societies. They are the priesthood of modernism, the texts they study are its bibles, the authors its gods.

The modern university that emerged from the Enlightenment to serve the needs of the nation state through the application of scientific rationalism is still with us. It is still the legitimate university, but signs that all was not well with it came in 1968 when students and academics in Paris staged a revolt against the authoritarianism of the modern university and its failure to address the issues of the time. This was the year that Philip Coombs (1968) reflected global concern that education was preparing people for the past instead of the future. *Les évènements* in Paris rumbled on around the universities of the world and down through the years that followed, manifesting itself in a variety of guises as feminism, cultural theory, postmodernism and now as a form of globalisation ironically called anti-globalisation.

In 1977 Roland Barthes announced the 'death of the author' (Barthes 1977). By this he meant that once a text is published it is the reader who gives it meaning. Readers become the new gods creating their own individual virtual worlds from the bits of information provided by a text. Many will remember the way in the past some academics behaved as though they were minor deities. Anyone who is teaching today in a university will encounter students who expect to be treated as something very special. Jacques Derrida taught the intelligentsia to deconstruct the meaning in texts and to find that there was no single universal meaning (Derrida 1974). Jean-François Lyotard defined the postmodern condition as 'incredulity towards meta-narratives' in which he included both religion and science (Lyotard 1984: xxiv). Critical theory in its many forms has attacked the theoretical structures that have held together the modern university and modern society. The effect has been to erode the episteme of modernism that universities have maintained and the consequent worldviews by which we cooperate in what we see as civilisation. When we are all gods, who is left to believe in us?

Kuhn's concept of a paradigm can be applied to the idea of a university itself. Could we then see a paradigm shift in the way the medieval university became the modern university and argue that we are undergoing another shift from the modern to the global virtual university? The scientific revolutions that Kuhn regarded as paradigm shifts really were revolutions. It is not possible to reconcile genesis with geology. Equally the industrial revolution really was a revolution. Life in pre-industrial societies was radically different from that in industrial societies. The change between the medieval and modern universities was not of this order. It was more in the nature of an adaptation to the episteme shift of the industrial revolution.

Paradigms on paradigms

If you found yourself transported to a thirteenth-century university somewhere in Europe you might not understand the Latin people were using and people might stare if you were a woman or not properly gowned, but you would have little difficulty in recognising that you were in a university. From the founding of Bologna University in 1088 there has been strong institutional continuity in universities. They have continued to hold lectures, seminars and tutorials that cover a fixed curriculum. They still have faculties, deans, rectors, chancellors and vice-chancellors, and students have been writing assignments, arguing, getting drunk and taking Bachelors and Masters degrees for almost a thousand years. These are components of the university paradigm that everyone recognises. Most medieval universities survived and transformed themselves into modern universities and new universities still follow the traditions of the medieval universities. The philosophical paradigm of what was taught and researched shifted from theology to rational scientism as the university adapted to the epistemic shift from the medieval to the modern, but the institutional form of the university stayed relatively constant. What was taught changed, but how it was taught has remained the same. We could, therefore, think of a paradigm of the medieval–modern university that has lasted with little change over 900 years.

A question that faces us in designing a global virtual university for the future is whether it will continue within the norm paradigm of the university as an institution. Can the university paradigm adapt to the epistemic shift of the information revolution and the philosophical shift of the postmodern? Will we continue offering degrees, using traditional titles, completing terms and holding medieval rituals where the participants dress in the mock medieval finery of monks to graduate students, or will there be the kind of disjuncture that took place between the Greek idea of a university and the medieval institution of a university?

If you were now transported to a class in ancient Greece would you recognise it as a university? Many American universities echo ancient Greece in their architecture so that the classic surroundings would suggest a university, but we have no evidence that there was any kind of classroom or formal sequence of lectures or that degrees were awarded. You might be startled by the scant attire of

Figure 1.2a The University of Virginia founded in 1819 is an expression of Thomas Jefferson's belief that a new university for a new country should be based on the example of ancient Greece

Figure 1.2b Victoria University of Wellington, only 100 years old, looks back to the influence of the medieval church

Figure 1.2c Waseda University's clock tower subtly mixes European gothic with medieval Japan

Figure 1.2d Leeds University's Library Tower when it was built was an art deco symbol of the modern

Figure 1.2e National Chung Cheng University founded in 1989 makes its links with early Chinese civilisation

Figure 1.2f Universitat Oberta de Catalunya. The Open University of Catalonia founded in 1996 has a classical exterior but there are no students on these premises. It houses the offices of the virtual university

the students, but they would be intelligent, schooled and adult and women were part of the Greek university tradition. However, what would seem strange to anyone who has attended a modern university would be that instead of telling you, the teacher in ancient Greece would be asking you. Knowledge was not something to be accepted as it was passed down, but to be sought and endlessly renewed through questioning.

Glenys Patterson draws the distinction between the university as an idea and the university as an institution (Patterson 1997). What the medieval and the modern university have in common is an institutional paradigm. What the modern university shares with the Greek-Alexandrian university is the idea that a core function of a university is a search for truth. This is the universal of a university that transcends epistemes. It is the academic freedom to test received knowledge, the restless probing of the norm paradigm that throws up the seminal ideas that lead to revolutions and epistemic change.

There is something paradoxical in the idea of questioning knowledge in an institution dedicated to the continuation of knowledge and at times universities become the means for maintaining the status quo rather than questioning it. When it becomes impossible to question the paradigm of what is taught, when norm paradigms become dogma, when radical thinkers have no place, then the idea of a university dims, and they become mere institutions, universities in name not nature.

The Greek philosophical paradigm did not sit easily with the mainstream theological philosophy of the early medieval university. However, there were tenuous links across the Dark Ages between the ancient Greek-Alexandrian university and the medieval–modern university. Irish monasteries in the sixth to eighth centuries, remote monasteries in the Appennines, the University of Constantinople (AD425–AD1453) and centres of study in the Islamic world kept the ideas and knowledge of ancient Greece alive. It was with the Renaissance that Greek rationality was renewed in European universities. From the Renaissance came the Enlightenment and the emergence of the rational scientific way of explaining the world that provided the philosophical basis of the modern university. Today any overview of a subject in the arts or sciences will begin by recognising its roots in ancient Greek thinking. Every time a subject carries a suffix such as -logy or -ology, -graphic or -graphy we are reminded that it had its origins in the universities of ancient Greece. How far back does the university paradigm extend?

One could argue that the Greek idea of a university began with a woman. Sappho's college in Lesbos provided a complete education for a community of young women in the seventh century BC. It was regarded by Marrou as the equivalent to an Academy of Music and Drama because of its focus on dancing, music and its 'ideal of beauty aspiring to wisdom' (1956: 34). However, we have little idea of the level or content of what was taught and the first real evidence of something that could be regarded as a university comes from what we know from later writings of the school Pythagoras founded at Crotona in Southern Italy in 518BC. It was a community of adult people of both genders drawn from many places that lived together and were engaged in profound philosophical study on subjects that still engage us, at a level that would challenge any modern academic (Dewdney 1999). From the Pythagoreans we can trace a continuous tradition of Greek scholarship that lasted up to the final sacking of the great library of Alexandria in AD640. Then comes a gap of between four and five centuries before the first medieval university. This was not a paradigm shift. It was the Dark Ages.

Does the university begin in Greece with Pythagoras? Many of the ideas that Pythagoras brought as a teacher to his school in Crotona have their origins in his travels and studies in the ancient centres of civilisation in Africa and Asia. He spent some twenty years studying mathematics in the temples of Egypt. Builders there used a knotted rope that was a practical application of what today we call Pythagoras' theorem (Dewdney 1999). The buildings and organisation of Pharaonic Egypt could hardly have been possible without advanced knowledge and an associated system of tertiary level instruction. There were sources in ancient Egypt as well as Greece for the founding of the great library in Alexandria. In Cairo the university of al-Azhar with its foundation in AD969 claims to be the oldest continuous university and the college mosque of al-Zaituna in Tunisia has a similar ancient history (Gibb 1939).

Pythagoras was captured in Cairo by the army of King Camyses and taken to Babylon. Four tablets found near the site of Babylon and housed in Yale University show that the Babylonians were able to apply Pythagoras' theorem over a thousand years before he was born (O'Connor and Robertson 2002). Babylon was a great metropolis and centre of learning. The Babylonians were outstanding mathematicians and occupied the ancient land of Sumer which is regarded as the cradle of written language and classroom education (Kramer 1963).

For some five years from his Babylonian captivity until his return to Greece the movements of Pythagoras are not clear and legend has it that he went to India and China. Applications of his famous theorem (though not the proof) were described in Indian Vedic sulbasutras that were extant three centuries before him. Moreover, his philosophical ideas include the transmigration of souls across species that is similar to the Hindu belief in reincarnation. There were settlements of learned men in India involved in higher education from 600BC (Mudaliar 1960). This seems to have been the origins of the university of Taxila in Northern India that attracted hundreds of students from many places and was famous for its schools of medicine and philosophy when Alexander invaded India (Raza 1991). Buddha was contemporaneous with Pythagoras and it was with the emergence of Buddhism that what can be clearly recognised as universities appear in India (Siqueira 1943). The University of Nalanda in Bihar came to rival Alexandria as a centre of study. At one point it had 1,500 teachers and 8,500 students, a teaching ratio any university could be proud of. Students came from China, Nepal, Tibet and Korea. Entrance examinations were strict, the average age of students was twenty and they were taught a broad range of sacred and secular subjects. There were similar rival universities at Vallabhi in Gujarat and Vikramshila in Bihar (Raza 1991).

There is a Chinese proof of Pythagoras' theorem and his concept of the interaction of contraries seems to be the same as the Chinese idea of yin and yang.

Confucius (551–479BC) was another contemporary of Pythagoras and although there was an earlier form of higher education, it is Confucius who is seen as inspiring higher education in China. Confucianism held that education prepared people for public life by cultivating virtue and wisdom and harmonious relations. Higher education was closely linked to examination for entry into the civil service.

It would seem that there were early centres of higher education in Asia and Egypt that we may think of as proto-universities. However, it is around 500BC that we have the extraordinary coincidence of Pythagoras, Buddha and Confucius establishing not just universities *per se*, but paradigms of what universities should be. The philosophical content of what they taught was different, but what each of these philosophers had in common was a search for truth that involved a teacher– student relationship between intelligent literate autonomous adults. It seems unlikely that this first flowering of universities took place in the ancient civilisations of China, India, Mesopotamia, Egypt and Greece without them being aware of each other. They were linked by great trade routes. The story of Pythagoras is one of mobility. It is not difficult to imagine academics of yore conferencing by camel along the ancient Silk Road.

The Christian paradigm in medieval universities was matched by the Hindu, Buddhist, Confucian and Islamic paradigms in Asian universities. However, Asia does not appear to have had an equivalent to the Enlightenment. The early flowering of universities in Asia, with the exception of the madrasas of Islam has faded over the centuries. By contrast the last 500 years has seen the European university paradigm spread around the world. Initially, especially in North and South America, universities were part of the process of colonisation and subscribed to the medieval theological tradition. However, the last 200 years have seen the global spread of the idea of the modern university which has proved remarkably adaptable wherever it has been implanted.

If any particular event can be seen as inaugurating the modern episteme it is the American Revolution. It marked the emergence of a democratic nation state based on rationalism. A new kind of university was needed to match a new kind of nation: a university based on empirical science, democratically accessible and dedicated to the service of the state. The USA developed remarkable diversity in its tertiary education, but it was the emergence of the modern university in Germany and the way it integrated teaching and scientific research that most influenced the way American universities developed. It is in the USA that the modern university has reached its apogee and it is from the USA, as well as from Europe, that the modern university has been seeded in Latin America, Africa and Asia.

Today, overseas students form a considerable component of classes in the English language speaking universities of the developed world. They study in a second language and learn to apply knowledge in the way of the West. Some of these students will take the opportunities Western universities offer to become part of the process of globalisation. Some will go back to their own countries and adapt what they have learned to their own language, their own context and their own culture. Many will be aware that the roots of their culture lie in the universities of antiquity that existed long before the modern university. The university paradigm that we trace back to Romano–Greek–Alexandrian civilisation in the Mediterranean has shared roots with the early universities of Asia. Over almost 3,000 years the university paradigm has drifted Westward until it has come full circle back to Asia. It has seen epistemic changes and clashes with time and place, but the basic paradigm has proved remarkably durable. Today, as they probably were in the days of Pythagoras, universities around the world are remarkably similar, as they would be, because they are all examples of the same paradigm. However different the form a global virtual university may take to fit the episteme of the future, it will need very good reason to depart from the basic university paradigm.

Paradigms are communication systems

In linguistics and communications studies the word 'paradigm' refers to a communication system in the abstract and is used in opposition to 'syntagm' which refers to an actual manifestation of communication from a paradigm (Fiske 1990).

All messages, therefore, involve selection from a paradigm and combination into a syntagm. All the units in a paradigm must share characteristics that determine membership of that paradigm, thus letters in the alphabet paradigm, numbers in the numerical paradigm, notes in the musical paradigm. Each unit within the paradigm must be clearly differentiable from other units; it must be characterised by distinctive features. Just as the paradigm is governed by shared characteristics and distinctive features, the syntagm is determined by rules or conventions by which the combination of paradigms is made – rules of grammar and syntax (Watson and Hill 1996: 123).

This is not in contradiction with Kuhn's use of paradigm. Universities are communication systems. The idea of a university is a paradigm. An actual university is a syntagm. Cambridge University has survived the medieval episteme to become a modern university and no doubt one day there will be a Virtual Cambridge University. Cambridge already is a global university. It draws its staff and students from every country in the world and has managed to maintain a degree of autonomy from the state thanks to having chancellors and vice-chancellors who were prepared to give their all. Like other distinguished universities with an international reputation, its brand name transcends its location. Such universities are going to be tempted to expand globally by going virtual. In its different incarnations Cambridge is a syntagm of the overarching university paradigm.

Universities as institutions are universities because other universities accept that they are universities. The process called *ad eundem* (to the same level) is applied to students seeking to transfer from one university to another. This establishes whether the student's previous experience was in a university that can be recognised as a university because it fits the university paradigm. Today universities are such a fundamental part of society that they fall under scrutiny from students, government, employers, accrediting agencies and the media to ensure that they do what universities are supposed to do and comply with the paradigm that states have of a modern university (Hanna 2000: 22–3). It is here that we can appreciate the effect of an episteme on the university paradigm. Agencies that accredit universities expect them to fit the paradigm in its modern form. They have little difficulty accepting the equivalence of universities of similar ranking in other countries. They do have difficulty with universities that claim to be virtual and global and that, while apparently functioning as a university should, do not have the form of a university. They accredit some virtual universities and not others and it is clear that the idea of a global virtual university is not established. However, if any organisation tried to establish a university where all communications would be in Latin, women would not be allowed and academics could be sued for teaching anything that did not comply with the Bible, they would have real problems. The medieval university is finished. For that matter, think of trying to establish a university in the style of classical Greece where, apart from the language problem and the peculiarities of the dress code, student and teacher were wont to engage in what Patterson (1997) calls the tradition of educative eros.

Universities are educational communication systems

Educational systems are a special kind of communication system in which there are four critical factors: teachers, students, knowledge and problems. The core communication process is one where teachers interact with students to help them apply knowledge to problems (Tiffin and Rajasingham 1995). This is as true of universities as it is of kindergartens with the difference that one is at the top and the other at the base of the educational process in society.

The terms teacher and learner are used in a broad sense to mean people who have these roles in relationship to each other. It also allows for the roles to be reversed, as frequently happens today in a postgraduate course where a mature professional student may in the course of a seminar take over the role of teacher. What is critical of the teacher-student communication axis in education is that it is interactive. The student has to be able to ask for help and the teacher has to be able to find out if the student needs help.

The use of the terms 'knowledge' and 'problem' is also relative and refers to the domain of knowledge that applies to a particular class of problems. The knowledge–problem axis is embedded in the content of student-teacher interaction.

This model is based on Lev Vygotsky's notion of a Zone of Proximal Development (ZPD). A ZPD comes into existence when someone finds they do not know how to resolve a particular kind of problem and turns for help to someone who does and who thereby takes on the role of teacher (Vygotsky 1978). This implies that there exists some abstract body of knowledge that can be applied to the particular class of problem a learner is addressing and that the teachers are teachers because they know how to apply knowledge and learners are learners because they do not. When the learner can apply the knowledge then the ZPD no longer exists for that learner.

Vygotsky saw this process as being embedded in culture. A particular class of problems is dealt with by applying a paradigm of knowledge that is culturally sanctioned. An attempt to solve a specific problem in a culturally appropriate way is a syntagmatic expression of a knowledge paradigm. The process of acquiring knowledge paradigms begins from the moment a child is born. It is parents and family who are the first teachers and the paradigmatic body of knowledge a child is learning is that of the culture into which the child is born. When the child goes to school the paradigmatic body of knowledge they are expected to acquire is approved by the state, as is the examination system that checks that students are able to apply the knowledge in the curriculum to appropriate classes of problems. Legal systems ensure that people continue to solve problems in approved ways out of school and there are penal systems for those who fail to conform to this. A doctor may consider euthanasia the best solution for a terminally ill cancer patient in pain, but in many countries could face criminal charges for practising this. At the apex of the educational system are the universities preparing the judges, the lawyers, the doctors, the civil servants and the teachers who will be responsible for ensuring that the apparatus of a state functions in accord with the national hierarchy of paradigms as they exist in a particular episteme.

The *sine qua non* on which the paradigmatic organisation of states depends, upon which all education since time began depends, is the simple interaction between teacher, student, knowledge and problem. It is the basic function of universities to do this at the topmost level of educational systems, at an advanced level, with mature students. These are basic components of any university paradigm, no matter the era or country. It is the nature of these components and the style and means of communication between them that vary with the episteme. What is meant by students, teachers, knowledge and problems in a global virtual university and how the interaction between them is effected is the subject of Chapters 3–7.

In conventional educational systems the technologies that make the educational communication system possible are those of transport and buildings. Teachers and students travel by road or rail to come together in classrooms. They bring with them knowledge and problems that may be in their heads, their textbooks or their notebooks. Knowledge will also be housed in libraries but it will have been brought there in the first place by transport systems. The school, college or university has support systems for administration, relaxation and personal needs, but the core process takes place in classrooms. These provide sheltered environments for the face-to-face communication process called a class which is where education in the Vygotskian sense happens. Students, teachers, knowledge and problems can also be brought together by postal services and with the help of film, radio, television and computers, but transport systems and buildings still remain the primary enabling technologies for education.

The radical difference between a virtual university and all previous universities is that students and teachers and knowledge and problems come together as bits of information not as atomic substance. Telecommunications and computers replace roads and buildings. The Internet has facilitated this process and while as yet the numbers involved in no way match those of conventional education, the turn of the millennium has seen a multiplication of virtual schools, colleges and universities on the Internet. However, the Internet is in transition. At the beginning of the twenty-first century it is still primarily dependent on the narrowband tele-communication systems set up for different purposes in the last century. This means that the interaction between teacher, student, knowledge and problem is essentially asynchronous. It is based upon email and the World Wide Web.

The first generation of virtual universities approximate to open universities using the Internet instead of the postal service. The dynamic of synchronous face-to-face communication that has been possible in the conventional class, which explains its survival for some 4,000 years, has yet to emerge in the virtual class. Until it does the Internet may supplement, but does not threaten the conventional mode of instruction.

How universities differ as communication systems

What makes universities unique is the search for truth, whatever that is conceived to be. Research and questioning have always been there, but it is in the modern university that we find a clear acceptance that there should be a unity of teaching and research. This is derived from the founding philosophy of Humboldt University of Berlin, known for this reason as the mother of modern universities. Universities with strong postgraduate studies and research traditions in the Humboldtian tradition expect that their teachers have research qualifications, are actively engaged in research and demonstrate its standing by publishing regularly in research journals.

From the origins of universities in Greece and Asia, academics derive a sense of mission akin to that which drives doctors and priests. Universities are where the approved paradigmatic knowledge of a society is created, consolidated, critiqued and renewed. It is why universities are respected, called on to pontificate on their subjects and seen as the conscience of society. Even the medieval university encouraged research, secure in the knowledge that, if properly done, it could only reaffirm that all phenomena are a manifestation of God's will. Otherwise the researcher was a heretic and went to the stake. Today a search for truth in research would be defined as something that can attract funding.

The knowledge–problem axis remains in research communication, but the teacher–student relationship is replaced by one of interactive questioning between fellow researchers until an answer is found. The teaching process begins when a zone of proximal development opens up and closes when students can apply knowledge to problems. The research process begins when a zone of paradigmatic questioning opens up (why does the knowledge not solve all the problems?) and is closed when the query is resolved either by an addition to the existing knowledge paradigm or by a new knowledge paradigm which is seen to solve the problem in a better way than the old paradigm.

What makes one paradigm better than another? William of Ockham applied the principle of parsimony. Einstein similarly sought simplicity (Schroeder 1991). The recognised procedure today is to report the results to a research journal and undergo a peer review. If the research paper is accepted and published as a contribution to the existing paradigm it becomes part of the knowledge about that subject and hence a part of the paradigmatic body of knowledge taught within an educational system and thus part of the episteme within which people understand their reality. If the research findings do represent grounds for a paradigm shift they will not be published lightly and will not be accepted readily by the knowledge community concerned.

The change from the medieval to the modern took place over centuries in the universities of Europe. Humboldt University of Berlin may claim to be the mother of the modern university because it was founded in 1810 on the principle of integrating teaching with research, but the University of Halle also claims to be the first modern university because when it was founded in 1694 it abandoned religious orthodoxy in favour of the scientific approach and adopted the national language instead of Latin. It also awarded the first doctorate to a woman in 1754 whereas it was not until 1869 that Girton College for women was founded at Cambridge. By contrast the change taking place in universities today from the modern to what we would see as the global and the virtual is happening so rapidly that academics are actually aware of it. We suggested the events in Paris in the 1960s marked the start and the pace of change is quickening, but the technological infrastructures that make a global virtual university possible are not yet in place and the equivalent to a Humboldt or a Halle has yet to be founded.

What then is a university?

In sum, what are the universals of universities across the ages and around the world?

Any syntagmatic expression of the universal university paradigm would be a spacio-temporal field where people interact in the roles of teachers, students and researchers to study the application of knowledge to problems at an advanced level in a way that questioned accepted knowledge and sought to improve knowledge in what would be seen as a search for truth. It would be at the apex of the educational paradigm of the society it served, preparing people for professional roles and having a key part in validating the corpus of knowledge that constitutes the societal paradigm. What constitutes the society, the knowledge and the problems and who are the teachers, students and researchers and how the quest for knowledge is pursued depends upon the episteme within which the university exists.

A paradigm is a communication system in the abstract, but its syntagmatic application requires an actual communication system which in universities means some kind of institutionalised communications technology such as libraries, lecture theatres or the Internet. We can say that all universities have systemic structures that will not function without feedback and control systems, support systems and inputs of information, energy and money.

Paradigms are systemic but the term paradigm does not carry the obsession with objectives that goes with a systems approach. People think paradigmatically and act syntagmatically. Objectives in a paradigm are self-referential. Thinking within the paradigm requires credulity in the paradigm and its purposes. The occasional student or academic might wonder why they are in a lecture and what the point of it all is, which is rather like going to a football match and wondering why the people in the funny costumes are chasing a ball around a field. Paradigms are only possible because people accept them on their own terms. However, those who are players in today's university need to ask themselves what they think they are playing at, because the game is changing.

What no one dares say

One of the delights of the globalisation of universities is the proliferation of international conferences. Here and in pre- and post-conference email chat, collegiality has gone global and thrives. With the gossip that accompanies academic discourse, chatting to colleagues from other universities who are unlikely to pass on any indiscretions, comes the realisation that the stresses and strains that have arisen over the last two decades in one's own university and that have come to seem so personal, are in fact widespread, at least in the universities that can still afford to send their academics to conferences. The talk is of a malaise in universities, a creeping corruption of the academic spirit. Academics with more than a decade of experience in universities believe that teaching standards are declining, research is compromised and intimidation by management rife, but as in the days of Henry VIII, most of them know to keep quiet if they want to avoid the chop. Even so, there is a growing body of literature being hammered onto university doors by fearless souls that amounts to a call for reformation (Hanna *et al.* 2000; Miller 1998; Barnett 1997; Biggs and Davis 2002; Slaughter and Leslie 1997; Marginson and Considine 2000; Readings 1996; Wortham 1999).

The episteme is changing and universities have change thrust upon them. To state the obvious, the information society is based on information technology and so too must be its universities. They have to have a virtual dimension. Nation states do not disappear, but much of their function is taken over by global corporates. Universities have to have global and corporate as well as national and public dimensions.

The epistemic change we are in at the global level does not have the kind of immediacy that comes with conquest or radical political change, nor will it have the century of enlightenment in which the modern replaced the medieval. Universities are in transition and know not whether they are fish or fowl. From within today's university, what is good and bad depends upon whether it is seen from the perspective of the new or old epistemes. John Fisher, the man who lost his head defending papal infallibility is also celebrated as the person who, almost single-handed, brought renaissance learning to Cambridge (de Hamel 2001: 29). Logic that would lead to the modern university and belief in medieval catholic theology coexisted in the same man. A similar polarity of mind can be found in Galileo, Keppler and Darwin and is a source of angst in today's academic.

The dilemma for universities is not dissimilar from that which faces ecotourism. The parks and leisure movement of the last century opened vast areas of private mountains and forests to the public. This was seen as making the beauty of nature available to everyone. However, by the end of the century the cumulative impact of ever-increasing numbers of tourists and sightseers was devastating the landscape and destroying that beauty. One hundred years ago university education was only available to a privileged few. Slowly, the doors have been opening to more and more people, but as they do, it becomes increasingly difficult to maintain the environment that existed when universities were the preserve of the elite. The social pressures to increase access to university education come as governments promise to reduce taxes. In response to this students pay an increasing proportion of the costs of universities yet governments demand greater accountability from universities for their use of government subsidies.

According to the OECD (2000) 37 per cent of all education is in the private sector and this is reflected in universities where what is paid by students and what is paid by the state rapidly approaches parity. From the perspective of the old episteme, the more government support is reduced the worse things get. Education is a public good and its privatisation is bad. From the perspective of the new episteme, however, the less the government contributes the better. State subsidisation is seen as the problem. According to the World Trade Organisation, university education is an information service that can be traded globally (World Trade Organisation: www.wto.org). State-supported universities are trading a subsidised service and that is unfair practice. The universities of North America and Europe which dominate global exports of university education are being as protective of their education as they are of their agriculture.

In this time of transition, universities lose their sense of direction and mission. We addressed the question 'What is the purpose of a university?' to academic colleagues and found ambiguity. However, Georgette Wang who writes about the information society (1994, 2000) answered in a way that transcended epistemes: 'To address the great issues of its time' (1999). It takes us to the question 'what are the great issues of our time?' It serves as a basis for designing a university of the future and leads to the next chapter on the technology that is transforming the episteme.

Chapter 2

Universities have IT

Information Technology (IT) a microelectronics-based combination of computing and telecommunications.

(Watson and Hill 1996: 87)

Virtual: Computing. Not physically existing but made by software to appear to do so.

(OED 1993)

It is not the technology itself that is important, but using the best technology available in the service of one idea: to enhance and globalize learning.

(Ferrate 2000: 15–16)

These kinds of robots will be able to traverse freely between the real world and cyberspace while existing simultaneously in both worlds.

(Shimohara 2001: 84)

Introduction

Conventional universities bring students, faculty, library and researchers together in buildings by means of transport systems. Virtual universities bring them together by means of computers and telecommunications. These are also the technologies that enable globalisation. Where the critical components of a conventional university exist as atoms, in a virtual university they exist as bits of information. The Internet made first generation virtual universities possible, with the World Wide Web providing the knowledge base that traditionally came with a university library and email accelerating what open universities already did. However, the Internet is in its infancy. This chapter considers the implications for virtual universities as Internet bandwidth and computer processing capability grow, as they most assuredly will. It explores the impact on the university paradigm of speech recognition, multilingual systems, wearable computing, wireless Internet, artificial intelligence, avatars, virtual reality and HyperReality. It describes the technological infrastructure in which universities will be enmeshed, in the not so distant future.

Will they still be struggling to catch up and adapt to technological change after it becomes inevitable, as happened with the introduction of the Internet, or will they take a lead in designing and developing the technologies in which knowledge will be embedded and in exemplifying how IT can be used in an information society? To what extent will universities shape information technology, and to what extent will they be shaped by it?

IT has only just begun

The term Information Technology (IT) was first used as recently as 1981 (Watson and Hill 1996). In 1986 we asked a class how many used a PC. Out of some sixty students, only three hands went up. When we said that computers would be made available and that all future assignments would be done on a PC the rest of the class was outraged. They were communications students not computer nerds. What did they need a computer for? By 1992 the question had to be reversed: who did not use a computer? Three hands crept up. And how many were using the Internet? Once again, three hands. Today, teachers, students and researchers in universities use computers and the Internet as readily as they use the phone.

We are in the middle of a massive change in the way we communicate in universities. It is happening quietly, quickly and globally, but the adoption of IT in universities as in society at large is far from plateauing. What we have seen so far is to the information society what the coming of the steam engine was to the industrial society. The equivalents to the motor engine, the electric engine and atomic power have yet to come.

The 1980s saw the introduction of desktop PCs, and the 1990s the arrival of the Internet on existing narrowband telecommunication infrastructures designed for telephones. What comes next will be a consequence of the growth of broadband digital telecommunication networks and computer processing capability and the continuing trend toward the miniaturisation and portability of information technology. These background technological trends will make possible the widespread introduction of artificial intelligence and distributed virtual reality. Universities will adopt these technologies as they have adopted computers and the Internet, because they are extensions of computers and the Internet and, like computers and the Internet, they will become part of the infrastructure of the professional workplace and of society in general. The question is not whether universities will adopt these new information technologies so much as to what extent they can afford to retain books and classrooms if they seek to compete in the coming global trade in tertiary level teaching.

What difference does IT make?

Over the last fifty years educational researchers have adopted quantitative methodologies in seeking to compare the outputs of any new medium of instruction, such as film, radio and television, with those of conventional classroom teaching.

The results have been remarkably consistent in showing that there is 'no significant difference'. Many doctoral students still use the same research methods to compare learning via the Internet with classroom learning with the same results (Merisotis and Phipps 1999). It is like comparing apples and pears by the rate at which they grow or by how much they sell for. Apples and pears are different fruits and comparing them in a way that takes the difference into account calls for qualitative not quantitative research.

We have been teaching conventionally in a face-to-face classroom situation and simultaneously with distance students by means of computers and telecommunications since 1986 and have sought to understand the difference through discussion with our students, colleagues and expert technologists. This was within a long-term action research framework which sought to discover how university instruction could be conducted in an IT environment. In 1992, a telecommunication company commissioned a conventional quantitative comparison of the learning outcomes of our classroom based students and our telestudents. The research found, surprise, that there was no significant difference. This pleased the telephone company sponsoring the research. They were able to argue that it was possible to get as good a university education with computers and telecommunications as through physical attendance at a university and that of course is a significant finding. From our qualitative perspective we were finding that there was a difference, not a statistically significant one, but a traumatic one. The apples and pears were not those students who attended class and those at a distance; rather they were students before and after the Internet. They were from different epistemes. The difference was not in what they learned, but in how they learned it. With the Internet, students began to take charge of their own learning. They emailed the authors of the texts they used about their theories. They found that some authors had revised their ideas and they passed this on to their fellow students. The trickle down of knowledge over time was suddenly bypassed and so was the intermediary position of the teacher. Students checked the curriculum of similar courses in other universities to see how they compared. What texts were they using? What kind of assignments were they set? How were they graded? Our students got in touch with students like themselves in other countries and compared experiences. They surfed the Web for resources and got together in international chat groups. Pre-Internet apple students think local. Post-Internet pear students think global. Both apple and pear students can answer the same examination questions, but they think differently and pears are in demand.

To function as a university, people interact by talking and listening and by reading and writing. Of course some subjects such as medicine, music, engineering and geology also require interaction with things, such as bodies, instruments, and machines and make use of images, but they still need language (sometimes an additional specialised language such as algebra or musical notation) transmitted by sound waves or light waves to mediate such interaction. Whether we read and write with paper or computers or talk and listen face-to-face or by telecommunications, it does not seem to make much difference to student ability to learn the abstract bodies of knowledge that universities deal in. In the last analysis it is language that matters in any subject that is measured with tests and exams. Universities in the future may operate very differently because of complex information technology, but what they teach and research and how they teach will still be embodied in language just as it has been for over 2,500 years, and even if it is possible to deliver an encyclopaedia in a second, there is unlikely to be a matching increase in our reading speed.

This is not to say that the choice of media of instruction is not important. Media define the circumstances of learning, they determine who can access learning and they do, in subtle ways, affect what we learn. Marshall McLuhan strove to articulate the changes that come with placing the same message in different media when he claimed that the medium modifies the message and that media are extensions of man (McLuhan 1964; McLuhan and Fiore 1967). McLuhan's own guru, Harold Innis, in effect argued that epistemes are the product of the dominant medium. Media that lasted like cave walls favoured continuity and were time binding, but they restricted spatial growth. By contrast media such as paper that could be easily transported were space binding and facilitated the growth of empire (Innis 1950; Innis 1972). McLuhan foresaw that electronic communications would create a new episteme which he likened to a global village. More recently Tapscott has described those who live in the episteme that comes with the Internet as the 'net generation': 'They have a different culture, psychology and approach to learning, consuming, working and playing than their boomer parents ...'(Tapscott 1998a: 2). Tapscott is looking at the impact of the first generation of the Internet. What is waiting in the wings was not foreseen by him or Innis or McLuhan.

Is it a real university if it is asynchronous?

Open universities essentially function asynchronously and have been doing so with some success since the UK Open University began in 1971. However, as Don Hanna notes, 'open learning is not universally accepted' (Hanna 2001: 7). First generation virtual universities also function asynchronously and they too raise the question: 'Are they really universities?'

In the modern university, programmes of study are valued in terms of the number of credits or points they contribute toward a degree. Credits or points are based on a quantitative estimate of the time involved in doing a programme, in particular the contact hours in lectures, seminars, tutorials and practicums that Hanna refers to as 'clock hours of seat time' (Hanna 2000: 7). These are fixed times for synchronous communication between students and teachers which are the *sine qua non* of conventional universities. Most of a university's efforts go into providing the rooms and teachers for this kind of communication. They are the main events of university instruction, where the teaching transaction can be seen to take place.

Students are also expected to spend time in private unsupervised study, reading and writing. Typically, they are set assignments that encourage them to look for the knowledge they need in their textbooks, class notes and libraries. In due course the assignments are marked and returned, providing students with feedback. This asynchronous interactive learning process has depended on printing and writing technologies and the medium of paper and before that on parchment and papyrus. A major expense for a university is a good library with space for study and another is the time teachers spend marking and providing feedback. However, since many students study outside the university with their own books and without supervision, the costs per student to the university of the asynchronous component are less than the synchronous.

This leaves us with a question that many people who have attended a university must at some time have asked themselves. As long as a person can read and write and has some self-discipline, why bother going to classes? To societies seeking to reduce the costs of tertiary education the question then becomes: instead of using transport systems to bring people together to communicate in classrooms, why not use the postal service? Better still, today, why not use the Internet?

Teaching by correspondence, supplemented by radio, television and various audiovisual media, was the initial basis for open universities, which have grown to become what John Daniel (1996) calls mega-universities. These universities are moving their correspondence functions onto the Internet to become, in effect, virtual universities. Their success would seem to suggest that asynchronous communication by the written word could be all that is needed for the instructional interaction of a university. This represents an enormous saving in the costs of a university (Bates 1995; Daniel 1996). Why do we need the synchronous spoken word? Why do we still bother with lectures that have to be given at fixed times and fixed places at the lockstep pace of the teacher when we can have them printed off, videoed, streamed on the Internet or cleverly presented with illustrations and effects on Webpages for perusal by students in their own time at their own speed?

It is evident that a lot of people *are* able to study for a degree by correspondence or by the Internet. There are plenty of people who never attend lectures, borrow lecture notes, and keep to themselves and the library, and to the irritation of those who do turn up regularly for lectures, most of them get through their exams and assignments creditably. Some people are by inclination autonomous learners who prefer to study by themselves in hours of their own choice. Among those who want to go to university there are many who live complex lives with families and jobs and children that make attending fixed classes difficult. For them the asynchronous communication systems of open and virtual universities are attractive and effective. After all, what is written, especially what gets published, is more carefully considered and organised than what is spoken. The speed of reading as distinct from the lockstep of listening varies with the individual and allows for reflection and re-reading. When university management seeks quality assurance and accountability it is easier to apply rigorous instructional design and control to what is written than to what is said.

Yet, students want to talk. We consistently find that the majority of our mature postgraduate telestudents will go to great pains to meet their teachers and peers. Open universities have from the first felt the need for some conventional classes or for study centres or block courses where students can meet for a few days of intensive interpersonal interaction. Virtual universities find there is a student demand for some kind of meeting even if it is only the quasi-synchronicity of a chat room or a local centre where they can meet with other students.

The legend is that lectures go back to the days before print, when they were a way for students to make their own copy of the text that was being read to them. Such practice may still exist, but this is not what drives students to seek opportunities for face-to-face contact. They want to be able to talk with each other as well as with the teacher and not just about knowledge and problems. The expectation may be that students should spend a certain number of hours reading and writing but the reality is that many of them will spend much of that time talking. There are often more people chatting in the restaurants, bars, cafés, quadrangles and walkways of a university than there are studying in its libraries and it is a fair guess that not all of them will be involved in academic debate.

However, where people in the same field come together, even though they may be chatting and gossiping informally, they are likely to make play with the concepts, ideas, theories, events and people that they have in common. In so doing, they may also take on the distinctive way of speaking and behaving that will identify them as someone taking say Law, Computer Science or Drama. They may dress, affect the styles and mannerisms and frequent the same social scenes as their classmates. They are being initiated into the network that becomes 'class of '03'. They are becoming players in their disciplinary paradigm and involved in its discourse in the sense that James Gee uses the term: '… a combination of saying the right sorts of things in the right way, while engaging in the right sorts of actions, and appearing to think and feel the right way and have the right sort of values' (Gee 1990: xv). It is by talking with the full flavour of face-to-face synchronous communications that people are encultured in universities. The lone learner retains independence of thought at the expense of being seen as an isolate.

The traditional university caters for both synchronous and asynchronous modes. First generation virtual universities that use narrowband telecommunications for the Internet cater only to the asynchronous mode. They make a virtue of this, marketing themselves as a no-frills way for autonomous learners to streamline getting a degree by cutting out the trappings and non-essentials of university life. In so doing, they are acquiring a reputation as degree mills (Bear 1994). And if there is an added value in the synchronous communication component of instruction, then they are second class universities, because conventional universities now use the Internet and computers *as well as* the conventional modes of communication. They have the best of both worlds.

It is in the traditional class that the synchronous and asynchronous modes of communication intersect. It is here that students and teachers talk to each other about the established corpus of knowledge on a subject. Students bring texts and teachers bring notes and powerpoint presentations. What was written and printed before the class comes alive in synchronous discussion. Whiteboards act as auxiliary short-term memory. Students make notes to augment their memory and knowledge goes back into asynchronous mode as teachers and students gather their papers together at the end of class. In the lockstep of the classroom process, as a group of people are all thinking and talking about the same thing at the same time, knowledge becomes plastic. It is in spontaneous debate that instruction becomes a live art. True it can be boring performance, but it can also bring about a lasting change in the way a person thinks.

Narrowband Internet and virtual universities

The dynamic communication that is possible in a conventional classroom has proved difficult to emulate with narrowband Internet. Traditional speech allows rapid intuitive interaction and the huge bandwidth available with face-to-face allows subtle sensory cues of gesture, expression, position and voice. Compare this to the clumsy click-to-talk audio, audiographic and videoconferencing systems available on narrowband Internet with their delays in response and their unreliability.

There is also a problem in the ambience the Internet is acquiring. The Web is the biggest collection of words the world has ever known and it is still growing, but it is fast becoming a virtual Tower of Babel. The first commercial use of the Internet was the infamous Green Card scam in the early 1990s (Canter 1994). Up to that time the Internet was developing as a medium of great promise for academics. It was a democratic virtual meeting place that traded in ideas and arguments. People talked of liberating knowledge and information and saw in the World Wide Web a new Museion of Alexandria open to the world. Then it was commercialised and became a virtual Shinjuku of massive corporate sites and flickering advertising displays, a vast seedy supermarket that is a setting for investment frauds. Cyberspace is living up to the unsavoury images portrayed in cyberpunk novels like *Neuromancer* (Gibson 1984) and *Snow Crash* (Stephenson 1992). Increasingly it is seen as a place to purvey pornography, where paedophiles lurk and hackers breed viruses. People now seek information on the Internet at their peril, not knowing what comes with it nor which database operators are buying access to their information-seeking habits. Howard Rheingold called it the frontier of society, a place where law and order had yet to emerge (Rheingold 1993). Universities set up watchdog mechanisms to restrict and monitor the use of the Internet, and ensure that students do not use it for cheating and that academics are caught if they visit dubious sites. The Internet as we know it is fast becoming a graffiti-ridden information slum. Its future as an academic medium falls into question not because of its capability but because of its associations and reputation.

Something similar happened with television. In many countries, especially developing countries, its early use was to educate and inform. Where there was no other form of schooling and literacy rates were low it could be surprisingly effective. However, television became a commercial medium seeking to attract audiences to its adverts by pandering to the popular taste for violence, sensationalism and exploitation of personal life. It has acquired a dubious reputation as a source of knowledge and a means of education. Video is used in universities, but a glance at the numbers using a university video library shows that its use is marginal. Television has played a role in the development of giant open universities such as Sukhothai Thammathirat Open University, the Korean National Open University and the British Open University, but with the possible exception of The China TV University System it has not developed the key role envisioned for it (Daniel 1996).

Broadband Internet for virtual universities

The Internet2 is a consortium involving 190 USA universities, a number of large corporations and a few international universities concerned with establishing the next generation of the Internet for educational purposes. Its research and development effort is concerned with determining the functions necessary for the global deployment of what it calls collaborative services. A high priority is given to

> developing gateways among videoconferencing technologies, the development of automated scheduling mechanisms, and videoconferencing support services such as monitoring capabilities. It is expected that outcomes from the research and development efforts will include the creation of white papers and best practices documents leading to eventual ratification by standards bodies.
>
> (www.Internet2.edu)

Internet2 seems to be preoccupied with resolving the problems of the past by making videoconferencing work on the Internet.

Videoconferencing has always been a technology looking for a role in education. It adds little to what can be done by audiographic conferencing other than images of people talking, something that can in fact be distracting. To get the kind of interaction that looks natural requires skilful directing, professional camera work and a talent for talking in front of cameras. Videoconferencing can work between two sites for dynamic interaction between a small group of people or to show someone lecturing. However, interaction between many people in many places is difficult to coordinate. The more sites that are involved the more difficult it is to see the participants and the changes in expression and body language which are the whole point of being able to see them. However, although the struggle to make videoconferencing work may prove to be a cure for a problem that does not exist, it could have beneficial side effects. Wherever there are cameras at a site, distributed virtual reality becomes possible.

The technical limitations of today's Internet will be resolved. Moore's Law continues to apply and computer-processing power continues to double every eighteen months. Wired and wireless telecommunications become more and more ubiquitous. Available bandwidth will increase. Computers will be worn from head to toe and we shall have Internet wherever we go.

To realise the potential that this brings, a better way is needed to interface with information technology than the hybrid of typewriter and television technologies called a PC. For a quarter of a century the personal computer has given form to the idea of IT as a mixture of computing and communications. However, it presupposes literacy and keyboard skills and it is difficult to see further development of the Internet as a mass medium, especially while it is based on today's software and yesterday's keyboard. As the basic technology passes the level of a Pentium 4 and 128 k bandwidth, driving a PC with a Querty keyboard and Microsoft Windows software is like driving a Mercedes on a motorway using the reins from a stagecoach. PCs cause repetitive strain injury to fast users, are difficult to handle for anyone who is arthritic, scare off people who cannot type, are unreliable, break down, get viral infections and become more difficult to use as time goes by.

A glance around any lecture theatre shows the extent of students who use spectacles and aging populations increase the number, yet computer monitors are designed for normal vision. People buy prescription spectacles to read from monitors that cost as much as the spectacles do. Yet what is on a computer monitor could be displayed directly on Head Mounted Display (HMD) units in three as well as two dimensions. Computers could be morphed into spectacles and, as natural speech user-interfaces assisted by auto-correcting syntax systems develop, people could read and speak instead of read and write. Datagloves make it possible to gesture, point and touch in virtual reality. The technology keeps shrinking. Wearable computing will develop to match mobile access to broadband telecommunications. Mobile sound systems have to improve on the clumsy handheld mobile phones that are burning our brains.

A new technical paradigm needs to be developed for interfacing with information technology that will be direct, intuitive, and sensual and like the way people interface with other people in the real world. A key component of such a paradigm could be the avatar.

Avatars

One day, when wearable computers linked to transceivers develop to the point where they are part of the weft of the clothes we wear, we can imagine that our avatar in a virtual reality could look and act and even feel like a replica of our physical selves. We could in fact come to feel even better in virtual reality than in physical reality. Cybersuits will become intelligent and autonomous, able to mould themselves to the shape of our bodies so that they can remedy physical problems we may have in mobility, eyesight and hearing. They will assist, protect and empower our movements (Drexler 1990) while shaping our virtual presence to the way we want to look and sound to others. Today we are at an early stage in this development where there are many limitations, not least of which is what we do with our bodies while we are venturing into VR.

In a class people are usually seated and communication is primarily done from the front and from the waist up. It is perfectly feasible with today's technology to

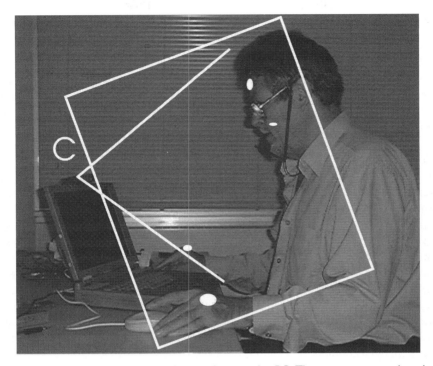

Figure 2.1   Basic situation for avatar for interfacing with a PC. The camera mounted on the computer has the person in a medium shot from the waist up (shown by two white lines). This allows an avatar to be made of that part of the person that is inside the rectangle. There is no need in a standard face-to-face classroom type interaction to see the back or bottom half of a person. Reflector patches on the hands and face are shown in white. They would transmit hand movements and facial expressions.

make an avatar for this situation that allows visual communication by hand and face and the front upper torso. Such an avatar could be operated from the security of a chair.

Avatars can be selected from a menu of avatar models or created by placing a photo of a person onto a standard avatar's head, but a 3D image of the front of the user's face that was mobile and reflected the person's expression could be effected using shutter glasses, reflector patches and a camera mounted on top of a PC. A software system would be needed that allowed a person to develop an avatar of their face and hands and the upper front of their body for themselves. By presenting their right and left profiles to the camera, it would be possible to create a 3D image. A neutral 'default' face would be established. Departures from this, as in a smile or nod, would then be recognised by changes in the positions of reflector patches on the face. Similarly, reflector patches on arms and hands would show how these moved. It would also be possible to save smiles, frowns and nods to use as emoticons. We could don our avatars like Pagliacci the jester putting on his motley so that we can laugh while we cry.

'My representation on the Net is not an inevitability of biology, birth and social circumstances, but a highly manipulable, completely disembodied intellectual fabrication' (Mitchell 1995: 12). Avatars do not need to be replicas of the person using them. They can be changed to make a person look older or younger, male or female, black or white. It is possible to borrow a friend's avatar or hire or buy an avatar and have telepresence as a tiger or mouse, or as Attila or Cleopatra. For many students being in a university is an opportunity to experiment with their persona and appearance. Classes could become less conventional in appearance. Students could explore the rhetorical relationship between what is said and who says it.

Do we need avatars in a virtual university? We are aware of no significant research that shows that it makes a difference to classroom instruction if teachers and students can see each other as distinct from being able to hear each other, unless of course the body is involved in the instruction as for example in learning to pronounce words in a foreign language. But this is not to say that there is no difference. There has to be. It is just that we do not know what it is or whether it matters. Instructional research has been preoccupied with the cognitive aspects of instruction and with measuring standardised outcomes. We lack the research methodologies that can take into account the affective aspects of instruction and the impact of smiles and frowns and laughter and explosions of anger. We are only beginning to recognise emotional intelligence (Goleman 1996) and the constructivist component in learning. We suspect the issue of telepresence in class will prove important. Our telestudents contribute in our classes as voices and there is a general feeling that they do not in consequence have full presence and participation. People like to be able to look round and see who is in a class. They are not pleased if they discover a lurker listening in on a virtual class without making their presence known. It is seen as a discourtesy. Part of a good class should be a sense that it is a safe place where it is possible to try opinions, ideas and new knowledge without being self-conscious or fearing ridicule and it could be that being able to choose how you want to look might help that.

Virtual class and HyperClass

We developed the concept of a virtual class in the mid-1980s with the idea that students and teachers in different places could come together synchronously with the aid of computers and telecommunications as virtual people in a virtual place (Tiffin and Rajasingham 1995). Initially we experimented with audiographic conferencing, but then became interested in the possibilities of distributed virtual reality. However, the more we pursued the idea of a virtual class, the more we realised how important it was for most students to meet in physical reality. Indeed, it seemed almost as though virtual meetings made them want to meet in physical reality. The paradox gave us pause. Would virtual reality really replace the traditional classroom which has survived for some 4,000 years?

Education prepares people for the larger environment of a society. While people in a future information society may make much greater use of virtual reality they will still eat, sleep and have babies in physical reality. People will still use rooms, so we will still need to prepare people to live in rooms and we will still have classrooms. But we also need to prepare people to live and work in VR. We need to know how to live and work in physical *and* virtual reality.

What seemed to be needed was a conjunction of the real world and the virtual world. This was the vision of Nobuyoshi Terashima, who as president of Japan's Advanced Telecommunications Research (ATR) communication laboratories between 1986 and 1996 led a team that developed a form of distributed virtual reality for teleconferencing that he called Telesensation (Terashima 1993). The technology allowed people who were physically present in different places to meet as telepresences to work together on a common task. Something similar was developed at a later date in the USA under the leadership of Jaron Lanier who calls it Tele-immersion (Lanier 2001). However, by then Terashima had revised the concept. In 1996 he began working on the idea of a spatio-temporal field of communication that makes connection not only between the real and the virtual, but between artificial intelligence and human intelligence. He named it HyperReality (Terashima 2001). It is an attempt to solve a fundamental communication problem of the future.

The concept of HyperReality (HR), like the concepts of nanotechnology, cloning and artificial intelligence, is in principle very simple. It is nothing more than the technological capability to intermix virtual reality (VR) with physical reality (PR) and artificial intelligence (AI) with human intelligence (HI) in a way that appears seamless and allows interaction.

The interaction of HI and AI is a developing function of communications and telecommunications. The interaction of PR and VR in HR is made possible by the fact that using computers and telecommunications, 2D images from one place can be reproduced in 3D virtual reality at another place. The 3D images can then be part of a physically real setting in such a way that physically real things can interact synchronously with virtually real things. It allows people not present at an actual activity to observe and engage in the activity as though they were actually present. The technology will offer the experience of being in a place without having to physically go there. Real and unreal objects will be placed in the same 'space' to create an environment called a HyperWorld (HW). Here, imaginary, real and artificial life forms and imaginary, real and artificial objects and settings can come together from different locations via information superhighways, in a common plane of activity called a coaction field (CF), where real and virtual life forms can work and interact together.

Communication in a CF (coaction field) will be by words and gestures and, in time, by touch and body action. What holds a coaction field together is the domain knowledge (DK) that is available to participants to carry out a common task in the field. The construction of infrastructure systems based

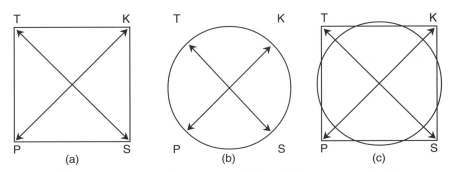

Figure 2.2 The basic elements and interactions of a class. (a) Using a conventional classroom.
(b) Using a virtual class on the Internet. (c) Using a HyperClass which conjoins a
conventional class with a virtual class.

on this new concept means that people will find themselves living in a new
kind of environment and experiencing the world in a new way

(Terashima 2001: 4–5).

Since 1992 we have been working with Terashima on the application of HR to
education and the design of a HyperClass and a HyperUniversity (Tiffin and
Rajasingham 2001). The idea of a global virtual university in this book is based
on the supposition that HyperReality or something similar will become a key part
of the infrastructure of developed societies within the first quarter of the twenty-
first century (Tiffin and Terashima 2001) (see Figure 2.2).

A HyperClass is a space where a conventional class is intertwined with a virtual
class in such a way that virtual components can interact with physically real components. The components are people, things and settings and the mode of interaction
face-to-face. The first experiments took place between Victoria University in New
Zealand and Waseda University in Japan in 1998 (Terashima 2001). To the Japanese
the New Zealanders were virtual and to the New Zealanders the Japanese were
virtual. In other words, whether the participants were virtual or real depended on
where they were in relation to each other. It was a form of teleconferencing where
the avatars, the setting and the objects of study were three dimensional and virtual
objects could be handled by and passed between the virtual and real people. In
2000 Nobuyoshi Terashima in Japan handed a disk to Lalita Rajasingham in New
Zealand and showed her how to put it into a computer. Rajasingham in her turn
passed the disk to Anne Gooley in Australia and showed her where it fitted. Then
Gooley passed the disk back to Terashima to complete the world's first HyperClass
between three countries. There are no technological limitations to the number of
centres and countries that can be linked together in a HyperClass in the future.

HyperReality or something similar will become available as an infrastructure
technology wherever there are broadband information networks. It will be widely
used for work and leisure and social purposes and because of this it will be used

by students and teachers and researchers in universities, whether universities think it is a good idea or not, or indeed whether it is a good idea or not. HR gives a choice as to whether to attend a university in virtual reality or physical reality and means that there are no limits to the number of students who can take a course or where they are located.

Terashima's concept of HyperReality, unlike Lanier's concept of Tele-immersion, has a further dimension. It is also a place where artificial intelligence can interact with human intelligence and which enables artificial life developed in virtual reality to cross into the physical world.

Artificial intelligence (AI)

Whether or not a machine can eventually be programmed to think in a way that can be recognised as similar to that of humans, or at least can pass Alan Turing's famous imitation game and appear to be human (Turing 1992), remains, half a century after Turing posed it, a question open for philosophical debate (Casti 1992). That computers can think autonomously on their own terms is not. It is this that should concern universities in the future.

There is an overlap between animal intelligence and human intelligence and we can recognise some areas in which animals are better equipped intellectually than humans. We have by selective breeding programmed dogs to do some things better than we can. Dogs have more olfactory intelligence than we do, so we use them to find things that smell. In return we feed and look after dogs. From this interaction we have developed a social relation with them that can transcend the original contract. In pre-computer days we held in awe people who could do what then seemed to be prodigious feats of memory and computation and regarded ability at chess as a hallmark of intelligence. In this form of intelligence computers have outgrown us. They can remember facts and figures and perform calculations and play chess in ways that no human can now match. The more intelligent they become in this way, the more useful they become to us. A researcher today without a computer is like a hunter without a dog and a student who leaves university without a symbiotic relationship with computers has little chance of surviving in the jungles of a modern society. We already have a symbiosis with computers whereby in return for providing us with memory and computation we nurture their development. Will social relations ensue? What better place to find out than a university.

So far AI has developed logical-numerical intelligence that can be applied in clearly defined domains. This is why it is so readily adaptable to the HR device of a coaction field and to the paradigmatic nature of university subjects. Wherever life is a game with clearly defined rules and objectives we should be able to play it with artificial intelligence.

There is little use of AI in universities today outside of computer science research but the idea of the Windows Microsoft 'office administrator' which has avatar form as a paper clip shows the direction AI could take, even if at the moment it simulates the intelligence of a troublesome two-year-old: trying to be helpful but in ways that are irrelevant to the task at hand; asking redundant questions at the wrong time but unable to provide help when it is really needed. However, it is a beginning and unless someone kills it off, could grow up to become really useful.

JITAITs

The Vygotskian approach supposes that the teacher is there when the learner needs them. A hand goes up in class, 'please, I don't understand', and the teacher comes over. This ideal is difficult to sustain beyond a primary school with small classes. In a university much learning is asynchronous. The learner has to wait for help and learning slows down. Getting feedback on an assignment a week or more after doing it is to lose the edge of all the questions the exercise produced. The idea of Just in Time Artificially Intelligent Tutors (JITAITs), as their name implies, is that they can be available whenever and wherever a student needs them. This has serious potential to improve instruction.

JITAITs are based on the concept of expert systems and intelligent computer assisted instruction (ICAI). These are effective where the domain of knowledge they address is restricted, paradigmatic and orientated toward problem solving. A JITAIT could, therefore, be an expert tutor on a subject that formed the domain knowledge of a coaction field in HyperReality. It would always be ready to help any learner in the coaction field and would improve as a tutor from each encounter with a learner, provided it received feedback from a human tutor. Such a JITAIT could come to take over many of the low level repetitive student–teacher interactions and is feasible now.

JITAITs could also act as personal tutors to individual students. They could search for information, keep track of where a student was in their individual programme of study and organise their learning activities. Interlinking intelligent agents that manage schedules, meetings, email and workflow are already used in office systems and the Web-based organisation of programmes of study that is taking place in universities around the world provides a framework for such a development. In time we could imagine JITAITs acquiring form and personality to act as a guide and mentor in a student's learning life in the manner of the servant-tutor pedagogue of ancient Greece.

Something similar could be developed to have a similar support function for university teachers, managing their email, class schedules, student assignments, marks and grades and linking with student JITAITs and university administrations. Essentially this is the addition of intelligence as office-based administration becomes automated and universities benefit from the applications of information technology that are taking place in the business world. A more interesting development for teachers will be when they get artificially intelligent secretaries with voice recognition that can be linked to the corpus of a teacher's email so that they know what, how and to whom a teacher is in the habit of writing and what is unsolicited junk. Since one of the main communicants for an academic is the university in which they work, since universities already spend an enormous number of hours devising 'official' paradigms of university communications (who is supposed to write what, to whom and when) and since everyone in a particular university could have the same model of artificially intelligent secretary, it might be possible to have happy universities where AI secretaries endlessly write to each other in bureaucratic harmony about bureaucratic things, while teachers get on with teaching.

What we have looked at so far are the kind of AI agents that can collaborate with people on specific tasks and have the appearance of intelligence that are becoming part of office environments. They will become part of the university IT environment and could take avatar form and be personalised. What we turn to next is more problematic.

Artifical Life in universities

Artificial Life (ALife) is a research paradigm founded by Chris Langton (Langton *et al.* 1992) which studies the nature of life from an IT perspective and experiments with the evolution of autonomous, intelligent artificial life forms which can range from the level of artificial brains which can self-replicate, to the level of societies of artificial brains connected through the Internet. Katsunori Shimohara (2001) sees the initial relationship of humans to ALife as being similar to the relations of humans to pets. For the kind of 'rich communications' that take place between humans and pets ALife would need to be equipped with 'mechanisms for artificial emotions'. To sustain a relationship with a human, ALife pets would also need to have autonomy, creativity and an attractive character. ALife creatures would also need to be aware of themselves and others and able to adjust their boundaries to different people and situations (Ibid.: 83).

ALife has a long way to go before it becomes more than tamagotchi-like experiments with AI pets, but ALife is programmed to evolve on the principles by which Darwin believed all life evolved. Unlike other life forms, however, intelligence in ALife is cumulative from generation to generation and in theory should evolve faster. There will come a point when it will be intelligent enough for us to ask: 'Is it not time for ALife to go to university?' What role would ALife take in a university? That of students going to classes and playing tennis and dating (ALife does breed), or that of servants to humans along the lines of JITAITs, or, heaven save us, that of ALife professors lecturing and researching and being profound?

Shimohara sees ALife taking form as virtual characters that evolve in cyberspace, but are also able to take robotic form in physical reality. They would be creatures of HyperReality, living entities that are virtual and real, that can co-exist with us in our avatars and allow us to co-exist with them as robots. For the first time ever we will be able to communicate with creatures that can see the world as we see it and whose world we can see as they see it. In a relationship where it is possible to interchange viewpoints with an alien creature, who is the possessor and who the possessed? Such questions and the very idea of ALife are as bizarre today as the ideas once were that the earth circled the sun, that Hertzian waves could carry messages through walls and that the Internet could be used for education. But it is time for universities to address the logic of ALife development and the implications that ensue from the perspective of the coming rather than the departing episteme.

If we are going to have intelligent albeit artificial creatures living with us and working with us in the future, then perhaps they should be studying, teaching and researching with us in our universities. We need to learn to live with ALife before it develops complexity so that we have a better chance of achieving symbiosis with it. We have managed this over time with other life forms such as cats and dogs and we do not want ALife creatures to go feral. Better to have them studying with us in our universities than studying by themselves in their own universities.

Who gets to play God?

Television did not seriously come of age until direction was wrested from the hands of studio technicians who knew how to make the cameras work, by the artists and writers who knew what pictures they wanted. Film became an art when Charlie Chaplin took control of directing. The most advanced ship of her time, the Varga, sank in the first gust of wind because people who were not sailors dominated her design. At some point, university academics need to regain the involvement in the design of IT applications for universities they had in the early days of the Internet which, for a short and now forgotten time, began to look like an educator's Eden.

IT is imposed on many universities by administrators who buy software systems and require academics to adapt to it. The Internet is used by virtual universities with a mission to make money. The direction being taken by Internet2 lacks academic vision. The information technology that is coming to us can open the door to extraordinary advances in education, but equally it can become an instrument of standardisation and automation for replacing the rich variety of university life. Every major new idea in universities has come not from the state, the church or from business, but from scholars. It is time for academics to drive developments and tell the information technologists what is needed, before the new infrastructures are in place and universities again find themselves adjusting to a hand-me-down technology.

Five and a half million and the numbers still rising rapidly; they said it was going to be the biggest lecture ever held. It was a public lecture and the speaker was someone very special. Shirley, a newly enrolled grad student, was overawed by the occasion.

In front of her was the speaker's podium. Behind it the vast screen showed a moonscape, transmitted live from Moonmission. It showed a full earth shining high in the sky. And how it shone, because sparkling blue light was being superimposed on it to show how many people in what countries were jacking into the lecture. North America, just coming into view, was a great blaze of light, as was Europe in the centre and the Pacific rim of Asia. But there was little light across a great band that ran from Africa across the Red Sea, the Persian Gulf and the roof of the world to Mongolia and Siberia. True it held the great deserts of the world, yet, Shirley thought, these were the areas where humanity had its roots and where civilisation had begun and the first universities had held their lectures. If this had been 1,300 years ago everything would have been reversed. It was Europe then that was in the Dark Ages and North America a warrior's wilderness.

Shirley looked behind her at the vast auditorium of the HyperTheatre. It was designed as a semi-amphitheatre on the lines that Pythagoras 2,500 years ago had argued made for the perfect classroom. It blended into the mountains beyond and it seemed as though the vast audience stretched up their slopes, those in the far distance no more than pixels in the virtual reality. She felt lonely in this multitude and wondered if there was anyone present she knew. Still thinking about the ups and downs of universities over the millennia, she ran a query to see if her Iranian friend was one of the lights from Tehran. To her delight he was and they clicked smiles and waves at each other as they zoomed in together and adjusted their avatars to sit side-by-side. Shirley was about to ask after his family when she got a message that her new teacher wanted to contact her. As she accepted, Prof. Sam appeared at her side and she found herself surrounded by avatars of people wearing the same coloured academic gowns as herself. Everybody began introducing themselves. What a nice way to begin a programme of study, Shirley thought, warmed by the telepresences around her and a sense of collegiality with the worldwide audience.

A warm buzz rose from the multitude as others searched for and found friends. Shirley had read that the sound of warm welcoming words had been digitised from rustling leaves, while cool, critical chatter came from the rattle of bare branches and applause from the sound of breaking waves.

Just at that moment the light dimmed, the sound faded and he was there on the podium. Like each one of the millions present, Shirley could see him clearly directly in front of her and it seemed as though his wonderful smile was just for her. Even as an avatar, his charisma enveloped her.

'My friends,' he began, 'Benjamin Franklin once said that a well-educated citizenry is the best guarantee of democracy. So I am come to this university, to talk about democracy, real democracy, the final democracy, global democracy.'

A great roar of applause began to roll in.

Chapter 3

Instruction in universities

Instructing is done to help people learn. It can be done well or badly. Sometimes it is difficult to tell which of these ways has been chosen.

(Gagne 1974: 3)

The possibility of the emergence of ... a new instructional paradigm raises the whole question of paradigms and how they change.

(Heinich 1970: 25)

Introduction

Vygotsky posited that there are two planes of activity in education, the intra-psychological of the learner and the inter-psychological of the learner's relations with others in the role of teachers (Vygotsky 1987). At one level there is communication between students and teachers about the application of knowledge to problems and at another level communication within the learner and within the teacher about the application of knowledge to problems. The roles of teacher and learner are relative to, dependent on and interwoven with each other. They are interlocked communications from the opposite poles of the learner–teacher axis. We call the combined communication interaction of teaching and learning 'instruction' and since it is a communication system, an instructional system in the abstract is a paradigm.

This chapter looks at university instruction as a paradigm within the university paradigm. How does instruction in a university function as a communication system, what are the techniques, technologies and media that made instruction possible in the past, how are they changing today and what will they be like in the future with the kinds of information technologies forecast in the previous chapter? We attempt to describe the instructional paradigm of the modern university and that of a global virtual university of the future. Parts of the future paradigm are already apparent in the current paradigm and parts of the current paradigm are seen as continuing in a future instructional paradigm.

Table 3.1 Characteristics of university instruction in the new and the old epistemes

The old episteme	The new episteme
• Teacher-centered	• Student-centred
• Knowledge-based	• Problem-based
• Lockstep learning	• Flexible learning
• Authoritarian	• Democratic
• Individual study	• Group study
• Face-to-face and paper	• Internet
• Classroom	• HyperClass
• Teacher-administrated	• Computer-automated

Episteme in university instruction

As a communication process, instruction has to match the communication processes of the episteme in which it takes place. There is no point teaching students to write with a quill on parchment when the world is using computers. How people teach and learn, as well as the content of instruction, have to accord with societies' expectations of how things are done and this is more than being able to use the current media of communications. From the point of view of our episteme, Socrates is a heroic figure dying with the dignity of a great teacher, but from within his own episteme he was an unrepentant corrupter of youth. The design of instruction in a university needs to reflect the mores, manners and styles of communication of the society it serves. In more authoritarian times teachers were not questioned. We move into an episteme of user pays where the customer is king and students want service. This does not mean that instruction is any better or worse if it privileges students above teachers or *vice versa*.

If it were possible to make a fresh start and design a system of instruction for universities for the new episteme that was unimpeded by any existing rules, regulations or traditions, is there any clear best method in the present or from the past that we should take into the future? University instruction these last fifty years has been full of fads, but nothing has emerged that is manifestly better than anything we have seen over the last 2,500 years. The tempo of change quickens in universities with the Internet and computers, but this too does not mean instruction is getting better.

There are good teachers and bad teachers and good students and bad students and the good universities are good universities not because they have some special system of instruction, but because they get the best teachers and the best students, and the ratio of teachers to students does not seriously exceed 1:10 which means that it is possible to have more teaching taking place than in universities with larger ratios.

At the beginning of the last century the fastest humans could travel was at the speed of a galloping horse, now they can fly above the speed of sound. Health in developed countries has improved to the point where people now live almost twice as long as they did 100 years ago. During this time there has been no evident improvement in instruction in universities or indeed at any level. University students do not learn twice as much or twice as fast as their predecessors. Instruction is where transport and medicine were 200 years ago. It has yet to find its Stephenson, Pasteur or Lister. Its practitioners use lectures like doctors of yore used leeches, because it's what university teachers do, not because they know what they are doing in any deep sense.

Instruction in the modern university accords with a well-defined paradigm where students and teachers interact in the application of knowledge to problems by means of lectures, seminars, tutorials, texts, assignments, tests, and exams. Special subjects may have other components as well, but these are the basic elements and their syntagmatic application has a sequential syntax. Exams come at the end, lectures are at fixed times on a weekly basis and instruction is chaptered into semesters or terms. The paradigm has proved remarkably durable and while there are grounds for concern as to its efficiency and effectiveness, it has worked for nearly 1,000 years in the sense that most people who attempt degrees get them and are mostly satisfied with them. Therefore, rather than regard university instruction as we know it as a mindless template we have sought to analyse the system that makes it work in a modern university. In doing so we realised the extent to which the Internet is assuming basic communication functions of university instruction. It opens a window of opportunity to shift to the instructional paradigm described at the end of this chapter. However, what we appear to be seeing is the old paradigm being reinvented in the new media with the danger that, far from improving instruction in universities, it could make it worse.

The instructional paradigm of the modern university

Figure 3.1 shows the instructional paradigm of the campus-based modern university as a communication system in the abstract that enables teachers (T) to help students (S) apply a knowledge paradigm (K) to a related domain of problems (P). These, along with an administrator (A) are the key inputs. The output is students who are competent practitioners of the knowledge paradigm (S+), students who are not (S–) and research initiatives (R).

The traditional means of implementing instruction in a modern university is still by face-to-face and paper media. However, the growth of the Internet as a medium of instruction brings a virtual dimension, which is shown by a shadowed input.

There are five subsystems within the instructional system for organising, paradigm acquisition, syntagm practice, in depth instruction, and evaluation and certification. The media that make them possible are shown as inputs to the subsystems and they fall into two categories: traditional media and the Internet. Each subsystem is followed by what we see as the critical cybernetic question that should be asked if they are to function effectively. Arrows show where the negative feedback from these questions should be directed. This is not to say

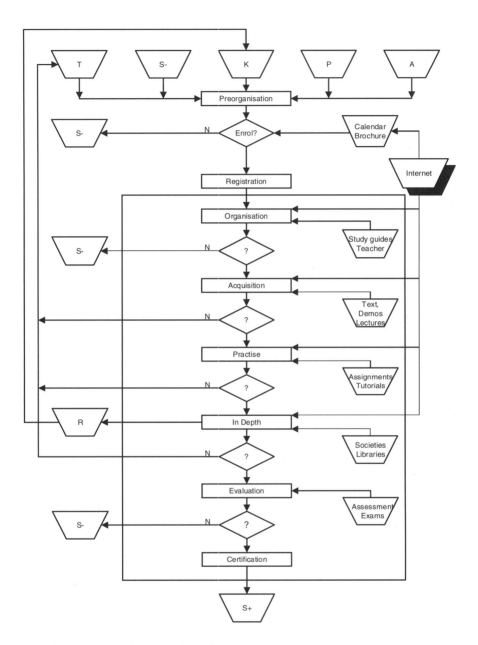

Figure 3.1 The instructional paradigm of the conventional campus-based modern university

these questions are actually asked or that there really is feedback, but where they are not there is a problem.

The system is shown at the level of a term or semester length programme of study. This is the basic operational unit of universities. It is what teachers are contracted to teach and students pay to take. However, these instructional processes are fractal. They can be seen at the level of instructional events in a class that last a few seconds, at the level of an assignment, a lecture or the whole course of study that leads to a degree.

Organising instruction

For instruction of any consequence to take place it has to be organised and there has to be an organisation. The development of universities as institutions with thousands of students and hundreds of teachers has meant that their use of time and space for instruction has to be coordinated before instruction can even begin. This external organising process involves designing programmes of study at the semester level that follow the formula of lectures, texts, assignments and exams, and seeking the approval of committees of academic peers who ensure that the design conforms to a university's very own paradigm of a programme of study. While every university jealously guards its very own instructional template, worldwide they seem remarkably similar.

Once a programme is accredited it can be fixed in the concrete of a university's calendar, which becomes the reference point for the brochures and advertising that present the design to students to help them decide whether they want to enrol.

Universities run a cottage industry as a factory with little flexibility. They are surprisingly effective in this in that they produce qualified students and they run on time. But they do not do this efficiently, as anyone who has ever undergone the trauma of enrolment day must agree. Many universities are now set on becoming businesses, but one wonders how they can survive as such if they continue to make it so difficult for their customers to get the service they want. Will universities that do cater to their customers put those that do not out of business or will students be prepared to continue to accept poor organisation if the quality of instruction is good?

One reason for the confusion that surrounds registration in a modern university is that the parties involved have conflicting objectives; students want to study what they want to study, academics want the best students they can get or, at the very least, students with prerequisite competencies and university administrators like airline administrators want to fill all the seats available. If there is a big demand for a programme of study then the objectives of its teachers and the administrators can be attained, but many students are left unsatisfied when the programme's quota of students is filled. The dissatisfied students now apply for their second choice and, if that is full, their next choice. In this way students cascade over from course to course until finally all places are allocated and the administration is happy. However, this leaves unhappy students studying subjects in which they have little interest and unhappy academics who have had to accept marginally qualified uninterested students. The problem is well-known, but universities have not been listening to student feedback. They do not need to; student numbers around the world are increasing faster than student places in universities. It was this that created the opportunity for a first generation of virtual universities that gave students what they wanted.

Changes are now taking place in the modern university. The new mode of university administration looks to business models of efficiency and pressures teachers to take notice of student feedback and improve the organisation of their programmes. Webpages for public access now provide an online version of a university's calendar and subject brochures and more and more it becomes possible to register online. Students are selecting instead of being selected. They can surf the Web for their university. Indeed as universities begin to allow students to take electives from other universities, it even becomes possible to shop online for individual programmes of study.

The internal organisation of a programme of study is often not much better than its external organisation. Students are often left with uncertainty as to what is expected of them. The detailed internal design of a programme of study needs to be communicated and its implementation managed. Socrates would not last a minute in a modern university. He had no lesson outline or set content, his lessons seem to have gone on for as long as his students could stand him interrogating them and there appears to have been no concern for set timetables and the formal organisation of classes. Of course there was a design to his instruction, but it was not explicit (Plato 1952). It was in his head and he could draw on it at any time to re-organise his instruction according to the way they answered his questions. We know it as the Socratic method. It is a way of organising instruction at the micro level.

Good teachers are like Socrates endlessly designing and redesigning instruction to manage their day-to-day interaction with students. It is a largely intuitive process derived from memory of how they were taught when they were students reinforced by the departmental memory embodied in a good secretary-administrator. Unlike Socrates, however, today's teachers have to accommodate the micro level of instruction in the macro level of university organisation.

The organisation of instruction seems set to undergo radical change with the growing adoption by universities of Internet-based platforms such as Blackboard (www.blackboard.com). Blackboard seeks to provide a total university communications environment, which includes administration, campus and collegial activities as well as instruction. Teachers can design and manage instruction much as they already do, but with more organisation and a much greater variety of functions and tools than they would normally employ. It becomes possible to build banks of questions, automate test procedures and review statistical analysis of how students are progressing. Did you ever wonder whether anyone ever read the course readings? It is possible to check student hits on individual course materials and correlate that with their test scores. Students in turn can organise their instruction, check their progress and directly access a greater variety of course materials because they can go to off-campus sites. Teachers are propelled into the basics of instructional design: they define objectives, match them with assessed outcomes and look to how they can improve learning resources. Academics begin to think systemically about what they are doing, helped by a genre of do-it-yourself books that explain how to adapt courses to the Internet (Hanna *et al.* 2000; McCormack and Jones 1998; Porter 1997; Hall 1997; Williams 1995; Schweizer 1999; Ryder and Hughes 1998; White and Weight 2000; Driscoll 1998; Cahoon 1998; Palloff and Pratt 1999).

This development brings efficiency, removes ambiguity and standardises instruction. It has the capability to improve that part of university instruction that is training. But university instruction, while it may involve training, is an educative process that addresses the individual and allows a knowledge paradigm to be questioned. There is a danger that the new software could entrench an already fossilised system. University instruction should allow for Socratic chaos. Perhaps when such systems become capable of synchronous communications, they will.

Paradigm acquisition

If university subjects are paradigms, then learning a subject means acquiring a paradigm. People need to know knowledge before they know how to apply it.

A fundamental way of getting knowledge is from an explanation. Ausubel argued that the acquisition of clearly organised stable bodies of knowledge was the most significant factor in learning new subject matter and in consequence advocated good expository teaching (Ausubel 1967). Robert Gagne took a similar position with his concern for clear analysis of learning hierarchies, by which he meant an organised set of interlinked intellectual skills which can best be learned in an optimum sequence (Gagne 1977). Clear explanation of a knowledge paradigm synchronously in lectures and asynchronously in text has been and still is a defining instructional process in universities.

Today teachers are putting their explanations on the Web. The software systems that academics are encouraged to use to design and manage their courses can also be used to house course texts, workbooks, lecture notes and powerpoint materials. Pioneering university teachers have been broadcasting lectures on the Internet since the mid-1990s. One-way videostreaming of lectures does not allow audio interaction, but students can download and view a lecture whenever and as many times as they want and then interact with their teachers asynchronously by email.

A Web search on a keyword with academic connotations is likely to find the pages of university programmes of study on the subject. Students search the Web for courses similar to the ones they are taking or want to take to compare them. As universities become more commercial and competitive their instructional materials become part of their marketing. If well-presented lectures attract fee-paying students then it becomes worthwhile to invest in the design of subject matter that can be accessed on Webpages.

Figure 3.2 A medieval lecture in astronomy at Oxford (Compotus Maualis ad Usum Oxoniensium, printed by Charles Kyrforth 1519, courtesy of Anders Piltz and Blackwell Publishing, Oxford). A clock, hourglass and candle ensure that the lecture begins and ends on time. The size of the lecturer and the two students reflects their relative importance. The students are making notes. These were called reportatio (carrying home) and were regarded as an effective aid to memory, but in danger of destroying a sense of the wholeness of knowledge. At the bottom students are shown debating the content of a lecture (disputatum) rather in the manner of a seminar (Piltz 1981). The only paradigmatic difference between then and now is what appears to be a birch cane in the hands of the lecturer.

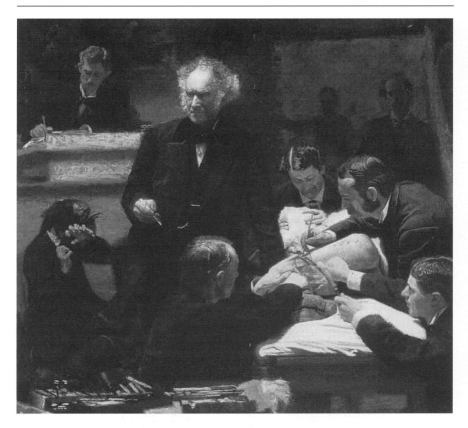

Figure 3.3 'The Gross Clinic' by Eakins Thomas 1875 (courtesy of Fred Ross, Chairman, Art Renewal Centre). Professor Gross lectures as his assistants operate on a leg. He explains as he demonstrates. The picture highlights his head, which is the location of paradigmatic knowledge on the subject, and the operation that is a syntagm of that knowledge. Behind the professor a student takes notes and one can see how the seats are banked theatre style. Even so, it is obvious that it is not easy to see what is happening to the patient.

Since Socrates, teachers have been pushing students to find for themselves the knowledge they need. A special aspect of knowledge acquisition in a university is that students are expected to supplement what they learn from lectures and texts with their own explorations of the relevant literature. Subject literature grows, like the number of students searching it. Today the Internet brings some relief to the pressure on space in libraries. Knowledge in the form of film, video, audio and three-dimensional graphics becomes increasingly available on the Web.

Besides making it easier to access texts, the Web allows students to break away from the traditional longitudinal sequencing of lectures and traditional texts by the use of hypertext. This allows students to navigate knowledge in ways that best suit their individual cognitive structures. It becomes possible to remap knowledge and shift between textual and audiovisual explanations blurring the distinction between lecture and text. This is an area where in the future students could be assisted in their searches by intelligent agents.

Teaching someone how to do something by showing them is another ancient instructional method. Even hens use it with their chickens. A demonstration is a syntagm performed by a teacher to illustrate how to apply a knowledge paradigm. Where a subject is abstract in nature like mathematics and philosophy the demonstration often involves the use of a blackboard and is closely linked to explanation. However, where a subject is syntagmatically manifested in physical reality it may not be so readily linked to theoretical explanation. Medical interns accompany doctors on their rounds, geologists and geographers take students on field trips, scientists have laboratories and departments of education attach their students to schools. Direct face-to-face demonstrations in real time carry their own tension and excitement. It is awe-inspiring to watch a skilled pathologist conduct an autopsy and progressively reveal the story of a person's body, but there are limitations and sometimes dangers in face-to-face demonstrations. In an autopsy only a small handful of people can actually see what the pathologist is doing and if the diagnosis of death proved to be Ebola those who did have a good view might not appreciate it.

A key factor in a demonstration is being able to see and hear clearly as the demonstrator directs attention and relates paradigm to syntagm. When demonstration involves detail it is only clear to the small group who can gather round the demonstrator. Film and video have overcome this to some degree with their ability to site cameras for optimum observation, for example, on the forehead of a demonstrator or in a spotlight. It is possible then to zoom in and out and to make the subject accessible to an unlimited number of people in safety, over and over again. As television and video become digital and definition improves, it becomes possible to integrate them into Webpages and to give students some control of how they see the demonstration.

The critical question for this process is whether students have acquired the knowledge paradigm and teachers do take note of this feedback. It comes at them from the level of nods of understanding in a class to the results of tests, assignments and exams. That a student has acquired the concepts, facts and theories that constitute a knowledge paradigm can be checked before moving on to practise, but the two are closely interlinked and it is often in practice that it becomes clear whether a student has acquired the knowledge paradigm at a depth which allows them to apply it, as distinct from memorising it.

Syntagm practice

Academics are often accused of living in ivory towers out of touch with the real world, of knowing knowledge but being incapable of applying it. It is indeed possible to simply teach and learn the knowledge paradigm without taking the next step and learning to use it. Universities are sometimes guilty of examining students to verify that they acquired the paradigm, but not that they could apply it, which is like learning what tennis is, without ever playing it.

The distinction between knowing a paradigm and applying it is clear in subjects that have their referents in reality, such as medicine, engineering and education, where syntagm practice takes place in laboratories, practicums and in real life. The key question 'can the student apply the knowledge paradigm?' becomes clear and teachers and tutors can see the answer for themselves and do something about it.

When a subject is entirely contained in words the distinction between knowing the knowledge and knowing what to do with it is not always clear. It is easy to verify that a student knows history, philosophy or literature, but not to measure if they can apply them. We can hardly expect that all students will go out to make history, philosophise or write a book. Students do apply what they learn from these subjects, but in ways that are subtle, individual and difficult to measure. A consequence is that written assignments are often set in ambiguous terms with an emphasis on length, suggesting that it is quantity that counts and that the number of words signals the importance of the problem. This ignores feedback from employers and the world at large that it is quality and brevity that count. The Web could provide an alternative way of doing written assignments by setting them within a purposeful context. The filmmaker Peter Watkins in a film for the BBC called *Culloden* (1964) introduced a docudrama style that showed the battle as though it was live coverage of the event. He wanted the viewer to feel that they were there and challenged by the historical or philosophical questions it raised. The Web is an excellent medium for this kind of situational exercise.

The change taking place in syntagm practice is in the use of computers and the Web for written assignments. Student assignments need no longer be full of spelling mistakes, grammatical errors and indecipherable handwriting. Computer spell checks, grammar checks, AutoCorrect and style analysis can improve student writing and eliminate many of the traditional marking chores of a teacher. Instruction can focus on whether a student can apply knowledge as distinct from whether they can write a lot.

Today there is growing interest in problem-based learning and collaborative and cooperative instructional practices that reflect the way professional practice increasingly involves teamwork. This may involve people located in different places who have to work as a virtual team. The Internet encourages the development of online communities of practice that prepare students for this (Hanna 2000).

In-depth instruction

Universities have an ideal of study as a profound experience which is at odds with the 'What do I have to do to get a degree' approach of many students. Research at Gothenberg University (Svensson 1976) and by Marton and Saljo (Marton 1976) showed a difference in the way students studied academic papers. Some sought to memorise while others looked for meaning. A distinction was drawn between deep and shallow approaches to study which has since been researched more widely, in part because deep approaches are seen as desirable in universities and in part because there is a strong correlation between shallow study and student dropout and failure rates. This raises the question of whether there are interventions that could lead students from shallow to deep study approaches (Kember and Harper 1987).

When shallow study students were habitually asked deep questions they tended to persist in their shallow study approach, but when deep study students were given shallow questions they tended to adopt shallow study approaches. Moreover, when deep study students came under heavy workloads or had little freedom to explore their learning or interest in the subject matter or did not perceive its relevance to their needs, they tended to adopt shallow study approaches (Ibid.). These factors are under the control of teachers and suggest that we could think of shallow and deep study being matched and related to shallow and deep teaching practices. We would argue that a special attribute of university instruction should be to promote deep study in conjunction with deep teaching. We term this in-depth instruction and would see it as something that begins as students become proficient in the application of a paradigm and begin to contextualise, socialise and critique it. It is the path to becoming part of the community of paradigm practitioners and being involved in the ethical values and issues of professional practice.

In depth instruction has similarities to the term deep learning as it is used by Fred Litto (1999) as something that refers to the whole approach to being a student. Litto goes so far as to suggest that enabling deep learning is something that has to be built into the very design of an educational institute and the ethos in which it is founded. A university needs a strong campus life with a good library, societies and teachers ready to engage in what in the medieval university was known as *quodlibetum* (a disputation on a question about anything). It draws attention to the strong situated learning perspective of Marlena Scardamalia (Hewitt *et al.* 1997) who argues that the learner cannot be unaffected by the context in which they learn. If this is the case it has profound implications for designing a global virtual university.

Deep study students, as they become proficient in a paradigm, seek to become part of the community of practitioners associated with it. They want to try new applications, join societies, attend conferences, write articles and get jobs and esteem. What we would identify as a characteristic of a deep practice teacher is that they do not see their role beginning and ending at the classroom door. It is the role of good academics to introduce their students to their knowledge paradigm community. The Internet is making this easier as it becomes a vehicle for promoting collegiality in the community of a subject paradigm. Students explore the Websites of international societies and associations for themselves, they email students in other countries about upcoming conferences and when they find an interesting citation in a text they look for the author on the Web and get in touch with them by email.

The social and cultural context of a subject paradigm is elusive. Its existence is evidenced by its absence. One of the first virtual universities, the Open University of Catalonia, designed an instructional system that initially was strictly instructional. Students were dispersed and studied at home on the Internet and there were no classrooms. However, feedback from students showed that while they were satisfied with the instruction they were receiving, they wanted a social life with it. They wanted to meet and talk to each other and socialise what they were learning. Somehow it seems in the process of chatting about a course over coffee, as people talk about what they are studying and the people involved, a subject gathers social meaning and values. Students see their subject through the eyes of their peers and from within their episteme. The OUC set up a virtual café. Students who lived close to each other could get together as a small group over a drink and then link to chat with similar student groups via the Internet.

There are many cybernetic questions for in-depth instruction but a key one would be: 'Can a student critique the knowledge paradigm and its application?' Negative feedback is something a teacher should address, but it is also an issue for the university itself because, while a teacher can set the immediate context for a programme of study, it is the university that sets the wider context of campus culture.

When students and teachers question the knowledge paradigm they open the door to research initiatives, which could lead to publications that could in time modify the knowledge paradigm. This renewal from critique is the dynamic at the very heart of the university paradigm. Today university administrations in seeking efficiency look to uncoupling teaching and research and see savings from not needing an infrastructure for in depth instruction. Instruction then becomes training and the institution a university in name only.

In our search for efficiency we forget what can be lost when we have no time for ourselves in a university. We need time-out for what Foucault called the 'cultivation of the self'. He noted that in ancient times this was thought of as a 'cultivation of the soul' (Foucault 1990: 43–6). Learners need to be able to reflect on what they are learning. The pressure to pass through the university experience as quickly as possible is at the expense of the maturation that allows a student to find his or her own place in a knowledge paradigm (Foucault 1990).

Evaluation and certification

The instructional process is intensely cybernetic. Every one of the interactive processes described above should have a feedback system that seeks to improve the way it performs. Feedback is needed from the level of classroom question and answer to the setting, marking and grading of assignments and exams. Formative evaluation provides feedback to teachers and students to improve performance. Summative evaluation is the final evaluation of a student when, on the basis of final examinations or internal assessment, a teacher recommends to the university administration that a student be given credit for taking the course or otherwise. It is the university that awards the credits and ultimately a degree, but it is the teacher who traditionally evaluates whether a student can in the last analysis apply a knowledge paradigm and critique it.

We return to some of the problems inherent in a system where evaluation is entirely in the hands of the teacher in the sections on accreditation and assessment in Chapter 9. However, at this point we would note that feedback in interactive communication systems is two-way. Teachers and students alike look for the nod or smile that says they are going in the right direction and just as teachers give final feedback with grades, students now routinely evaluate teaching performance when they complete a programme of study.

Good teachers in traditional instructional programmes tend to be good at the tactical level of reacting to feedback from individual events of instruction. They are not so good at the strategic level of reacting to feedback at the macro level. It is university administrations in their search for efficiency that address questions as to what proportion of students pass at what grade and with what degree of satisfaction and how many drop out or decide against doing the programme of study and why. Administration systems now have information management systems that allow them to scour a university's databanks for long-term trends and universities begin to evaluate the utility of degree programmes after students have entered the workforce. Such information can be used to improve programmes of study. It can also provide the basis for commercial decisions as to which programmes of study to invest in and which to cancel.

The Internet encourages feedback and evaluation from students to the extent that many university teachers find themselves overwhelmed by the sheer volume of it. Responding to student emails becomes a significant part of a teacher's job. This kind of feedback is qualitative in nature with individual students expressing themselves directly and sometimes emotively to the teacher. It can give teachers deep insight into the needs of their students and their own performance; however, if student comment is overwhelmingly negative and sometimes it can be deliberately so, it can cause considerable stress. An unpleasant phenomenon of the Internet known as flaming is when people send a stream of heavily critical email. Universities find they have to monitor email and chat rooms to stop students flaming each other and their teachers. Flame wars can erupt on a campus that involve whole departments and faculties, but is this any worse than the riots that occasionally happen in universities as a way of providing feedback?

Instructional paradigm for a virtual global university of the future

We turn now to the kind of instructional paradigm that could exist in a global virtual university of the not too distant future. It would be embedded in the technology described in Chapter 2 and retain the universals of university instruction described above, while seeking to address the problems in the current instructional paradigm. It starts to become possible as the conventional instructional paradigm moves onto the Internet and will mature in a broadband Internet environment. However, a basic form of what is described here would be feasible today.

Again the instructional paradigm is shown as a communication system in the abstract that enables teachers (T) to help students (S-) critically apply a knowledge paradigm (K) to a related domain of problems (P) with the help of an administrator (A). These will still be key inputs in the future. However T now encompasses professors responsible for programme content, tutors and JITAITS and there is a new key input in the form of systems designers (D). Where the previous instructional paradigm applied to the physical reality of a campus, this one takes place in HyperReality, specifically in the kind of HyperClass described in Chapter 2 where the design and management of instruction will involve the preparation and development of coaction fields for subject paradigms. Figure 3.4 shows all the elements of the instructional paradigm as lying within a HyperClass except for the shadowed box that shows a traditional class option.

There are six subsystems within this instructional paradigm: self study, interaction with JITAITs, interaction with tutors, interaction with professors, attempting assignment and certification. These subsystems achieve the traditional functions of organising, paradigm acquisition, syntagm practice, in depth instruction, evaluation and certification, but in a different way.

A syntagm of instruction occurs in a spatio-temporal field. The instructional paradigm of the modern university that we described above is based on programmes of study that last for a semester (term) and take place on a campus. The paradigm we describe here for a future global virtual university is based on weekly time units in a HyperClass.

This paradigm, in contrast to the traditional paradigm, is student-controlled. Instead of the students being selected for a programme of study, it is the students who select the programme. They do this by interacting with the university's Webpages. These pages are the portal to the instruction and would be designed to catch the attention of anybody searching the Web to find out how to apply knowledge x to problem y. Keywords in x and y would be used as attractors and the knowledge and its problems would become part of marketing. Having caught the attention of a potential student, the Webpages would show what the instructional unit has to offer, who the professor is, what they have published on the subject, what prerequisites are needed and what the level of study is. If the prospective student decides that the one week HyperClass unit can help them learn to apply x to y and that they can cope with the level of instruction, they can sign on, pay a fee and be given a password that lets them enter the HyperClass. Registration would take five minutes not five hours.

The first interactive process is called self-study. We could think of it as a student's HyperCarrel in their HyperClass, a place where they, not the teacher, can organise their instruction, where they have a map of exactly where they are in their studies and what comes when, where and with whom, where they can call up texts and readings or browse online libraries, where they can follow a work guide, try self-marking or computer-marked exercises or computer assisted instruction

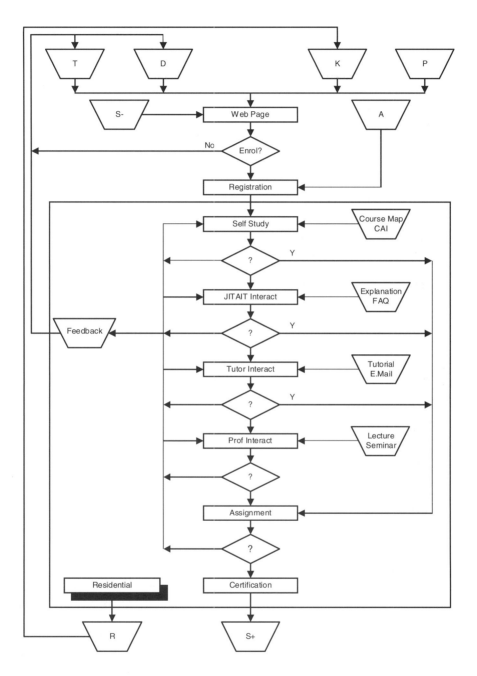

Figure 3.4 Instructional paradigm for a global virtual university

(CAI), check their grades and progress, do some emailing, see if any of the other students they are involved with want to chat online, call up their JITAIT or tutor, review a copy of a lecture or seminar or work on their assignment. Apart from the JITAIT, most of these features are already available with the Blackboard-type Internet instructional environments that are being adopted by universities.

The next interactive process is with a Just In Time Artificially Intelligent Tutor (JITAIT) that is an expert system on the basic question: how does one apply knowledge x to problem y? JITAITs were described in Chapter 2 and, as their name indicates, are available anytime. They could be embodied in an avatar. At its most basic, a JITAIT would be a system that responded to Frequently Asked Questions (FAQs) with a repertoire of answers that would expand with use. When it cannot answer a question it refers it to the human tutor and thereby steadily improves its ability to answer. JITAITs would progressively deal with the redundancy in instructional interaction.

Tutors, similar to the teaching assistants in the US university system, could be recruited from postgraduate students. As they enrolled, students would be put into small groups of 10 to 12 and allocated a tutor who would meet with them electronically for scheduled tutorial sessions. The elementary questions students may have about their assignment would be dealt with at the level of the JITAIT, leaving human tutors to concentrate on in-depth instruction, helping students articulate complex difficulties, acquire habits of deep study, interact with their peers in the tutorial groups and contextualise knowledge and problems. Since there is no competition between students, they are free to work with each other on assignments. Questions that the human tutor could not deal with would be passed on to the professor.

The professor with responsibility for the academic content would give a lecture on the subject and later conduct a seminar. The lecture could be a synchronous event like that described at the end of Chapter 2 or it could be a HyperReality recording. Interaction with large numbers of students would be via email. The professor could also give a synchronous seminar towards the end of the week that would allow direct interaction with moderate-sized groups of students. The seminar would be used to revisit the basic issue addressed in the assignment from the perspective of the students and the questions they had raised in tutorials and assignments.

This instructional paradigm is problem-orientated and each stage has the student addressing just one question: can they critically apply knowledge x to problem y? If they think that they can (Y in Figure 3.4), then they are encouraged to try an assignment that will demonstrate this and to keep working at the assignment through the week using the different kinds of instruction available to them.

The tutors would mark assignments, referring any difficult issues to the professor, who would also have responsibility for monitoring marking standards. In time, computer-assisted assessment would take over much of this work. Students who complete the assignment and demonstrate they can apply x to y would exit the HyperClass with a certificate of proficiency and a feeling that at last they were able to solve the kind of problem that had brought them to the instructional unit in the first place. A student who still did not know how to apply knowledge x to problem y could repeat the unit. However, in a commercially-operated university a repeat that involved further synchronous interaction with professors and tutors might involve a further cost.

The system is shown as having a residual component in physical reality from the old paradigm because we do not see the traditional format based on traditional media disappearing. The shadowed box in Figure 3.4 could be a follow-up week in a residential international centre or a conventional university campus, an idea that is discussed in Chapter 9. Such an extra week of conventional instruction would provide a conventional context for in-depth instruction and for the development of ideas leading to published research.

Positive and negative feedback on every process is provided to everyone to improve performance. The JITAIT learns from feedback from tutors. Tutors get feedback from students and from the professor. The professor gets feedback from students and tutor. The students get feedback from JITAITs, tutors, peers, and professors and from the self-study system. System designers would receive automated feedback from the system as a whole as to how effectively each process was functioning. This would be matched to the feedback from the administrator about the numbers of students who registered, dropped out, failed and passed as well as details of marketing costs. From this what was taught would be iteratively redesigned and expanded or reduced according to demand.

Basic cybernetic control of the system could become a function of computer-assisted instructional design (CAID), which uses feedback from each iteration of instruction to improve its design (Tiffin 1996). In principle, CAID is like a management information system. The detailed level of quantitative feedback about every possible interaction in the system should make iterative optimisation of instruction possible at a very different level from anything we have in universities today.

A system like this is organic in the sense that it would grow or decline in response to student demand and how well it addressed that demand. A HyperClass system of this nature could start with a small number of students and with the professor acting as tutor to sort out initial problems and would grow with success. The use of JITAITs is a key factor in allowing student numbers to grow, while the quality of instruction improves and costs are reduced.

HyperSubjects in HyperClasses

A HyperClass is a shell for instruction in a HyperReality environment, just as a classroom is in the physical environment of a campus. It is somewhere students can meet with professors and tutors for lectures, seminars and tutorials and, like a conventional class, it will have blackboards and audiovisual aids. It can be a venue for a HyperTutorial, a HyperSeminar, a HyperLecture or even a giant lecture like that described at the end of Chapter 2. Unlike a conventional classroom there are no limits to the number of people who can attend.

The HyperClass would have more functions than a conventional classroom. The HyperClass can be a library, a personal study carrel, a place to meet with JITAITs, a point of departure as a telepresence into coaction fields of practice or a portal into other virtual classes in other universities.

University classrooms are generic environments where different subjects can be taught. Terashima postulates that coaction fields can be embedded in coaction fields without limit provided their attributes are not in conflict (Terashima 2001: 11). HyperSubjects can be embedded in a HyperClass. Where it would be difficult to conduct an anatomy class in a conventional classroom, there should be no problem conducting a class on HyperAnatomy within the framework of a HyperClass.

Brazil has a fascination with the use of images in education. Samuel Pfromm Netto studied the way different media framed the content of education in different ways (Netto 1998). The Brazilian documentarist Benedito Duarte sought objectivity in what he portrayed. His film of a necropsy won many prizes for the clarity and accuracy with which he approached the subject. Yet, just as Netto noticed how the choice of media affected content, Duarte found within the single medium of film that every shot involved so many choices of camera lens, angle and movement and of lighting that he was forced to an intense appreciation of how accidental and subjective the portrayal of phenomena is. As in Eakins Thomas's picture (Figure 3.3) it shows one perspective, at one point in time, in one particular frame of reference.

It is possible in HyperReality to have a telepresence anywhere there is a camera linked to a telecommunication system. The more cameras there are covering different facets of a scene, the more detailed and immersive the virtual reality that can be created. It becomes possible for students in a HyperClass to follow their teacher through the blackboard into a virtual reality of a physical reality. They could be telepresences at an actual autopsy of a suspected case of Ebola anywhere in the world and in safety see what is happening from any perspective, zooming in on details, looking over the shoulders of professionals as they do their job and windowing lab reports and X-rays. If the pathologist is wearing a camera on their forehead every student could have the viewpoint they will need when they practise.

The first HyperClass between Waseda University in Japan and Victoria University of Wellington in New Zealand took as its subject ancient Japanese ceramics. This involved making virtual simulacra of a collection of ceramics. To do this each priceless artefact had to be carefully moved onto a pedestal from which it could be photographed as it revolved. When they were safely archived in virtual reality they could be taken out in the HyperClass and casually passed back and forth between Japan and New Zealand (Tiffin and Terashima 2001).

Chapter 4

New academics for old

Every teacher is always a pupil and every pupil a teacher.
(Gramsci 1971: 350)

They [the streets of Sialkot in 180BC] resound with cries of welcome to teachers of every creed.
(Sacred Books of the East, vol. xxv: 2–3; in Edwardes 1961: 64)

How much worse will it have to get for these clever chaps to change?
(Hills 2001: 17)

… faculty must begin to design instruction and not just deliver instruction.
(Olcott 2000: 274)

The processes by which professors are appointed bear some relation to papal elections.
(Tight 2002: 30)

Introduction

Teachers are a universal of the university paradigm. As universities change to adapt to the new episteme so too must the teachers, not only in the way they teach but in the wider role they play as academics.

In Chapter 2 we defined teaching as a communication process that took place within the teacher as well as with the learners. We saw that the overt communicative acts of lecturing, questioning and marking are being modified by the new media and methods of instruction. The way a teacher thinks does not change so readily. For many, being an academic is more a way of life than a job they can leave as they exit the car park. Today university administrations seek to define the teacher paradigm. Job descriptions in the contracts of teaching staff require them not only to teach, but to behave and comport themselves in ways that fit university mission statements, but do not allow for the affective component of personal commitment and sense of vocation that many teachers have.

This chapter outlines a future teaching paradigm and a new kind of teacher and academic hierarchy. In our view there would continue to be published professors at the apex with a supporting level of tutors or teaching assistants, but we conceptualise the introduction of Just in Time Artificially Intelligent Tutors (JITAITs). They will be the 'new' academics.

New teachers for old

John Tiffin was giving a paper in Vienna. One of his newly minted doctoral students was in the audience. Also in the audience was his own doctoral supervisor, Bob Morgan, whom he had not seen for many years. John introduced his old professor to his ex-student saying, 'Meet the man who was your real teacher.' He then proceeded to give a lousy paper and duly received a caustic evaluation from his old professor to the amusement of his own student.

Robert Morgan was one of the founders of the instructional design movement that has so influenced education over the last forty years. Many of his doctoral students went on to teach in their turn and in so doing many of them pass on not only a subject paradigm, but also Morgan's way of teaching it. Yet all he did was to sit and talk and ask questions. The method is as old as the idea of a university. It was the way of Socrates who was the teacher of Plato, who was the teacher of Aristotle and so it has been passed down for at least 2,400 years.

Julia Kristeva introduced the idea of intertextuality by which she meant the way meaning in a text is made up of the meaning from other texts (Kristeva 1969). There is intertextuality in the way a teacher's teaching is made up of the teachings of their past teachers. Most of us can remember what we thought were bad teachers as well as good ones and teachers try to emulate the good ones and avoid being like the bad ones. Simplistically this might suggest a Darwinian process at work and that teaching should progressively evolve. However, what is a good teacher to one student is a monster to another and what constitutes good teaching in one episteme and one country may not be so in another. There is little sign that teaching has improved over the ages. We still look back to the Greeks for good example.

Yet, withal, some elements of the paradigm of university teaching seem almost archetypal. Societies have always wanted their professors to be wise, altruistic and concerned for the public good. The crucial idea of a teacher in the medieval university was that they had an authority based on the dignity of their knowledge (Verger 1992). This does not fit easily with the new transactional view of teaching as an information service, but it is an expectation people continue to have of university teachers that is evidenced whenever they fall from grace. We will need to care about the reputation of teachers in a university of the future.

So what is it that university teachers actually do? The immediate answer is 'teach' and it is with this that we are primarily concerned, but we need to recognise that in hard fact most teachers probably spend only a third of their time teaching. The other two thirds are spent on research and administration, especially administration. They also get involved in public life.

Teaching

Is there anything in the way academics teach that can be said to transcend nation, culture and time and so needs to be incorporated in a university of the future? The neo-Vygotskian communication model defines the role of a teacher as helping students to apply knowledge to problems. What differentiates the university teacher is that they also help the student critique the relationship between knowledge and problem because they are involved in research.

Chapter 3 examined the critical communication processes involved in university instruction. These are interactive processes, and today's students take a greater part in these processes than their predecessors did, but it is still the teacher who has the primary responsibility for initiating instruction. This means that a university teacher should be able to: design and manage instruction, explain and demonstrate how knowledge is applied to problems, set assignments, tests and exams that allow students syntagm practice, evaluate student performance, provide feedback to improve it, motivate students, engage students in dynamic interaction so that they can sensibly critique the knowledge–problem relationship, introduce them to the community of knowledge in the subject paradigm and help them to research, contextualise and reflect on what they learn. Along with these capabilities go the communications skills of knowing when, for how long, in what tenor, in what sequence, with which students and in what setting, to explain, demonstrate, question and judge. The job also calls for sensitive management of the multitude of contingencies that occur in the teacher–student communication axis.

Teaching in a university is complex and demanding and it is not always obvious when it is being well done. Griffith University did a metastudy of what constitutes good teaching in a university (http://www.autc.gov.au/caut/rrgt/chapter2.html). Drawing extensively on papers from the UK, USA, and Canada, the report makes the point that because there are so many different aspects to teaching, good teaching is hard to define and no single system of evaluation can ever measure it. There is no 'right' way to be a good teacher.

Studies of teachers and teaching are usually based on the supposition that teaching is the independent variable and learning the dependent variable and that teaching is responsible for learning. Yet the teacher–learner communication axis is one of interaction that can only function with what in cybernetics is known as circular causality. A teacher initiates a communication to a student which causes the student to communicate to the teacher which causes the teacher to communicate back to the student. The exchange or the class may come to an end, but the ripples of circular causality may not. They carry through to the next class or into an assignment or an evaluation. A Cambridge don describes how she was given a low evaluation by a student for 'assistance with essay writing'. This lead her to check the student's essay grades only to discover that the student had not presented any essays. When she asked the student how she had reached the evaluation the student explained that it was her judgement of the assistance she would have got had she written an essay (Beard 1995: 7). Instruction is a two-way process in which teacher and learner are interdependent. If we can accept that new born children can turn the people around them into teachers (Gopnik *et al.* 2001) then surely we can suppose that university students have some responsibility for their own learning and for the way their teachers teach them.

When states paid students to go to university and student grants depended upon teacher assessment, the assumption was that students had only themselves to blame if they failed. University teachers were regarded more as content providers than teachers and learning as a function of student intelligence and application rather than the outcome of teaching. There was little by way of feedback to teachers to improve their teaching. Today, the pendulum is swinging to the other extreme. As paying customers, students blame their teachers for their failings. They want to know why they do not have good grades when they paid good money and did the things they were told to and if the teacher does not reconsider their grades they are prepared to go and see the teacher's 'supervisor', give the teacher a bad evaluation or, if they find others who are dissatisfied, to take action as a class.

A wave of litigation is sweeping through universities as students argue that they have been cheated, that they were sold a programme of study under false pretences, that they cannot get jobs with their degree and that their teachers were ineffective. Sometimes the students have a case and unlike their universities they are prepared to go public. Many such actions are settled out of court.

The response of universities to this situation has not been to increase teacher salaries and improve student to teacher ratios, but to apply the notion of quality assurance. This is a guarantee without a guarantee. The universities' customers are assured that they can have confidence in what they learn because of the controls put in place by the university.

University teachers come under increasing scrutiny that is intended to ensure that they actually do what teachers are supposed to do. The problem of course is that we do not know what good teachers do that is good and whatever it is, it cannot be separated from what their students do. However, the new breed of university administration with its roots in business culture has little sympathy for what smacks of mystique and is prepared to standardise those teaching processes that can be observed and understood by the student customer. In so doing they create an environment for neo-Taylorism in universities.

Scientific management, the brainchild of Frederick Taylor (1856–1915), held that the manufacture of a product could be divided into a sequence of tasks that would allow people to do the tasks they were best at, as distinct from trying to complete the whole product (Kanigel 2000). We can see something like this happening in universities with moves to separate teaching, research and administrative functions. Carried to its logical conclusion teaching itself could be subdivided into its component processes so that different people could be assigned to do different parts. In Taylorist terms people who are good at lecturing would lecture, people who are good tutors would tutor, people who enjoyed marking (and who knows, there may be such) would mark and so on.

Taylorism led to Fordism and the assembly line factory. Making manufacturing a sequence of distinct definable acts meant that factories could be automated first for piecework and later for robotisation. This deskilled the workers and shifted the design function from traditional craft knowledge acquired by workers through apprenticeship to a specialist function controlled by management. This raises the spectre of instruction being broken down into small clearly definable tasks that can be conducted by computers and of the craft knowledge that a teacher has becoming the property of the university that employs them.

Academics do not spend all their time in high-level interaction with students. A great deal of their time is spent on mundane repetitive low-level interactions such as marking fixed-answer tests and answering what on the Internet are known as frequently asked questions (FAQs). In Chapter 3 we described how JITAITs could be used in the future for such repetitive teaching tasks and how this could free teachers for the more demanding roles. However, we also noted that JITAITs get smarter. We can imagine that while at first JITAITs will take over the low-level automatic jobs in teaching, they will in time become capable of more demanding tasks. This raises concerns about the replacement of humans by computers, as the process of standardising and automating teaching expands. The commercialisation of universities will create pressures to computerise instruction because the biggest cost to a university is the academic staff and it is the need to increase staff proportionately to the increase of student numbers that inhibits profitable expansion.

Universities are not garages that pump knowledge into people. They are an expression of the highest aspirations of a civilisation. Some parts of instruction can be automated but some cannot. Applying Taylorism to tell the difference may not be a bad thing. It is as silly to think of universities in a couple of decades still being totally taught by humans as it is to think of them being totally taught by computers. We suggest a possible future teaching hierarchy that differentiates the roles of human intelligence and artificial intelligence in teaching.

An academic hierarchy for the future

The pedestal of the teaching hierarchy of the future will be computerised. From a teacher's perspective, the bottom level of teaching activities includes marking tests, exams and assignments with predetermined answers, collating marks and providing data on student activity, such as attendance and subject results. Such automatic activities can be done by computers and most teachers would be happy to let computers do them.

The second level would be tutoring. It is where teachers interact with students to guide their learning. It involves listening to students, comprehending the difficulties they have in mastering a subject and its application, eliciting performance, being able to explain and demonstrate, monitoring student practice, marking assignments, tests and exams where answers are open-ended, providing detailed feedback and answering questions. It requires considerable one-on-one or small group communications and is the reason that low teacher to student ratios make for good instruction in a university. This level is labour intensive and, as they become commercial, universities will look for ways to reduce costs by automating tutoring.

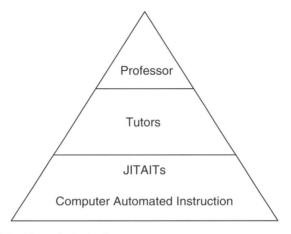

Figure 4.1 Teaching hierarchy in the future

'I am the group tutor,' said Shirley. 'There are nine of us in this HyperTute at the moment. They are all studying to be teachers and are interested in how you teach your theorem and in you yourself.'

Pythagoras smiled at her and gently inclined his head. 'I can answer questions about my life and teach you how to apply or prove my theorem, but my instructional design is classified. However, I am allowed to explain why I teach as I do.'

'That sounds fine,' said Shirley. 'Now I want you to meet the others.' She glanced up at the toolbar that was always at the top of her vision when she was in HyperReality and saw that he had finished accessing her basic bio. He would be checking each of them out in turn as he did his group intro-protocol. The Pythagoras avatar was a demo model of a new range of JITAITs from HyperTutonix Inc., based on famous philosophers. Sam the professor for EDU 505 (New Tutoring Techniques) had been lecturing on their application and had set them an assignment to see how far it was possible to use a JITAIT to teach Pythagoras' theorem to a class of fifteen-year-olds. To begin with they were familiarising themselves with the JITAIT in a HyperTutorial run by Shirley who had just got a part-time position as a tutor.

Shirley found the visual detail of the avatar remarkable and the emoticons so natural that the thing seemed to have a personality. According to the brochure it could access up to four overlapping coaction fields.

'Are you from Afghanistan?' asked Ahmed, the student from Egypt.

'No' said Pythagoras, 'I am Greek.'

'Then why are you wearing a turban?' said Ahmed.

'I spent part of my life in Egypt and Babylon and am often depicted with a turban in recognition of the way I blend Asian and European thinking.'

Someone else asked Pythagoras where he had taught and he swept his arm to the scene behind him. The Pythagoras avatar came as part of a HyperSubject package that included exercises and settings and the tutorial was set in an imaginative rendering of the site of Pythagoras' School at Crotona in Calabria. The tutorial group appeared to be sitting within a curve of colonnades on a rocky promontory with the Gulf of Taranto in the background. Pythagoras explained that there had been an inner circle called the mathematicoi, who lived at the school and dedicated themselves to study. They were allowed to talk and debate. Then there was an outer circle called the akousmaticoi who lived independent lives outside the school and attended classes but were not allowed to participate in discussions.

Sounded like the difference between taking a course and auditing it, thought Shirley. Why did universities draw distinctions between people and create hierarchies? What, she wondered, was the difference between her and this avatar that it was only too easy to think of as the real thing. She noticed how the group spoke with respect to what after all was nothing more than some clever programming, as though it actually was a reincarnation of Pythagoras. Was reality just appearance?

The group had now switched to asking questions about how Pythagoras taught his famous theorem.

'No one actually knows how I taught, except that I explained my theorem with geometry. Algebra which provides a popular explanation today developed after my time.'

'Does it make a difference?' asked the Japanese student.

'Look at the floor,' said Pythagoras. They all glanced down and saw that it was laid in a pattern of square and triangular tiles that corresponded to the theorem. 'You can,' said Pythagoras 'pick up the tiles and check their spatial correspondence to the theory whereas with algebra the theorem becomes an equation.' Behind him a window appeared showing the Pythagorean formula.

Shirley began to feel despondent. Would there be any need for human tutors like her in the future when you could get performance like this from a JITAIT? How could she match the production skills of HyperTutonix, a company that intended marketing Pythagorean philosophy and mathematics to the whole world? The avatars were beginning to look sexier than the humans and they did not eat, sleep, lose their cool, or go to the bathroom.

'How many languages can you do this in?' asked the American student.

'Besides the three languages that this tutorial group is using at the moment, I can handle another two languages synchronously out of a total of 25 languages available for my subjects and it will be possible to update with new languages. I also check individual vocabularies from student biodata and adjust my vocabulary accordingly.'

A murmur went round the group as the implications for them as future teachers sank in.

'What about practice?' asked another of the students.

'The bank of questions that can be accessed through me now links abstract questions to practical exercises,' replied Pythagoras. 'Students select a question, analysis of the answer picks up where they are having problems, and I in my role as Pythagoras advise them on where they are going wrong. My process speeds are such that I can respond to learner problems as they apply the theorem. Background patterns in the learners build up so that if there are any inexplicable anomalies I can bring them to the attention of a group tutor.' He turned so that they could all see him smile at Shirley.

'Could you do an exercise with one of us,' asked Ahmed, 'so that we can see how you go about it?'

Pythagoras pointed to one of the Doric columns in the background. 'Would you care to use my theorem to measure the height of that column?'

'In feet or metres?' asked Ahmed.

'Whichever you wish,' said Pythagoras. 'The height will be the same.'

Shirley could not help herself. 'Everything is numbers,' she interrupted.

Pythagoras smiled at her and a message windowed at the edge of her vision: 'Not understood.'

'I thought your philosophy was based on the idea that all reality is numbers,' said Shirley.

'My philosophy coaction field is not open,' Pythagoras replied. 'Shall I open it so that I can answer your questions?'

Suddenly Shirley felt much better. She grinned: 'No, keep it shut'.

There was a ripple of applause from her students.

Pythagoras just smiled.

As the story seeks to illustrate, JITAITs will improve and increasingly take over some traditional tutoring functions. It will be many years before they get to the level of this Pythagoras JITAIT, but there is nothing inherently impossible in what is described. A basic version of such a JITAIT is possible now and we are working on an experimental version.

The third level of the hierarchy is that of the master professors. Here we would find teachers in the old fashioned sense of content providers. They would be people who had achieved academic stature through research and publications and, therefore, really did have content to provide. They would have responsibility for the knowledge paradigm. If Pythagoras was alive he would be among them. Their primary purpose would be to communicate a synthesis of the subject matter in a way that brought it up to date, placed it in context and encouraged students to question it. Professors would do this by lecturing and giving seminars.

Figure 4.2 Components of the HyperTutorial with Pythagoras (copyright Nobuyoshi Terashima). This is a coaction field developed by Nobuyoshi Terashima from a design by John Tiffin. It will serve as the basis for an experiment between Terashima at Waseda University in Japan, Lalita Rajasingham at Victoria University of Wellington in New Zealand, Fred Litto at the University of Sao Paulo in Brazil, Minako O'Hagan at the University of Dublin and Anne Gooley at the Queensland Open Learning Network which will seek to implement the elements of the Pythagoras story above. The hypothesis is that it is possible to teach the application of Pythagoras' theorem in HyperReality with a JITAIT in more than one language to students who are in different countries and come together as avatars.

Instead of being salaried employees, such professors could relate to their universities in the way authors relate to their publishers. Richard Katz believes such a development has 'the potential to change US education in profound ways' (Katz 1999: 48). Indeed it could radically change education everywhere. A global virtual university would be a means whereby no matter where a professor lived they could be available to students worldwide. Such professors would enter into a contractual relationship to retain their intellectual property and receive royalties for each student taking their programme. This could mean students paying different fees for different programmes. Professors of music might want to give master classes to a small number of students and do their own tutoring, in which case the rates charged to the students and the proportion that goes to the professor would be very different from the case where there was a class of millions. Here the professor would have to leave all the interaction to a network of tutors in different countries in order to focus on the media events of their virtual lectures. These might well be open to the public, attracting new students and giving them a feel for the level and nature of study. Because of its size, the cost of such a course could be lower and the professor, who would be using the lectures to market a book, might negotiate a lower royalty.

There is little incentive for today's university teachers to work hard at being good teachers. Promotion, praise and prestige come through published research, citations and the ability to attract research grants. Hence the idea of a new teaching paradigm which separates the functions of the teacher as subject expert seeking recognition and success through publishing, from the functions of the teacher as guide seeking success and promotion in the tutor role.

In some countries it is not unusual for university teachers to act as tutors in one programme and course coordinators in another. What is different about this proposed hierarchy is in the relationship teachers at different levels would have with the university. Tutoring would be a relatively stable job where tutors were paid a fixed rate for the number of students they were responsible for, or in the case of senior tutors, the number of tutors they supervised. Those seeking to offer programmes of study at the master professor level would submit them first for accreditation which would be on the basis of academic merit, not commercial feasibility. The risk is taken by the professor who would be dependent on royalties from the students who enrol. If numbers were low, they might do their own tutoring and perhaps also tutor on other programmes. They could have a role as a professor and as a tutor. Whether someone in the role of professor continued with a course if numbers remained low would be their decision in a virtual university where there were no costs involved in keeping a course on the books.

A global virtual university of the future facing global competition would research what the market wanted and would be prepared to pay whatever induce-ments were needed to attract the professors who could deliver it. Professors would find their own level in an academic agora in which they could make more money than any teacher has dreamed is possible or far less than a beginner tutor.

JITAITs can take over many of the traditional tasks of a teacher but could they ever replace human tutors or be used at the professorial level? Given the clarity of the components of Pythagoras' theorem, the logic of their relationships and the way they form a precisely defined domain, instructional designers could programme a comprehensive system of instruction that included tutoring and the semblance of a professorial role. Pythagoras' theorem is taught each year to many millions of learners around the world and a multilingual teaching system like this would seem to have enormous commercial potential. Imagine a series of JITAITs called 'great paradigmatists of the past' that had Aristotle teaching deduction, Einstein relativity, and Darwin evolution.

However, the essence of teaching in a university is to encourage questioning of the paradigm and while a JITAIT can respond to frequently asked questions it does so from within the logic of the paradigm with examples of syntagms for demonstration and problems for practice that have been selected because they fit the paradigm. A JITAIT would not be able to deal with contradictions arising from different contexts and epistemes and problems that do not fit with the paradigm. It requires a human with deep knowledge of a particular knowledge paradigm and an open critical mind, the kind of person we imagine a real professor to be to cope with paradox in a paradigm.

Administration

The list of what is expected professionally of a good university teacher makes no mention of what universities actually require of a teacher. This typically includes participating in committees, writing references, brochures and reports, preparing for reviews, attending weekend staff retreats, going on software familiarisation courses, interviewing prospective students. The list is endless. In the past much of the burden of academic administrative work was alleviated by competent secretarial staff. They were the legendary university dragons that had spent their working lives at a university, loved the mystique and knew where all the bodies were buried. They have long been retired and today's breed of business administrators sees it as efficiency to expect academics to do their own secretarial and administrative work. And this has increased with the demand for more reporting, monitoring and accountability. Professors now spend much of their time doing the work of secretaries. It is a reverse form of Taylorism in which they do a job they are not competent at for a salary way above that of someone who could do the job properly.

The tasks at the bottom level of the teaching hierarchy are where teaching traditionally merges into administration with the collection and collation of marks and grades and, as we have seen, we can expect these to become increasingly automated. Already the development of Websites and associated software is making it possible to automate the way enquiries from prospective students are dealt with. While the example of the application of Taylorism to manufacturing gives cause for concern as to how it could be applied to teaching, greater separation of teaching from administration can only be a good thing for teachers.

What is being lost in today's university is traditional collegiality, the process whereby academic colleagues working through committees controlled what was taught and how it was taught and sought in theory to preserve the notion of academic freedom and curiosity-driven research. In this spirit academics were happy to engage in the management and administration of universities. Unfortunately, they were inefficient and resistant to change. They sought to stop the clock rather than face up to the need for change as universities moved into a new episteme. Forward thinking academics have shifted their sense of collegiality to the colleagues they interact with on the Internet. Collegiality has already gone global and awaits a university with matching vision.

Who are the teachers?

In a future global corporate virtual university can anyone be a teacher? In terms of gender, ethnicity, culture or creed we would hope so. The only discriminators, we believe, should be that tutors should have skill in teaching in a subject

Figure 4.3a Complete faculty of Victoria University of Wellington in 1908 (Copyright J.C. Beaglehole Room, the Library, Victoria University of Wellington.)

Figure 4.3b The faculty of the School of Communications and Information Management, Victoria University of Wellington in 1999. The total number of faculty in 2002 is 611.

paradigm and professors the scholarship manifest in their publications. It should be possible for any specialist in some serious field of study to have the same responsible freedom to teach their specialism that they would have in publishing their research in an academic text. There is no equivalent freedom in today's universities where what is taught is prescribed by the university, within the ethics of the university and increasingly within commercial constraints imposed by the university.

The citizens of Crotona destroyed Pythagoras' school and sought to kill its teachers, students and alumni. The library at Alexandria was destroyed in turn by Romans, Christians and Muslims. German universities under the Nazis saw Jewish academics forced to flee. In 1933 the Council for Assisting Refugee Academics (CARA) was established to help them. Raymond Hoffenberg, its president, argues that the climate of bigotry today is if anything worse than it was in the days of the Nazis (Macleod 2001). Yet, as CARA can show, the record of the academics forced to flee universities because of their ideas is quite extraordinary in terms of later recognition of their contributions to knowledge in the form of Nobel Prizes. It is often the lone dissident voice that strives for the truth beyond the episteme that in time is seen as a great scholar and it is the special strength of a university to tolerate their difference and a special shame when they do not. It is the reason behind the tradition of tenure whose replacement by fixed-term contracts will see universities lose teachers with passion, loyalty and commitment.

There is a universal in teaching in a university that is quite at odds with the idea of a teacher as providing a commercial service. It is the pastoral obligation of a teacher to strive for a truthful, caring relationship with their students and to act as the conscience of society by speaking out on critical issues and if necessary challenging the status quo no matter how difficult or unpopular this may be. University teachers have striven for this in the light of the country and culture they share with their students. The records of Human Rights Watch, Amnesty International, UNESCO and the Network for Education and Academic Rights show that from Egypt to Ethiopia, Palestine to Israel and China to Afghanistan teachers have been harassed, imprisoned and tortured and have lost their jobs and even their lives maintaining the high traditions of their profession. In a global virtual university they will need to maintain such standards at a global level. This may be the single biggest issue that faces the future university.

Chapter 5

Old students for new

... higher education shall be equally accessible to all on the basis of merit.
(Article 26, Universal Declaration of Human Rights adopted and proclaimed
by the General Assembly of the United Nations on 10 December 1948,
New York United Nations 1950)

A sizeable new university would now be needed every week merely to sustain
current participation rates in higher education. New institutions are not being
created at this frequency. A crisis of access lies ahead.
(Daniel 1996: 4)

... universities should allow improved access by working class people, people
of colour, women in non-traditional professions and members of marginalized
communities, particularly people living in subaltern spaces.
(Torres 1998: 244)

We admit today that education begins with birth and ceases only with death.
(Trindade 1993: 16)

The more you learn the more you earn.
(Tony Blair, cited in Spring 1998: 6)

Introduction

Article 26 of the Universal Declaration of Human Rights is a noble ideal, but is it
remotely attainable? Not, according to John Daniel, if it is to be accomplished by
the expansion of conventional universities (Daniel 1996). But it is possible to
address this giant new market with global virtual universities that are commercial
and take the world rather than the state as their market.

It is the extraordinary growth in demand for tertiary level education that provides
the driving force behind the emergence of a global trade in teaching at the university
level. With it goes the question of how those who want to go to university can
afford it. A partial answer is provided in the reduction of costs that is possible
with a global virtual university.

This chapter examines the nature of the genie that the UN invoked half a century ago when it declared that higher education should be 'equally accessible available to all'. Who are the 'all', what is the student paradigm they want to be a syntagm of and how is this possible?

Growth in student numbers

The British Prime Minister, Tony Blair, established a benchmark when he said: 'we are committed to 50 per cent of our young people getting a university degree' (*The Guardian* 22 July 2002). If we think that 100 years ago less than 3 per cent of the people in the UK had any form of higher education then proposing such an increase is like proposing to extend a nation's riparian rights over the sea from a three-mile limit to a fifty-mile limit. It vastly changes the profile and resources of a country, other nations see it as setting an example to be followed and it raises the question: why stop at fifty?

Britain is a wealthy country that recognises that the knowledge and the skills of its people are to an information revolution what its coal seams were to the industrial revolution. All developed countries have similar intentions to see tertiary education expand as a way of growing their economies. The world is at the beginning of an explosion of higher education. The most important thing about the university students of the future is that there will be so many of them.

In 1950 there were 6.5 million enrolments in tertiary education worldwide. In 1997 there were 88.2 million. It would not be unreasonable to suppose that sometime in the first decade of the third millennium there will be over 100 million and approximately three quarters of these enrolments will be in university or equivalent institutions (UNESCO 2000: 71). Much of the expansion in university student numbers has been in the developed countries where approximately a third of the relevant age cohort is enrolled in university (Ibid.). There exists internationally a broad measure of agreement that the core mission of higher education is expansion (UNESCO 2000). Growth in tertiary enrolments in the populations of China, India, Indonesia, the Philippines, Pakistan and Bangladesh has hardly begun. The world population that is now 6.1 billion has doubled since 1960 and is projected to reach 9.3 billion by 2050 (UN Chronicle 2002). On top of this there is a trend to lifelong learning which means that more people will spend more time in universities.

Table 5.1 Tertiary enrolments (millions) by continent, 1950–97 (UNESCO 2000: 67)

	1950	1960	1970	1980	1990	1997
World total	6.5	12.1	28.1	51.0	68.6	88.2
Africa	0.1	0.2	0.5	1.5	2.9	4.8
Asia/Oceania	1.2	3.2	7.4	14.6	23.9	36.1
Europe	2.5	4.5	9.0	16.4	18.9	21.8
Latin America/Caribbean	0.3	0.6	1.6	4.9	7.3	9.4
Northern America	2.4	3.7	9.5	13.5	15.6	16.0

In democracies there is still a tendency to expect the growth in demand for university education to be met by an incremental expansion of existing state education systems funded through taxation. In principle this is an equitable way that allows access to universities by merit, but even wealthy states have difficulty sustaining university growth to match the demand. There is the massive capital cost of constructing buildings and developing transport infrastructures. Then there are the high ongoing costs of maintenance, support systems, salaried staff and the administrative costs of ensuring that students are selected on merit and merit their selection.

Global virtual universities are not supported by governments and must, therefore, be commercial. They make no pretence at being equitable, but are more economic than conventional universities. There is no large capital cost involved in setting up the software and hardware for a virtual university. If students pay for themselves and there are no selection procedures and no need for campus support systems, administration costs can be greatly reduced. Previous chapters have shown how teaching costs could be reduced and information technology used to reduce the costs of expansion. The increased demand that is seen as a problem for the old generation of state universities becomes an opportunity for a new generation of commercial global virtual universities which see the expanding demand for university education as a business opportunity in a sellers' market.

The changing demographic

With the exponential growth in student numbers comes a change in the composition of the student body. For most of the two and a half thousand year history of universities students have been a small privileged elite of mainly young men. This has begun to invert. To what extent will a global virtual university facilitate the changes?

One of the hallmarks of the modern university is the way it has gradually opened its doors to women students and teachers so that now the proportion of male to female students around the world is approaching parity. In Europe and North America, where women have had access to university education for over a hundred years, there is a clear majority of women students. In other parts of the world a catch-up process has been taking place since 1950. The convenience and ease of access of a global virtual university for women will help this trend.

Table 5.2 Percentage of females in tertiary enrolments by continent 1950–97 (UNESCO 2000: 68)

	1950	1960	1970	1980	1990	1997
World total	32	33	38	44	46	47
Africa	21	20	23	27	33	38
Asia/Oceania	17	24	30	34	38	40
Europe	40	37	42	49	50	53
Latin America/Caribbean	24	32	35	43	49	48
Northern America	32	37	41	51	54	55

Could the trend continue so that the university of the future will be primarily female? The assumption of male hegemony that dominated universities half a century ago seems to be giving way to an assumption of male inadequacy (Jones 2000). The spiral of silence (Noelle-Neumann 1984) that saw women as a minority keeping their thoughts to themselves in a class could see males becoming what Ardener (1973) calls the muted group. The growing number of women graduates means a growing number of women driving the professions and taking over management. There is still a predominance of men in top positions in the professions but they came from universities at a time when men were still in a clear majority. A change may be working its way through the system. It would seem possible that control of universities and ultimately of society could at some time in this century swing from men to women (Tiffin 2001).

Besides a gender balance, universities look to a culture balance. There was no tradition of discrimination in the ancient universities. There were Chinese scholars in India, and Islamic scholars in Europe. The development of theological universities brought discrimination by creed. The establishment of the European university in colonies in the sixteenth and seventeenth centuries brought discrimination by race. However, today walking through the campus of a European, North American or Australasian university is to see students from many countries, creeds and cultures freely intermingling. Could we then say that the United Nations Article 26 of the Universal Declaration of Human Rights has been achieved?

Religious bigotry, racial prejudice, cultural antagonism and political fanaticism are still with us and at the turn of the millennium provide the purposes for global conflicts. This is inevitably reflected in discriminatory attitudes within universities. How easy would it be for a blonde Protestant American to study in a Pakistani madrasa and voice a Western woman's opinion, or for a bearded Pakistani to enrol in an American university and express an Islamic perspective on women? How many university students languish in the wastelands of refugee camps because of their race, creed or culture? Nations support universities to educate people within the national culture. Universities are happy to take the money of overseas students, but universities are territorially tied to the state that accredits them as a university. They require all students to conform to the laws and social norms of their nation and speak its language which is likely to be English because the trade in tertiary level teaching is predominantly in English (Crystal 1997).

In 1950 over half the countries in the world had fewer than 1,000 students enrolled in universities and a quarter had no universities or tertiary institutions. Today there are few countries that do not have at least one tertiary level institution and there are over twenty countries with over a million tertiary enrolments (UNESCO 2000: 68). There is progress, but who caters to the university needs of minorities, of diasporas and of cultures with no written language? One of the first virtual universities on the Internet was the Open University of Catalonia that uniquely addressed the Catalan minority of Spain. There are proposals for a university to address Celtic culture. The Tamils are developing a virtual university. So are the Maori of New Zealand and the Native American community of the

USA. To a culture with no homeland of its own, whose members are a minority in many countries, virtual universities seem an ideal way to keep their language, traditions, arts and history alive.

A global virtual university does not have a homeland and it is possible for students of different races creeds and cultures to mingle freely and on equal terms. It offers something more. Students are not typed by their appearance. They can choose their gender, creed and culture and be anyone they want to be.

Would anyone want to be old? Until recently to be old as a student was to feel singular. People went to university directly from school. Such people now constitute barely half the university population in the USA (Dirr 1999). Universities are becoming communities of adults of any age rather than extensions of the school system. As in medieval times they become a way of life to which alumni return over and over again. A global virtual university of the future with no obligations to taxpayers for the efficient use of their money instead of seeking to rush people through the university experience could encourage them to take as long as they want over their studies. Instead of three years at university it could become normal to spend six years or more. Just as there need be no limits to how long a student took over a programme of study so there need be no limits to how quickly a student moved through a programme of study in a global virtual university other than the basic unit of a week. Participation in the life of a university need not be something that is only done while undertaking study. It could be like membership of a club entitling a person to ongoing participation in its intellectual, social and cultural life.

Students are getting older. The last century saw a doubling of life expectation in developed countries and the trend is expected to continue (http://www.oecd.org). In developed countries the proportion of the population above current retirement ages increases. The success of the University of the Third Age, which since its foundation in Toulouse in 1973 has expanded to every continent except Africa, suggests that elderly people could become a major component of the student population. In the USA Indiana university took a lead in 1983 in building a retirement community on the edge of campus for elderly students. Penn State University and the University of Florida are now doing the same thing. However, although the elderly are healthier than in the past, getting around conventional universities with their sheer size is daunting. In a virtual university the elderly can move about and socialise with people who have similar interests as easily as anyone else. In a virtual university no one can tell your age unless you do.

It is not only the elderly who want to go to university but have problems doing so. Prisoners, disabled people, hospitalised and housebound people are among those who have problems of time or access. There are also people who are shy or isolates by inclination who do not like the social bustle of a campus. For such people a virtual university is a simple, undemanding, convenient way to go to a university. They can be present as telepresences and attend class as avatars and keep their privacy and anonymity. Some people prefer the virtual to the real.

Students are on the right side of the bell curve

If a university is open to all and sundry does this not reduce the average level of student intelligence and will this not lead to a reduction in the standards of universities and the degrees they award? We have proposed a university where it is up to the prospective student to decide whether they have the prerequisite competencies for a course of study. The cost of a week-long module of instruction would not be very different from the cost of buying a book and, as with a book, one could expect that the customer could work out for themselves whether they could understand the content. This does not mean that the level of content has to be reduced to make it accessible to everyone. The standards to be achieved are made quite clear and anyone who wants to strive for them can take as long as they want and get as much tuition as they need and are not in competition with anyone except themselves. There is no need for a global commercial university to be locked into the way that state education systems cull by the norm curve.

'A statistician uses a bell-shaped curve the way an internist uses a stethoscope' (Gleick 1987: 84). Both are devices for measuring variance from the norm. If the factors measured by a stethoscope are graphed for a population they will tend to take the outline of an old fashioned bell. Most of the measures group around the mean. The further from the mean, the fewer the instances until they tail away at both extremes. The more doctors find that a patient's respiratory and cardiovascular rates are at variance from the norm, the more they become concerned to remedy

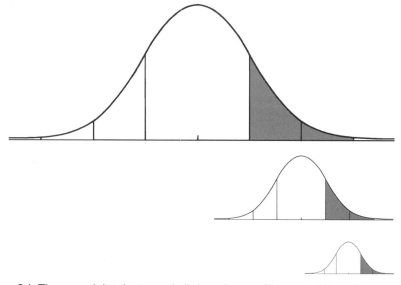

Figure 5.1 The normal distribution or bell-shaped curve. The vertical lines show standard deviations from the mean in positive and negative directions. The three distributions show how students with marks above the first standard deviation are progressively selected for advancement.

the situation. The idea of a norm curve has been established in education where deviations from the norm are also seen as requiring intervention.

Educational systems as a whole and universities in particular are interested in people with good alphanumeric skills. From primary school to the doctoral level in universities, a continuous process of culling takes place in accordance with the concept of the normal curve of distribution applied to the results of tests, exams and assignments that favours people with dexterity in written language and mathematics. It is the top ranking masters students who become doctoral students, the top ranking bachelors students who become masters students and the top ranking secondary school students who go to university.

There is no official form of progression for the people who are habitually in the bottom tail of the norm curve, but those who fall into this category at school are regarded as being 'at risk' (Herrnstein and Murray 1996), because they are likely to form a substantial element of prison populations. For them the equivalent of getting into a doctoral programme is getting a life sentence in prison.

There is danger that the application of the normal curve in education could polarise society. There are arguments that this is already happening in the USA as it becomes a meritocracy and that we are seeing the emergence at one extreme of a cognitive elite and at the other feral outcasts. Although the majority of people (the middle of the bell curve) are in neither group, stress is put on the structure of society by the pressures from the extremes (Herrnstein and Murray 1996; Lebedoff 1981).

Universities use ranking systems to cream off the cream of those who are skilful with words and numbers and it is with words and numbers that the world is run. There has always been some resentment of this. The division between town and gown is as old as universities. It is still there in the way that populists in countries such as the UK, Canada, USA, Australia and New Zealand refer to products of universities as the 'thinking classes', the 'chattering classes', the 'chardonnay set' or the 'nerdy intellectuals'. But what happens as the number of those who go to university passes parity with those who do not? Do we see the emergence of a two caste society: Unis and Antis? Imagine some summative norm curve made up of all the norm curves which measure possession of all the desirable factors in life superimposed on each other: income, health, house, safety, pension etc., where positive is on the right and negative on the left. On which side would we find the people who were good at school and went to university? From which side will the senior positions in government, commerce and the professions be filled? The UNESCO Report on World Education points to the emergence in industrial countries of an ' "underclass" minority of young people in precarious employment outside the formal education system, lacking the skills and competencies needed for full participation in the modern economy' (2000: 71). Article 26 promotes higher education *on the basis of merit*. It promotes meritocracies which could divide societies.

A global virtual university of the future by removing academic entry criteria could bypass the culling by the norm curve in conventional education. There need be no reduction in standards in opening the doors to wider participation in student life that credited people with whatever progress they did make. In contrast to the norm referencing of student performance a university could make clear its criteria of assessment as something to be achieved at a standard that was set externally to the university and would stand independent scrutiny. An example of this is a driving test. Driving a car requires acquisition of a knowledge paradigm that is at least as intellectually challenging as most semester length university programmes of study, yet the majority of people manage to pass a driving test and they go on to practise in an environment where mistakes are deadly. This is to credit people by reference to fixed criteria in contrast to crediting them by reference to a norm curve that inherently assumes that some will do better than others. There is no ranking of the people who take a driving test as there is in an educational system. Certification is something that is unaffected by how many pass or fail.

An even more complex knowledge paradigm than driving is happily acquired by the vast majority of children who go to primary school. Teachers at this level seek to ensure that all their students can read and write. It is in the secondary school that the selection process begins and it revolves around selection for higher education. We need to make it possible in some way to open the doors of universities so that everyone has the opportunity at some time to participate in a university and to have what progress they do make there, however small, recognised. Nation states provided equal access to primary education and then sought to do it with secondary education. Perhaps it is at a global level that we need now to contemplate this at a tertiary level. Global virtual universities would seem to provide the means to universal university education, but they have no governmental support. They need to charge for the education they provide.

Who can afford to go to university?

Is then the only requirement for being a university student that one can afford the cost? The poor scholar is as much a part of student tradition as the student prince. In the past they survived in penury, acting as servants to richer students, doing part-time work, finding patronage, getting a scholarship, taking religious vows so that the church would take care of their fees or by begging. The expansion of student numbers in the second half of the last century was largely achieved by using taxpayers' money to make it possible for students of merit to go to university. Today, growth is made possible by universities becoming businesses and requiring students to pay an increasing proportion of their costs through student loans and cost recovery programmes. There are signs in some countries of a student debt problem developing (UNESCO 2000: 70). Students who do the student thing of falling in love now find that marriage to a fellow student is impossible because their joint student debt would cripple a future together. The poor student returns in another guise. Today they make up the ranks of taxi drivers, waiters and sex workers in university towns.

The sheer cost of a university education could limit the expansion of student numbers if universities continue in the conventional mode and governments continue to cut their funding. The possibility that a virtual university can improve the quality of what is taught as student numbers grow while reducing costs well below that of conventional universities holds out hope for making university education increasingly accessible.

Who will control universities?

The first medieval university in Europe was that of Bologna which had its beginnings in student guilds. Students elected the Rector and the Executive Council. Students decided how many lectures should be held and what constituted terms. They rented rooms for classes and hired and fired professors. They decided what lecturers should do and how they should conduct themselves and fined them when they were negligent in their duties (Patterson 1997).

The Bologna model was copied by most of the early medieval universities established south of the Alps in Europe. This contrasted with the universities established in northern Europe based on the example of the University of Paris where the professors were in charge. It was this model that finally prevailed in the sixteenth century (Ibid.).

There has always been tension between students and teachers over the control of universities. In the modern state-subsidised universities where teachers' salaries were paid by the state not by students, academics ruled. In today's neoliberal world it is management, not teachers or students, who are in control. However, as students pay an increasing proportion of their fees, they could become once again the ones who call the tune.

Student rule conjures images of rebellious adolescents invading Chancellor's offices and declaring university communes, but Patterson (1997: 46) notes that 'One reason the student group was able to organise itself so successfully may have been that the Bologna law students were older than the usual undergraduate student' and that a reason students lost control of the medieval universities was that they were not there permanently. Today the student population is in fact becoming more mature and is acquiring a lifelong commitment and investment in the university. If the publishing model of academic involvement were to be introduced, it would see the upper echelons of teaching less involved with the university as an institution. The battle for control of the heart and mind of the university would then be between business management and students.

Recently we have become the recipients of alumni magazines from our old universities. How they found us after gaps of up to half a century is a remarkable feat of detection and reflects well on the databases they have developed. Presumably they feel it is time we made our wills. They sell nostalgia. Would we like some pictures of the old place, some memorabilia or to travel in academic company? As universities become businesses, alumni are targeted as a source of money, which they may well be. However, a sleeping giant is being woken.

Students become alumni and the alumni of a long-established university are a very large and often very influential body of people and their numbers grow as the university grows. These days they can be mobilised by the Internet. From a thin interest in the university of their youth and a token representation on a board of governors, alumni could come to represent millions of ex-students many of whom have an ongoing interest in the activities of the university and in undertaking further studies. Unlike the new breed of university administrators, alumni have a vested interest in maintaining and improving the quality of their university's degrees. Alumni want to see standards go up, because it means that the value of their qualifications is enhanced. When parents and children and even grandparents find themselves studying at the same university, there is concern for tradition. It could be that it is as they become alumni that students become the primary controlling body of the university of the future. A global virtual university could encourage such a development by involving students as stakeholders. They could acquire share options with their degrees (Sinclair 1998).

New learning styles

The intrapsychological and interpsychological processes of learning mirror those of teaching. The roles of teacher and student only exist in relation to each other. The communication between them is like that between dancers. They both need to know the instructional dance and it helps that teachers first learned to do it when they were students themselves. However, when the dance changes, as it is doing, then both the dancers must learn the new steps. In the past the teachers led, now it is the students' turn to lead. The student of the future needs to be a more proactive learner than the student of the past. They will need to accept responsibility for their own learning and the design of their own instruction. It will be up to them to maximise the learning situation for their own benefit.

The pendulum swings in favour of the student on the teacher–student axis and on the knowledge–problem axis in favour of problems. Problem-based learning is at the moment in its infancy and something that is particularly associated with Australia, Canada and the UK in fields of medicine and law. Increasing use of this approach may bring about a more critical attitude towards established bodies of knowledge. We may see students as players questioning the rules of the game rather than seeing teachers as umpires questioning whether the players know those rules. As students become older and more mature and return to universities to upgrade their skills, they bring with them a fund of practical knowledge as problem-solvers along with questions about the knowledge paradigm and why it does not always seem to work. Such mature students may well know far more about problems than their teacher. Many bring with them a critique of the subject paradigm and are a valuable source of case studies. This means that they challenge the orthodox dogma of a subject paradigm. The role of student as a relatively passive recipient of a teacher's guidance changes to that of questioning and challenging a subject.

Professional problem-solving takes place more and more in teams. Mature students going to university are accustomed to working in groups to solve problems and want a learning environment that reflects this. They want to be able to compare their problem-solving approaches with fellow students who could be fellow practitioners in the future. Instead of competing with their peers, they need to collaborate with them and increasingly to collaborate in virtual teams. Part of learning to apply knowledge to problems is to be able to do it in heterogeneous groups of people in different countries, from different age cohorts, different cultures and different languages.

Pedagogical JITAITs

In 1995 we postulated the idea of a student having their own personal JITAIT that would cater to their individual learning needs in the manner of the personal pedagogues of ancient Greece. Unlike a subject JITAIT that is specialist in a particular knowledge paradigm and improves by practice with many students, a pedagogical JITAIT would specialise in the way one particular student learned and would improve by practice with that student's interactions with different subjects. Like a subject JITAIT a pedagogical JITAIT could take the form of an icon to be clicked on, or assume avatar form, or be a quiet voice like that of a close friend looking over a student's shoulder at the same scene.

> He had been with her since she was a child. Of course in those days he looked like a cartoon. He would roost somewhere up in the right hand corner of her computer-generated virtual reality and any time she raised her hand to him he would blink and look at her and be ready to help. He knew exactly where she was in her studies and that she hated to be told how to do things, preferring to try to work them out for herself, but he was so good at suggesting things she could try when she was really stuck. She got her first datasuit when she was in high school and then Woo became like a real owl. When she wanted him all she had to do was look at him and he would fly over and perch on her shoulder. His gentle whisper of encouragement and advice helped her through the bad patch when her parents divorced. It was through his guidance that she became a teacher herself. He was with her all through her time at the Trans-Pacific Teleteaching Training College. By that time she knew he was in touch with other virtual teachers. With them he organised the virtual classes and it was through those links that he was able to advise her on how to relate to the other students with all their different cultures...
>
> Now that she was a teacher herself, Woo was still there for her. He knew so much about her. All she had to do was whisper his name and she could feel his grip on the shoulder of her datasuit, ready to listen to the problems she was up against and look for the knowledge she needed. Trouble was when she had to lift her HMD (Head Mounted Display) unit off to deal with the real world.
>
> (Tiffin and Rajasingham 1995: 152–3)

A personal JITAIT such as this is a more complex and problematic idea than that of a subject JITAIT such as the Pythagoras example.

The physical side of student life

If there is one thing we have learned over the years from our students it is that while they may be fascinated with the new modes of learning, most of them still want to meet, even if it is only occasionally, in old-fashioned real reality where they can eyeball each other and have a meal, or a game of tennis, or an affair. They want to play at being an old-fashioned student in old-fashioned physical reality.

The advertising agencies who now market universities know this and play not only on the fact that a degree will bring a better job and income but delicately hint that it is a top class singles club. The earliest glimpses of student life in the Greek and medieval traditions suggest that student life has always had a wild side. Student behaviour in the classical period was 'characterised by irresponsible actions, fainéantism, excessive drinking and womanising' (Eyben; cited in Kleijwegt 1991: 117). There are references to 'gangs of late Roman student-hooligans, terrorizing Athens and Carthage' (Kleijwegt 1991: 121). Cambridge University came about from academics fleeing town and gown violence at Oxford (Preston 2002). The stereotype of the student living a life of ideals and love affairs in rowdy taverns and cafés has some basis and still attracts. There are many students who say that what they really want is the shortest route to a degree and please cut out the

(a)   (b)

Figure 5.2 (a) Advertisement for an MBA programme at Bradford University (permission from Bradford University and Brahm). (b) 'Man in a Doorway' by L.S. Lowry (source: Paintings of L.S. Lowry (1964) London: Book Club Associates: 85). The old image that Lowry portrayed of the industrial north of England as a dour working man's world that turned its back on anything different is morphed into that of a lively young woman looking forward to a management role in an information society.

trimmings, and no-frills-click-here-for-degree-virtual-universities have risen in response to them. But getting a real degree is like having a real baby. Most people know that they have to go through the pain and problems as well as the pleasures that go with getting them, yet they still want to do the full syntagm. Many of the people who want to go to university want to be university students and do what university students do in the fullest sense.

Students can socialise in virtual campuses, but it will be a while, if ever, before they will be fully satisfied with *la vie bohème* in VR, however exotic it may become. Some things just cannot be done virtually. Chapter 9 looks at the idea of student centres around the world where students and teachers could meet in physical reality for in depth study and for renewing the ancient traditions of being a student.

Plagiarism

There is another more pragmatic reason for having student centres dispersed around the world in physical reality. The Internet has made it easy to find answers to assignments, find people who write assignments for a living and to copy other people's work.

Plagiarism is an old student vice, but today, thanks to information technology, it has become a major problem. In the last analysis, therefore, the only way to be reasonably certain that a student really does know how to apply the knowledge from a programme of study to a class of problems is to examine them in old-fashioned physical reality with an invigilator who can check from their documentation that they are the real person behind the virtual person who took the course of study. If they want a degree, students will have to get real for their exams.

This is to police the problem rather than to address it. A major part of what universities do is to hand down knowledge. Traditionally the purpose of much university examination has been to ensure that the knowledge had been handed down. Students down the years have learned by heart great chunks of knowledge in order to repeat them in tests and assignments as exactly as possible often in the sincere belief that that was what was wanted and it often has been what was wanted. When students are asked to prove Pythagoras' theorem in an examination they are not expected to originate a new proof. Teachers themselves reiterate the work of their predecessors even if they do add to them and make changes. They would never complete their lectures if they were to meticulously cite all their sources.

Plagiarism is something that students copy rather than originate. Academics plagiarise, vice-chancellors have had to resign because they plagiarise and even universities plagiarise. A better solution is needed than endlessly informing students that plagiarising is wrong. It might help if some of the pressures to complete assignments on time were removed, if students were given assignments, tests and exams that called for deep study and individualised responses and if they were in an episteme that did not see knowledge as property to be made private and kept private.

Chapter 6

Play the game
Knowledge in universities

Lying tales are necessary for the education of citizens.

(Averroes 1966: 129)

I believe that in collaboration with common greed – the nearly absolute dominance and authority of the reductionistic scientistic view of nature and knowledge is one of the reasons for our environmental problems and for our problem of understanding what life, intelligence, and consciousness are.

(Brier 1992: 61)

The rules of the universe that we think we know are deep buried in our processes of perception.

(Bateson 1979: 35)

I define a paradigm as a model that exhibits a closed logic. It means that our attempts to break out of a fixed pattern of thinking are constantly defeated – by running headlong into our own premise.

(Beer 1992: 1)

Paradigms are also normative, telling the practitioner what to do without the necessity of long existential or epistemological consideration. But it is this aspect of paradigms that constitutes both their strength and their weakness – their strength in that it makes action possible, their weakness in that the very reason for action is hidden in the unquestioned assumptions of the paradigm.

(Patton 1978: 203)

How exquisitely the individual mind to the external world
Is fitted-and how exquisitely, too
The external world is fitted to the mind.

(Wordsworth 1895: 755)

Introduction

Knowledge is a universal of the university paradigm. As the university changes with the new episteme so too does the knowledge it teaches and researches and a key question to be addressed is what shape knowledge will take in a global virtual university of the future.

Knowledge in universities forms a communication system and so has paradigmatic and syntagmatic dimensions. In theosophical universities there is only one knowledge paradigm, but in the modern university knowledge takes paradigmatic form at the level of the different subject disciplines that are taught. University degrees certify that holders are proficient in the application of a knowledge paradigm. The community the university serves provides a field of practice for the professionals it produces. We see knowledge as the totality of the interaction between its literature, artefacts, databases, the organisations that use it and everyone involved in it, whether as teacher, learner, practitioner or the person it is practised on. In this sense it has characteristics of a self-organising communication system.

This chapter will address the changes taking place in knowledge that come from the Internet, which is making professional knowledge available outside universities and taking over many of the functions of university libraries. Future changes in the nature of knowledge lie in understanding the way knowledge is perceived. Two technologies that enable this are multilingual knowledge systems and three dimensional time-variable modelling of phenomena in HyperReality coaction fields. A key issue that universities will need to address is the growing commercialisation of knowledge.

What is knowledge in a university?

If there is one thing above all that we associate with a university, it is knowledge. The function of a university is often seen to be the creation, storage and dissemination of knowledge. Today's student as customer sees it as what a university has to sell and university administrators look for ways to bank it. Management consultants conceptualise universities as 'knowledge providers'. The Vice Provost of Columbia University which boasts that more of its BAs have won Nobel prizes than any other college, states that the 'University creates, transfers, assembles, integrates, and exploits knowledge'. He sees the university taking a 'Knowledge Capitalist Approach' which amounts to 'bundling Columbia knowledge capital with that of other knowledge-creating enterprises' (http://www.columbia.edu/cu/osi/Deans Day/DDknowledge_univ.htm).

Yet, if someone were to go to a university looking for knowledge they might be greeted with puzzlement. Is it what is in the library, in a department, in a course of study or in the head of an academic? Knowledge resides in all these, but in the modern university we are not accustomed to think of knowledge as a single entity, rather we tend to think of knowledge in terms of the subjects offered, as science, mathematics or anthropology. When science tumbled the Humpty Dumpty of theologically based knowledge off the walls of the medieval university, there was no attempt to put the pieces together again in the modern university. If anyone tried today, they would find that the pieces do not fit. There is no longer a universe of knowledge as the term university might imply. Knowledge in the modern

Figure 6.1   'Margarita philosophica' by Gregorius Reisch, printed by Sebastian Henricpetri in Basle 1583 (courtesy of Anders Piltz and Blackwell Publishing, Oxford 1981: 16) How knowledge was seen in Europe at the end of the sixteenth century. The figure of Grammar passes the alphabet to a schoolboy with one hand while in the other she holds the key to the house of knowledge. In the ground floor people are learning grammar. The floors above are occupied with a hierarchy of subjects represented by their founding figures. Pythagoras is in the tower, but he is associated with music and it is Euclid in the next window who gets to be remembered for geometry. At the top is Peter Lombard making the link between metaphysics and theology. His 'Sententiae' (Sentences) written in the twelfth century explained the relationship between faith and knowledge and was, with the Bible, a basic textbook in theology until the sixteenth century (Piltz 1981: 16). It must have been a major factor in holding the medieval knowledge paradigm together. Can we imagine a modern text that will still be in use in 2400?

university is to be found in separate subject paradigms, which manage to coexist in the same university by not speaking to each other.

Not only has knowledge been broken into a multiplicity of subjects, but the way subjects themselves are seen varies from university to university, from country to country and from language to language. Where the medieval universities of Europe had a common language in Latin, modern universities use the written language of the nation that supports them. Yet anybody who has studied in more than one language will intuitively recognise some truth in the Saphir Whorf Hypothesis, otherwise known as the theory of linguistic relativity, that the way we think depends upon the language we think in (Whorf 1956). Are such knowledge paradigms as anthropology, sociology, philosophy and education the same in different languages? Can even the sciences be the same?

The languages used by universities continue to multiply. Not only does every nation want a university operating in its national language, but every culture wants its own university operating in its own language. Even in the same university, with the same common language, among people who socialise together in the common room, we can find the same subject addressed from different perspectives in the different discourses of different disciplines. For example, if students were looking for knowledge on the impact of information technology on human communications, a subject that is at least as critical to an information society as, say, engineering was to an industrial society, then they can find courses on the subject being offered to them by departments of communications studies, information science, information technology, information management, computer science, cognitive science, business communications, mass media studies, linguistics, sociology, or courses with e- as a prefix, as in ecommerce, elearning etc. And what they would learn in each case would be different and quite possibly contradictory.

The postmodern mood of the turn of the millennium sees virtue in multiple knowledges on the same theme (Lyotard 1984). Constructivism argues that knowledge is individual to each of us (Burleson 1989). As Boulding wrote half a century ago,

> Communication between the disciplines becomes increasingly difficult and the republic of learning is breaking up into isolated subcultures with only tenuous lines of communication between them … One wonders whether science will grind to a stop in an assemblage of walled-in hermits each mumbling to himself words in a private language that only he can understand.
> (Boulding 1958: 4)

The growing fragmentation and lack of consensus as to what constitutes knowledge creates a context for chaos. If a language means all things to all people it is babble. If knowledge is whatever an individual thinks it is, then there is no paradigm and no way people can communicate and cooperate in its application. If knowledge is a paradigm that varies according to the subject studied, then its wider application in society will be as confusing as letting people skilled in different versions of football play in the same game. If knowledge is a paradigm that varies according to the country or culture, then global issues can only be addressed from the perspective of that country or culture.

'Truth is in the search for truth' (Tehranian 1999). Science still seeks a theory of everything and a key task for a global virtual university of the future should be to seek to make a new whole of knowledge even though the search may be in vain or, if successful, destined in its turn to become another Humpty Dumpty. Chapter 8 looks at an approach to a unified curriculum.

Knowledge is paradigmatic

Bert Shaw was apprenticed as a boy in 1896 to a printer. The knowledge of how to mix colours was passed on to him from older craftsmen. He stayed with the same company for fifty-five years and watched the company grow into a modern corporation and his job change. By the time he retired, the management had acquired the chemical formulas for a vast number of colours and no longer needed his old skills. Or so they thought. The possible combinations of colours is virtually infinite and so are the demands of customers and the printers would from time to time find a large contract depended upon their producing a colour that only old Bert Shaw knew how to mix. However, he had a long memory and in retirement was resentful. He would not divulge what he knew of colours until the managing director came in person to ask him. He never charged for showing how to mix a colour, because, he said, no one had charged him for the knowledge. He did not see it as something he owned. It was knowledge that had slowly accumulated over the centuries from the practical experience of craftspeople who passed it on secretly by showing how it was done. One wonders what the company did with the knowledge they got from Bert Shaw, but he would smile and say all they had got was a formula for a colour. In the terms we are using, he gave them a syntagm, not the paradigm. When Bert Shaw died, the knowledge paradigm of colour mixing that he knew became extinct.

Bert Shaw's kind of knowledge is not exactly what we have in mind when we think of knowledge paradigms in universities. Tacit non-verbal knowledge, the kind of knowledge that is embodied in the domestication of plants and animals, farming and horticultural practices and pottery and carving, had to be translated into written language or mathematics to become knowledge in the university sense. Later in this chapter we look at changes taking place in university knowledge and the way non-verbal knowledge paradigms are being digitised, but for the moment we look at university knowledge as something that is essentially in written language and mathematics.

In its syntagmatic application knowledge in a university is normally made explicit in writing, mathematical notation or speech. In this form, like information, it can be stored, transmitted and processed and regarded as a commodity. In the paradigmatic abstract, the concepts, generalisations, theories and beliefs of knowledge that are held in common by its practitioners are also coded in language.

Linguistics recognises a paradigm hierarchy in language: written words are a syntagmatic expression of an alphabet paradigm and sentences are syntagms from the paradigm of a language. University knowledge is yet another order of syntagm–paradigm organisation above that of language where the elements of the paradigm are systems of meaning (Halliday 1989). These we would see as referring to the theoretical structures in university knowledge. Like the relationship between the alphabet and language there is a relationship between the paradigm formed by an individual theory and the paradigm of a discipline constituted of a number of related theories. The syntagmatic application of the elements of a subject knowledge paradigm, that is its praxis, would then be governed by selecting theories according to the syntax of a discipline, applying the ideas within the theories according to the syntax of the theory and doing this in appropriate language.

Stephen Littlejohn has for over a quarter of a century been seeking in editions of *Theories of Human Communication* to describe the discipline of communications studies from the sum of the theories involved. He is a paradigm maker extraordinaire. His book is widely used as a university text in courses on Communications Studies. For a multitude of students it is their introduction to the paradigm. There are seven editions. Each one is an iterative attempt to make the paradigm more systemic and to reflect what theories are actually being taught and what are not, what are in fashion and what are out. As he acknowledges in each edition, he consults extensively with people who are teaching the subject in universities. In a subject that lacks any core theory and that is little more than a loose association of many theories, he has acted as a catalyst by summating what many people think it is into a coherent structure. He writes that

> in a sense a way of knowing is like a game. It is selected because it is believed to be most appropriate in light of the problem being tackled. It comes with a set of rules that one is obliged to adopt during the course of the game. When playing the knowledge game, the scholar does not usually question the assumptions or rules though on other occasions these assumptions and rules may be hotly debated.
>
> (Littlejohn 1992: 11)

Knowledge becomes syntagmatic as it is applied and made explicit in words and deeds. If this involves cooperative action between people, as for example in surgery, then there needs to be common agreement as to the components of that knowledge, their syntax, purpose and theoretical structure. This means that there must be a community of people who 'know' the paradigm and 'know how to' syntagmatically apply it. Such a group of practitioners of a knowledge paradigm constitute a communication network in their common use of the paradigm. The paradigmatic bodies of knowledge taught in universities as subjects or disciplines are maintained by such communication networks. At one level they consist of organisational links between university departments, professional associations and societies, libraries, publishers, corporations, foundations and research institutions that are all engaged in the same disciplinary field with a common concern for the maintenance of the subject and its standards. At another level there are the collegial and working links between the individuals in these organisations who think of themselves as professional practitioners in the same field. The network also exists in the literature of the knowledge paradigm in the way authors link intertextually across time as they cite each other and in the filtering processes of publishing, which ensure that new texts are embedded in the referential network of the subject. It is the sum of the interactions within and between the individuals, the organisations and the literature derived from a particular knowledge paradigm that constitutes knowledge as we know it in our episteme. What then are the interactions?

Subject knowledge as a self-organising system

The long-established subjects of university knowledge such as law, medicine and philosophy have long outlasted the people and organisations that have professed them. They have an autonomous existence independent of the people involved in them, are dynamically self-renewing and manifest characteristics of a self-organising system. The key to this existence would appear to lie in the way the paradigmatic dimension is continually informed and changed by feedback from its syntagmatic expressions.

To explain this, imagine a university knowledge paradigm such as medicine, law or education as a multilevel edifice like that in the centre of Figure 6.2. A clock tower represents the special occasions such as conferences when all the practitioners and professional organisations are called together for keynote addresses and intense interaction about new issues that confront the paradigm. Such occasions motivate and provide the sense of identity, renewal, purpose, and dedication that hold the paradigm together. The tower is seen as supported at one level by organisations concerned with the maintenance of the knowledge paradigm (libraries, publishers, research institutions, and professional associations) and at another level by organisations concerned with the syntagmatic application of the knowledge (in medicine it would be hospitals, health authorities, biotech corporates and medical insurance companies). The university department or faculty that addresses the knowledge paradigm would have a central location in the building. The steps to the edifice are occupied by people going into the university to learn to become practitioners and by qualified practitioners going out to deal with the problems in real life that the knowledge paradigm addresses. Others stay within the edifice to teach, do research and provide support.

Knowledge in explicit form exists in the libraries, the literature, the documentation of case studies, the reports, files and databases of the organisations and individuals. Implicit knowledge exists in the brains of the individuals who make the organisations function and practise the knowledge. Knowledge as a self-organising communication system exists in the cybernetic interaction that takes place between all the components of the knowledge edifice of a university subject.

Figure 6.2 The edifice of knowledge. To conceptualise knowledge we return to the medieval metaphor of a building though it has now become a large rather corporate edifice sitting in the centre of a modern metropolis which houses the community where the knowledge is practised. The city is seen as surrounded by the physical reality of the problems the knowledge ultimately addresses.

If we allow that every individual has their own unique knowledge of a subject because of the way they approach it in the light of their experience and genetic makeup, then we recognise that although they may apply a paradigm in a syntagm according to the semantics and syntax of the paradigm, they do it in their own way. As professional practitioners apply knowledge to real-life problems they get positive or negative feedback, which affects the way they deal with similar problems in the future. If they work in a team or for an organisation there is also the feedback they get from, and give to, the team and the organisation. Feedback in complex systems is fractal and operates at the levels of individuals, groups, organisations and at the level of a knowledge edifice as a whole.

The city from which the knowledge edifice in Figure 6.2 rises stands for the community in which a subject knowledge is located. It houses the people on whom the paradigm is practised; they are the patients, the audiences and the customers. They are the consumers of subject knowledge. Like the crowd at a football match or the audience at a play, the people in the community of practice become pseudo-experts on the subject knowledge, or as it were para-paradigmatists. As such they too provide feedback to the knowledge edifice. Are the nation's doctors, teachers and lawyers doing a satisfactory job? Individuals complain, the media air opinions, questions are asked of government, civil servants investigate, professional associations and academics convey their views through conferences and at elections politicians promise change. Every time a practitioner syntagmatically applies the knowledge paradigm, however minor it may seem in the broader scale of things, feedback filters through to the knowledge system as a whole and, however slightly, modifies the paradigm. Alternatively, chaos theory would see a single incident at the edge of the paradigm (think of a doctor who helps a patient die in a country where euthanasia is illegal) triggering a massive reaction in the press with the potential to bring major changes to the paradigm.

Finally we come to the foreground of natural objects in Figure 6.2, the ground on which the community and all knowledge edifices ultimately stand; the physical reality that knows nothing of language or paradigms. From this reality comes a feedback that has no cultural or political bias or knowledge of statistical procedure. The earth gets warmer or cooler. Species become extinct or survive. Wars and peace happen. However much feedback within the community of practitioners and the community on whom they practise optimises a knowledge paradigm (think of the millions who pray to different gods for answers to their problems) ultimately it is feedback from physical reality that exposes the paradoxes in a paradigm.

So far we have been concerned with first order cybernetic interaction in knowledge paradigms. We turn now to second order cybernetics, also called the cybernetics of cybernetics. One of the founders of this particular knowledge paradigm, Heinz von Foerster, likened it to 'looking at looking itself' (von Foerster 1990: 1). From the perspective of this chapter it could be likened to knowledge of knowledge itself. It is the interaction in knowledge that takes place from observation of the application of knowledge. First order cybernetics is when a doctor or engineer or journalist applies the knowledge they learned in a university and uses feedback as to how effective they were to improve their performance. Second order cybernetics is when they question the knowledge itself. It is the circularity of interaction whereby studying what is known changes what is known. Simply to read a sentence in a text on a subject or to listen to the argument of a fellow practitioner is in some way, however small, to modify the subject. This means that, simply by being part of the knowledge edifice, a person changes the knowledge edifice. Even if a professional in a knowledge field does not change their thoughts on their subject, the fact that they have not changed them affects their relations with their fellow practitioners. Heraclitus said, 'The river where you set your foot just now is gone' (Haxton 2001: 27). We could similarly say that we never participate in the same knowledge paradigm twice. It is the special nature of a university knowledge paradigm to induct the ability to interweave first and second order cybernetic interaction in the individual. To play the game and yet to think about why we play the game.

University libraries and explicit knowledge on the Internet

We have looked at subject knowledge as it is known in universities as an amorphous cybernetic set of interactions between people and institutions engaged in the profession of a particular subject. It has attributes of language and of games and seems to have a life of its own. It exists in the abstract and in its applications, but most of all in books. Traditionally these have been the bricks in the edifices of university knowledge because in the last analysis it is written knowledge. Access to knowledge has in some ways become easier today.

Published texts hold knowledge together over time and give it continuity. Richard Dawkins suggested that ideas (which he called memes) have qualities like genes that lead to them being reproduced over and over again (Dawkins 1976). Michael Pollan points out that apple trees like humans do not fall true to seed. Every seed in every apple of an apple tree would produce a different apple tree whose every apple would in turn reproduce differently. Four thousand years ago the Chinese learned to clone trees by grafting them. It was then possible to persistently produce a particularly tasty apple (Pollan 2001). When we copy a text we clone it. The invention of printing allowed knowledge to be cloned like apple trees. Today readers and editorial boards decide what knowledge is worthy of cloning. However, Pollan also points out that there is danger in the trend today to clone only the very best apple trees. We lose the diversity that has allowed apples to proliferate and survive in so many environments. Similarly, knowledge needs a balance between selecting and standardising and allowing innovative diversity. Universities traditionally provided such a balance in the campus interaction between the domesticated knowledge in cloned texts and the wild ideas that spontaneous talk can generate. Today the Internet introduces a new kind of diversity.

Figure 6.3 Leiden University Library 400 years ago (courtesy of Leiden University Library, Collectie Bodel Nijenhuis). A quick count suggests that there are less than a thousand books. Today this library has 2.7 million books. Knowledge was divided into seven subjects the largest of which was theology. Contrast this to the diversity of subjects in a modern university library and the relative place in it of theology. Chained Libraries like this were common. They reflect the value books held and suggest that knowledge capture is not something new. To study students had to come to the library and they had to stand which would discourage them from staying too long. Access to knowledge has become easier.

The storage of knowledge in university libraries is closely associated with the traditional role of a university as a guardian of knowledge. Umberto Eco in *The Name of the Rose* (Eco 1983) describes a medieval university with a secret library within a library guarded by fanatical monks who are prepared to murder for the knowledge it contained. King James I of England on visiting the Bodleian at Oxford was moved to say, 'if it were so that I must be a prisoner, if I might have my wish, I would desire to have no other prison than that Library and to be chained together with so many good Authors' (Burton 1913: 105).

The great library of Alexandria sought to have a copy of everything written and to be a true universe of knowledge. University libraries in the Middle Ages sought to reflect a comprehensive corpus of knowledge. However, over the last fifty years particularly, there has been such an extraordinary expansion of explicit knowledge that even in developed countries university libraries cannot keep pace. In the universities of countries such as Bolivia and the Philippines queues form to use limited collections of books held together with tape.

Now we have the World Wide Web. The biggest library ever known is available to anyone with Internet access. In the early days of the Web it was seen as having the potential to be a superlibrary, available to anyone, anywhere, anytime. It was taking up the task of liberating knowledge that public libraries began. In this spirit some wonderful sites like Principia Cybernetica developed that sought to organise and universalise knowledge in a manner reminiscent of the encyclopaedist movement of the Enlightenment. The Web has the potential to solve the library problems of universities in the developing world as well as the developed world. However, as we noticed in Chapter 2, the Web has developed its own set of problems. It was never specifically designed to be a university library and has grown so huge and indiscriminate that searching it and evaluating what is found becomes increasingly difficult. The Web begins to reflect the chaotic fragmentation of contemporary knowledge. It becomes a giant dump of text which places knowledge and wisdom side-by-side with data and information and responds to a search by offering a fourth grader's exercises along with the works of Plato. And this is only a beginning. The Internet accumulates images and sounds and as it becomes broadband could become a graffiti-ridden wasteland of moving images and three-dimensional simulacra.

The comprehensibility of knowledge depends upon paradigmatic organisation. Einstein argued that it implied 'the production of some sort of order among sense impressions, this order being produced by creation of general concepts, relations between these concepts and by definite relations of some kind between the concepts and sense experience' and he cites Immanuel Kant as realising that the postulation of a real world would be senseless without such comprehensibility (Einstein 1982: 292). How do we structure self-maintaining paradigmatic organisation on the Internet? Many universities have allowed libraries to develop in departments or faculties and to specialise in a particular knowledge paradigm. This is being paralleled on the Web where subject sites are emerging that are dedicated to a particular knowledge paradigm. They offer a comprehensive cover of professional journals and texts and provide facilities for chat groups and focus issues for students and academics in the field. Increasingly, however, this comes at a cost and continues to encourage the separation of knowledge paradigms.

In preparation for classes, teachers seek to distil the essence of a body of knowledge and adapt it for the coming presentation. They prepare teaching notes, handouts, audiovisual aids and study guides or workbooks. These explain the knowledge in published texts in the light of the teachers' own experience. They are seen by students as highlighting the aspects on which they will be tested and by teachers as their own copyrightable version of subject knowledge. The process is at least as old as the medieval university (Piltz 1981). However, it may be about to change. Academic staff are being encouraged to incorporate their teaching materials into the integrated Web infrastructures their universities are building or buying. Whether teaching materials and content remain the property of teachers when they are on a university's server is becoming a bone of contention.

Multilingual knowledge and the Internet

In the early days of the Internet an action research programme sought to use the new medium to advise a community of dairy farmers on better practice. It followed the traditional pattern of development communications by assuming that knowledge was something that university-trained specialists had and farmers needed. As long as these roles were maintained the project had little success. In 1992 Noel Bridgeman re-organised the project by developing an online community of people involved in dairy farming where knowledge flowed in whatever direction it was wanted. It quickly became apparent that dairy farmers had unique specialist knowledge from their interaction with the physical reality of the place they farmed and from the folk knowledge derived from long-term practice of farming in their particular environment. The academics involved found themselves to be learners as well as teachers. A new kind of dynamic was developing in the interaction between the knowledge professionals and the professional practitioners. However, there was yet another aspect. Dairy farmers and academics around the world as they surfed the Web became aware of the group and joined the interaction. Knowledge was cross-fertilised between different countries and the Website (www.grazel.taranaki.ac.nz) became global (Bridgeman 1997). But only to those who were literate in English.

Over the last fifty years English has become the language of globalisation. It is the dominant language of the media, communications, trade, education and research. By far the majority of the world's alphanumeric knowledge is in English. David Crystal (1997) points out that it is not simply that a third of the world's population in some way uses it, but that it is the first language of the world's most powerful country. There is a close association between knowledge, power and universities. Greek was the language of Alexander the Great as well as Plato. Latin was the language of the Roman Empire as well as the medieval universities. Arabic was the language of the Koran and therefore of the universities established with Islamic expansion (Crystal 1997).

Today serious postgraduate studies in almost any country need good mastery of written English. Advancement in universities around the world depends on publication and publications are more valued if they are international and to be international they have to be published in English. Universities that teach in languages that have no tradition of research literature translate or adapt English language texts. Teaching English as a second language has become a major aspect of the new trade in teaching. Students from non-English speaking countries flock to the universities of the English speaking countries.

Knowledge may have widespread application and utility because it is in English and obviously professionals want to learn how to apply knowledge in the hegemonic language, but is knowledge intrinsically any better for being in English than if it were in Latin, Greek, Hindi, Mandarin or Arabic and how would we establish that it were so? Is knowledge language-bound and different when it is in different languages? Are there universals in a knowledge paradigm that are independent of language? If there were, could they be expressed equally in different languages? These are key research issues for a university of the future. If we are to think in terms of global societies, global virtual universities and the globalisation of knowledge then it should be possible for dairy farmers and agricultural specialists of any language to access Bridgeman's Internet dairy farmers site.

To some degree universities have always been polyglot. Medieval universities in Europe fought unsuccessfully to be monolingual and would even employ spies to catch students talking to each other in anything but Latin (Patterson 1997). Until the Second World War many European universities still required students to have a qualification in Latin or Greek and many universities hold that postgraduate students should have a second language of relevance to their field of research. A rounded university education in many countries traditionally meant fluency in more than one language. What we are looking at in multilingual approaches to knowledge, however, is more related to the way Websites allow someone accessing them to select a language in which to interact, or responds to them in the language their email address would indicate they used. Corporate and institutional Websites present themselves as a paradigmatic body of knowledge about what they are, what they do, how they do it, what they see as their purpose and what their rules and regulations are, and they do this in different languages. When global corporates, organisations and institutions present themselves multilingually on the Internet, it is time that we had a university that can present knowledge multilingually.

In the Advanced Telecommunications Research (ATR) laboratories in Japan a research group works on making it possible for people in different languages to hold a conversation with a travel agency about booking a hotel room. The same basic principles make possible the kind of multilingual class that was described in Chapter 4 for teaching Pythagoras' theorem.

Knowledge in coaction fields

HyperReality occurs in coaction fields where objects and people derived from physical reality and virtual reality and human intelligence and artificial intelligence can interact purposively in the application of a specific domain of knowledge. Like a football field, a doctor's surgery or a classroom, it is a space for the syntagmatic expressions of a paradigm. It will be possible with HyperReality to have HyperGames, HyperSurgeries and HyperClasses where the people may be real or virtual, and derived from human or artificial intelligence and they will be able to interact by speaking in different languages (Tiffin 2001; Terashima 2001).

Learning to apply geographical knowledge, medical knowledge or knowledge of how to drive a car to problems presented in alphanumeric or diagrammatic form on a classroom whiteboard in a classroom is very limiting. Stories of the consequences are legend: students who pass a multiple choice question on what a volcano is, but cannot recognise that their school stands on the slopes of one; medical students who can write an essay on a disease, but cannot recognise the symptoms in a patient; people driving away after passing the written driving test and failing to observe a rule of the road which they had just correctly given on paper. This is the problem of the transfer of learning from classrooms to real-life situations. It is a problem that is seldom addressed because of the way knowledge learned in classrooms is tested in classrooms. Solutions to problems are examined in the way they were learned, alphanumerically. This is quite different from testing the application of knowledge to real-life situations in real-life situations.

The HyperClass introduces a new dimension to education by directly juxtaposing knowledge with the kind of problems that have a referent in physical reality. It is not easy to take someone living in Britain on a field trip to a volcano, and to ensure that they can, in safety, see the volcano erupt. It is difficult to present malarial students in delirium to students at medical schools in Japan where the possibility of malarial patients is remote. Most driving schools teach within the reality of the roads on which the student is likely to be tested, but they do so in safe conditions and try to avoid the nightmare freak conditions which one day the learner-driver is going to have to face. HyperReality can take a class to an active volcano, to the bedside of a patient in crisis or to a critical traffic situation. At the same time it can window key knowledge that students should have in mind while they study the problem and try to solve it.

The means to do this lie in the application of the capability … to develop a three-dimensional virtual reality in one place from images garnered by cameras in another place. It allows the development of virtual reality simulacra of case studies from a problem domain. An eruption of a volcano can be recorded by an array of videocameras at different sites and these could be combined and converted into a virtual reality simulacrum of a volcano erupting that could be a case study for future HyperClasses. Medical students in North America could accompany a doctor in Africa on her rounds through a malaria ward. Observations of malaria patients could be related to the kind of four-dimensional human atlas we already find on the Internet that allows us to view the functioning of organs in 3D. It is common practice to have videocameras permanently stationed at dangerous traffic intersections. These could be used to create VR libraries of problem case studies that include dangerous conditions. A learner-driver could then drive a virtual car through a virtual reality of a specific intersection in which they could be faced with a vast array of different situations.

Where students are faced with practical problems in today's education and training systems, their comprehension of the problem domain is limited by their perspective of time and space. To a human, a volcano is something very big whose formation and existence is a matter of millions of years. By contrast, a malarial parasite is too small for a human to see and its life cycle is brief. Motorists may sense the size and speed of their vehicle in relation to that of other road users, but they cannot see the way they use the road from the perspective of other drivers and pedestrians. In a HyperClass it would be possible to augment reality by switching viewpoints with another driver or by taking a helicopter view of the section of road that presents the particular problem under study. Similarly it would be possible to have a fly-over virtual reality of a volcano, to window a satellite view of the extent of an eruption or compress the time scale of the volcano's history so that it can be viewed as it changes shape with each eruption. It would be possible to compress the history of a patient with malaria and compare appearances at different times or to take a micro-perspective of what was happening in their blood during a delirium

(Tiffin and Rajasingham 2001: 121–2).

Medicine, geography and transport studies are fields of study where the knowledge paradigm is grounded in physical reality. We have sought to explain these paradigms in words, because in words it was possible to discuss them in the abstract. The use of drawings, photographs, films and actual cases illustrate, but are no more than specific syntagmatic examples. They can supplement paradigm acquisition but they cannot express the generic nature of their subject. For that we have needed words. What we are suggesting is that information technology is beginning to make it possible to generate paradigmatic knowledge mathematically by aggregating actual syntagmatic instances of a phenomenon.

Language is the classic case of a paradigm and provides an example where the process is happening. Dictionaries list the component elements of a language and as long as there have been universities there have been teachers and books to explain the syntax, semantics and pragmatics of the way the elements can be combined and used. People seek to write and speak in conformity with the paradigm, but it is not an automatic process and they change it and thereby change the paradigm of the language and the dictionaries and texts have to be rewritten. In an age of collectors, James Murray put together the Oxford English Dictionary by using a volunteer force of dedicated readers which even included an incarcerated mad murderer to garner every word of the English language no matter how esoteric and record its first usage no matter how obscure (Winchester 1998). In an age of computers John Sinclair (1987) designed the Cobuild English Language Dictionary based on the principles of corpus linguistics. Corpus linguistics involves the use of computers to record, measure and analyse the actual use of written or transcribed language. In effect, a language paradigm based directly on syntagmatic usage can be housed in a computer. The syntagmatic input and therefore the population of words on which the paradigm is based is limited quantitatively by current computer technology, but in theory it would be possible to think of a paradigm of language as it is used on the Internet which would be endlessly changing to reflect actual usage as it happened. It shifts the teaching of language from the syntactic logic of the traditional paradigm to the patterns of actual usage emerging from corpus linguistics, from language as it should be to language as it is.

Something similar is happening in geography. In *The Nature of Geography* Richard Hartshorne examined the way geography as a knowledge paradigm is based on the cross-referential writings of its great European and American thinkers (Hartshorne 1939). An examination of the texts referred to reveals that they too form an intricate network of intertextual references. Referring to this literature Hartshorne later wrote, 'Geography is what geographers have made it' (Hartshorne 1960: 8). One would have to note that geography was, therefore, what American, British, French and German geographers made it by writing about it. It was not what Chinese, Arabic or Hindi writers made it, or what the people who lived in the places that were the objects of study wrote about it. However, geography is no longer what Hartshorne and other geographers wrote. It is no longer a literary paradigm. It is being computerised. However, whereas words are made by humans and are discrete, the elements studied in geography are not. Whether a hill is a mountain or a river a stream is a human distinction that makes them characteristic components of the classical geographical paradigm and geography has developed by characterising them in terms of their significance to humans. Geography in the modern university had a preoccupation with coalfields and oilfields and sea routes because those were the factors that mattered to the nations that supported their departments of geography.

Now, Geographical Information Systems (GIS) express the spatial interactions of geographical phenomena in quantitative form as four-dimensional models. Linked to telemetric systems that measure anything from the flow of a stream to the flow of traffic it becomes possible to study changes in the landscape as they occur. As with the Cobuild Dictionary it becomes possible to model the paradigmatic form of geographical phenomena as something plastic that changes with syntagmatic input. A landscape can show erosion as it happens, as it has happened in the past and as it could happen in the future with different levels of precipitation. Where in the past what was significant provided the basis for studying a landscape, now what is significant emerges from the model that reflects an actual landscape or component of the landscape. Since the computer-based model does not carry the connotations and selectivity of language, it can be used by people from different disciplines and different languages. A computer-generated model of a cyclone or of a wave, based on an aggregation of syntagmatic exemplars, can anchor geographers, meteorologists, climatologists, physicists, engineers, architects and marine architects on the same phenomena in a way that written texts have failed to do.

The human body is a more discrete and seemingly accessible world of study than the biosphere and anatomists have long sought with illustrations and exemplars to express it visually, but the paradigm of anatomy has primarily existed in words. Techniques such as cadaver sectioning and magnetic resonance imaging have

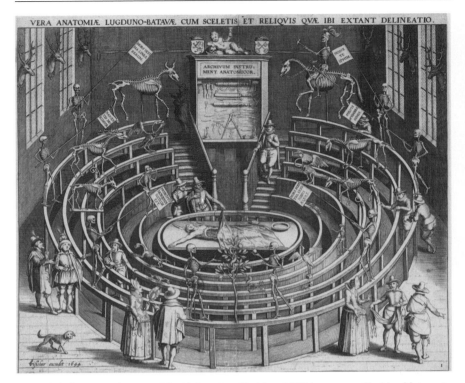

VERA ANATOMIÆ LUGDUNO-BATAVÆ CUM SCELETIS ET RELIQVIS QVÆ IBI EXTANT DELINEATIO.

Figure 6.4 Anatomy theatre of the University of Leiden, 1610 (courtesy of Leiden University Library, Collectie Bodel Nijenhuis). The anatomy paradigm is still part of the overall theological paradigm. The skeletons carry banners that remind everyone of their mortality. In front are skeletons representing Adam and Eve complete with snake and tree of knowledge. An elaborately dressed lady is being shown a human pelt. Appearance is superficial. Dissection of cadavers took place over several days and was only done in winter, skeletons were studied in the summer, a unique case of a university calendar having a rational relationship with the curriculum. Dissections were open to the public as a form of theatre.

been used to develop three-dimensional atlases of the human body or various parts of it. The Visible Human project of the National Library of Medicine (USA) makes it possible to fly over three-dimensional anatomical images which are available on the Internet (http://www.crd.ge.com/esl/cgsp/projects/vm/). The Vesalius project at Columbia University uses the data from the Visible Human project to develop an interactive learning environment which uses three-dimensional anatomy models that can be manipulated in real time (http://www.hoise.com/vmw/01/articles/vmw/LV-VM-05-01-5.html). Surgical techniques can be practised on virtual people and it becomes possible to study the underlying structures of the human body as they relate to each other and as they function in different time frames or as the body ages.

Currently human atlases are based on the dissection of individual cadavers. This amounts to a paradigm based on a single syntagm, but it will in time be possible to generate generic representations of humans from a broad base of bodies and to do this at different stages of their life. We keep records of X-rays and electrocardiograms of people with medical problems, but we can imagine in the future, with growing concern for healthy lifestyles, that it could become a norm to keep regular records of different aspects of the body that in sum provided a composite picture of the person over time.

Imagine a video camera set up in a bathroom so that it could take a series of full-length pictures of a person as they stood on something similar to bathroom scales that revolved. This would give a relationship between weight and shape and a record of daily change. Kids could watch themselves grow up and adults could see the effects of their habits. Add information about the norms for a person's age and height and artificial intelligence with the ability to analyse trends and a repertoire of caustic comments and it becomes a decision-support system for self-maintenance. This is knowledge of an individual's topography, but automatic measurement of a number of internal factors could be part of the technology in a smart bathroom or datasuit of the future. Telemetering of such things as blood pressure is already feasible and one day we might have access to individual genetic profiles that indicate what symptomatic factors need monitoring. It would make sense for such information to be made available to a person's health services. Through them information could go to a national medical system. It becomes possible to aggregate the data to form something like a Cobuild Dictionary for human anatomy. It would present a paradigm not in words but as a four-dimensional virtual human that could be manipulated to show how it would appear according to such factors as age, gender and regional location and it would be endlessly changing as the population it represented changed. Similarly it is possible to build paradigmatic knowledge of animals and plants and their organs and even their cells and how they relate to their DNA and atomic structure and vary across time and space. The process whereby science has gathered encyclopaedic knowledge of the physical world in words is starting to be repeated in four-dimensional virtual reality.

Like anatomy and geography, transport studies is a knowledge paradigm based on physical reality. The transport studies paradigm has to conform to the anatomy paradigm. It is humans that travel and medical and transport researchers jointly study what happens to human bodies in crashes. Transport studies also has to conform with the geographical paradigm because roads and railways are built into landscapes. The development of paradigms in words made it possible to obscure or avoid any lack of congruity between different knowledge paradigms. The development of paradigms as four-dimensional virtual realities makes discrepancies between them obvious. It forces researchers from different fields to seek to reconcile differences between their paradigms. It suggests that, as we begin to build a virtual version of the world in the manner that HyperReality makes possible, it will reverse the fragmentation of knowledge we have seen taking place through the modern university.

Where anatomy and geography are based on the givens of human bodies and landscapes, transport studies is based on the artificial reality of transport systems created by humans. As a body of knowledge it has been orientated more toward what could be, rather than what is. Transport studies have always been a knowledge paradigm that envisions futures. However, the development in HyperReality of knowledge paradigms that mirror the phenomena of the real world impels us to consider how things can be changed in fields other than transport studies. So we see geography developing 'what if' decision-support models of the impact on landscapes of things like climatic change and medicine becoming involved in the genetic design of its subject.

Will the application of information technology to the study of phenomena have the same effect on how we paradigmatise knowledge as telescope technology had when it got into the hands of Galileo (and continues to have with the Hubble Telescope)? Knowledge could become more closely and directly aligned to its objects of study. Scientific knowledge has always been based on mathematics. However, while the 'truths of mathematics do not obey our wishes or our fears' (Dewdney 1999: 5) we have interpreted the mathematics of science through language, with all its associated cultural ambiguity.

Knowledge in HyperReality takes only one form in response to a specific mathematical query. It is the same form for whoever studies it, whatever their language, politics or persuasion. Knowledge in this form allows international, interdisciplinary and multilingual approaches and, like a telescope, makes it possible to look ahead without bias. A HyperClass makes knowledge in this form accessible for teaching. The coaction field in HyperReality is designed to allow syntagmatic interaction with knowledge in this form, but it means that the exploration of knowledge in this form in HyperReality will be conducted in conjunction with artificial intelligence.

The commercialisation of university knowledge

At an after dinner speech to a conference of bankers some twenty years ago a hypothesis was put to them: would they lend $1 million on the security of a piece of property valued at $4 million? The bankers looked at each other and shrugged. They could see no problem in such a deal until one of them thought to ask where the property was. The speaker pointed to his head. He was talking about intellectual property. Twenty years ago the bankers laughed at the very idea of intellectual property being used as security. Today they would not.

Knowledge is capital in a knowledge society, but has never been seen that way in a university until recently. The term 'academic freedom' refers to a tradition where academics were seen as seeking knowledge for its own sake without regard for utilitarian purpose or commercial gain. With the tradition went a freedom to speak out on issues of public concern and tenure meant that academics could do so without fear of losing their jobs. Today's university sees growing restrictions on academic freedom. Universities become businesses. The question then arises as to who owns the knowledge in a university, who owns the explicit knowledge that academics produce as they write books, articles, papers and teaching notes in the company's time. In some universities in recent years academics have been startled to find that teaching materials they stored on their university server and the Webpages they so carefully prepared on their university's site have become the property of the university. There are cases where 'universities are entering into agreements, sometimes private, with private sources to market and sell copyrightable instructional materials outside the university. A number of universities have entered into confidential agreements, purportedly without consultation with their faculties' (Tallman 2000: 196). Do these universities, one wonders, harangue their students on plagiarism? What they are doing is not in keeping with an academic's traditional right to retain copyright to the lectures they give and the books and articles they write in university time, but it is in keeping with modern corporate practice. Who owns copyright of instructional materials in a university is an issue of growing concern in universities as they become knowledge businesses in a knowledge society and as the possible extent of income from global markets becomes apparent (Tallman 2000).

In the past, a corporate's capital was seen to consist of its tangible assets. Of course the plans, formulas, blueprints, research findings, patents and copyrights that were part of a private enterprise have always been seen as having value. The difference today is that there is an aggressive process of acquisition of knowledge, not only of explicit knowledge in concrete form but also of knowledge that is implicit in an employee or even of knowledge that is held in common by a community and, as it were, is in the public domain. Knowledge workers might find they have to sign a document that stops them using knowledge gained while working for one company outside that company. Museums and art galleries claim rights to the copies that can be made of national treasures that embody knowledge of the past and of people long dead. Pollan (2001) points out that the patented potatoes Monsanto sell to farmers around the world are descended from wild potatoes grown on the Andean Altiplano which were first domesticated by the ancestors of the Incas seven thousand years ago. The communal knowledge of potato growing that existed amongst these Amerindians for thousands of years was embodied in a crop that has been a boon to humanity. The knowledge that is embodied in a potato is now seen as the property of a multinational corporate, but there is no recognition of the contribution of the people whose knowledge led to the domestication of potatoes in the first place. There is no royalty from Monsanto to the poverty stricken descendants of the Incas and unless they can pay they have no access to the genetically modified descendants of the potatoes they still till (Pollan 2001).

In the first universities in Greece and India, people sought knowledge with the guidance of teachers. In the theological universities, knowledge was divine and ultimately unknowable but one tried to understand it with the help of teachers and books. In the modern university knowledge became discoverable, quantifiable and formulaic. Now knowledge is seen as something that can be purchased or captured. The idea of 'knowledge capture' seems to have its origins in 'expert systems'. These are computer programs, which can be used to respond to a domain of problems by mimicking human experts. The idea is to 'capture' the expertise of recognised experts in a field and deduce the common knowledge paradigm they use. Simplistically this is expressed as cause and effect rules: 'If the problem manifests conditions X, Y and Z then apply procedures A, B and C with n per cent confidence'. The vision behind expert systems is that, as more and more experts contribute, it becomes a synthesis of all the expertise in a community of knowledge and more expert than any individual expert. Being a computer program and cybernetic, an expert system has the latent ability to iteratively improve its expertise from every contributing case study and every contributing expert.

What constitutes knowledge in the head of an expert or in the heads of many experts has proved fuzzier and more elusive than was first imagined and super-expert knowledge machines are yet to emerge. However, the direction behind the idea is still there: computers improve and programming becomes more sophisti-cated and able to handle fuzzy concepts and to learn. The nature of new IT-based knowledge such as we see it in anatomy, geography and the human genome facilitates the quantification of knowledge and its expression as a computer algorithm that is patentable. In the past business spoke of data management systems and then of information management systems, now they talk of knowledge management systems by which they mean the whole process of capturing, controlling, keeping and using the knowledge generated by their employees and garnered from their customers. As universities become commercial corporations will they move to adopt such systems? For over 2,000 years universities have sought to manage the knowledge of students and teachers. Let us hope they have as little success in the future as they have had in the past.

The pursuit of knowledge

Some knowledge can be formularised and codified in ways that make it amenable to information technology. In Chapter 4 we suggested that the dreary repetitive part of teaching that consists of checking the same answers to the same questions or controlling the administrative aspects of teaching could be done by JITAITs who would be operating from the kind of knowledge that academics would surely be only too happy to let computers have. A lot of knowledge can be automated. Rule-bound paradigmatic knowledge can be lodged in expert systems. It is the other end of the knowledge spectrum we should be concerned with. Where academics are engaged in the pursuit and dissemination of new knowledge, it would be a travesty of a university that let its administration scavenge at their heels for knowledge that could be incorporated. If a university is to be true to the ideal of pursuing knowledge it will need to privilege its academics and find a balance with the forces of commercialisation and automation. It may be that a system is needed like that described in Chapter 4 that approximates the role of knowledge-producing academics with that of an author and sees them paid a royalty for the knowledge they make explicit.

Knowledge lies between information and wisdom. To an Asian it is on the way to wisdom, part of seeking truth as an abstract ideal. To a Westerner it is information that has been given structure and animation by humans, something essentially utilitarian that provides the power behind 'knowing how' to do something. This Western hierarchical view of the place of knowledge is mirrored in the way the knowledge paradigm that addresses computer technology has emerged over the last fifty years. In the early days of computers their function was said to be that of data processing. Departments of computer studies sprang up in universities to teach the data processing paradigm and academics argued about computopias (Masuda 1985). In 1976 the term information technology was introduced and people began to talk of information processing, an information revolution and a coming information society (Dordick and Wang 1993). Around the world departments of information science, information systems and information management mushroomed in universities. Today we talk of knowledge processing and introduce courses in knowledge management in preparation for a knowledge revolution leading to a knowledge society. Will there come a day when computers process wisdom, will we teach it and could it lead to a wise revolution inaugurating a wise society? If ever there was a wise computer we suspect it would have the wisdom to keep the fact to itself.

Chapter 7

The problem's the thing
Research in a global virtual university

So the best we can do is to build ourselves an artificial world in our minds, populated with theories and idealisations. Then when we try to understand something in the real world, we shift the problem into the relevant part of our imaginary world and solve it there in the hope that the solution will apply equally to the real world.

(Hudson 1984: 117)

I would advocate a return to the Great Problems to reverse the trend toward fragmentation and incoherence in the sciences.

(Casti 1992: 498)

As a scientist, I have been an explorer looking for new worlds, not a harvester from safe and productive fields, and life at the frontier has shown me that there are no certainties and that dogma is usually wrong.

(Lovelock 2000: 5)

Introduction

We have used the term 'problem' to refer to the object of knowledge because it is often used in that sense and is the least unsatisfactory term we can think of. Sometimes we use application as a synonym, but it is too referential to knowledge to be generally applicable. We recognise that in the application of knowledge there are possibilities as well as problems and it would have been nice to have an English word that handled this. We stayed with problem because it matches the idea of knowledge as solving something and as with teacher and student the two ideas exist only in relation to each other. We see knowledge and problem as lying at the ends of an interactive axis of people-mediated communication. When people do things to things because of what they know it is a form of communication. To arrest a criminal, to do open heart surgery or to write a computer program are applications of knowledge to problems that are manifestly acts of communication, though they do not readily fit current models of communication which see people not problems as the ends of communication. However, if we can accept that a communicative interaction takes place when knowledge is applied to a problem then this interaction can be regarded as a syntagm of the knowledge paradigm.

So is the class of problems that a knowledge paradigm addresses part of the knowledge paradigm or is it paradigmatic of itself? Where knowledge is a human invention and defines its own problems as for example in the case of theology, literature and management, then knowledge and problem form their own yin and yang relationship where the existence of one depends on the other. The problems of chess are the purpose of chess. However, where a problem domain has its referent in physical reality as in the case of the sciences, medicine and geology, problems can be perceived in terms of the knowledge paradigm and addressed by the knowledge paradigm, but do not necessarily respond to the knowledge paradigm. The pill that appears to be the solution might kill. A paradigm shift might see a problem disappear. Transmuting lead to gold is no longer a problem now that we no longer believe in alchemy. On the other hand a cyclone is a cyclone is a cyclone whether we think it is the wrath of God, a category of tropical storm or chaos theory at work.

Problems (and possibilities) are of course something that people perceive and universities have traditionally perceived them in their own special way. In the form of tests, assignments, exams and research they are quite definitely paradigmatic. This chapter looks at how we give problems entity in universities by problematising them. The purpose behind this is to look at the role of problems in universities as the objects of knowledge and the subjects of research.

Research addresses the correspondence between a knowledge paradigm and its problem domain. Questioning the adequacy of the knowledge paradigm could challenge what is socially acceptable, politically correct or culturally appropriate in an episteme. When it does, it poses a dilemma for a university. Does it keep faith with its basic mission to search for truth, or does it keep faith with the world-view of the society that supports it? Caught between epistemes universities face this dilemma anew.

This chapter examines the structure of problems and their interconnectedness in order to address the nature of research in a global virtual university and lay the foundations for what it should teach.

Privileging problems

Universities swing between the extremes of the knowledge–problem axis. Medieval universities privileged biblical knowledge, but the Enlightenment saw a swing to problems the Bible could not answer concerned with the physical facts of geology, biology and geography discovered in the explorations of people like Darwin, Humboldt and Cook. Modern universities were based on the problems raised by scientific study. They built new bodies of knowledge to explain the nature and potential of the rocks, soils, climates, vegetation and locations of the countries they served and their colonies. The industrial revolution was founded on the applications of science and technology, and scientific rationalism is the orthodoxy of the modern university.

With the advent of postmodernism and growing concern for the long-term problems arising from the excesses of industrialisation, there has been a swing back to problems. Today's students do not want to find themselves driving taxis and waiting table. They want knowledge that works. Older students who have been in professional practice return to universities with questions that arise from the limitations of the knowledge they gained from their first degree. They want to address problems they are encountering in practice and are sometimes dismayed to find how remote from reality university knowledge can be. There are computer companies, television companies, and newspapers that will not employ graduates from departments of computer science, television production and journalism. They argue that it is easier to train from scratch someone who has a good degree in another subject than to retrain someone who has become proficient in a knowledge paradigm that does not fit with current practical professional problems.

The problem with problems

We do not really know what problems are. *The Encyclopaedia Plus of World Problems and Human Potential* (1996) finds them 'strange nebulous entities having a shadowy existence'. *Collins Cobuild English Language Dictionary* (Sinclair 1987) calls a problem 'A situation or state of affairs that causes difficulties for people, so that they try to think of a way to deal with it. It is something that people perceive'. In other words a problem is a problem because we perceive it to be a problem. Academics are comfortable with the idea of problem-solving as long as it is seen from within their discipline where what constitutes a problem is taken for granted. Robert Gagne who sees problem-solving as the highest order of skill that can be taught felt the real issue was problem-finding (Gagne 1973).

Chapter 6 examined the way knowledge is held together by first and second order cybernetics. Negative and positive feedback in first order cybernetics hangs on the question as to whether a knower of a knowledge domain can solve a problem from the set of problems it addresses. Negative and positive feedback in second order cybernetics hangs on the question as to whether the knowledge can solve the problems it addresses. Problems with solving problems that lie within the knowledge paradigm (as distinct from within the knowledge practitioner) form research problems. However, the distinction between first and second order cybernetics in applying knowledge to problems is not neat. Every time a problem is addressed the outcome reflects on the knowledge as well as its knower and percolates over time through the knowledge paradigm and in subtle ways re-shapes it.

From the perspective of this book, problems are problems in universities because they are what knowledge paradigms seek to resolve. The medieval theological knowledge paradigm sought to answer all problems, but knowledge in the modern university comes in discrete paradigms that address specific domains of problems. Dealing with a specific case from a specific problem domain is regarded as a syntagm of the knowledge paradigm. Practitioners of a knowledge paradigm identify problems (problematise) in the terms of their knowledge paradigm. A poem, a painting, a performance might not seem like a problem except to a poet, painter and performer. An open question for any discipline is whether the problems it addresses are a construct of its knowledge paradigm, or whether its knowledge paradigm is a construct of its problem domain.

Research problems

Research in universities has come to be dominated by the way that it is communicated. To achieve promotion and prestige in a university an academic must publish according to a strict paradigm such that it:

- is expressed in written language. It carries greater weight if the language is English
- addresses a problem that the existing knowledge paradigm does not adequately address and demonstrates that this is the case from a search of related literature that shows the extent of knowledge on the problem
- addresses a problem that is ethically acceptable to the knowledge community
- proposes some kind of hypothesis that resolves the problem
- explains how the research was done so that other researchers can verify the procedures and the results
- draws conclusions about the hypothesis from the results
- explains how valid, reliable and generalisable the research is
- cites all references and provides a bibliography to show how it is enmeshed in the communication network of the particular knowledge paradigm it addresses
- is in the house style of the research journal or conference to which it is submitted
- goes through some kind of peer review process which in effect decides whether it constitutes a professional syntagmatic expression of the research paradigm.

How many editorial boards would accept a research paper that had no bibliography because it was original, or no 'search of the literature' because no one had written on the subject? Who would take seriously research that took the form of a film, a poem, a product or an invention or a virtual reality?

The research publishing paradigm has a powerful logic to it and brings discipline to the research process, but the form in which research is presented can become more important than the research itself. Promotion for academics depends primarily upon the extent of their research publications and the extent to which they are cited. Many academics respond by publishing widely on trivial issues that are faultlessly formulated. In many graduate schools the emphasis has shifted from ability to resolve a research problem to ability to apply the research publishing template. Doctoral dissertations are sometimes evaluated by people unfamiliar with the subject area, but expert in the research presentation paradigm. It is not what is researched, but how the research is communicated that matters.

In the research publishing paradigm, aspects of a research problem that cannot be measured and described alphanumerically are not reported. The presentation of a problem and hence the way it is perceived by readers is shaped by the way it is written and the data manipulated. The use of citations means that many aspects of a problem are seen in terms of other research reports from other contexts. Readers of a research report in their turn interpret what they read according to their own cognitive structures. The research paradigm is a process for reconciling research problems to a knowledge paradigm, but it is also one that can progressively mask any differences between the way a problem is seen in the knowledge paradigm and the way it actually is.

If research was conducted, recorded and reported in HyperReality, it would be possible to present three-dimensional, time-variable simulacra that made it possible to study correspondences between paradigmatic knowledge, syntagmatic reality and projected future syntagms. A model of the cyclone paradigm could be contrasted with a model of an actual cyclone and it would then be possible to develop models of what the cyclone could become as the variables change. The cyclone under study would be the same cyclone to everyone involved in the research. People 'reading' the research would be able to manipulate the variables for themselves and examine the model from multiple perspectives (Tiffin 2001).

Commercialisation of university research

University research today is being increasingly commercialised. Industry and business find that university postgraduate students are a source of cheap research labour. Universities that are government subsidised can undercut independent research institutes. To universities short of resources and encouraged to fend for themselves, outside sources of funding for research are attractive, but the more universities look toward commercial funding of research, the more research ceases to be a public good, open to criticism and inspection. Peer reviews, publishing and placing dissertations in university libraries keep research honest. Privately funded research may be tagged as commercially sensitive and kept secretive. In the pursuit of research grants, university departments give weighting, in the way they select and promote staff, to people who can bring in research grants. The resources departments have for research may be used to attract externally funded research. Increasingly, research is restricted to that which is externally funded or to an area where a department can be seen as having some special research capability that will attract funding. Research becomes something that benefits university finances rather than the community or the individual academic seeking to conduct curiosity-led research.

Is the modern university a place for basic research anymore? What little we know about research breakthroughs suggests that they come from unusual people who are not conformist. 'The men responsible for technological innovations ...

during the beginning of the Industrial Revolution were non-conformists who had been excluded from the universities and learned their science indirectly while pursuing their trade' (Senate Special Committee 1970: 21 http://www.cultural economics.atfreeweb.com/art_ed_ni.htm). Academics when they meet today talk not so much about their research as about the obstacles they face to doing it. They lack time and finances and have difficulty in getting proposals accepted if they do not carry funding, or conform to policy or the demands of committees. The Enlightenment took place in the declining years of the medieval university and it took place largely outside universities. Would an independent thinker like Voltaire or Diderot, wanting to do original creative research that carried the philosophical connotation of a search for truth, be able to do it under the aegis of a modern university?

Even researchers have to eat and Diderot and Voltaire prospered with patronage from benevolent despots and mistresses (Bradbury 2000; Bodanis 2000). Their present day equivalents are benevolent corporates and funding agencies whose palaces are the great corporate edifices in science parks where talent, technology and finances come together in major research themes, provided they are based on technology. Japan's Advanced Telecommunications Research (ATR) laboratories are a research centre in Kansai Science city surrounded by the research headquarters of large Japanese corporations engaged in information technology. ATR does basic research into the future of information technology. It gets its backing and support from the Japanese Government and from the telecommunications and computer industries. The neighbouring corporates apply the results of this basic research. ATR is staffed by top Japanese IT researchers with a sprinkling of researchers from other parts of the world. Universities establish colleges nearby so that their postgraduate students can seek entry into the research industry. Research parks like this create an environment for researchers from universities and industry to co-mingle in the development of the technological environments of the future.

Problematisation

Shirley was walking down the road to her apartment wearing her HMD unit so that she could negotiate an extension on an assignment with her professor Sam who was accompanying her as an avatar. Suddenly she was knocked down by a teenager who grabbed her handbag and ran off with it. As well as being a grad student, Shirley was a battle-hardened teacher who jogged every day and took karate. She picked herself up, straightened her HMD unit, flicked its camera to the front so that Sam could join the chase from her point of view and took off after her assailant. She quickly caught up with him, knocked him down, regained her handbag and put in a kick where it mattered to forestall any counter-attack.

'Problem in physical reality solved' she told Sam who had got a bit disorientated.

Things could have ended there, but Shirley was afraid that the mugger might do the same again, so drawing on her knowledge and experience as a teacher she gave the teenager a good stiff telling off while he was struggling to his feet. In so doing she shifted the problem into the virtual reality of language giving him a mental picture of what would happen to him if he ever tried to rob someone again. A sobered young man got to his feet and slunk off.

Sam was impressed, but as they discussed the matter Shirley could not help but worry about whether the problem really was solved. The guy was probably on drugs and he was wearing gang patches. This could be part of a pattern of street attacks on women, not all of whom could give as good as they got. She felt it her duty to report it, she told Sam, who in the circumstances had no problem giving her an extension and they ended their HyperMeet.

Later that day Shirley went to a police station where the incident was logged on the police computer. There was no recent report of similar attacks, but the police took a complete statement and got her to sign it. And that, she felt, was the end of the problem, though she noticed that the police looked at her oddly as she left.

Two days later Sam called Shirley. 'Did you have to kick that lout so hard? He has been to the hospital and the police. They have been in touch with the university about you and are considering laying charges. Apparently their computer shows a growing trend for women to take the law in their own hands and assault young men they say threaten them.'

'But' Shirley said, 'you were there, you saw what happened.' 'Well, not exactly,' said Sam 'I was only there in virtual reality. The guy has the physical evidence of his bruises to support his claim. Look, why don't you go and talk to the Professor of Criminology. He is doing some research with the police on attacks like this for a report that will be the basis for some new legislation for compensating victims.'

'But who' Shirley mused to herself, 'are the victims?'

The story seeks to illustrate the elusive nature of problems in the way they are perceived by different people with different knowledge paradigms. Problems can exist in physical reality and virtual reality and be formulated and re-formulated at different levels by people with different knowledge paradigms. There is the problem in physical reality of the attack on Shirley, who in solving the problem creates another problem. These problems could have stayed at the level of the rough and tumble of everyday events that people deal with from their own individual knowledge resources, but this problem was outside the norm and could be part of a bigger problem involving the safety of society.

Both Shirley and the thief take the problem as they separately see it to professional problem-solving institutions. There is no ongoing crime scene for the police to go to, so they are dealing with a virtual problem invoked by the words of the complainants. In taking statements and entering information on the police computer the problem is re-conceptualised to fit the categories of problems in a police knowledge paradigm and database. However, the police have two virtual realities of the same problem. One fits the old police paradigm (robber attacks woman), the other fits an emergent paradigm (woman attacks robber). There is a paradox. It invites research and a court case to resolve it. Research findings can help define the socially acceptable paradigms by which problems are judged.

As the problem shifts from the way the police see it in terms of the police paradigm to the way the Professor of Criminology sees it according to the university paradigm of criminology to the way lawyers see it according to the legal paradigm, there would be an equivalent shift in language as the issues become increasingly abstract and theoretical and the perception of the problem shifts from an actual event to being part of a pattern of societal behaviour involving the cultural, ethical, political and legal issues of an episteme.

It could be that the Professor of Criminology finds that the problem neatly fits the theories he is expounding in a book he is writing on the basis of his report and his recommendations for new legislation to control aggressive behaviour in females. He will put his new book on his class reading list. The new knowledge paradigm it expounds can be applied to a new class of problem and Shirley's problem becomes a case study that is used as a practice problem in criminology classes. Alternatively it might happen that Shirley's subsequent summons for assault coincides with a TV programme on a trend for pack-attacks on female teachers by teenagers. There are mass demonstrations at her hearing which television turns into a nationwide issue. She is acquitted, the old paradigm is reinforced and a book on the case becomes a reading in feminist studies.

Chaos lurks where there is a lack of congruence in problematising between different knowledge paradigms. It is here that we see the problems that arise from the fragmentation of knowledge in modern universities and consequently in societies. University disciplines research the disjunctions between their knowledge paradigm and the problems it addresses and all too often the solution is to define an ever narrower problem domain and knowledge paradigm.

Problem structures

Shirley's problem is based on an actual incident, and according to the *Encyclopaedia Plus of World Problems and Human Potential* (1996) such problems are part of a vicious cycle: *Alienation → Youth gangs → Neighbourhood control by criminals → Psychological stress of urban environment → Substance abuse → Family breakdown → Alienation*. Such cycles are seen as vicious because they are self-sustaining and difficult to identify.

This particular vicious problem cycle is addressed piecemeal by universities around the world within the boundaries of existing disciplines. Criminology concentrates on the criminal, legal and policing aspects of the problem, sociology on alienation aspects, urban studies and social geography on the spatial aspects, psychology on stress and family breakdown and education on its own failure in the matter. If these different perspectives could be combined to allow a comprehensive study of the problem cycle as a whole there might be some prospect of resolving it, but interdisciplinary research is difficult to do in the modern university. Apart from the administrative difficulties created by the faculty system, academics have great difficulty in seeing things from the perspective of knowledge paradigms other than their own. So this particular problem, despite all the efforts of so many departments in so many universities, remains a growing problem of worldwide proportions, like terrorism, to which it is almost certainly related.

There is deep discontent in many countries at the failure of education (and hence with the educational paradigm taught in universities) to deal with the problem of youth alienation. Many solutions have been tried. Film, radio and television have been harnessed to the problems of education around the world. Today we look to the Internet for solutions and tomorrow we propose to find them in HyperReality, so it may be useful to look back at what went wrong with the last great educational panacea, educational television (ETV).

In the mid-1970s the Organisation of American States (OAS) funded an international research programme to find out why the millions of dollars that were being poured into educational television in Latin America to solve its educational problems were having so little long-term effect (Tiffin 1978). At that time the effectiveness of ETV was researched quantitatively by comparing test scores from teaching by television with those from conventional classroom teaching. Almost invariably the research showed 'no significant difference' and it was widely recognised that the phenomenon under examination was more complex than the research methodology used to measure it (Chu and Schramm 1968). However, the OAS wanted hard answers, so instead of fitting the research problem to the standard educational research methodology, a research methodology was devised to fit the problem. Called problem structure analysis (PSA) it approached the problem of why ETV was ineffective in Latin America by regarding it as a complex problem with a structure of interlinked and interdependent sub-problems. By identifying the sub-problems and the links between them, PSA sought to create a framework for designing solution strategies.

The research did indeed show an extraordinary complexity of problems within ETV systems in Latin America that in sum explained why it did not work and it was possible to trace the problems to the key decision to use the medium of television in the first place to teach conventional curricula which were based on words: the images that television provided at no small cost were redundant (Tiffin 1978). The Brazilian minister of education at the time asked if ETV was solving their educational problems or adding to them. The answer was, it was adding to them and the OAS withdrew its support for ETV projects. This did not solve the educational problems of countries like Brazil, where the problem cycle of youth alienation continues today and grows more vicious; it simply recognised that television as a treatment was not working and was becoming a problem in its own right. What it did suggest was a new research approach to problems that examined their complexity and the links between them.

An approach similar to this is taken in the *Encyclopaedia Plus of World Problems and Human Potential* (1996). This is an ongoing programme of the Union of International Associations, a Belgium-based clearing house that draws upon the documents of some 20,000 member associations and periodicals to identify problems. It has moved from a focus on describing individual problems to an elaborate analysis of the way world problems are interlinked. With this goes the key idea that attacking many persistent individual problems does not work in the long run because their links to other problems mean that they can regenerate when only one aspect of the problem is addressed. It suggests that tightly focused research solves symptoms rather than root causes. Such a thesis might explain the failure of world organisations and universities to resolve the great problems of our time with their piecemeal approach to research.

The future of problems

Scientists from Galileo to Einstein have conducted thought experiments, but the scientific community as a whole has been preoccupied with the observable measurable tangible world that is, rather than the intangible hypothetical worlds of what could be. Research in universities tends to be reactive rather than proactive.

The full consequences of global warming, genetic engineering, AIDS, and a global economy have yet to come, but the universities of the world are in the main geared towards the study of present and past problems that can be explained if not resolved with reference to existing knowledge paradigms that derive their authority from applications of knowledge to past problems. They address problems after they have impacted, not before and not in time to prevent them.

What is needed in a university of the future is a research paradigm that can project its thinking to address the problems of the future. In McLuhan's famous metaphor, 'We look at the present through the rear-view mirror. We march backwards into the future' (http://www.alibris.com/subjects/entertainment/feature-author).

Global problems

Most of us will have seen the kind of wildlife television documentary that looks at the drama of a pack of predators hunting a herd of herbivores. We can observe the problem from the perspective of the carnivores who need to kill in order to survive or from that of the herbivores who need to escape to survive or from that of the ecological whole that needs a balance of herbivores and carnivores. University research, however, has difficulty seeing problems from the perspective of an Islamic country as well as from that of a Christian country, from that of the rich who want economic globalisation as well as from that of the poor who do not. Modern universities are accredited and in the main funded by the nation state they serve and the research problems they address tend to be seen from the perspective of national survival. Now, as universities become commercial enterprises, they begin to see research objectives from the perspective of how big business can survive and thrive.

To suggest that research in the modern university was dedicated to the aims of the state and that in the future it will be dedicated to the ends of multinational corporates is somewhat simplistic. Many fields of research such as philosophy or mathematics have no immediate national or monetary bias, much of the patronage of research comes from genuinely disinterested foundations that owe their origins to business and many academics are international and humanistic in perspective. Since Rachael Carson's *Silent Spring* (1963) researchers have come to see the survival of our species as interlocked with the survival of other species and with the fate of the globe as a whole. But there is a need for a new sense of direction in university research that is independent of interests and dedicated to the issues of globalisation: not globalisation in the narrow neoliberal sense, but globalisation in a Gaian sense that recognises the interconnectedness of things (Lovelock 1988).

It is not just the problems of university research that need a global perspective, but also the methodology, the researchers, the language of research and the ethics of research. If problems are to be seen globally then we must seek to address the cultural differences in the way different people deal with a problem. We need to do research in multilingual teams that can deal with problems from the multiple aspects of different cultures. This may allow us to find common denominators at the heart of the problems which all people face.

We come back to the purpose of a university as being to address the great issues of its time. A glance at any newspaper in any country will reveal some story about freak weather conditions, medical concerns over new viruses, genetic engineering, free trade or the impact of information technology. They echo the way world problems are listed and mapped together in the *Encyclopaedia Plus of World Problems and Human Potential* (1996). These are the issues of our time and they come at us as problems of global dimension. The next chapter addresses the need for a global curriculum based on these problems.

Chapter 8

The curriculum of globalisation

A university, I should lay down, by its very name professes to teach universal knowledge.

(Newman 1996: 25)

... the new institution of the university which emerged to meet the over-whelming need to provide for the training of lawyers, schoolmasters and clerics to fill the ranks of the increasingly sophisticated administrations of both church and state.

(Bowen 1975: 105)

After centuries of intellectual effort man has forged for himself instruments and methods of thought upon which he can rely for a solution of his problems and for an understanding of the universe around him.

(Beck 1964: 17)

... a prehistoric tribe ... decided to introduce systematic education for its children. The curriculum was specifically designed to meet particular survival needs in the local environment and so included such subjects as sabre-tooth-tiger-scaring-with-fire. But the climate of the region changes and the sabre tooth tigers perish. Attempts to change the curriculum to meet new survival needs encounter stern opposition.

(Benjamin 1971: 7)

The curriculum is interwoven with the social fabric that sustains it.

(Smith *et al.* 1971: 16)

Introduction

The university curriculum is part of the university paradigm and is itself a paradigm. This chapter proposes a curriculum for a global virtual university that incorporates what is universal in university curricula. It looks at a university curriculum as an integrated whole, responsive not to national needs, but to global needs, not to the community of supply, but to the community of demand and not to rigidly defined objectives, but to the issues of the first global episteme.

The universals of university curricula

In the 1950s the British civil service was in the habit of sending a team around universities advising interested students as to what they were looking for in new entrants. Their subjects of study did not really matter as long as it was not something too freaky like psychology, nor did the level of degree, although a third suggested you were a bit lazy and a first that you were a bit of a boffin. What they were after was the right sort of chap. The process would not have surprised a Chinese university student prior to the nineteenth century. For 2,500 years the educational system of China was based on a progression of examinations for the civil service and the philosophy that the right kind of person would ensure the right kind of government for the right kind of society.

Since the earliest times universities have produced the senior servants of their societies as well as the members of professions such as law, medicine, and education. However, universities have also attracted idealists seeking knowledge for its own sake and trying to understand the nature of reality. Such people question the *status quo* and seek to change society. This polarity is at the heart of university curricula. Students learn to conform to the paradigm while at the same time questioning it. The nature of some subjects encourages conformity while others place more emphasis on critical thinking.

Producing professionals who address global problems

Complex societies need competent people well versed in the paradigmatic structure of their society to ensure its security and continuance. Law, medicine, engineering, education and theology are relative universals in university curricula. These are vocational subjects producing cadres of problem-solvers who share the same paradigmatic knowledge and network together through professional bodies.

Modern universities have been shaped by industrialisation and over the last century they have expanded their vocational degree programmes to include the professional roles that make an industrial society possible such as engineering, mining, geology, textiles and journalism. The USA in particular has extended the range of vocations considered suitable for study at university level. The information society has introduced another layer of complexity in society that calls for new skills and new kinds of information professionals. Universities find themselves faced with a need to further diversify the specialist professional programmes they offer. And now comes globalisation with yet another level of professional require-ments. A university of the future will need to prepare professionals at the level of a global society not instead of, but as well as, at the local level. This means adding a new global dimension to traditional subjects, so that we have global medicine and global law, and to the newer professions, to give us global transport studies and global business studies.

The MBA is probably the first degree programme to become global. Its origins go back over 100 years in the USA where students of Harvard Business School learned to manage in America. In the 1960s the MBA spread to Europe. In the last two decades it has spread around the world and become the most popular post-graduate programme of study. Like theology management studies is a knowledge paradigm of human invention that has no basis in physical reality, but works as long as people believe in the paradigm and as long as the paradigm conforms to the episteme. What the MBA did that made it so successful was to create a common style of management worldwide at a time when global business was booming. In MBA speak, they learned to talk the talk and walk the walk.

Subjects such as geography, oceanography and climatology always had a global dimension, but they were seen from the perspective of national advantage. The great schools of geography in France, Germany, Britain and the USA that developed in the second half of the nineteenth century did so in response to a need to explain and justify national programmes of expansion. Today we need to see the physical reality of the biosphere from a global perspective. We also need to introduce new subject areas that will develop cadres of global professionals dedicated to the processes that enable globalisation. Minako O'Hagan introduced the idea of teletranslation and argues that it constitutes a coming industry of global proportions that is necessary if globalisation is to work (O'Hagan 1996). Similar new professional fields with a focus on globalisation processes are ecommerce, disaster communications and aviation medicine.

The University of Hawaii applied the term Teleprofessor to Stan Harms in tribute to his vision of a world in which teleprofessionals could use telecommunications to work anywhere, while they lived wherever they wanted to. This is the kind of world a global virtual university would prepare people for and that is made possible by HyperReality. In such a world we will exist and be responsible at both the local and global levels. We do this already to some degree. As we drive into town listening to global news and wondering how it will affect the local economy we obey the highway code of the country we are in, yet we may pay a carbon tax for the contribution we are making to global warming. There is a growing need in the new professional areas of information technology for people who can address the duality of globalisation and localisation (O'Hagan and Ashworth 2002). A professional programme of study could be delivered in part from the curriculum of a global virtual university with a global perspective and in part from their local university with its local perspective.

The search for reality

The preparation of professionals to address the problems of globalisation is seen as forming one side of the curriculum of a global virtual university. We turn now to the other side and to the curriculum issues of those who go to universities with a sense of mission: to find themselves, to search for truth, knowledge and the meaning of life. Traditionally such scholarly seekers have looked to the humanities with their roots in Greek philosophy and skills in language or to the sciences or to the subjects that seek to be scientific about humanity such as sociology, anthropology and psychology. These knowledge paradigms have in common a search for the nature of reality. Pythagoras' belief that it was all numbers is still as good as any other and fits the digital age. It reminds us that the search is as old as universities and constitutes a universal. We would argue that the mission of a university to understand the nature of reality has become fractured and is in need of renewal.

At the University of Geneva at the beginning of the last century, Ferdinand de Saussure taught the first scientific approach to the study of language (de Saussure 1983). Instead of looking at the way language is used he examined the nature of language itself and so opened the way to realisation of how language structures reality, a step that the philosopher Ernst Cassirer compared to that of Galileo's new science (Cassirer 1945: 99).

Today we have structural linguistics, psycholinguistics, sociolinguistics, sociology, anthropology, mass media studies, journalism, corpus linguistics, psychology, cognitive science, communications studies, computer science, information science and informatics; all, in their various ways, study how we arrive at mental realities from physical realities.

Sigmund Freud, a contemporary of de Saussure, gave us a convincing explanation of how we do this as individuals (Freud 1997). Emile Durkheim another contemporary of de Saussure gave us a rationale for doing this at the level of society (Perdue 1986). Claude Levi-Strauss sought to explain how it is done at the level of cultures (Levi-Strauss 1972). Shannon gave us a model for how we communicate mental realities between ourselves as a species (Shannon and Weaver 1949). The discipline of Communications Studies evolved to try and synthesise all the hundreds of theories that have been thought up over the last hundred years to explain the problem. But these different knowledge paradigms fail to form a consensus. Indeed, many are at odds with each other. Theories of how mass media provide our mental realities polarise between those that claim limited effect and those that claim the effect to be powerful (Littlejohn 2002). Nor are we any wiser from a new wave of subjects such as cognitive science, information science and neurophilosophy that seek to understand how we understand in order to mimic it with information technologies.

The modern university has arrived in the third millennium with a plethora of knowledge paradigms all seeking from different perspectives to resolve the question that has been at the heart of universities since their beginnings: what is reality? That there are now so many approaches to the question would be healthy if the scholars advocating the differing paradigms were in open dispute with each other as they would have been in classical and medieval times. They cannot all be right. It is quite likely that none of them is right. In the curriculum outlined in this chapter they are placed adjacent to each other in a programme of study that would seek to question the anomalies between them.

The modern university permits these different explanations of reality provided they appear to comply with the paradigm of scientific rationalism, which begins to feel like requiring acknowledgement of papal infallibility at the time of the reformation. There are flaws in the scientific approach that need addressing. In particular as we noted in Chapter 7 in the way science is communicated. It seeks to explain the physical reality outside us to the virtual realities within us. Yet as we have noted previously, this is only possible through a medium and every medium and every channel in every medium has a different range of capabilities and a different set of restrictions and will show a different version of reality because of this. We have also noted that it requires language, but that every language provides a different interpretation of everything that we know and every choice of every word and the syntactical order in which they are placed embodies a different meaning for every individual. We may have shifted from a theological to a scientific paradigm but we still see reality darkly and distortedly through the lenses of language, culture, the senses and media. Scientists use microscopes or telescopes to see aspects of the world that are outside our standard sensory capabilities, but they have no 'languagescopes' with which to relate what they see to the billions of neural connections that light up in consequence in the vastness of their brains. This is not to deny science, but to say that until its methodology allows for how people perceive what science perceives, the validity of what it purports to explain is questionable. This is the America waiting to be discovered in the time of a global virtual university.

A fractal and organic curriculum

Students buy and teachers teach programmes of study in semester (term) sized chunks. Students cannot buy half a semester or the third week in a semester or spread things across a double semester or buy two weeks one year and the rest the next year or do the first weeks in one university and the rest in another. No two universities ever have the same timetable, so it is never possible for people who are mobile to pick up a programme of study in a new university from where they left off in their old university. To put it mildly, the way universities offer instruction is not user-friendly. The only service that is as uncompromising is that offered by prisons.

Instead of semester length programmes of study we have suggested that the basic unit of instruction that students pay for could be a one-week modular unit of instruction like that described in Chapter 3. There would have to be some fixed tutorials and seminars in the week, but with large numbers of students broken into small groups these could be repeated at different times. Moreover, the week could be repeated as many times as there was learner demand. Chapter 4 outlined the way professors responsible for the syllabus could be paid by royalties on the number of students who enrolled in their classes. Professors could operate at the level of individual weekly HyperClass units and be paid royalties on the number of students completing a one-week unit. These one-week units could be aggregated to make up a semester length programme towards a degree, they could be taken by themselves or as part of any combination that learners as customers decide to put together for their programmes of study.

Figure 8.2 shows how this would work. At the first level is a one-week modular virtual class on 'globalisation'. A person who wanted to study the practical issues raised in this week can shift down a fractal level to where the one-week unit becomes the introductory first unit of a semester length programme of study on globalisation that has a minimum of twelve weekly units covering different aspects of globalisation including a unit on the 'globalisation of education'.

Anyone who wanted to study 'the globalisation of education' in greater depth than a one-week unit allows could again shift down to a third fractal level to do a semester length programme on the 'globalisation of education' to which the week-long unit on the subject now serves as an introduction. The programme on the 'globalisation of education' has a one-week modular unit on 'the idea of a global virtual university' that in turn forms the introduction to a semester length programme on 'global virtual universities' at a fourth level. At this point we have arrived at the level of this book and the weekly units can be thought of as similar to the chapters in this book. So we can imagine that there is a unit on the idea of a global curriculum, which corresponds to this chapter. Could anyone interested in this subject shift down to a fifth level and take a semester length programme in it? In theory yes, but while there is a considerable literature on virtual universities and the globalisation of education and some of them touch on curricular issues, there is no emergent paradigmatic body of knowledge on global curricula as yet. At this point we have in effect reached the research pedestal for university education as it applies to the issues of globalisation.

The idea of allowing a basic twelve to fourteen weeks for a programme of study is to match the usual length of a semester in a conventional university. There is, however, no reason why there could not be sixteen, twenty or forty modular weekly virtual class units from which students could select. If we accept the idea of student as customer who can choose what they will study and in what sequence, then a fractal curriculum of this nature allows for students to select from a smörgåsbord of subjects to suit their individual needs.

A fractal curriculum allows students to design their own learning by making their own interconnections between modular week-long units. Tracking the demand for different weekly units and the frequency with which students take the same path in putting together their own semester length programmes would provide a basis for facilitating instruction that reflected what students want.

There would be design but it would be at the level of the weekly units where professional instructional designers responsive to detailed iterative feedback from students would be engaged in designing HyperClass environments in the manner described in Chapter 3. The more students want a unit, or a particular path through the units, the more there would be investment in design and development and the more frequent and available the instruction offered. It is an organic system of instruction that grows in response to student interest.

An issues curriculum

In the remote parts of the Amazon jungle, in the loneliest islands of the Pacific, in the Sahara and the Congo and on the roof of the world in the great massifs of Asia, ordinary people watch television and listen to radio. In the past, in the main, illiterate people knew what was happening where they lived and literate people knew about their country and the countries it was involved with. Now, in a way without precedent, everyone, even the humblest, even the illiterate, knows about world events. This is 'technocultural' globalisation (Green 2002: 69). When the media clamour to the world that the World Trade Centre has tumbled and the USA has declared war on terrorists and that refugees are a problem and that violent storms wreak havoc, these become global issues, which more and more, the ordinary people of the world see as linked to the local issues that directly affect them. Even if, as critical scholars point out (Schiller 1991; Giddens 1991), the global voice and the agenda it sets is from the rich to the poor, from the developed nations to the developing nations, that very fact becomes part of the agenda of the silent listeners. Even if commercial control of the media means that much is not said and much is biased, there are some journalists who like some scholars remain true to their calling and search for the truth. Sometimes, something gets through that has the ring of reality. People identify with the storms stories, with the AIDS stories, with the stories about Jews, Christians and Muslims because these things are happening to them too.

It is with issues like these that a university should be involved and it is with them that a global university curriculum needs to begin. However, in developing a curriculum for a university the subject matter of such issues needs to shift from the emotive, simplistic, single issue statements of the media and the village meeting. The phenomena of globalisation need to be organised into a body of thought that seeks to discover the fundamental elements that constitute globalisation, how they interrelate and what they mean. If university subjects are paradigms, then developing a curriculum for globalisation means considering globalisation as a paradigm, albeit an emerging one that, as yet, is not clearly perceived. Globalisation is not a designed system arising from human logic, like the United Nations. We may seek to control it through organisations like the United Nations, the World Trade Organisation, the Kyoto Protocol and the International Court of Justice, but globalisation is developing independently of human control and exhibits the characteristics of a self-organising system with potential for chaos.

Initially the term 'globalisation' was used to describe an economic paradigm, a neoliberal free market game of global monopoly that all countries are encouraged to play until it becomes the only game in the world. But monopoly is a game where the rich tend to get richer and the poor unless they have a lot of luck, get poorer with stops in jail. The raw syntagmatic applications of globalisation as an economic paradigm have failed to take into account the ecological impact, demographic issues, the erosion of democracy and the impact of new technologies that accompany it. The way globalisation is played is as an economic paradigm

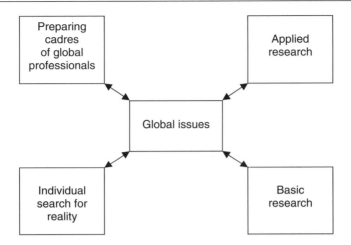

Figure 8.1 Basic interactions in an issues driven curriculum

that impacts on every aspect of life on a finite planet and has already gone beyond the point where people might say: 'we don't like the game and would rather play something else'. It has become a much bigger game than anyone imagined. The rules and elements are no longer determined solely by the human players. We are not even certain what they are.

It is from the question 'what is globalisation?' as it emerges from the events of globalisation, that the rest of the curriculum would grow. There is no agreed globalisation paradigm. Globalisation studies have not been established and nobody has written a defining text. Yet, like some Golem, globalisation is there among us growing rapidly while we argue as to whether humanity should love it or destroy it. What we need to do is go beyond its basic appearance as a commercial phenomenon to include its ecological impact, effect on cultures and communications and the implications this has for the way we educate, trade and cope with pandemics.

What follows is a suggestion for a programme of study consisting of one-week modular units that can be amalgamated into semester length programmes of study of between twelve and sixteen weeks which would examine each of the critical processes that would seem to be involved in the emerging paradigm of globalisation where the economic element is only one of a number of sub-paradigms.

The issues are linked to the universals of university curricula, the programmes of study that provide cadres of professionals and allow the investigation of reality with the difference that these are put into a global rather than national context. The curriculum addresses the interlinked issues of globalisation, the reality of the issues and the skills that are needed to deal with them.

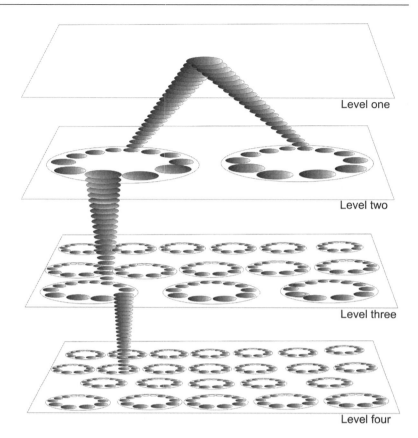

Figure 8.2 Design for a global curriculum. The curriculum is seen as having four levels. The grey buttons represent week-long units. At the top level there is only one such unit. At the other levels week-long units are clustered in oval shapes that represent seminar length programmes of study. The grey funnels show a fractal shift where a week-long module at one level becomes the introduction to a semester length programme at another.

Level one of a global curriculum: an introductory week

The curriculum is seen as starting from a single one-week module that addresses the question: 'What is globalisation?' This would be the point from which the curriculum would grow. It could be offered free to anyone anywhere via radio, television and the Internet and would reflect global issues as they happened, although it would approach them as symptomatic of deeper issues. It would seek to be a weekly media event that reacted to world events, generated debate, invited comment from world figures and distinguished thinkers, and provided a point of lecture in this week could be like when HyperReality, or something like it, becomes available.

Ausubel modernised the Aristotelean belief that what one taught should first be anchored in what was already known (Ausubel 1967). As the images of some event circulate the world, that is what people know about. That is where study begins. The Sophists in ancient Greece gave free lectures in the agora not only to market their skills but to demonstrate the relevance of their curriculum to the issues of the times. This is what the opening virtual class on globalisation would seek to do: market by example, demonstrate its methodology and go straight to the heart of what it sought to teach and research, with the difference that instead of using a marketplace, a global virtual university would use global mass media linked to its Webpages.

Level two of a global curriculum: two basic programmes

At the second level would be two semester length programmes of study: one addressing the practical aspects of globalisation, the other the theoretical; one concerned with professional problem-solving at a global level, the other with the question of the new reality that globalisation brings. These would be introductory programmes, but each of the one-week units that constitute them could be expanded into semester length programmes in their own right at the third level. Neither the list, nor the brief descriptions of syllabi are intended to be definitive. They are starting points. They would change with every iterative application to allow the programmes to grow in response to those involved so that they become an expression of what people around the world want to know and study about globalisation. The issues would define themselves. The two basic programmes are not intended to set students in one direction or the other. A student could put their own programme together with selections from both the basic programmes.

Globalisation: the practical issues

Globalisation
The one-week introductory virtual class unit at the first level.

The globalisation of business and commerce
This addresses the economic paradigm of globalisation. Since it is what most people first think of as globalisation, it grounds students in what they are familiar with.

Global demographics
Who are the players in globalisation? Where are the rich and where are the poor? Where are populations growing and where are they aging? Where are they moving

from and to? This could include such issues as refugees and poverty and could create a dialectic with the previous unit.

Global education

The film classic *All Quiet on the Western Front* begins with a patriotic teacher enthusing his students with the glories of the German nation so that proudly, and full of the idealism of youth, they march off to the horrors of the trenches of the First World War. There they face young men like themselves who have also been taught pride in their nation. National education systems have taught people to be good citizens of their nations. What kind of educational system is needed that will make them good global citizens as well?

Global ecology

Globalisation is played out on a finite planet. We have become aware of global warming and of the consequences of the old technologies of the industrial society, but what will be the consequences of genetic engineering and nanotechnology, the growth and movement of peoples, increasing tourism and affluence? How do we find sustainable growth?

Global resources

Economic globalisation has led to heedless exploitation of the finite resources of the planet: fish, forests, soil, minerals, water and humans. The very existence of humanity depends upon these resources. The globalisation paradigm needs to allow for sustainable and equitable use of global resources.

Globalisation of transport

Globalisation has been with us since Magellan first sailed around the world. It is the remarkable development in transport technology over the last quarter of a century that has enabled the rapid mass movement of people and goods. Yet technological developments in transport are set to accelerate. How sustainable is this aspect of globalisation? How do we prepare for it?

Globalisation and information technology

Where transport permits the free flow of goods and people, information technology permits the free flow of knowledge, ideas and information. Like transport technologies, information technologies are still developing. In the future globalisation will take place in a broadband telecommunications environment where computer processing power will become part of what we wear and physical reality and virtual reality will blend in a HyperReality. What will be the global impact?

Globalisation of work

The mind work that characterises the information society can flow between countries. This can mean new industries springing up in developing countries and it can also mean exploitation of workers and child labour.

Globalisation of leisure

Entertainment became global when Charlie Chaplin's films were shown in every country in the world. Increasingly, affluent people take their leisure by travelling to other countries. Sports are played at a global level. The Olympic games and football's World Cup are broadcast to a global audience. Could this create a common sense of being global or will it provide new grounds for cultural clashes?

Global health and the globalisation of medicine

Conventional universities prepare practitioners to address the health needs of a nation. Health practitioners are also needed to address global needs. The transport processes of globalisation accelerate the spread of epidemics while the Internet raises possibilities of telemedicine. Global catastrophes and the illnesses of poverty call for global remedies.

Global communications

Globalisation is effected by communications between people in dyads, groups, organisations, nations and cultures using telecommunications and travel. The effect can be one of cooperation, conflict or domination. It involves language and culture, translation and interpretation.

Global security

At the time of writing, the United States has declared war on terrorism. The last century saw a hot war against fascism and a cold war against communism, but these 'isms' were associated with specific countries and pitted nation against nation. The advent of globalisation sees the emergence of new security issues where the danger is covert and perhaps unimagined by security forces; a city could be held to ransom with a hidden nuclear bomb or a plague let loose via the airways of the world. There are also natural disasters resulting from global warming, earthquakes, famines and disease.

Global governance

If the game of globalisation is to be played according to rules, a system of governance based on law that represents the people of the world as a whole is needed. The world community advocates democracy within nations, but at the heart of the objections that come from the demonstrators at conferences on global issues is the simple fact that there is no global democracy. The United Nations is the nearest we have to world government, but it is based upon a democracy of nations in which some are more equal than others. It does not represent the people of the world. We have yet to hear the cry of 'No globalisation without representation' and the idea at first glance seems impractical, but could the development of information technology make it feasible in the future?

The impact of new technologies on globalisation

Transport and information technologies made globalisation possible. This in its turn makes possible the rapid worldwide diffusion of new technologies such as genetic engineering, nanotechnology and robotics. They become part of the globalisation paradigm though what they are, how they will impact and what their role will be, is not yet clear.

Applied research on globalisation

How do we make globalisation work in a way that is benign for most people and for the planet? What are the elements of a paradigm that is partly a human construct, partly a consequence of the planetary forces invoked and still emergent? How do we devise the new technologies and control their application? Who will be the researchers and what methods and languages should they use?

Toward a practice of globalisation

People of nation states seek to live together through the practice of respect for each other under the rule of law and government in the kind of organised harmony that we think of as civilisation. How do we live together as global citizens?

Globalisation: the theoretical issues

This programme addresses the underlying philosophical issues of how we perceive and paradigmatise globalisation. It does this by taking conventional subject paradigms that address the nature of reality but are normally studied separately and giving them a common focus on the issues of globalisation.

Globalisation

This would be the one-week virtual class unit from the first level that introduced 'Globalisation: the practical issues'.

- Epistemological issues of globalisation
- Linguistics and globalisation
- Scientific perspectives on globalisation
- History of globalisation
- Evolution and globalisation
- Philosophy of globalisation
- Sociology of globalisation
- Theological perspectives on globalisation
- The rhetoric of globalisation
- The communication of globalisation
- The economics of globalisation
- The ethics of globalisation
- Basic research on globalisation
- Toward a theory of globalisation.

Level three of a global curriculum

Any one of the one-week units that make up the semester length programmes listed above could serve as the introductory unit to a semester programme at this level. The way they could be further developed is illustrated in Figure 8.2.

Level four of a global curriculum

As with levels two and three this consists of semester length programmes of study that are expansions of the one-week virtual class modular units in level three. Units at level four can in their turn be expanded into semester length programmes. However, we have found, as in the case of education described earlier in the chapter, that programmes of study at this level tend to be based on ongoing research. They are at the edge of the knowledge, problems and issues of globalisation. Level four in effect becomes the research pedestal of the curriculum from which new programmes of study would be built.

Is a global curriculum feasible?

This curriculum is for autonomous learners anywhere who have the motivation and language skills to take advantage of it. They can take it in whole or in part, for interest or for a professional qualification, as part of a degree in a conventional university, or as a course in a global virtual university. Unlike the faculty-based curricula of conventional universities, it is unitary and syncretic and gives weight to the need to find the knowledge to deal with the problems of globalisation rather than providing the knowledge in the expectation that it will resolve problems.

The curriculum is designed for delivery in the first place at a postgraduate level. As the knowledge of globalisation becomes an established paradigm it will begin to seep down through the educational system. Undergraduate courses will develop and the study of globalisation will in time permeate through the school system.

The feasibility of developing such a curriculum has been tested by asking academics from around the world to design programmes that would fit the model. Doing this, suggested the hierarchy of levels. At levels two and three academics with a reputation in specific aspects of the field expressed interest in leading a one-week modular unit and in designing an expanded semester length version. They were able to indicate other academics that could be approached to give units within a semester length programme. However, there came a point where the fractal levels could not be extended further because people were involved in original research.

The four levels can be thought of as a pyramidal hierarchy. Level four lies on a pedestal of research that is seeking to understand and paradigmatise what is unknown in globalisation while the one-week introduction to globalisation that forms level one links into popular thinking and current concerns with the issues of globalisation.

While there is a basic sequential structure that would suggest students enter at level one or two and explore their way downwards to the research roots of globalisation, the structure is intended to make it possible for students to combine their own choices of units into their own programmes of study. They need not be restricted to any one level in doing this, so they can, as it were, look at different topics in general or in detail. The same modular unit may occur in different programmes. Recognising these overlaps helps a student to formulate a programme of study parsimoniously. However, it is anticipated that common paths would emerge and that curriculum design would react to this, re-shaping the semester length programmes on offer.

A cautionary syntagm

Sam was giving the second HyperSeminar in a series for doctoral students on paradigm design in curriculum development.

'Last time,' he said, 'we looked at natural paradigms in curricula. Any questions on the assignment before we go on?'

'Yes' said Shirley. 'I want to do pregnancy. It is a natural paradigm that is pretty important to a lot of us, but I have not been able to find any examples of it as a subject in universities.'

'Have you checked out medical curricula?' asked Sam. 'Yes,' said Shirley, 'but you have to be a medical student. It's a knowledge paradigm where pregnancy is the problem. What about the other side? What women need to know about pregnancy and not just the medical side, what about the poetry of pregnancy?'

'Good point,' said Sam, 'and it makes a lead into this seminar on paradigms as human inventions.'

Sam clicked up a series of paintings by Colin McCahon and asked the students to deduce the painter's paradigm. They found it difficult and he explained: 'McCahon was a controversial New Zealand painter who broke the conventional paradigm of painting by painting words as objects or as part of the landscape. By doing so he established a new painting paradigm and I guess this is now accepted because his pictures are hung in galleries around the world and fetch large sums of money.'

There was a murmur of interest and the group explored what made something become paradigmatic. Then Sam put up another image.

'There is a similar painting paradigm in Japan. This is an example by a Japanese artist called Tihsllub. By the way do any of you read Japanese?' There was no response. 'A pity because these Japanese characters that take the form of a range of mountains are haikus, brief poems that express the beauty of the mountains and forests and you can see how the Japanese characters resemble the trees which cover the slopes. If you look at the sky above the mountains, you can see how the characters now depict clouds that look dirty. They are intended to suggest pollution. These dramatic slashes down the mountains that wipe out the words symbolise the way polluted rain is destroying the forest.'

The class was moved by these ideas and took time to compare McCahon with the Japanese artist. They loved the way Tihsllub had a woodgrain effect as a background and how this suggested a sunset. Some felt that Tihsllub was more polished than McCahon. Then Sam switched the image 180 degrees so the clouds were now on the bottom of the picture.

'Does it matter,' Sam asked, 'if I turn the picture upside down?'

'Yes,' said Ahmed, 'it does not follow the syntax of the paradigm. The writing is upside down and the clouds are on the bottom.'

'What if I told you,' said Sam, 'that this is the correct way to read Japanese characters?'

The class was puzzled. The picture looked quite different. Sam now turned the picture 90 degrees so that the clouds were on the right. 'If the writing was in English, it would be this way up.'

'It does not make sense anymore,' said Ahmed.

'What if I tell you,' said Sam, ' that the clouds are prices in Yen?'

What was Sam up to Shirley wondered. How could clouds be prices? Then she suddenly realised. 'It's a list of something and their prices,' she exclaimed.

Sam smiled, 'Thank you Shirley, it is indeed a menu from a restaurant.'

'Then what are the black slashes?' someone asked.

'They're items that have been crossed off the menu,' said Sam. A ripple of amusement went through the class as they realised how they'd been tricked.

'So there isn't a paradigm,' said Ahmed.

'Yes there is,' said Sam. 'This is a syntagm from the paradigm of menus.'

'So there is no McCahon paradigm?' Ahmed asked.

'I invented Tihsllub, but McCahon really was a famous painter, although the art world still argues as to what his paradigm was or if he ever had one. The point I am seeking to make is how do we determine the validity of paradigms? How much of what we teach are paradigms that will one day be perceived as meaningless or flawed or indeed frauds? How many subjects in a university have as little value as my Tihsllub?'

The French student, Denise, said, 'Prof, where did you get the menu from?'

'A small restaurant in the mountains behind Kyoto,' said Sam, 'it looked so attractive I asked if I could have it.'

'Prof, you have shown us how easy it is to invent a paradigm and get people to believe in it,' said Denise, 'but why did you keep that menu? Surely it was not because you wanted to be reminded of the food available that day? In Japan even the most humble of things are given meaning beyond their function.'

Figure 8.3 Tihsllub 'Mountains'

> Sam looked hard at Denise. 'You know Japan?'
> 'I lived there for many years,' said Denise.
> 'Then you knew all along that I was playing a trick.'
> 'Yes of course,' said Denise, 'but although I knew it was just a game, I still got to see mountains in a menu.'

The Doctor Fox lectures on 'Mathematical Game Theory as Applied to Physician Education' were presented to three groups of psychiatrists, psychologists, social workers and educators who warmly evaluated them for the interest they stimulated, the way they were presented and their content. Yet the lecture was a jumble of contradictory statements, double talk, non sequiturs and meaningless references delivered by an actor with an impressive delivery and fake *curriculum vitae*. Out of a total of 55 subjects most of whom held Masters or Bachelors degrees, no one realised that it was a hoax (Naftulin *et al.* 1973). There are other such examples and they raise the question: 'How valid is what we study in a university?' The power of such paradigms as medicine and mathematics is manifest in their applications and historical continuity, but how many of the new subjects solemnly taught in today's universities will still be taught in twenty years' time? How valid will their application be in ten years' time? The implication of the Fox Lecture is that 'the extent to which students are satisfied with teaching and even the degree to which they feel they have learned, reflects little more than their illusion of having learned' (Ibid.: 635).

Scientists believe that in mathematics they have a pure paradigm uncluttered by the linguistic labyrinths in which a Dr Fox can hide, a paradigm that can explain the world and allow them to develop technologies to master it. They are neo-Pythagoreans believing that everything is ultimately numbers. Dewdney (1999: 2) posed the questions: 'Is mathematics discovered or created and why is mathematics so incredibly useful in the natural sciences?' He describes how he took these questions to noted mathematicians who lived in Greece, Egypt, Venice and Oxford and were steeped in the mathematical traditions of these places and how they answered them in a way that made sense from their different perspectives. But, Dewdney himself is left like the mathematician poet Omar Khayyam, who lived nearly a thousand years before him and wrote:

Chapter 9

Global corporate

Education and the global economy are envisioned as having an interdependent relationship. Competition in the global economy is dependent on the quality of education.

(Spring 1998: 6)

Universities are one of the causes of globalisation as well as an effect of it.

(Marginson and Considine 2000: 48)

The focus of a business is profit, the focus of a university is knowledge.

(Mason 1998: 151)

If the WTO has its way … trade in education will be open to global competition and is expected to surpass all other trade in the service sector…It is therefore not too difficult to see why predatory entrepreneurs and cash-strapped vice-chancellors find online delivery an attractive opportunity.

(Dhanarajan 2001)

Introduction

The Internet has made it possible to bring students, teachers, researchers, knowledge and problems together by means of telephone systems and computers. This is the basis for a virtual university. The economic advantages are enormous. Already there are hundreds of first generation virtual universities on the Internet. The majority are conventional universities, seeking with varying success to adapt their existing courses to the Internet in search of bigger markets, and open universities switching from correspondence courses to ecourses. Some seek commercial advantage by forming consortia. Some are degree mills. Some target diaspora cultures like the Celts, the Tamils and the Maori. None of them, however, has attempted to radically rethink the very nature of a university if it is to address the needs of a new episteme hallmarked by information technology and globalisation. This has been our aim in writing this book.

The previous chapters examined the universals of the university paradigm and how they are likely to change in the future. All purposeful systems need a control subsystem and a universal requirement of universities is some system of management. In the modern university management was until recently in the hands of academics who saw the purpose of a university in academic terms and in the context of the state that supported them. Now university management has adopted the MBA mode and increasingly sees its mission in monetarist terms. Universities in the future will need to be self-supporting and competitive in the worldwide trade in teaching that comes with globalisation. This final chapter explores the organisation of a global virtual university as a global corporate and the key issues that it will face if it is to retain its academic purpose.

The idea of a global university

Like all universities a global virtual university would bring teachers and students together to study the application of knowledge to problems at an advanced level that involved research as well as teaching. It would have a campus providing support services such as libraries and a space for people to socialise and contexts for in-depth instruction. Bachelor's, master's and doctoral degrees would be offered and these would need to be comparable in quality and weighting to conventional universities.

Where a conventional university may have an extension on the Internet, but is essentially based in the atomic reality of a physical location, a global virtual university would exist in the digital reality of the Internet, although it would also need to have extensions in physical reality for assessment purposes which could also provide optional experiences in situated learning. A global virtual university of the future will also be different from the first generation virtual universities that now exist in narrowband Internet, in that it will take advantage of the more advanced information technology infrastructure that can be expected over the next twenty years. When people design a bricks and mortar university they look as far into the future as they can and make provision for expansion. Similarly, a global virtual university should be designing its place in a future of broadband telecommunications and vastly increased computer processing power. This will make possible the kind of environment described as HyperReality where virtual reality and physical reality and human intelligence and artificial intelligence intermingle. Such technological infrastructures make it possible to construct virtual campuses with a rich environment not only in the artistry of its architecture, but in the multitude of activities that make a university an exciting place.

The application of artificial intelligence to instruction and administration makes it possible to develop instruction in a way that is scalable. Every additional ten to twenty students does not mean employing an extra teacher and building a new classroom. The more students who enrol, the lower the *per capita* cost and the better the quality of the programmes offered, because there is more money to invest in materials and to attract top academics. A global virtual university has the potential to improve the quality of its programmes above that of most universities, while at the same time reducing the cost of a degree programme to well below half that of conventional universities. Where the costs of building and maintaining conventional universities and their associated transport systems will increase over time, the *per capita* costs of global commercial virtual universities will decrease. A global virtual university could become very big business.

To a virtual university on the Internet it does not matter where teachers and students are physically located. It becomes possible to have a university that is orientated toward global and regional rather than national and local issues. However, such a university cannot, like conventional universities, look to local and national sources of support and accreditation. Global virtual universities have to be corporate entities to survive and may have to find accommodation with national universities for accreditation until such time as global accreditation is readily available. Where universities supported by states seek to restrict entry to universities and the time taken over a degree programme, a corporate global virtual university would seek to maximise entry and encourage students to remain students for as long as they wanted. Whether someone was fit to take a programme of study would be for them as customer to decide. The quality of degree programmes would be controlled by the standards and rigour of assessment and exams procedures.

Instead of selling university instruction in semester or term length units it could be sold in week length units. Students could do a degree programme incrementally and as quickly or as slowly as they want. They could take twenty weeks over a degree if they already had most of the background knowledge or twenty years if they enjoyed being a student.

No conventional university could find the teachers to cope with the kind of expansion that could be possible with a global virtual university. Successful programmes of study where student numbers rise rapidly represent a problem in conventional universities and limits have to be imposed. The lecture theatres available are not big enough, more staff are needed and at the very least a year will pass between recognising the need for new staff and getting them, by which time numbers might have shrunk as rapidly as they rose. In a virtual university where the teachers were paid on a per student basis, all that would be required would be an electronic exchange of contracts. The teacher could start within the hour. Their income would depend on the rise and fall of their student numbers and in effect on the quality of their teaching and the demand for what they taught. They could earn far more than university teachers earn today, or far less. For the first time teachers would be paid according to the degree of their success.

Good academics find this challenging. When we tested the idea out with internationally respected academics, within a month almost fifty had indicated willingness to teach in this way. Of course most of them already had an academic post. At the moment academics in the main have freedom to give an occasional programme of study outside their university provided it does not interfere with their regular teaching and research programmes. Offering a seminar and lecture for a week on the basis of a book they have written is not a major commitment. If, however, the weekly unit proved successful and the demand for it grew, the teacher might have to come to some accommodation with their university or make a decision to freelance for a global virtual university, which would mean trading the security of tenure for the possibility of a large income and global recognition.

There would need to be some kind of academic board similar in function to an editorial board of an academic journal that would ensure the quality of the courses and the credentials of the teachers, but the basic criterion applied would simply be that the proposed course of study was based on an academically acceptable published text of international standing. How many programmes of study in conventional universities are taught by the person who has published the set text?

A global virtual university in the global virtual agora

In the Vedic tradition from which the universities of India emerged, one of the duties of students was to beg for their guru. By giving alms, the community voluntarily supported higher education. The idea of a university *pro bono publico* has roots in the Greek as well as the Asian tradition. Still today, senior academics and university managers are expected to take their (virtual) begging bowls to alumni, big business and government. Of course they have a more up-market and commercial approach to mendicancy.

Almost as ancient is the tradition of paying for higher education. The Sophists in the fifth and fourth centuries BC contracted in the marketplace for the full training of a youth over a period of three or four years for a thousand drachmas (one drachma was a qualified worker's daily wage) (Marrou 1956). It does not feel so very different from what universities charge students today.

Private and public education have coexisted for almost as long as there have been universities. The Chinese university traditions go back to private academies that existed at the same time that Confucius (551–479 BC) was developing his model of education as something open to everyone regardless of class (Du 1992). The medieval university expected students to pay, but patronage from the church and feudal lords made it possible for poor students with ability to go to university (Crane 2002). Today, around the world tertiary education is still primarily state supported, but private tertiary education accounts for some 37 per cent (OECD 2000). It will grow because what Anne Duin and her colleagues (2001) call the Learning Marketspace is opening up on the Internet.

If current trends continue, by 2010, the population of Internet users should be well on its way toward its second billion. If, however, it was conservatively estimated at 1 billion, then the potential market for global virtual universities by that time will be in the order of 800 million people. This is based on the NUA Internet Surveys that indicate that approximately 80 per cent of Internet users are above the age of 16 and hence potential students for a global virtual university (http://www.nua.ie/surveys/index.cgi?f=VS&art_id=905354750&rel=true).

The people who are on the Internet are the most economically advantaged people in the world and those most likely to make use of a global virtual university. If one were to think of an average student doing just one semester length programme of study per year at a cost of US$1,000, the size of the potential market at the end of the first decade of the new millennium is in the order of US$800,000,000,000,000.

The major proportion of the huge loans that students incur in getting a degree is not spent on paying for courses. It goes on the lifestyle of the student. This may be the bare basics of transport, accommodation, food and clothing, but it can include the literature, entertainment, sport and travel that are part of student life. Clustered around any campus are shops and services offering banking, travel, books, pendants, sports, societies, clubs, gymnasia, healthcare, career guidance and counselling. Looking at the commercial value of university education in terms of course fees is like looking at the travel industry in terms of seats on planes. The real money in travel is in the value added components of insurance, duty free goods, land transport, hotels, entertainment and everything that makes tourism one of the biggest industries in the world. The big money in university education has always been in the lifestyle involved. The size of the market for global virtual universities by 2010 is likely to double with value added for associated services. This is only at the beginning of the expansion of university education forecast in Chapter 5. University education is set to become to the information society of the future what the oil industry is to the industrial society of today. This is not simply because of the size of the market, but because it is what universities provide that fuels and makes possible a society dependent on knowledge.

Much of the current angst in universities arises from academics contemplating the impact of expanding student numbers without a corresponding increase in resources or any financial incentive. Where business people see more customers, academics see declining standards. Universities desperately need the efficiency and common sense that is inherent in good business practice. They need to attract students, remove the regulatory and administrative barriers to university entrance, let the customer decide what they want and provide it, let good teachers and good researchers get good money and let bad teachers and poor researchers go. Universities have to get out from under the shadows of the state and become businesses, but they must not in the process lose their integrity as universities. We have sought to understand what this is by looking for the universals of universities and the dangers that face universities as they embrace a commercial modus. The business model that is being applied to universities today seems to be that of a sausage factory. Publishing or the theatre, where there is respect for the content of what is marketed, make better examples of the relationship that is possible between service providers and their business handlers.

Accreditation

The term 'accreditation' derives from the Latin *credere*, to believe in. A paradigm only exists among the people who accept that it exists and who thereby accept the ideas, rules and values by which it can be played. This is a form of belief. Until recently people believed in universities. They had a mystique. They housed the high priests of scientific knowledge; they were the conscience of society; they accredited the lawyers, doctors and teachers that society believed in. This is no longer the case. People distrust science. They question their doctors and lawyers and sue them for malpractice. They litigate against their *alma mater* when they find their degrees do not get them jobs. Universities are losing credibility.

This is not the first time that faith in universities has faltered. It happens whenever the episteme shifts. In a world where universities are becoming global and virtual, the way universities are accredited along with their degree programmes, their teachers and their students needs to be addressed anew.

The modern university is accredited by the nation in which it is located. This may be a regulatory procedure established by government or it may be voluntary and subject to regular review as in the USA or it may take the form of a founding charter or an act of parliament. Once accredited a university can normally accredit its own programmes of studies and degrees and is seen as autonomous. However, both the external and internal accrediting processes of a university involve evaluation and this is something that depends upon the episteme a university finds itself in.

The ancient Greeks arrived at their values through a process of rational thought. The Islamic universities and the European medieval universities took their values from theology. The value system of the modern university was based on scientific rationalism. However, the episteme is shifting. Capitalism has become the dominant ideology. Money has always been a way of valuing things. Now it has become the one way of valuing things that everyone can recognise. The value system of globalisation is derived not from Christianity, Islam, Confucianism, Buddhism or Scientism, but from monetarism. At the turn of the millennium, universities perforce find themselves monetising their values, because that was in turn what the governments of their state were doing, because that in turn was what the world at large was doing. The ideal of the nation state as a welfare state is in retreat. Public services provided by the state come under close monetarist scrutiny and this includes the university sector.

By business standards universities were managed inefficiently by academics. They were open to criticism in terms of their use of public funds. The last decade of the twentieth century saw a movement around the world to replace the administration of universities by academics, for academics, with the administration of academics by management of students. An industrial model of efficient business management was introduced into universities. Now they are seen as providing information services and students are seen as customers. Quality is no longer ensured by tenure or sabbaticals or paying good salaries to attract good people, but by the principles that built the pyramids: standardising the basic operational units, rigorous control of the workers and an occasional crack of the whip.

Assessment

In an article entitled 'How necessary are universities?' Alan Peacock looks at the problems of getting accredited and quotes Adam Smith, 'When a man has learned his lesson very well, it surely can be of little importance where or from whom he learned it' (Peacock 2001: 6).

In an Adam Smith world, it would be the assessment system that was accredited, not the teaching system. This would mean a national assessment system for degrees that are national in nature and a global assessment system for degrees that are global in nature. It would then be possible for anyone paying a cost-covering fee to sit certifying examinations. As long as the assessment procedures were a cheat-proof rigorous test of whether the candidate could apply a knowledge paradigm to a relevant set of problems and question the process, does it matter where, or how, or for how long, they learned to do it? If assessment procedures were applied blind, assessors would not know whether a candidate had studied under a great name at a prestigious university or anonymously in a diploma mill or in fact if they had ever even been to a tertiary level educational institution. It would be possible to compare instruction between universities from valid premises. Autonomous learners could study by themselves. Why does a person have to go to a university to get a degree? Would not an independent system of examination, in principle similar to the old Chinese civil service exams, be fairer than the current system? Universities the world over accept the International Baccalaureate as a universal entrance qualification, why not then an International BA as a universal exiting qualification?

Every university has a unique set of regulations about the content of a degree programme: who can take it, how they will be evaluated and what a student must do to gain a degree. Although universities look over each other's shoulders in various ways, especially when they are in the same country or field of study, the hard fact is that there is no generally agreed operational definition of what exactly constitutes a degree or a degree programme or the standards by which they are assessed. There is no global equivalent in a university subject paradigm to TOEFL (Testing of English as a Foreign Language) and IELTS (International English Language Testing Service). Yet English language universities depend on these international tests of proficiency in the English language paradigm when they admit students who are not native English speakers. There is no way of comparing a degree in a particular subject in one university to another. Each university offers its own unique curriculum delivered in its own unique way to its own unique standards, by its own unique set of teachers. And here we come to what every student knows is the wild card in the pack: the teacher. Because in the last analysis it is the teacher in a university who decides exactly what is taught and how it is taught and who then proceeds to both set and mark the tests, assignments and examinations which decide a student's grades.

Students quickly learn which courses are easy and where the marking is soft and how to select a programme that will get them through a degree with the minimum effort. The system has always been open to abuse and it is has been to the great credit of teachers in the modern university that they have maintained a concern with objective assessment. But today there is pressure from students and administration to improve the grades awarded. Grade inflation is widespread in the USA, even among the prestigious universities, according to Harvey Mansfield, a professor of government at Harvard University, who in the spring term of 2001 provoked an uproar among his colleagues by giving his students two grades: an official grade that conformed with the inflated grade level at Harvard which sees 50 per cent of students getting A grades and a private grade which rated students at what he thought they were really worth (Mansfield 2001).

To be valid, the assessment process should be separated from the teaching process. This is not to say that teachers should not set and mark tests and assignments. That is formative evaluation and part of the teaching process. Here we are concerned with the final summative evaluation of a student's ability to apply a body of knowledge to a class of problems. This needs to be assessed by a body of experts external to the teaching process. It is the basis for certification for professional practice and evaluates not only the student but also the teacher and the teaching institution.

When students do asynchronous assignments by themselves some of them will cheat by passing off someone else's work as their own. It seems to be a fact of university life that probably goes back to Pythagoras (was that really his theorem?). The only way to be sure that a student has the ability implied by a degree or diploma is to get them, in person, under the supervision of a neutral expert or invigilator to actually apply the knowledge paradigm to an arbitrarily selected instance of the set of problems the knowledge addresses. In the last analysis, examination and supervised practice remain the only dependable basis for certification.

We have suggested for a global virtual university a three-tiered study system where students could accumulate weekly units to form semester length programmes of study which in turn could be accumulated for a degree. A bachelor's degree would be awarded, as is fairly standard in universities, on the completion of twelve such semester length programmes of study each of which would have a final examination. Such certifying examinations should be designed, delivered, marked and graded under the supervision of an accrediting board, in physical reality, under strict supervision, at sanctioned centres where the student would need to present documentary evidence that they were the person who had enrolled for the examination. Without such a system, no virtual university would be taken seriously, indeed without such an examination system, no university should exist.

Apart from establishing a level playing field for awarding degrees, there could be benefits, especially for globalisation, in the standardisation of practice that would ensue. Take the case of information theory, cybernetic theory and systems theory. These are well-established, universally accepted, interlinked knowledge paradigms that have no special cultural connotations and are taught in universities around the world in a variety of languages. It should, therefore, be possible to establish a universal curriculum and assessment system in these subjects. This would in fact be a very sensible thing to do, because together they form the knowledge paradigm on which the information technology infrastructure of globalisation is based. A sector of the International Telecommunications Union known as the ITU Telecommunication Standardization Sector (ITU-T) has the task of standardising the concepts and procedures of the knowledge paradigm by which telecommunications functions globally, in order to foster the growth of the emerging global information infrastructure. International study groups develop recommendations for new developments which become the agreed international standards. It is this that enables global telephony, the Internet and the coming broadband environment. Without the international interoperability of equipment and services that this standardisation makes possible there would be no globalisation. Not surprisingly, the ITU-T has a strong interest in gaining consensus on the description techniques used for telecommunications standards and in training and education. It would make sense to involve an organisation such as ITU-T in accrediting and assessing instruction in the theoretical structures that underpin the international telecommunications paradigm (as well as the international computing paradigm).

Subjects that seek to be acultural and operate at a global level, such as mathematics and medicine, could also seek to establish internationally agreed curricula and assessment systems through professional associations and societies. Such accrediting and assessment systems should be in as many languages as is viable.

Not all knowledge paradigms are global in nature. Interpersonal communications, group communications and organisational communications, unlike the techniques and artefacts of information technology, do not function in the same way in Japan as they do in the USA. A national curriculum and assessment system on human communications that included these knowledge paradigms would need to be devised for Japan and for the USA. Where knowledge paradigms are specific to a state, such as state law, or cultural, such as the Islamic Shariah, or language-specific, as in the case of Portuguese literature, national or cultural or language-specific accrediting and assessing systems would be needed, but these should still be external to individual universities and therefore able to provide unbiased measures of competency.

Brand names

If a degree was a degree no matter where a person studied would it matter where they studied? We do not buy services simply on utilitarian grounds. We do not necessarily go to the cheapest restaurant we can find to satisfy hunger. We want to enjoy the experience. The university paradigm involves more than teaching people to apply knowledge.

People are prepared to pay for brand names. Study at Heidelberg, Cambridge or Yale carries cachet. Such universities attract distinguished scholars as well as good students. Depending on time and place and point of view, big name universities can be seen as imbuing intellectual honesty or as inculcating narrow-minded bigotry. A West Point graduate and a graduate of an Islamic university may have equal grades in navigation, but very different world-views. Where a person studies and who they study under and with are not measured by exams, but say things about the social and cultural context in which people obtained their degree and the network of professional associates they are likely to have.

It may be that the first global virtual universities will develop as extensions of universities that already have a global reputation. The idea of virtual Bologna or

Cambridge universities in a virtual version of their campus in a virtual version of the cities they are named after may one day prove too difficult for these universities to resist.

For geographers there is cachet in studying at the University of Wisconsin-Madison, for instructional designers at Florida State University, for aviation medicine at Otago University because in these subjects these universities are world leaders. We might see virtual universities of global medicine, global transport, global information technology and teletranslation which by virtue of garnering the best academics, databases, researchers and professional support could become expert in specific fields not as yet addressed by conventional universities.

HyperCampus

Chapter 8 described a curriculum for a global virtual university that addressed the issue of globalisation itself as a basis for returning to the ideal of a university dealing with the universe of knowledge. For that curriculum to be taught in a context that encouraged in-depth instruction requires a virtual campus that could capture the imagination in the way the spires of Oxford did in the past.

We attempted to describe such a campus (Tiffin and Rajasingham 1995), basing it on the principle that a university is a meeting ground for teachers, students, knowledge and problems. These were represented by four virtual buildings on each side of a quadrangle. The corners had footpaths that could lead to virtual gardens, virtual sports fields, virtual shops and virtual theatres. We felt that it is not enough to bring the elements of a university together; the environment should generate intellectual excitement. A new architecture was needed that was unconstrained by the laws of physics, invested with artificial intelligence and an imaginative expression of the hopes and possibilities for the future that a university should present to its community. JITAITs could stroll the quad and be endlessly available to talk, the trees that line the quad could sing choral arrangements while their leaves danced and the statues of great philosophers could be accosted about their ideas.

Before she left the campus, Shirley wanted to visit the Towers of Teaching. She moved back into the quad first and was delighted to find that it was programmed to have a day. It was now early evening and there seemed as many people as ever, but then she remembered that [the university] stayed open all the time and was available to anyone from any country. Lights were coming on and the last of the sun was touching the tops of the towers. Was it true, she wondered, that the taller the towers in which the great teaching dons had their chambers, the higher the esteem in which they were held? She pointed at the imposing entrance to the towers and triggered herself into a virtual reality that was, with its oak walls and balustraded staircase and the faintest of choral renderings of 'Gaudeamus igitur,' the very epitome of a grand old university.

(Tiffin and Rajasingham 1995: 160).

In 1996 one of our master's students Liz Mirams designed a basic version of this virtual campus on the Internet and we experimented with classes where participants from different locations joined as avatars. We demonstrated the virtual campus at a number of conferences and would ask colleagues from different parts of the world to participate as avatars.

What we are talking about here is simulating what HyperReality could be like by projecting three-dimensional graphic virtual realities onto a large screen in a darkened room. The effect is helped by selecting a neutral avatar to represent the audience and then switching to the avatar's subjective viewpoint so that members of the audience can identify with the perspective of their avatar. On one occasion the audience as avatar met with the avatar of Mirams who proceeded to show them around the virtual campus she had developed. They visited the virtual research laboratories, the virtual library, the virtual student union and finally the 'Towers of Teaching' with its portrait gallery of academics. The audience avatar was then led to a virtual window and invited to look through it. When it did, the audience found themselves looking at the backs of their own heads. In a virtual version of Plato's cave, the image they were looking at in front of them through the window in virtual reality came from a video camera placed behind them.

Afterwards a number of people from the audience said that until they worked out how the effect was achieved they had a sense of dislocation. Like all immersive new media we only start to appreciate their possibilities and limitations as we begin to use them. A new factor is involved in a HyperCampus which we can think of as telepresence. It raises a major research question as to the impact of HyperReality and virtual reality on the human psyche (Schuemie *et al.* 2001).

Organisation of a global virtual university

Figure 9.1 reflects how a global virtual university could be organised from a student's point of view. It shows the way they would encounter it while searching on the Web for any subject that might link them to any aspect of the university or any part of a subject taught or researched in the university. The site would be designed like a spider's web to catch ideas and their owners.

As a visitor to the global virtual university's Website, a prospective student could, as is becoming routine with university Websites, study the curriculum, examine the background of the teachers, see what was available in the library, what research was being done and how the university was governed, managed, administered and who owned it. Wearing shutter glasses or an HMD unit, they would also be able to explore the virtual reality of the campus as a full immersion experience. In Figure 9.1 the visitor is in the centre of the quadrangle looking toward the library. The fractal building on the right is the research centre and on the left is the teaching centre. Entering any of these buildings is in turn to enter virtual realities within virtual realities which the visitor could explore, but interaction within the site would not be open to them.

The visitor could at any point decide to join the university. All that need be involved would be a basic Internet transaction with a credit card. Within seconds

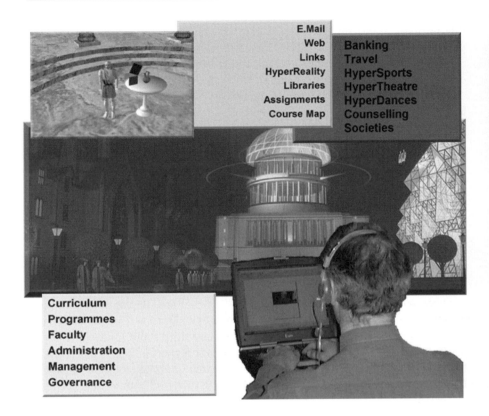

E.Mail
Web   Banking
Links   Travel
HyperReality   HyperSports
Libraries   HyperTheatre
Assignments HyperDances
Course Map   Counselling
            Societies

Curriculum
Programmes
Faculty
Administration
Management
Governance

Figure 9.1 Organisation of a global virtual university from a student's perspective. The view
of a virtual campus in the centre is from the frontispiece of Tiffin and Rajasingham
1995 *In Search of the Virtual Class: Education in an Information Society.*

they would have a password as an enrolled student and an avatar with which to
have an interactive telepresence on campus. The avatar could have a gown, perhaps
with a hood in the colours of their subject so that they could recognise fellow
students with whom they had something in common. In the manner described in
Chapter 2, the avatar could look like the person it represents and reflect their
facial expressions. It would also be possible to adjust the avatar cosmetically so
that it looked more the way the person wanted to be seen or it could be anything
at all.

The only criterion for joining would be that it would be the student's responsibility to decide what subjects to take in what sequence and whether they were
capable of the study involved. If a student found that they had chosen badly, the
consequences of dropping out would be relatively small as they would be paying
at a weekly rate. Nobody has to worry about accommodation, campus security
and parking. Academics do not need to attend offices, staff rooms or endless

committee meetings. Communication between administrators and teachers would involve little more than agreeing contracts. A considerable amount of university administrative work would simply disappear or be automated.

A student could even join as nothing more than a student, paying a monthly or annual fee for full interactive campus rights that allowed them to socialise with other students, go to campus events such as guest lectures, virtual theatre, virtual sports fixtures and use such online facilities as the campus travel agent, bank, insurance services, health services and shops with their student discounts. It would be possible for a person to enjoy student life without having to study, but hopefully they would want to, even if only to audit an occasional week-long modular unit where they could participate in tutorial groups, seminars and lectures but need not do the assignments. The fee for this would be less than for someone taking the weekly module toward a degree with its associated assignments.

When academics run universities they fail to operate them as businesses. When business people run universities they fail to operate them as universities. Universities need to be businesses in the future to survive, but if in the process they become degree factories, they will not survive as universities. Some form of joint management is needed, with a CEO responsible for business and a rector responsible for academic management. Both should see themselves as having to work together and that this would involve compromise. The university has to be a business and the business has to be a university and a dynamic tension between business and academe should be recognised as key to development. The governance of the university should support this polarity. Boards of governors should be equally drawn from academic stakeholders and business interests. This would also need to be reflected in the shareholders. One possibility suggested by John Sinclair (1998) is that on graduation students acquire a share option in the university. In this way, the alumni would become a powerful voice in governance concerned with maintaining the value of their degree and the good name of the university.

Global study centres

One of the key things we have learned is that most, though not all, students want to meet in real reality. The more they communicate in virtual reality the more they appreciate physical reality. We have been surprised at the number of our students who have paid for international travel and accommodation to meet with fellow students and professors from other countries who have taken part in our classes by telecommunications. It seems to have little to do with paradigm acquisition and syntagm practice, but a lot to do with situated learning. Virtual campuses have the potential to be very exciting places, but they will need to be balanced by real meetings in real places. This suggests a link between teaching and tourism which is already evident in subject-specific academic tours of historical and classical sites. Study centres could be established in places of great natural beauty or cultural interest where students from different countries who have studied together in virtual reality can meet in physical reality with their professors in a follow-up that would provide in-depth instruction in a pleasing social and cultural milieu which also provided facilities for tourism.

Another possibility could result from global virtual universities developing affiliations with conventional universities, which would allow virtual students to hold block sessions while using the facilities of a conventional university.

Business sees universities as '... an industry ripe for the unbundling of activities' (Duderstadt 1999: 13). A popular feature that has developed in recent decades in many cities is the food mall. Different franchise outlets for food from different countries are laid out around a common restaurant area where people can sit down and eat the food from the different vendors. Could there come a day when conventional universities adopt the basic principle involved and become vending outlets for a variety of competing virtual universities, while the sporting, recreational and social functions of the traditional campus provided a common ground for students to date and dance and play no matter what university they had joined? Many food malls now sell fusion cuisine that mixes food from different cultures. Perhaps we will see something similar in the development of courses that draw on different universities. This suggests a future where students can take different programmes and different parts of programmes with different universities.

The civilising mission

What is now the University of Wisconsin-Madison (UW) is a modern university. From the beginning, like the land grant universities and other state universities of the USA, UW dedicated itself to the needs of the state that founded and supported it. It taught the managerial and governing classes the laws, the philosophy, the medical practices, the accounting procedures, the language and the cultural values which came with the people who established the new state of Wisconsin. It researched the state territory in terms of its geomorphology and drainage, its geology and soils, its flora and fauna and climate. Departments of cartography and geography mapped and measured and sought with statistics to explain causal relations between the physical attributes of the state. Precise empirical research explained phenomena in quantitative terms and taught people how to apply and take advantage of such studies in such fields as agriculture, forestry, mining and engineering. The peoples of Wisconsin have prospered.

A new episteme based on the utility of physical reality replaced that of the Amerindians. Black Hawk and his people did not fence off land and buy and sell it as a commodity or think of it in terms of individual ownership. In this the Sauk were like other tribal people with no written language and hence deemed lacking in civilisation. Similar actions to the Black Hawk wars took place throughout the nineteenth century as America expanded west, Russia expanded east, European powers scrambled for Africa, Australasia and as much of Asia as they could get and Argentina, Brazil and the other newly independent states of Latin America extended their dominion in the manner of the USA.

Figure 9.2a A historical marker reads 'Black Hawk, Sauk Chief retreated through these grounds, July 21 1832 pursued by militia and US Regulars' (photograph with kind permission of D.E. Hanna).

Figure 9.2b The grounds are those of the University of Wisconsin which was founded sixteen years later (photograph with kind permission of D.E. Hanna).

Ethiopia had a written language at least as ancient as that of Rome, yet it was not an industrial nation, and in the scramble for Africa, Italy sought to colonise it. The ruler Menelik was, like Black Hawk, a brilliant tactician with battle-hardened troops, fighting a modern army with primitive weapons. Unlike Black Hawk, however, Menelik had a large army and managed to defeat the Italian army at the battle of Adowa. As a result Menelik found himself in possession of the guns of a modern army. He turned them against the tribal peoples on his borders who had no written language and were in their turn regarded by the Ethiopians as uncivilised. Menelik's armies pushed south, east and west to establish the borders of the Ethiopian empire. Some hundred years later the Italian army had its revenge. A silent League of Nations heard Haile Selassie argue in vain that Ethiopia was a nation like the rest of them. The developed countries did not see it that way and Italy was left to colonise it. But in the vagaries of the Second World War, Haile Selassie managed to regain his empire. One of the first things he then did was to found a university. Ethiopia is now a long-standing member of the United Nations and has two universities. Since the Second World War every nation has sought to acquire some kind of university even if, like the University of the South Pacific, it is shared. Like having an army, a judiciary and a flag, getting a university is seen as a rite of passage to internationally acceptable statehood.

The means of nineteenth-century empire was the muscle of industrial technology: guns, ships and railways. What decided whether a particular territory was civilised, as distinct from being in need of civilising (*pace* Ethiopia), was whether the people had a written language and had adopted rational scientific and technological practices. To have these, a nation needed a system of advanced education. The civilising mission of the modern university has been to bring science and technology along with better health and education and notions of democracy to the nation it serves.

What then will be the civilising mission of global virtual universities and who will they serve? They may emerge from the universities of English-speaking nations to extend their cultural hegemony. They may serve as the knowledge arm of global corporates as they replace nation states in the way that nation states replaced tribal society. They may become global corporates in their own right, the equivalent in the knowledge society of the oil industry in an industrial society. They may become a global grassroots movement like the Greens or *Médecins sans Frontières*, providing a counter-ideology to the neoliberal approach to globalisation.

The territories to be explored and claimed are the virtual worlds within us and those without in the growing jungles of information technology. What needs civilising is what we know today as globalisation. The professionals a global virtual university will produce are those who will work at the global level. The individuals it should inspire are those who seek insight beyond the trammels of national, cultural, linguistic and research paradigms. The search as always in a university is for wisdom in the search for truth.

Bibliography

Ardener, E. (1973) 'Some Outstanding Problems in the Analysis of Events', in M. Chapman (ed.) *Edwin Ardner – The Voice of Prophecy and Other Essays*, pp. 86–104. Oxford: Black.

Ausubel, D.P. (1967) *Learning Theory and Classroom Practice*, Toronto: The Ontario Institute for Studies in Education.

Averroes, R.I. (1966) *Commentary on Plato's Republic*, Cambridge: Cambridge University Press.

Barnett, R. (1997) *Higher Education: A Critical Business*, Buckingham: Open University Press.

Barthes, R. (1977) *Image, Music, Text*, London: Fontana.

Bates, A.W. (1995) *Technology, Open Learning and Distance Education*, London: Routledge.

Bateson, G. (1979) *Mind and Nature: A Necessary Unity*, first edn, New York: Dutton.

Bear, J. (1994) *Bear's Guide to Earning College Degrees Non Traditionally*, California: C and B Publisher.

Beard, M. (1995) 'Don's diary', *CAM: Cambridge Alumni Magazine*, Easter: 7.

Beck, F.A.G. (1964) *Greek Education*, London: Methuen and Co.

Beer, S. (1992) 'About flat earths: cybernetics and human knowing', *A Journal of Second Order Cybernetics and Cyber-Semiotics*, 1, 1: 1.

Benjamin, H. (1971) 'The saber-tooth curriculum', in R. Hooper (ed.) *The Curriculum: Context, Design and Development*, Edinburgh: Oliver and Boyd in association with the Open University Press.

Biggs, J. and Davis, R. (eds) (2002) *The Subversion of Australian Universities*, Wollongong, NSW: Fund for Intellectual Dissent.

Blackboard, available: http://www.blackboard.com/ (7 November 2002).

Blair, T. (2002) 'General election speech May 2001', in J. Sutherland, *The Guardian*, 22 July 2002.

Bodanis, D. (2000) $E=MC^2$: *A Biography of the World's Most Famous Equation*, London: Macmillan.

Boulding, K. (1958) *General Systems Theory: The Skeleton of Science*, Chicago: Aldine.

Bowen, J. (1975) *A History of Western Education*, London: Methuen.

Bradbury, M. (2000) *To the Hermitage*, London: Picador.

Bridgeman, N. (1997) 'Application of information technology to rural communities: case study Taranaki', unpublished PhD Thesis, Victoria University of Wellington.

Bridgeman Dairy Farmer Website, available: http://grazel.taranaki.ac.nz/grazel/ (7 November 2002).

Brier, S. (1992) 'Cybernetics and Human Knowing', *A Journal of Second Order Cybernetics and Cyber-Semiotics*, 1: 61.

Burleson, B.R. (1989) 'Paradigm exemplars', in B. Dervin (ed.) *Rethinking Communication: Paradigm Exemplars*, Newbury Park, CA: Sage.

Burton, R. (1913) *The Anatomy of Melancholy*, Volume II, London: Belle and Sons.

Cahoon, B. (1998) 'Teaching and learning internet skills', *New Directions for Adult and Continuing Education*, 78: 5–13.

Canter, M. (1994) *How to Make a Fortune on the Information Super Highway*, New York: Harper Collins.

Carson, R. (1963) *Silent Spring*, London: Hamish Hamilton.

Cassirer, E. (1945) *Structuralism in Modern Linguistics*, in B. Malmberg (ed.) *Readings in Modern Linguistics*, The Hague: Mouton.

Casti, J.L. (1992) *Paradigms Lost: Images of Man in the Mirror of Science*, London: Abacus.

Chu, G.W. and Schramm, W. (1968) *Learning from Television: What the Research Says*, Washington, DC: National Association of Educational Broadcasters.

Columbia University Online, available: http://www.columbia.edu/cu/osi/DeansDay/DDknowledge_univ.htm (7 November 2002).

Coombs, P.W. (1968) *The World Educational Crisis: A Systems Analysis*, New York: Oxford University Press.

Crane, N. (2002) *Mercator: The Man who Mapped the Planet*, London: Weidenfeld & Nicolson.

Crystal, D. (1997) *English as a Global Language*, New York: Cambridge University Press.

Daniel, J.S. (1996) *Mega-Universities and Knowledge Media, Technology Strategies for Higher Education*, London: Kogan Page.

Dawkins, R. (1976) *The Selfish Gene*, Oxford: Oxford University Press.

de Hamel, C. (2001) in Peter Richards 'Treasury of learning', *CAM: Cambridge Alumni Magazine*, Easter, 33: 28–33.

de Saussure, F. (1983) *Course in General Linguistics*, London: Duckworth.

Derrida, J. (1974) *Of Grammatology*, Baltimore: Johns Hopkins University Press.

Dewdney, A.K. (1999) *A Mathematical Mystery Tour*, New York: John Wiley and Sons.

Dhanarajan, G. (2001) 'Changing expectations of global education: charting a new course', Keynote presentation 15th Annual IDP Education Australian Conference Sydney: University of New South Wales, 25–28 September 2001.

Dickson, T. (2001) 'UK universities and the state: a Faustian bargain?', *Journal of the Institute of Economic Affairs*, 21, 3: 23–9.

Dirr, P.J. (1999) 'Distance and virtual learning in the United States', in G. Farrel (ed.) *The Development of Virtual Education: A Global Perspective*, Vancouver: Commonwealth of Learning.

Dordick, H.S. and Wang, G. (1993) *The Information Society: A Retrospective View*, Newbury Park, CA: Sage.

Drexler, E.K. (1990) *Engines of Creation*, London: Fourth Estate.

Driscoll, M. (1998) *Web-based Training Using Technology to Design Adult Learning Experiences*, San Francisco: Jossey-Bass Pfeiffer.

Du, R. (1992) *Chinese Higher Education*, Basingstoke: Macmillan Press.

Duderstadt, J.J. (1999) 'Can colleges and universities survive in the information age', in R.N. Katz and Associates (eds) *Dancing with the Devil: Information Technology and the New Competition in Higher Education*, San Francisco: Jossey Bass Inc.

Duin, A.H., Baer, L. and Starke-Meyerring, D. (2001) *Partnering in the Learning Marketspace*, EDUCAUSE Leadership Strategies, Volume 4, San Francisco: Jossey Bass Inc.

Eco, U. (1983) *The Name of the Rose*, London: Secker and Warburg.

Edwardes, M. (1961) *A History of India*, London: Thames and Hudson.

Einstein, A. (1982) *Ideas and Opinions*, New York: Crown.

Encyclopaedia Plus of World Problems and Human Potential [electronic resource] (1996) fourth edn, Union of International Associations, Munchen, New Providence: K.G. Saur.

Ferrate, P.G. (2000) Prologo to the Spanish edition of J.Tiffin and L. Rajasingham (1995) *In Search of the Virtual Class: Education in an Information Society*, Barcelona: Universitat Oberta de Catalunya.

Fiske, J. (1990) *Introduction to Communication Studies*, London and New York: Routledge.

Fordham University Online, available: http://www.fordham.edu/halsall/source/vitryl1.html (7 November 2002).

Foucault, M. (1970) *The Order of Things*, New York: Pantheon House.

—— (1990) *The Care of the Self: The History of Sexuality: Volume Three*, trans. R. Hurley, London: Penguin.

Freud, S. (1963) Reprint 1997 *General Psychological Theory*, New York: Touchtone Books.

Gagne, R.M. (1973) Personal communication, Wisconsin University, Tallahassee.

—— (1974) *Principles of Instructional Design*, New York: Holt, Rinehart and Winston.

—— (1977) *The Conditions of Learning*, New York: Holt, Rinehart and Winston.

Gardner, H. (1983) *Frames of Mind: the Theory of Multiple Intelligences*, New York: Basic Books.

Gee, J.P. (1990) *Social Linguistics and Literacies: Ideology in Discourses*, London, New York and Philadelphia: Falmer Press.

Ghosh, J.C. (1939) 'Universities of India', in E. Bradby (ed.) *Universities Outside Europe: Essays on the Development of University Institutions in Fourteen Countries*, London, New York and Toronto: Oxford University Press.

Gibb H.A.R. (1939) 'The University in the Arab Muslim World', in E. Bradby (ed.) *Universities Outside Europe: Essays on the Development of University Institutions in Fourteen Countries*, London, New York and Toronto: Oxford University Press.

Gibson, W. (1984) *Necromancer*, New York: Ace Books.

Giddens, A. (1991) *The Consequences of Modernity*, Cambridge: Polity Press.

Gleick, J. (1987) *Chaos: Making a New Science*, London: Cardinal.

Goleman, D. (1996) *Emotional Intelligence: Why It Can Matter More Than I.Q.*, London: Bloomsbury.

Gopnik, A., Meitzoff, A. and Kuhl, P. (2001) *How Babies Think: The Science of Childhood*, London: Wiedenfield and Nicolson.

Gramsci, A. (1971) *Selections from the Prison Notebooks of Antonio Gramsci*, New York: International Publishers.

Green, L. (2002) *Technoculture: from Alphabet to Cybersex*, Sydney, NSW: Allen and Unwin.

Griffith University Online, available: http://www.autc.gov.au/caut/rrgt/chapter2.html (7 November 2002).

Hall, B. (1997) *Web-Based Training Cookbook*, New York: John Wiley and Sons.

Halliday, M.K.A. (1989) *Spoken and Written Language*, Oxford: Oxford University Press.

Hanna, D.E. (2000) 'Higher education in an era of digital competition: global conse-quences', in D.E. Hanna and Associates (eds) *Higher Education in an Era of Digital Competition: Choices and Challenges*, Madison, WI: Atwood Publishing.

——— (2001) 'Open and flexible learning; an environmental scan', in C.Latchem and D. Hanna (eds) *Leadership for 21st Century Learning, Global Perspectives from Educational Innovators*, London: Kogan Page.

———, Glowacki-Dudka, M. and Conceicao-Runlee, S. (2000) *147 Practical Tips for Teaching Online Groups: Essentials of Web-based Education*, Madison, WI: Atwood Publishing.

Hartshorne, R. (1939) *The Nature of Geography: A Critical Survey of Current Thought in the Light of the Past*, Lancaster: Association of American Geographers.

——— (1960) *Perspective on the Nature of Geography*, London: John Murray.

Haxton, B. (2001) *Fragments: The Collected Wisdom of Heraclitus of Espherus*, New York: Viking.

Heinich, R. (1970) *Technology and the Management of Instruction*, Washington, DC: Association for Educational Communications and Technology.

Herrnstein, R.J. and Murray, C. (1996) *The Bell Curve: Intelligence and Class Structure in American Life*, New York: Simon and Schuster.

Hewett, D. (ed.) (1999) *Neap Tide*, Ringwood, NY: Penguin.

Hewitt, J., Scardamalia, M. and Webb, J. (1997) 'Situated design issues for interactive learning environments: the problem of group coherence', *Annual Meeting of the AERA*, Indianapolis, April 1997.

Hills, G., Sir (2001) 'Who owns the universities? The battle for university independence and against the dependency culture', *Journal of the Institute of Economic Affairs*, 21, 3: 12–17.

Hooper, R. (ed.) (1971) *The Curriculum: Context, Design and Development*, Edinburgh: Oliver and Boyd in association with the Open University Press.

Hudson, R. (1984) *Invitation to Linguistics*, Oxford: Martin Robertson.

Innis, H.A. (1950) *Empire and Communications*, Oxford: Clarendon Press.

——— (1972) *Empire and Communications*, Toronto: University of Toronto Press.

Internet2, available: www.Internet2.edu (7 November 2002).

Johnston, S. (1997) 'Examining the examiners: an analysis of examiners' reports on doctoral theses', *Studies in Higher Education*, 22, 3: 333–48.

Jones, S. (2002) 'Y: The descent of Man', *The Observer*, 29 September.

Kanigel, R. (2000) *One Best Way: Frederick Winslow Taylor and the Enigma of Efficiency*, London: Abacus.

Katz, R.N. (1999) 'Competitive Strategies for Higher Education in the Information Age', in R.N. Katz and Associates (eds) *Dancing with the Devil: Information Technology and the New Competition in Higher Education*, San Francisco: Jossey Bass Inc.

Kember, D.H. and Harper, G. (1987) 'Approaches to studying research and its implications for the quality of learning from distance education', *Journal of Distance Education*, 4, 2: 15–30.

Khayyam, Omar, *Rubaiyat*, trans. E.J. Fitzgerald (1859), London: B. Quaritch.

Kleijwegt, M. (1991) *Ancient Youth: The Ambiguity of Youth and the Absence of Adolescence in Greco-Roman Society*, Amsterdam: J.C. Gieben.

Kramer, S.N. (1963) *The Sumerians at Sumer*, Chicago: University of Chicago.

Kristeva, J. (1969) *Semeiotike, Recherches pour une Semanalyse*, Paris: Editions du Seuil.

Kuhn, T. S. (1962) *The Structure of Scientific Revolutions*, Chicago: University of Chicago Press.

—— (1977) 'Second thoughts on paradigms', in T.S. Kuhn (ed.) *The Essential Tension: Selected Studies in Scientific Tradition and Change*, Chicago: University of Chicago Press, 239–319.

Langton, C., Tayler, C., Doyne, F. and Rasmussen, S. (eds) (1992) *Artificial Life II: The Proceedings of the Workshop on Artificial Life*, Sante Fe, February 1990, Redwood City, California: Addison-Wesley.

Lanier, J. (2001) 'Virtually there', *Scientific American*, April 1.

Lebedoff, D. (1981) *The New Elite: The Death of Democracy*, New York: Franklin Watts.

Levi-Strauss, C. (1972) *The Savage Mind*, London: Wakefield and Nicolson.

Littlejohn, S.W. (1992) *Theories of Human Communication*, Belmont, CA: Wadsworth Publishing Co.

—— (2002) *Theories of Human Communication*, Belmont, CA: Wadsworth/Thompson Learning.

Litto, F. (1999) Personal communication, Rio de Janeiro.

Lovelock, J. (1988) *The Ages of Gaia: A Biography of our Living Earth*, Oxford: Oxford University Press.

—— (2000) *Homage to Gaia: The Life of an Independent Scientist*, Oxford: Oxford University Press.

Lyotard, J-F. (1984) *The Postmodern Condition: A Report on Knowledge*, Minneapolis: University of Minnesota Press.

Macleod, D. (2001) 'But what now', *Guardian Weekly*, 13 February, available online: http://www.guardian.co.uk/GWeekly/front/0,3936,181083,00.html (14 November 2002).

McCormack, C. and Jones, D. (1998) *Building a Web-based Education System*, New York: John Wiley and Sons.

McLuhan, M. (1964) *Understanding Media: The Extensions of Man*, New York: Random House.

—— and Fiore, Q. (1967) *The Medium is the Message*, New York: Bantam. Available online: http://www.alibris.com/subjects/entertainment/feature-author (7 November 2002).

Major-Poetzl, P. (1983) *Michel Foucault's Archaeology of Western Culture: Toward a New Science of History*, Brighton: Harvester.

Mansfield, C.H. (2001) 'Grade inflation: it's time to face the facts', *The Chronicle of Higher Education*, 6 April, 47, 30: 24.

Marginson, S. and Considine, M. (2000) *The Enterprise University: Power, Governance and Reinvention in Australia*, Cambridge: Cambridge University Press.

Marrou, H.I. (1956) *A History of Education in Antiquity*, New York: Sheed and Ward.

Marton, F.S.R. and Säljö, R. (1976) 'On qualitative differences in learning – 2: outcome as a function of the learner's conception of the task', *British Journal of Educational Psychology*, 46, 115–27.

Mason, R. (1998) *Globalising Education: Trends and Applications*, London: Routledge.

Masuda, Y. (1985) 'Computopia', in T. Forester (ed.) *Technology Revolution*, Oxford: Blackwell.

Merisotis, J.P. and Phipps, R.A. (1999) 'What's the difference? Outcomes of distance vs. traditional classroom-based learning', *Change*, May/June: 13–17.

Miller R.E. (1998) *As if Learning Mattered: Reforming Higher Education*, Ithaca: Cornell University Press.

Mitchell, W.J. (1995) *City of Bits*, Cambridge, MA: The MIT Press.

Mudaliar, A.L. (1960) *Education in India*, London: Asia Publishing House.

Naftulin, D.H. Ware, J.E. and Donelly, F.A. (1973) 'The Doctor Fox lecture: a paradigm of educational seduction', *Journal Of Medical Education*, July, 48: 630–5.

Netto, S.P. (1998) *Telas que Ensinam: Media e aprendizagem do cinema ao computador*, Sao Paulo: Editora Alinea.

Newman, J.H. (1902) *Newman's University Sketches*, G. Sampson (ed.), London: Walter Scott Publishing Co.

—— (1996) *The Idea of a University*, F.M. Turner (ed.), New Haven: Yale University Press.

Noelle-Neumann, E. (1984) *The Spiral of Silence: Public Opinion – Our Social Skin*, Chicago: University of Chicago Press.

NUA Internet Survey (2002) 'IntelliQuest: almost 80 million Americans Online', available online: http://www.nua.ie/surveys/index.cgi?f=VS&art_id=905354750andrel=true (5 November 2002).

O'Conner, J. and Robertson, E.F. (2000) '"Pythagoras' theorem" in Babylonian mathematics', available online: http://www-history.mcs.st-andrews. ac.uk/history/HistTopics/Babylonian_Pythagoras.html (5 November 2002).

O'Hagan, M. (1996) *The Coming Industry of Teletranslation*, Clevedon: Multilingual Matters.

—— and Ashworth, D. (2002) 'Translation-mediated communication in a digital world', in G. Samuelson-Brown (ed.) *Facing the Challenges of Globalization and Localization*, Clevedon: Multilingual Matters.

Olcott, D.J. (2000) 'Redefining faculty policies and practises for the knowledge age', in D.E. Hanna (ed.) *Higher Education in an Era of Digital Competition: Choices and Challenges*, Madison, WI: Atwood Publishers.

O'Leary, D.L. (1980) *How Greek Science Passed to the Arabs*, London: Routledge and Kegan Paul.

Organisation for Economic Cooperation and Development (2000) *Investing in Education: Analysis of the 1999 World Education Indicators*, Paris: OECD. Available online: http://www.oecd.org (7 November 2002).

Palloff, R.M. and Pratt, K. (1999) *Building Learning Communities in Cyberspace: Effective Strategies for the Online Classroom*, San Francisco: Jossey-Bass.

Patterson, G. (1997) *The University from Ancient Greece to the 20th Century*, Palmerston North, New Zealand: The Dunmore Press.

Patton, M. (1978) *Utilization-Focused Evaluations*, Beverley Hills, CA: Sage.

Peacock, A., Sir (2001). 'How necessary are universities?', *IEA Journal of the Institute of Economic Affairs*, 21, 3: 6–11.

Perdue, W.D. (1986) *Sociological Theory, Explanation, Paradigm and Ideology*, Palo Alto, CA: Mayfield Publishing Company.

Perez, C. (1983) 'Structural change and the assimilation of new technology in the economic and social systems', *Futures*, 15: 357–75.

Piltz, A. (1981) *The World of Medieval Learning*, trans. D. Jones, Oxford: Basil Blackwell.

Plato (1952) *Plato's Phaedrus*, trans. R. Hackforth, Cambridge: Cambridge University Press.

Pleumarom, A. (1994) 'The political economy of tourism', *The Ecologist*, 24: 142–8.

Pollan, M. (2001) *The Botany of Desire*, New York: Bloomsbury.

Porter, L.R. (1997) *Creating the Virtual Classroom: Distance Learning with the Internet*, New York: John Wiley and Sons.

Preston, D.S. (2002) 'The evolution of the English university mission', The Idea of Education Conference, Mansfield College, Oxford, 3–4 July 2002. Available online: http://www.inter-disciplinary.net/Preston%20Paper.pdf (26 November 2002).

Raza, M. (1991) 'Higher education in India', in M. Raza (ed.) *Higher Education in India: Retrospect and Prospect*, New Delhi: Association of Indian Universities.

Readings, B. (1996) *The University in Ruins*, Cambridge, MA: Harvard University Press.

Reagan, T. (2000) *Non-Western Educational Traditions: Alternative Approaches to Educational Thoughts and Practice*, Mahwah, NJ: Laurence Erlbaum Associates.

Rheingold, H. (1993) *The Virtual Community: Homesteading on the Electronic Frontier*, Reading, MA: Addison-Wesley.

Richards, P. (1995) 'King and martyr', *CAM: Cambridge Alumni Magazine*, Easter: 13–14.

Ryder, R.J. and Hughes, T. (1998) *Internet for Educators*, Upper Saddle River, NJ: Prentice-Hall.

Sayer, A. (1984) *Method in Social Science*, London: Routledge.

Schiller, H. (1991) 'Not yet the post-imperialist era', *Critical Studies in Mass Communications* 8, 1: 13–28.

Schroeder, M. (1991) *Fractals, Chaos, Power Laws: Minutes from an Infinite Paradise*, New York: Freeman.

Schuemie, M.J., Van Der Straaten, P., Krijn, M. and Van Der Mast, A.P.G. (2001) 'Research on presence in virtual reality: a survey', *CyberPsychology and Behavior*, 4: 2, 183–201.

Schweizer, H. (1999) *Designing and Teaching an On-Line Course: Spinning your Web Classroom*, Boston: Allyn and Bacon.

Senate Special Committee, (1970) 'Cultural economics: collected works of Henry Hillman Chartrand', available online: http://www.culturaleconomics.atfreeweb.com/art_ed_ni.htm (13 November 2002).

Shannon, C.E. and Weaver, W. (1949) *The Mathematical Theory of Communications*, Urbana: University of Illinois Press.

Shimohara, K. (2001) 'Artificial life in HyperReality', in J. Tiffin and N. Terashima (eds) *HyperReality: Paradigm for a Third Millennium*, London: Routledge.

Sinclair, J. (1987) *Collins Cobuild English Language Dictionary*, London: Harper Collins.

—— (1998) Personal communications, 20 September.

Siqueira, T.N. (1943) *The Education of India: History and Problems*, Humphry Milford: Oxford University Press.

Slaughter, S. and Leslie, L.L. (1997) *Academic Capitalism: Politics, Policies and the Entrepreneurial University*, Baltimore: The Johns Hopkins University Press.

Smith, B.O., Stanley, W.O. and Shores, J.H. (1971) 'Cultural roots of the curriculum', in R. Hooper (ed.) *The Curriculum: Context, Design and Development*, Edinburgh: Oliver and Boyd in association with the Open University Press.

Sobel, D. (1999) *Galileo's Daughter*, London: Fourth Estate.

Spring, J. (1998) *Education and the Rise of the Global Economy*, Mahwah, NJ: Lawrence Erlbaum Associates.

Stephenson, N. (1992) *Snow Crash*, New York: Bantam Books.

Svensson, L. (1976) *Study Skill and Learning*, Gothenburg: Acta Universitatis Gothoburgensis.

Tallman, J. (2000) 'Who owns knowledge in a networked world?', in D.E. Hanna and Associates (eds) *Higher Education in an Era of Digital Competition: Choices and Challenges*, Madison: Atwood Publishers.

Tapscott, D. (1998) *Growing up Digital: The Rise of the Net Generation*, New York: McGraw-Hill.

—— (1998a) 'Introduction: alliance for converging technologies', in D. Tapscott, A. Lowry and D. Ticoll (eds) Associate Editor Natalie Klym, *Blueprint to the Digital Economy: Creating Wealth in the Era of E-Business*, New York: McGraw-Hill, 1–16.

Tehranian, M. (1996) 'The end of university?' *Information Society*, 12, 4: 441–7.

—— (1999) Personal communication, PTC Conference, Hawaii, 19 January.

Terashima, N. (1993) 'Telesensation – a new concept for future telecommunications', in *Proccedings of TAO First International Conference on 3D Image and Communication Technologies*, Tokyo, Japan.

—— (2001) 'The definition of HyperReality', in J. Tiffin and N. Terashima (eds) *Hyper-Reality: Paradigm for the Third Millennium*, London and New York: Routledge.

The Australian, 26 June 2002.

The Economist (1997) 'Inside the knowledge factory', 4 October: 3–5.

The Virtual Human Project, available online: http://www.crd.ge.com/esl/cgsp/projects/vm/ (7 November 2002).

The Weekend Australian, (2001) 'Teachers oppose WTO agreement', 25–26 August: 13.

Tiffin, J. (1978). 'Problems in instructional television in Latin America', *Revista de Tecnologia Educativa* 4, 2: 163–265.

—— (1996) 'In Search of the Virtual Class in "The Virtual University"?', in G. Hart and J. Mason (eds) *Proceedings and Case Studies*, Melbourne: University of Melbourne

—— (2001) 'The HyperReality Paradigm', in J. Tiffin and N. Terashima (eds) *Hyper Reality: Paradigm for the Third Millennium*, London and New York: Routledge.

—— and Rajasingham, L. (1995) *In Search of the Virtual Class: Education in an Information Society*, London and New York: Routledge.

—— and Rajasingham. L. (2001) 'The HyperClass', in J. Tiffin and N. Terashima (eds) *HyperReality: Paradigm for the Third Millennium*, London and New York: Routledge.

—— and Terashima, N. (2001) 'HyperMillenium', in J. Tiffin and N. Terashima (eds) *HyperReality: Paradigm for the Third Millennium*, London and New York: Routledge.

Tight, M. (2002) 'What does it mean to be a professor?' *Higher Education Review*, 34, 2: 15–32.

Torres, C.A. (1998) *Democracy, Education and Multiculturalism Dilemmas of Citizenship in a Global World*, Lanham, MD: Rowman and Littlefield.

Trindade, A.R. (1993) *Basics of Distance Education: The Conceptual Panorama of Distance Education and Training*, Oslo: European Distance Education Network.

Turing, A. (1992) *Mechanical Intelligence*, Amsterdam and New York: Elsevier Science.

UN Chronicle (2002) 'The state of world population 2001: an opportunity to Johannesburg', *UN Chronicle*, 1 September.

UNESCO (2000) *World Education Report 2000: The Right to Education: Towards Education for All Throughout Life*, Paris: UNESCO.

Universal Declaration of Human Rights (1948) Available Online: http://www.un.org/ Overview/rights.html (20 November 2002).

Verger, H. (1992) 'Teachers', in De Ridder-Symoens (ed.) *A History of the University in Europe*, Vol. 1, Cambridge: Cambridge University Press.

von Foerster, H. (1990) 'Ethics and second-order cybernetics', paper presented to the International Conference on systems and family therapy, ethics, epistemology, new methods, Paris, 4 October 1990.

Vygotsky, L.S. (1978) *Mind in Society: The Development of the Higher Psychological Processes*, Cambridge MA: Harvard University Press.

—— (1987) in R.W. Reiber (ed.) *The Collected Works of L.S. Vygotsky: Problems of General Psychology*, Vol. 1, New York: Plenum Press.

Wang, G. (1994) *Treading Different Paths: Information in Asian Nations*, Westport, CT: Ablex Publishing.

—— (1999) Personal Communication.

—— (2000) 'Introduction', in A. Goonasekera and J. Servaes (eds) *The New Communication Landscape*, London: Routledge.

Watson, J. and Hill, A. (1996) *A Dictionary of Communication and Media Studies*, London and New York: Edward Arnold.

White, K.W. and Weight, B.H. (eds) (2000) *The Online Teaching Guide: A Handbook of Attitudes, Strategies and Techniques for the Virtual Classroom*, Boston: Allyn and Bacon.

Whorf, B.L. (1956) *Language, Thought, and Reality*, New York: Wiley.

Williams, B. (1995) *The Internet for Teachers*, Foster City, CA: IDG Books.

Winchester, S. (1998) *The Surgeon of Crowthorne: A Tale of Murder, Madness and a Love of Words*, London: Viking.

Wordsworth, W. (1895) T. Hutchinson (ed.) *The Poetical Works of William Wordsworth*, London: Oxford University Press.

Wortham, S. (1999) *Rethinking the University: Leverage and Deconstruction*, Manchester: Manchester University Press.

Index

REFRAMING BOLLYWOOD

REFRAMING BOLLYWOOD

THEORIES OF POPULAR HINDI CINEMA

AJAY GEHLAWAT

www.sagepublications.com
Los Angeles • London • New Delhi • Singapore • Washington DC

791.4309

First published in 2010 by

SAGE Publications India Pvt Ltd
B1/I-1, Mohan Cooperative Industrial Area
Mathura Road, New Delhi 110 044, India
www.sagepub.in

SAGE Publications Inc
2455 Teller Road
Thousand Oaks, California 91320, USA

SAGE Publications Ltd
1 Oliver's Yard, 55 City Road
London EC1Y 1SP, United Kingdom

SAGE Publications Asia-Pacific Pte Ltd
33 Pekin Street
#02-01 Far East Square
Singapore 048763

Published by Vivek Mehra for SAGE Publications India Pvt Ltd, typeset in 10.5/12.5 Goudy Old Style by Diligent Typesetter, Delhi and printed at Chaman Enterprises, New Delhi.

Library of Congress Cataloging-in-Publication Data

Gehlawat, Ajay
    Reframing Bollywood : theories of popular Hindi cinema/by Ajay Gehlawat.
        p. cm.
    Includes bibliographical references and index.
    1. Motion pictures—India. 2. Motion pictures—Social aspects—India. I. Title.

PN1993.5.I8G44   791.430954–dc22   2010   2010014828

ISBN: 978-81-321-0472-8 (HB)

The SAGE Team: Elina Majumdar, Aniruddha De, Rajib Chatterjee and Trinankur Banerjee

To the true Bollywood fans, Sylvie and Asha,

and to Jaya, a possible future fan

Contents

Acknowledgments

This book would not have been possible without the generous support, encouragement and feedback of numerous individuals, including Peter Hitchcock, Judy Milhous, Giancarlo Lombardi, Alison Griffiths, David Savran, Gayatri Spivak and Robert Stam. I would also like to thank the participants and panelists at the CHOTRO 2 Conference at the Indira Gandhi National Centre for the Arts in New Delhi, for their helpful feedback regarding Chapter 3, as well as the participants and panelists at the Media Fields 2: Infrastructures Conference at the University of California, Santa Barbara, for their questions and comments regarding the make-up of the Bollywood film. I would also like to thank the Center for Lesbian and Gay Studies (CLAGS) at the City University of New York Graduate Center for their generous support in developing Chapter 4, and Sonoma State University for providing me with an RSCAP summer grant to further develop this manuscript. An earlier version of Chapter 2 first appeared as an article in *Quarterly Review of Film and Video*—I would like to thank the publishers for kind permission to reprint it here. An earlier version of Chapter 3 is forthcoming in the collection, *Ethnographies* (Devy et al. 2010). I would like to thank the editors for their kind permission to include it in its expanded version here. I would also like to thank the editorial staff at SAGE, as well as the anonymous reviewer, for their feedback and suggestions which were extremely helpful in finalizing this manuscript. Last but not the least, I would like to give a heartfelt thanks to my family for their consistent love and support throughout the years—in particular, to my parents, my brother and sister and, most of all, my wife.

Introduction: Reframing Bollywood

Typically, books on popular Hindi cinema, or 'Bollywood', begin by presenting all the figures associated with this industry—how many hundreds of films made per year, how many millions of daily viewers, etc. For the purposes of this study, however, it would be more effective to start by examining the figures associated with critical studies and theorists of this industry: in the 1970s, they numbered in the single digits; in the 1980s, the number rose to over a dozen; and by the end of the 1990s, with over two dozen theorists of Bollywood, this latter form could be considered a constituted field of production in the realm of Film and Cultural Studies. In the past decade alone, nearly a dozen new books have been issued on the subject, including Vijay Mishra's *Bollywood Cinema: Temples of Desire* (2002); Jyotika Virdi's *The Cinematic ImagiNation: Indian Popular Films as Social History* (2003); Raminder Kaur and Ajay Sinha's edited collection, *Bollyworld: Popular Indian Cinema through a Transnational Lens* (2005); as well as two separate anthologies both entitled *Global Bollywood* (Gopal and Moorti 2008; Kavoori and Punathambekar 2008). This upsurge in publications is itself symptomatic of the growing interest in Bollywood films as objects of critical inquiry.

An initial question underlying much of the recent discussion surrounding this cinema is one of naming: What, precisely, is 'Bollywood' and what does such a name, or naming, imply? Rajinder Dudrah claims that Bollywood is 'the moniker for popular Hindi cinema from Mumbai' (formerly Bombay) and argues that the term has become 'an important catchword in the vocabulary of global South Asian popular culture' (Dudrah 2006: 13). At the same time, as Ranjani Mazumdar has noted, 'India has four powerful film industries located in different parts of the country, each addressing cultural specificities and contexts' (Mazumdar 2007: xxxiv). It is, thus, indeed 'more fruitful to talk of popular cinemas,' as Wimal Dissanayake has noted, 'rather than one popular cinema' (Dissanayake 2003: 215). Yet, while the Bombay-based Hindi film industry's designation as India's 'national cinema' remains a point of contention, it would seem that the Hindi film industry is 'unquestionably nationally dominant' (Gopal and Moorti 2008: 12). This comes despite the Tamil and Malayalam film industries' numerical outpacing of the Hindi film industry (in terms of total number of films annually produced), as popular Hindi cinema maintains its dominance in terms of revenues and reception, with each Hindi film on average generating more revenues than all the other non-Hindi cinemas combined (Gopal and Moorti 2008). A primary reason for this continued dominance is that popular Hindi films are released in all five of the distribution territories including the overseas market which, in the 1990s, became the biggest territory (Mazumdar 2007).

The question of what the 'Bollywood' moniker implies has also become a subject of increasing debate. While some theorists see it as a condescending or trivializing term, others see in this 'epithet' a mimicry that is 'both a response and a dismissal' (Virdi and Creekmur 2006; Jaikumar 2003). Even as some view it as 'affectionate domestic shorthand' for the popular Hindi film industry, others see in it a hybrid element, simultaneously 'mock[ing] the thing it names and celebrat[ing] its difference' (Prasad 2008; Waugh 2001). Suffice to say, the question of whether this term is 'a pejorative or subversive description ... remains unresolved' (Gopal and Moorti 2008). My primary aim in invoking this term, however, is to signal my focus in this book on popular Hindi cinema, whose circulation and domination remain unmatched in part due to the status of Hindi as the most widely spoken language in the country (Trivedi 2008). Yet, as Harish Trivedi notes, the language employed in Hindi cinema has been 'all kinds of Hindi', inflected by numerous other dialects and languages including Urdu, Bhojpuri, Punjabi and 'Hinglish' (Trivedi 2008: 202–03). My underlying concern, then, is in identifying Bollywood as *a* nationally (and globally) dominant cinema without it necessarily functioning as *the* national, i.e., 'Indian', cinema. Mazumdar has aptly noted the tendency in film studies to frame Third World cinemas as national cinemas. It is precisely for this reason that I have chosen to employ the

term 'Bollywood' and define it as popular Hindi rather than Indian
cinema, so as to avoid a nationalizing discourse and to simultaneously
emphasize what Gopal and Moorti call 'the global orientation of this
formation' (Gopal and Moorti 2008: 4).

It is also key to note at the outset that the Bollywood film is a
particularly hybrid art form, blending theatrical and cinematic elements
as well as First World and Third World cinema methodologies, plus
an assortment of Western and indigenous genres such as the musical,
dance drama and melodrama, to name but a few. Such a blending, also
referred to as *masala* (a spicy mix), is precisely what has previously been
belittled in the theorization of Bollywood. Even as Satyajit Ray, for
instance, called the Bollywood film 'a well-mixed potpourri of popular
entertainment', he directly linked this composition to an audience
comprised of 'tired untutored minds with undeveloped tastes' (Ray
1976: 73). Indeed, this syncretic art form has been and continues to be
primarily situated within a theatrical model, stemming from previous
models applied to the study of Indian theatrical performances. Along
with suggesting aesthetic distinctions, the application of this model is
based upon, even as it subsequently reaffirms, a devotional paradigm,
also associated with older, theatrical models, in which the implied
native/Indian/'Hindu' viewer is assigned a primitive and primarily
religious perspective.

At the same time, a Brechtian theatrical paradigm is denied
Bollywood. Beginning with Satyajit Ray, theorists of Bollywood have
consistently dismissed the possibility of a Brechtian interpretation of
the Bollywood film due to various reasons, including the alleged lack
of such an intention on the filmmakers' part. Whenever Brecht and
his aesthetic conventions are summoned in a discussion regarding
Bollywood, they are invoked as a contrast to this latter form which,
in comparison, is labelled a 'conventional cinema' (Kazmi 1999).
Such a positioning—theatrical yet non-Brechtian—also works to sever
Bollywood's potential relationship to what Teshome Gabriel labels a
'Third Cinema', in which the film exhibits its marks of production
as 'a polemic comment on the way things are in their "natural"
reflection' (Gabriel 1989a: 46–47). Because Bollywood is identified as
a commercial, or conventional, cinema, critics tend to immediately
associate it with 'Western conventions', such as concealing its marks
of production. Simultaneously, the Bollywood film is labelled 'doubly

degraded', as it is seen not only as mere entertainment but also as a form derived from and imitative of its Western counterpart.

Given this state of affairs, my intention in this work is to reframe the Bollywood film and, in the process, its implied viewers and the previous and continuing scholarship on this cinema. Just as the Bollywood film, rather than neatly fitting into any one category, defines itself through its parody and transgression of each, such a critical intervention will be achieved through a combination of fields and approaches, including the filmic, theatrical, ethnographic and postcolonial. This fusion of approaches is itself emblematic of the larger scope of this work, namely, to destabilize the positioning of Bollywood within any one sphere of reference and, rather, to illuminate how several spheres of meaning are simultaneously at play in its construction. By doing so, I hope to demonstrate how applying a variety of critical tools can enable a more comprehensive reading of the films.

OVERVIEW: BOLLYWOOD STUDIES

Beginning with Satyajit Ray's collected essays, published in 1976, and Kobita Sarkar's *Indian Cinema Today* (1975), Bollywood has historically been relegated by Indian scholars to a B-rate status. The films themselves are seen as crude imitations of Hollywood productions, even as their implied viewers are subsequently seen as the infantile masses for whom such crude entertainments are devised. 'If you think in terms of tired untutored minds with undeveloped tastes needing an occasional escape through relaxation', Ray writes, then 'the best prescription' becomes the Bollywood film precisely as it has been formulated, namely, as simple, escapist fare for simple-minded audiences (Ray 1976: 73).

Such a paradigm is further formulated during the 1980s by critics such as Chidananda Das Gupta, Ashis Nandy, Kishore Valicha and Sudhir Kakar. Numerous theories, for example, have been proposed by both Indian and non-Indian scholars on the issue of sexuality as mediated through the song and dance sequence in the Bollywood film. Although these views are varied, nearly all tend either to criticize what they consider to be the 'vulgar' erotics of these sequences or simultaneously to blame said vulgarities on Indian sexual mores, which are subsequently considered, in comparison with those of the

West, puritanical. Kakar, for instance, likens the Bollywood film to 'daydream' and claims that the reason for its resounding success in India is due to the Indian psyche's ability to 'regress temporarily to childhood modes'. This is because 'in India the child's world of magic is not as far removed from adult consciousness as it may be in some other cultures' (Kakar 1989: 28–29).[1]

This 'infantilizing' trend continues into the 1990s, even as it is further solidified by the appearance of critical work which supplements this 'fantasy' reading via the theory of *darsana*, or devotional viewing. Even as the number of critical works increases and diversifies during this decade (incorporating, for example, television programming and viewing habits in India and the diaspora), they become even more firmly yoked to a religious paradigm. Thus, both Marie Gillepsie and Ananda Mitra not only focus solely on a religious television serial but furthermore view a pre-determined religious perspective as the 'key with which to unlock the interpretive frameworks' of such televisual programming (Gillespie 1995a; Mitra 1993). Simultaneously, crucial components of the televisual experience such as what Raymond Williams called 'flow' are either unmentioned or downplayed (Williams 1975). All interactions with the medium by Indian audiences are filtered through cultural suppositions which preclude a structural analysis, so that the televisual experience becomes, first and foremost, an articulation of the *'religious world view'* that these people allegedly manifest, consciously or unconsciously (Gillespie 1995a: 358). Underlying principles of the apparatus, such as flow, are paradoxically used to reformulate the predominance of this 'religious world view' and to connect 'the religious and social practices in a continuous and interrelated chain' (Mitra 1993: 94).

This conflation of infantilizing and devotional paradigms culminates with the appearance of Madhava Prasad's *Ideology of the Hindi Film* (1998), in which this US-educated, Indian-based critic employs the psychoanalytic film theory of Christian Metz to the study of Bollywood. Naturally, Prasad uses Metz's famous distinction between the theatrical and cinematic experiences as a way of positioning the Bollywood film within a theatrical model and, thus, its implied viewer as again lacking the requisite cognitive skills for film viewing. Prasad examines the Indian cinema-goer's relationship to the Bollywood film primarily through the devotional paradigm, even arguing that moments that might otherwise be labelled 'Brechtian', for example, instances of direct address, are the result of the implied (Indian) viewer's religious constitution. A key equivocation upon which such formulations reside is that of 'being Indian' and 'being Hindu'. Whereas, to some extent, this equivocation is manifested by the culture at large (which may synonymize 'Hindustan' and 'India'), a key distinction remains: being 'Indian' does not mean being 'Hindu', and vice versa. The equivocation, however, remains and through it, the onslaught of ad hoc theorization which uses this linguistic loophole to position the art form within a primarily religious rather than semiotic frame of analysis.

Even as Bollywood critics have taken increasingly theoretical approaches, they tend to consistently use such approaches only to re-invoke infantilizing/devotional paradigms, themselves implicitly or explicitly based on a pre-constituted audience. Two recent examples of this paradoxical trend can be found in work of Ravi Vasudevan and Ashish Rajadhyaksha. Even as Vasudevan begins by stating, 'Especially important here is an agenda of moving beyond the deployment in Indian cinema of a rhetoric of traditional morality and identity to a focus on how cinematic address, the way spectators are positioned in terms of vision, auditory address, and narrative intelligibility, may complicate and rework the overt terms of narrative coherence', he still claims that 'the task here' is 'identifying how the "darsanic" locates characters and is responded to by them' (Vasudevan 2000b: 134, 139). Rajadhyaksha, meanwhile, begins by making the apologist argument, claiming that what he 'wants to do here' is develop 'a theory of the cinema that can account for the Indian cinema' (Rajadhyaksha 2000: 269). He then proceeds to delineate Laura Mulvey's famous argument regarding the voyeurism of classical Hollywood cinema only as a way of yet again describing 'the difficulty Indian (and generally non-Western) filmmakers have with the concept of "story-telling" as in Hollywood cinema' (Rajadhyaksha 2000: 276). 'Wherever it happens, and however it happens', Rajadhyaksha concludes, 'it appears to be generally the case' that the implied viewer of Bollywood resists the 'Hollywood Mode of Production', instead becoming 'a citizen subject who fully incarnates his symbolic authority' (Rajadhyaksha 2000: 293).

It is precisely now, as Dissanayake notes, 'with something ... approaching critical maturity' in the field, that the time has come to 'examine the various pathways that have been cleared in order to gain a deeper understanding' of Bollywood and, in the process, 'to identity some significant gaps and potentially fruitful lines of inquiry that yet need to be pursued' (Dissanayake 2003: 203). Similarly, it is only by 'paying close attention to the structure of narrativity' in this cinema that we can truly appreciate its cinematic discourse and, in the process, enable the idea of active spectatorship to permeate a field that all too frequently finds recourse in a facile model of the implied viewer as passive 'victim' of larger discourses beyond his/her control (Dissanayake 2003: 205, 212). However, to do so, it must first be acknowledged that, more often than not, it is Indian and Indo-diasporic scholars who employ 'Western lexicon' or immediately read Bollywood's filmic negotiations within 'Eurocentric hermeneutics' (Dissanayake 2003: 214; Desai and Dudrah 2008: 2). The solution, however, does not necessarily entail the invocation of 'indigenous frames of reference' (which, indeed, all too often lead to 'the equally perilous trap of essentialism or cultural exceptionalism') but, instead, lies in the careful re-examination of previous applications of the so-called 'Western lexicon' of film and media theory to the study of Bollywood cinema, as well as in how these theories may indeed reshape indigenous frames of reference (Dissanayake 2003).

REFRAMING: ENVISIONING NEW PARADIGMS

In order to liberate the study of Bollywood from these theoretical constraints, a crucial first step is to situate it within a filmic paradigm. This is not to deny the theatrical aspects of the Bollywood film but rather to locate them as functioning in an essentially cinematic frame. The key difference between these two registers, as pointed out by Walter Benjamin and Christian Metz, is an ontological one (Benjamin 1988; Metz 1982). As Metz notes, 'In the theatre, actors and spectators are present at the same time and in the same location, hence present one to another ... But in the cinema, the actor was present when the spectator was not (=shooting), and the spectator is present when the actor is no longer (=projection)' (Metz 1982: 63). This 'missed encounter' between spectator and actor becomes the basis for the former's interaction with the on-screen spectacle and one, furthermore, that allows for this viewer to engage in a specifically cinematic form of voyeurism—what Metz labels 'unauthorized scopophilia' (Metz 1982).[2]

Whereas Prasad employs Metz in order to define the Indian filmic interaction as 'theatrical', one in which the viewer's 'gaze then at once becomes, or is reminded of its, shamefaced voyeurism', I want to reconsider the implications of the basic tenets of the cinematic apparatus and, in the process, locate the implied viewer of Bollywood within a more cinematic frame. Foregrounding the technical aspects of the interaction between film viewer and film—the 'missed encounter', or what Benjamin describes as the loss of 'aura' in the filmic text—works to undermine theoretically the dominant religious perspective and simultaneously liberate filmic text and implied viewer from its limited/ limiting interpretive framework. By delineating how the film viewer actively participates in making the film's meaning, how he or she is present in a 'double capacity ... as witness and assistant' (Metz 1982: 93), my aim is to destabilize the construction of passive 'Hindu' with an essentially reverential gaze.

By focusing on the unique filmic components of the Bollywood film, such as the frequent use of playback sound and lip-synching, or the multiple scenic backgrounds and settings employed in song and dance sequences, a simultaneous shift from a religious to a postmodern perspective becomes possible. In particular, Jean Baudrillard's conception of the 'hyperreal' and Sumita Chakravarty's concept of 'impersonation' become effective theoretical devices that work to allow both Bollywood and its theorists to transcend some of the pitfalls of cultural truisms and paradoxically assert 'identity' through the absence of any such structured focal point (Baudrillard 1983; Chakravarty 1993). Through the metaphor of 'impersonation', it becomes possible for theorists of Bollywood to repudiate and subvert any exclusive reading of its mediations.

While Chakravarty deploys 'impersonation' as a way of constructing a narrative of Indian popular cinema and national identity, I would like to develop this concept further and, in fact, use it as a way of problematizing the concept of a national identity and, indeed, of Bollywood as a nationalizing discourse. In other words, my aim is to invoke the concept of impersonation as a disorienting principle, one that challenges rather than accommodates 'nationally inflected readings of Bombay cinema', highlighting in the process the very unstable and contaminated elements that constitute the crux of this cinema—the very same elements that Chakravarty attempts to downplay or disavow

(Chakravarty 1993: 5, 310). It is precisely because popular Hindi cinema continues to be invoked as 'India's sole model of national unity', that the concept of impersonation (as a way of appreciating this cinema's aesthetic form) should not be divested of its negative connotations (Chakravarty 1993: 310). By focusing on the so-called 'negative' aspects of this 'contaminated' cinema, it becomes possible to upset ossified discourses of the nation. Hence, while Chakravarty's 'modest aim' was to recuperate the idea of India as nation, my more ambitious goal in this study is to redeploy her concept of impersonation to demonstrate how Bollywood frequently and playfully disrupts the so-called narrative of the nation—and of national identity (Chakravarty 1993: 10).

Rather than positioning Bollywood within any one frame of reference, I believe it is more effective to see it as engaging in what Baudrillard calls 'ecstasy', namely, the simultaneous transcendence and dissolution of a form (Baudrillard 1987: 68). This concept shares a particular resonance with the previously mentioned trope of *masala*, the spicy mixing in which the typical Bollywood film engages. While the transition from *darsana*, or devotional viewing, to 'ecstasy', or to *masala*, may seem like quibbling over words, it is important to keep in mind, as Pierre Bourdieu has pointed out, that the constitution of language is reflective of social relations and social ranks, as well as crucial in reinforcing and/or recreating these relations and ranks (Bourdieu 1991). To see Bollywood as 'ecstasy' is not just a semantic shift; rather, it is one that reflects a reformulation of the antediluvian binarisms still informing the overwhelming majority of Bollywood criticism. Reframing Bollywood within such a postmodern frame produces a conception of 'Indianness' rooted in a dialectics of play that works to undermine, even as it extravagantly celebrates, those polar(izing) oppositions that critics continue to associate with its internal and external structures.

In other words, monolithic terms such as 'Indianness' and 'Indian cinema', as employed in these past and continuing instances, are themselves no longer effective, not because they reflect a juxtaposition and contamination but because they do not. Conversely, seeing Bollywood as deliberately engaging in 'impersonation' allows theorists to embrace precisely such contamination, thus allowing for a reformulation of both this cinema and its hybrid elements. As Chakravarty has noted, 'Impersonation implies a form of subversion, of the illegitimate (even the monstrous) masquerading as the real thing or person, generally

with the intention of displacing the legitimate' (Chakravarty 1993: 5).
The Bollywood film may thus be described as 'revamping schemas' to
'suit new purposes', a process of revision Noel Carroll calls 'amplification', in which cinematic innovations are devised by 'synthesizing
familiar schemas in fresh ways' (Bordwell 1997: 152–53). When applied to the dissemination of Bollywood films via television, such a reframing would similarly allow for elements such as the films' episodic
structuring and this structure's relationship to the 'flow' of television
programming, to put into question the essentially ethnographic assumptions regarding such interactions.[3]

Furthermore, in the process of reframing Bollywood in such a
manner, I hope to develop a new relationship between popular Hindi
cinema and theories of postcoloniality. Whereas postcolonial studies,
particularly in relation to Asia and even more particularly in relation
to India, have developed during the same period as Bollywood studies (1970s to present), the latter field has remained largely marginalized within the former. Simultaneously, Bollywood studies has largely
omitted these very theorists in its formulations of what may arguably
be, given the high rates of Bollywood production, distribution and
exhibition, a key arena for the negotiation of postcolonial identity,
particularly in the increasingly globalized world of the late twentieth/
early twenty-first centuries. Compounding this mutual failure of recognition, Bollywood more often than not draws only the dismissal of
predominant postcolonial theorists.[4]

What one gets, therefore, is a setting reminiscent of that in Philip
Dick's sci-fi classic, *Do Androids Dream of Electric Sheep?* (1969), namely,
one in which there are two police agencies simultaneously operating
in the same milieu, yet neither is aware of the other's presence. Along
with a gaping 'blind spot', this analogy illuminates how two sets of operators, situated within their own realms of investigation, map out their
own borders (even if these overlap) and then proceed to police them
with their respective disciplinary tools. Needless to say, these 'tools'
increasingly become 'weapons' in such usage, eliminating any and all
threats to theorists' self-contained, self-generating fields of knowledge
production. This inevitably works to enact the compartmentalization
and containment of both fields in the larger realm of Western systems
of classification.

It is my further ambition in this work, then, to de-isolate these two
trajectories of critical inquiry via the application of a postmodern praxis,

particularly building on Baudrillard's conception of the hyperreal as that which is always already reproduced (Baudrillard 1983: 146). This can hopefully result in a productive fusion for both Bollywood as a focus of study and for the larger realm of academic discourse in which it is situated and which, furthermore, works to situate. Indeed, just as Deckard, Dick's detective in the *Blade Runner* story, ultimately questions his own identity and wonders if he, too, might not be a 'replicant', the cross-pollination of Bollywood Studies with postcolonial and postmodern theories may work to implode arcane notions of authenticity and fixity both within the realms of academic discourse and in the Bollywood film. It is in this sense that this work will be building on previous scholarship such as Chakravarty's, even as it attempts to develop it further.

Reframing Bollywood is divided into five chapters, each addressing a specific area of controversial theorization. These paradigms include the religious frame, the musical frame, the subaltern frame, the (hetero)sexual frame and the 'crossover' frame. By examining this field's hegemonic paradigms, frame by frame, this book works to reshape the understanding of the Bollywood film and restructure its relationships with multiple disciplines, including film and theatre studies, postcolonial studies, queer studies, as well as the emerging terrain of transnational studies.

The first chapter explores how theatrical and religious paradigms are utilized by theorists of Bollywood as a way of overriding the implications of cinematic and televisual media, as well as what consequences this framing has for the aesthetic and cultural perceptions of Bollywood and its implied viewer. I am concerned here with how Bollywood films create private spaces in which erotic encounters frequently occur, thus contradicting the logic of the devotional paradigm which argues that such private spaces and representations are taboo in Hindi cinema.

The second chapter challenges the dominant perception of the Hollywood musical as forefather of the Bollywood film and, instead, presents the Bollywood song and dance sequence as a more radical, Brechtian form of narrative interruption than its Hollywood counterpart. In this manner, this chapter continues the examination of how older frames of analysis are invoked to position Bollywood, as well as how the Bollywood film form violates these paradigms in numerous ways. Using Jane Feuer's study of the Hollywood musical, this chapter performs a close comparative analysis of Hollywood musicals and

Bollywood films, including *Dil Se...* (1998) and *Aa Ab Laut Chalen* (1999), examining how Bollywood song and dance sequences differ in crucial ways in their structuring from those of Hollywood musicals.

Building on the previous two chapters, Chapter 3 is concerned with theories of reception, filmic literacy and subaltern agency as they relate to the screening of Bollywood films in Indian villages and among the socially and economically disadvantaged. This chapter critiques the notion of Bollywood as an 'oral cinema' and argues that the widespread viewing of Bollywood in Indian villages functions instead as a form of visual literacy. In doing so, this chapter applies key concepts from postcolonial theory to the study of Bollywood in a paradigm-shifting manner, challenging several key premises underlying the discourse of subaltern studies, as formulated by Gayatri Spivak, via a close reading of sequences from the classic Bollywood film, *Guide* (1965).

The fourth chapter considers the emergence of a homosexual subtext in contemporary Bollywood cinema, specifically focusing on the recent global blockbusters, *Kal Ho Naa Ho* (2003) and *Dostana* (2008). In the process, this chapter reconsiders the most recent scholarship on queer Bollywood spectatorship, including Gayatri Gopinath's book, *Impossible Desires* (2005), by questioning the implied repudiation of homosexuality in popular Indian culture, arguing instead that recent Bollywood films engage in such homosexual subtexts both knowingly and playfully. Drawing upon Judith Butler's concept of 'gender parody', this chapter also reveals and simultaneously destabilizes the larger ambivalence existing within Bollywood cinema—on the one hand, its infusion with and recognition of 'homosexual' elements and, on the other hand, its ostensible heteronormativity.

The final chapter considers the recent phenomenon of 'Crossover Bollywood' films and reformulates notions of 'Indianness' and Bollywood in an era of the non-resident Indian (NRI). Examining recent films such as *The Guru* (2002), *Bollywood/Hollywood* (2002), *Kabhi Khushi, Kabhie Gham* (2001) and *Bride and Prejudice* (2004), this chapter avoids reinvoking nationalist paradigms when considering such contemporary trends, instead arguing that Bollywood creates more fluid and transnational forms of cultural identity in the twenty-first century.

An underlying thread running through all of these chapters is a focus on the song and dance sequence in the Bollywood film, whether as a 'private realm' (Chapter 1), as a form of narrative interruption

(Chapter 2), as a way of reorienting both film and viewer (Chapter 3), as a 'queer' moment in an otherwise 'straight' narrative (Chapter 4), or, indeed, as a hyperspace through which characters traverse the globe (Chapter 5). This continued focus is an acknowledgment of Gopal and Moorti's claim that 'to talk of Bollywood is inevitably to talk of the song and dance sequence' (Gopal and Moorti 2008: 1). More than any other element in Bollywood films, the song and dance functions as a reframing device, allowing films and their characters to rearticulate their visions, desires and, indeed, viewers' understanding of both. Thus, such sequences are of paramount importance to my present study and serve as a recurring theme throughout the book. To make a definitional claim, I would argue that Hindi films without song and dance sequences would not be considered 'Bollywood' films. This does not necessarily entail the inverse proposition, however, that all films featuring 'Bollywood song and dance sequences' belong to this corpus—hence the phenomenon of 'Crossover Bollywood', films made in the West and in English that incorporate, or parody, elements of the typical Bollywood film, while maintaining their own distinct style(s) (to be discussed further in the final chapter).

A key question this book continually poses is: what are the effects of framing Bollywood in the ways that it has been up till now? One immediate result of these tendencies, I suggest, is to literally 'frame' Bollywood, that is, to prearrange it so as to ensure a desired (fraudulent) outcome, and/or to incriminate it falsely; to enclose it within certain limitations, to disenable it, to 'fix' it. *Reframing Bollywood* conversely opens up Bollywood to a multiplicity of meanings that challenge hegemonic claims regarding its composition and implied modes of spectatorship, thus repudiating any one fixed, essentialized meaning. In response to the dominant discourses surrounding and informing the study of Bollywood, this book offers a series of oppositional views—of Bollywood films, of their implied audiences and, indeed, of the latter's interactions with the former. To 'reframe', in cinematic parlance, implies a mobile, as opposed to static, frame. This is an apt paradigm for both a hyperkinetic cinema such as Bollywood as well as for the approach this book takes. In moving beyond the narrow frames of individual disciplines, this study, like the Bollywood film it addresses, attempts to create a conception of this cinema that not only draws awareness to all those elements overlooked by previous and continuing theorizations but also provides an underlying methodology that works to transcend and dissolve the very notion of essential otherness. Each chapter's particular intervention underscores the larger argument of this book—the usefulness of viewing Bollywood from multiple perspectives—even as readers are provided with an introduction to some of the key concepts and debates surrounding the study of popular Hindi cinema today.

NOTES

1. Here we see the classic 'Orientalizing' frame, critiqued by Edward Said, in which the 'Oriental' subject is relegated to an infantilized, 'natural' state (Said 1994). It is precisely this 'regressive haven' that Kakar claims 'Hindi films seem to provide ... for a vast number of our people' (Kakar 1989: 29).

2. Furthermore, it is important to note, as Metz himself does, that this discussion of cinematic voyeurism is not limited to Hollywood—'It doesn't even have to be Hollywood: the images of any film based on narration and representation—of any "film"' (Metz 1982: 91).

3. Rather than seeing the gods of religious television serials such as *The Mahabharata* as necessarily conveying a religious aura because the viewing audience has been pre-identified as 'Hindu', one might see these characters as 'impersonations' and these serials as being re-inscribed within an external flow of the televisual apparatus.

4. For example, even as Arjun Appadurai and Carol Breckenridge consider the cinema of Mira Nair to be 'a new sort of aesthetic presence', they dismiss Bollywood as 'B-grade' (Appadurai and Breckenridge 1991: 96, 98); similarly, Gayatri Chakravorty Spivak, even as she speaks of suturing 'the re-activated cultural axiomatics' of 'the subaltern cultures' into 'the principles of the Enlightenment', dismisses Bollywood films as 'embarrassing imitations' and '"adaptations" of moments from US MTV' (Spivak 2002: 195). Homi Bhabha, meanwhile, in a piece originally written in relation to a conference on Third Cinema, fails not only to mention Bollywood but cinema in general (Bhabha 1989).

Bollywood and its Implied Viewers

Popular Hindi cinema, or Bollywood, is one of the most prolific and widespread cinemas in the world. The theorization of this particular art form, a syncretic blending of a variety of tropes and genres, however, continues to situate it within a primarily theatrical frame, stemming from previous models applied to the study of Indian theatrical performances. Along with suggesting aesthetic distinctions, the application of a theatrical model is based upon, and subsequently reaffirms, a devotional paradigm (also associated with older theatrical models) in which the native/Indian/'Hindu' viewer is assigned a primarily religious perspective.

I am concerned in this chapter, then, with both delineating the structures and applications of these theatrical and religious models and examining how they are used to locate Bollywood and its cinematic viewer. Using Walter Benjamin's discussion of the work of art's 'aura' and Christian Metz's seminal characterization of theatrical and cinematic media and their crucial differences, particularly in terms of spectatorship, I want to explore how ancient (theatrical/religious) paradigms, in tandem with current 'postcolonial' theory, are used to override the implications of modern technological devices (for example, those of cinema and television), as well as what consequences this positioning has for the aesthetic and cultural perceptions of Bollywood and its implied viewers.

Bollywood is one of the few Third World film industries to have remained dominant in its national market in the face of the continued onslaught of Hollywood globalism (Pendakur 2003). The

typical Bollywood film is three hours long and conflates a variety of
filmic strategies into one production, often referred to as *masala* (a
spicy, mixed dish), including the musical, melodrama, Western, film
noir, action and soft-porn genres.[1] Music is of particular importance
to Bollywood—a typical film will include half a dozen songs, i.e.,
one every thirty minutes. In these songs, which are anywhere from
three to eight minutes, the technique of playback is employed. This
practice goes back to the 1930s when 'music doubling', i.e., using
professional singers to perform the actual music in synchronization
with the (already) filmed actor going through the motions of singing,
came into vogue. The cinema in India, however, engaged in a reverse
process: prerecording the song before the film shooting (Arnold 1991).
This strategy is directly linked to the popularity of both film songs and
playback singers, a handful of whom perform all the songs for all the
films released in the subcontinent (Pendakur 1990).

With the advent of this technique, directors could create songs
'without having to accommodate the particular vocal limitations' of
actors and actresses, thus liberating the latter from potential limitations
on their physical performances, for example, from engaging in more
complex gestures, movements and interactions (Arnold 1991). Even as
the film version of the song 'cannot include the traditional performance-
audience interaction and relationships because of its recorded nature',
it does become possible to 'simulate ... this interplay', and the manner
of performances on film is, indeed, now capable of being even more
'frequently dramatic and "showy"' (Arnold 1991: 149).

The song in the Bollywood narrative functions as a type of 'resolution' or interruption to what has come before. Dancing often accompanies these songs, as well as rather generic settings such as 'the rainy
forest', or 'the hill station', all of which ostensibly serve to heighten
both the dramatic tension of these nodes and the narrative in general.
Usually, these sequences feature a man and a woman who perform
an 'erotic interaction', during which they may go through a myriad of
changes in both costume and locale while lip-synching to the song. It
is these song-and-dance sequences that become the main focus, then,
when considering Bollywood within a theatrical/religious paradigm.

Numerous theories have been proposed by both Indian and non-
Indian scholars on the issue of sexuality as mediated through the song-
and-dance sequence. Although these views are varied, nearly all tend
either to criticize what they consider to be the 'vulgar' erotics of these

sequences or simultaneously blame such vulgarities on Indian sexual mores, which are subsequently considered—in comparison with those of the West—puritanical. For instance, Sudhir Kakar, a self-described 'distinguished psychoanalyst with a private practice in New Delhi', as well as the author of several books on both Indian sexuality and Indian art forms, finds the Hindi film 'perhaps closest to the daydream', and:

> [W]ithout passing any value judgment, that, relatively speaking, in India the child's world of magic is not as far removed from adult consciousness as it may be in some other cultures. Because of a specific thrust of the culture and congruent childrearing practices ... the Indian ego is flexible enough to regress temporarily to childhood modes without feeling threatened or engulfed. Hindi films seem to provide this regressive haven for a vast number of our people. (Kakar 1989: 28–29)

The Indian viewer, then, is a child to whom the Indian national cinema panders. One need not venture any further than another Indian critic to find validation for this view, for as Dr Kishore Valicha notes in his study of Indian cinema, 'Indian audiences accept such absurdities [i.e., those of the song-and-dance format] because of a deep conviction that love is comparable to music, and that true love is as pure as song' (Valicha 1988: 46). What is interesting in these instances is how the formation of 'the Indian' serves as a vehicle through which to examine the Bollywood film, as well as how, though technically 'from' this culture, both men's analyses relegate the Indian (and his accompanying thought processes, with specific regard to sexuality) to an infantilized, 'natural' state.

Both critics point out the inherent notions of purity embedded within the Hindu mind and subsequently read the Bollywood product through these preconceived categorizations. Sexuality, according to these Indian scholars, is viewed as a foreign entity by 'the Hindu psyche'—'sexual love', as Valicha notes, 'is also looked upon as the most severe hindrance to the spiritual development of the husband ... a man should, as far as possible, practise seminal thrift, for the loss of semen is considered weakening' (Valicha 1988: 45). Hindi cinema, then, can only mirror what has already been located within the greater culture, namely, those 'typical fears natural to a society that tends to repress sex' (Valicha 1988: 51). Thus, an indigenous model of identity is applied to the Indian psyche, which ultimately still finds the latter as epitomizing (or, in Kakar's words, 'flexible enough to regress to') an impaired sexuality.

A key equivocation upon which such formulations resides is that of 'being Indian' and 'being Hindu'. Whereas, to some extent, this equivocation is manifested by the culture at large (which may synonymize 'Hindustan' and 'India'), a key distinction remains in fact: being 'Indian' does not mean being 'Hindu', and vice versa. Similarly, the national cinema is more often than not referred to as 'Hindi' rather than 'Indian' cinema. This equivocation can be traced to some extent to the subcontinent's broad variety of official languages, as well as the (predominantly Hindi language) Bollywood film's domination of the film market (Pendakur 2003). Yet, it is not so much the language the film is made in as its formulaic tendencies that quintessentially define it as being a 'Hindi', or Bollywood, film. The equivocation, however, remains and through it, the onslaught of ad hoc theorization, which uses this linguistic loophole to position the art form within a primarily religious rather than semiotic frame of analysis.

This rather cyclopean and 'otherizing' view of the Indian/'Hindu' cinema viewer can be seen as stemming from an earlier and continuing theorization of this subject in relation to Indian theatre. At the beginning of the twentieth century, Indian theatre, as an object of study by Western scholars, is positioned within a religious framework—'It is', as 'Oriental' scholar A. Berriedale Keith wrote in 1924, 'a perversion of all probability to find in this item the trace of a primitive popular secular performance'—and (thus) contrasted with its other, namely, a Western secular model of theatre and theatricality, thus reaffirming its 'Otherized' status (Keith 1924: 51). Crucial to this criterion is its subsequent locating of the Indian (i.e., 'Hindu') spectator as a 'devotional subject'. As Keith says, 'It is indeed to ignore how essentially religion enters into the life of the Hindu to imagine that it is possible to trace the beginnings of drama to a detached love of amusement' (Keith 1924: 52).

To attempt to perform what later would become labelled 'interculturalism', i.e., the attempt to identify the implied spectator of Indian theatre as a 'modern [i.e., Western] mind', in other words, was (at least more clearly than now) seen as engaging in 'a delusion' (Keith 1924: 52). Interestingly enough, the 'postcolonial' critique levelled at 'interculturalism' from the other end of the century, by Yale-educated Rustom Bharucha, for instance, also bases its position on an essentialized notion of 'Indianness', which is both conflated with a 'devotional' paradigm and used to, again, contrast it with a 'Western' model (Bharucha 1990). Thus, even as Indian theatre scholarship shifts to a performative context (and, specifically, into the realm of the filmic) over the course of the twentieth century, an adherence to the notion of 'authentic Indianness' is maintained, thereby retaining Indian theatre's, and then cinema's, essential 'Otherness'.

In the 1920s, however, the idea that India's contact with Greece provided the 'necessary impetus' for the creation of Indian theatre was seen as 'perfectly legitimate', and subsequent attempts to ignore this possibility as 'idle' (Keith 1924: 57–58). By 1990, though these statements have become inverted (at least, in Bharucha's point of view), i.e., the 'perfect legitimacy' of seeing 'outsider' (i.e., Western) influences as providing the 'primary impetus' to 'Indian' texts is itself questioned for 'idleness', the essential binary (positing 'East', as represented by India, and 'West', as represented by the Occident) is maintained, thus allowing a Manichaean spectre to haunt Indian theatre and then film scholarship throughout the twentieth century, along with a temporal logic in which 'Indian drama rather is akin to the Greek than otherwise' (Keith 1924: 68).

Just as Keith posited the 'essentially religio[us]' nature of Indian drama, it is conceived at the end of the twentieth century, by both self-proclaimed 'insiders' (i.e., those coming from India) and 'insider/outsiders' (i.e., Westerners with a particular knowledge of India, through travel, study or combinations thereof), in essentially the same vein. Whether the pronoun employed is 'our' or 'their', whether a strictly 'theatrical' or primarily 'performative' model is applied, 'Indianness' continues to be equated with 'being Hindu'. Richmond, Swann and Zarrilli (three self-proclaimed 'insider/outsiders') reiterate Keith's sentiments, stemming from a colonial era, and simultaneously reflect the trajectory of scholarship's rather Mobius-like nature (from 'colonial' to 'postcolonial') through the following syllogism: 'The aesthetics of the [Indian] theatre are closely linked to the Hindu religious-philosophic base. Therefore, all forms of Hindu performance share common religious-philosophical assumptions' (Richmond et al. 1990: 7). That such a paradigm is simultaneously enacted from an insider and an outsider perspective works to shed light on both the alleged 'distinctions' between said positions/positioning and the complicity between these points in maintaining a decidedly 'otherized' notion of both Indian theatre and cinema and their implied viewers. Indeed, this trend is apparent since the very beginning of Indian film scholarship. One of the earliest book-length studies of the popular Indian cinema, Kobita Sarkar's *Indian Cinema Today* (1975), begins by characterizing Bollywood as an opiate—'the Indian cinema refuses to rise above the opiate level'; 'the latter [Indian commercial cinema, aka Bollywood] is mainly intended as an opiate, which demands nothing from the audience' (Sarkar 1975: 28, 155). Furthermore, 'because of the inability to say certain things outright it [Bollywood] has developed a meaningless, devious style that has been its greatest deterrent to maturity' (Sarkar 1975: 61–62). At the same time, 'a more mature type of film might have to await a more enlightened type of audience' (Sarkar 1975: 64). On the one hand, then, it is the Hindi cinema which attempts to 'delude audiences into believing their own delusions' and on the other, 'it is also the in-built resistance from the audience itself', that is to blame for this cinema's 'immaturity' (Sarkar 1975: 97, 100). In a similar vein, even as the roots of this 'resistance' are linked to a particularly Indian mentality, Sarkar claims 'this ultra-puritanism—it would seem, is a hangover from the Victorian outlook, grafted on to our system and fostered by a conventional morality' (Sarkar 1975: 102).

The Bollywood film and its implied viewer, then, would seem to have taken on the worst of both worlds. While it is 'possible' that they [the Hindi-film-going audience] 'have long had a sneaking suspicion that the world presented by the Hindi cinema does not exist', having been 'initiated into it, and doped consistently over a period of time with it, it has become standard "entertainment"' (Sarkar 1975: 131). In keeping with this form of back-handed compliment and these tropes, the critic Chidananda Das Gupta, after answering in the affirmative the question posed in his essay, 'Music: Opium of the Masses?', goes on to state:

> The opium of the music is, on the other hand, mixed with every dish that is served up to the audience. Once the audience has acquired the habit, it becomes immensely difficult for a lone man of good intentions to make it taste anything without that essential ingredient. (Das Gupta 1981: 31)

He proceeds to employ the 'tradition/modernity' binary, in which 'science has confused the Indian villager's philosophy and his pattern of living', to position Bollywood and its implied viewers as schizoid:

> The more the nouveaux riches rock and roll or twist and shake in blue jeans, the deeper becomes the schizophrenia between modernity and tradition in the Indian cinema. The all-India film thus paradoxically becomes the most effective obstacle against the development of a positive attitude towards technological progress, towards a synthesis of tradition with modernity for a future pattern of living. (Das Gupta 1981: 7)

This binary, indeed, becomes problematic, with Das Gupta concluding that 'the problem of being completely Indian and completely contemporary ... is echoing throughout the entire range of Indian art' (Das Gupta 1981: 39). Nearly twenty years later, Das Gupta seems to stick to his guns, claiming that the Indian audience 'has been brainwashed' and that, for 'most of them [Indian filmmakers], the conditions of practicing cinema are the conditions of religious art' (Das Gupta 1983: 40–41).

In another aptly titled piece, 'Music, Dance and the Popular Films: Indian Fantasies, Indian Repressions', Sanjeev Prakash, having affirmed on the first page the causal link his title implies ('Indian fantasies reflect Indian repressions'), appears to signal a change in methodology, declaring that 'attempts to dismiss serious analyses of film music and dance on the grounds that they are not "genuinely Indian" or are "hybrid", are probably as old as the sound cinema itself' (Prakash 1983: 114). Yet, immediately following this pronouncement, Prakash, paraphrasing musicologist Ashok Ranade, claims:

> It can be stated as an anthropological truth that in all cultures music is invariably employed to establish links with the supernatural—the element that enables mythology to have a firm base. The cinematic impulse in India was, therefore, congenitally bound with music. As primacy of vocal music in India is also an unquestionable trait, song dominance becomes almost automatic. (Prakash 1983: 114)

Here we see an Orientalizing essentialism again at play, where India becomes 'congenitally bound', both with music and, thus, a mythological predilection. Simultaneously, whereas Lothar Lutze points out that 'the coming of the film was not a process of destruction of indigenous culture by something alien, as some critics [for example, Das Gupta] would have it', he oscillates to the opposite extreme, echoing Prakash's essentializing sentiment in claiming that 'the Hindi film may well appear like a tree rooted deeply in Indian tradition and reaching out, fumblingly perhaps, into the space age' (Lutze 1985: 7). Similarly, while Prakash acknowledges a history of 'the creation of particular atmospheres through acoustic means' in India—what is sometimes referred to as *rasa*—he simultaneously claims that this 'elite, complex system did not find root in the popular film forms' (Prakash 1983: 116).

Thus, while being 'congenitally bound' with music, the 'roots' of the Indian cinema tree seem to preclude the possibility of a 'complex' hybridity and, furthermore, this should not come as 'surprising' (Prakash 1983: 116). The claim that Bollywood is 'a genre that defies easy categorization', then, seems belied by the ease with which critics have categorized it (Saari 1985: 16). Forced into a binary model where, 'as a rule, it cannot afford much shading in between', the Bollywood cinema is either seen as the schizoid manifestation of a worsening identity complex or the continued manifestation of 'deep-seeded' roots (Lutze 1985: 9). More often than not, one possibility becomes inexorably linked to the other, so that, for instance, even as this art form is seen as 'having evolved a broad framework of its own', it is 'congenitally bound' to 'the Hindu epics', necessitating that it be seen as 'a cinema that ... articulate[s] collective dreams' (Saari 1985: 23).

'It is precisely at this point', then, as Madan Gopal Singh says, 'that one is compelled to ponder the task proper' of the Bollywood film critic (Singh 1983: 120). To return to Kakar who, as noted earlier, approaches the Bollywood film as 'a collective fantasy, a group daydream', a disturbing parallel to earlier colonial discourse begins to manifest itself in the suggestion that the 'Indian' suffers from a dependency complex (Kakar 1983: 89).[2] When Kakar describes the Indian familial bond as 'so strong that even the loosening of the family bond, not to mention an actual break, may be a source of psychic stress and heightened inner conflict' (Kakar 1983: 91),[3] one can hear a trace of Octave Mannoni's colonialist characterization of the 'Madagascan':

It is the destiny of the Occidental to face the obligation laid down by the commandment *Thou shalt leave thy father and thy mother*. This obligation is incomprehensible to the Madagascan. At a given time in his development, every European discovers in himself the desire ... to break

the bonds of dependency, to become the equal of his father. The Madagascan, never! He does not experience rivalry with paternal authority,
'manly protest', or Adlerian inferiority–ordeals through which the European must pass and which are like civilized forms ... of the initiation
rites by which one achieves manhood. (Mannoni, quoted in Cesaire
2001: 60)[4]

Given this 'regressive' nature, naturally the cinema for such a one
cannot be too complex. Thus, Hindi films become 'contemporary
myths which, through the vehicle of fantasy ... temporarily heal for
their audiences the principal stresses arising out of the Indian family
relationships' (Kakar 1983: 97).

Interestingly enough, Mannoni surfaces in Christian Metz's discussion of the cinema as well, though here it is not quite the same Mannoni or, at least, not at first. Metz begins this section of *The Imaginary
Signifier* by stating, 'I shall say very little about the problems of belief in
the cinema' (Metz 1982: 71). One of the reasons for this, he claims, is
'because the subject has already been largely dealt with by Octave Mannoni in his remarkable studies of the theatrical illusion' (Metz 1982).[5]
Paraphrasing Mannoni, then, Metz asks, 'Since it is "accepted" that
the audience is incredulous, *who is it who is credulous?*' (Metz 1982: 72).
The answer is, 'of course, another part of ourselves'–'he' who is 'still
seated *beneath* the incredulous one' (Metz 1982). Although within the
parameters of Occidental psychology, this 'other part of himself' (the
credulous) is disavowed by the Western subject, when one grafts Mannoni's earlier views on the 'Madagascan' onto his subsequent theorization of the in/credulous spectator, one begins to see how 'the one
seated *beneath*' (the one to whom all this is 'incomprehensible') literally
becomes a necessary foil to the disavowing incredulity of the Western
subject. He is needed, in all his credulity (which must be maintained),
for the 'perfect organization of the machinery', namely, the colonial
discourse underlying Mannoni's claims (Metz 1982: 72). Following in
the latter's footsteps, then, one could claim Kakar attributes this type
of cinematic 'credulity' to the Indian via a psychoanalytic read 'from
within', as it were, relegating this subject, via Bollywood, to 'former
times', the time of myth, thus making the Hindi film 'a humble representative of the Hindu cultural ideal' (Kakar 1983: 97).

Such 'forcing-on' of the so-called 'religious world view' is further
exemplified by the theorization of the Indian viewer's gaze in relation

to the cinematic apparatus. M. Madhava Prasad, another Indian film scholar (also educated in the West), after reiterating the Metzian model of cinema viewing which stipulates the 'missed encounter' between film viewer and film actor as the basis for cinematic engagement, distinguishes this model from the one in which he places the Indian viewer, namely, that of the theatre-goer (Prasad 1998).[6] Key to this distinction for Prasad is the religious theory of *darsana*, a 'relation of perception within the public traditions of Hindu worship ... constituted by the combinations of three elements: the divine image, the worshipper and the mediating priest' (Prasad 1998: 75). Through this model, Prasad examines the Indian cinema-goer's relationship with the on-screen spectacle (particularly when of a 'sexual' nature) and posits that the depiction of sexual acts itself reflects this relationship.

Prasad examines the kiss as an example of such mediation. Though acknowledging that the ban on this act in films is of an informal nature, he directly links its absence to underlying social/religious convictions instilled within the Indian (Hindu) mind which views such an act—especially in its public display—as a transgression of morality. In explaining why this specific act is deemed 'offensive' even though, 'as everyone acknowledges, there is a great deal of sexual "vulgarity" in Indian films', Prasad posits that a distinction between 'public' and 'private' realms exists that 'undergirds the popular cinema as a national institution' (Prasad 1998: 90, 93).

> In Indian popular cinema we observe a tendency to resist the extra-communal tendency that Metz regards as constitutive of cinematic culture. The mandatory 'cabaret' scene in many Hindi films, marked by a tendency to frontal representation (where the dancer often looks straight into the camera, in violation of the 'recipe of classical cinema' which forbids such a direct address, and which originates in the logic of cinematic voyeurism), this spectacle is clearly 'theatrical' in Metz's sense. That which is offered as spectacle for the cinematic voyeur is distinguished by the fact that it 'lets itself be seen without presenting itself to be seen'. (Prasad 1998: 102)

Thus, unlike the Hollywood model, the Bollywood film only bridges the gap between screen and spectator through 'the effect ... of an underwriting of the voyeuristic relation by the Symbolic' (Prasad 1998: 103). This is due to the 'darsanic gaze' which characterizes the Indian (film) viewer, so that 'when the members of the couple turn to each other for a kiss, what occurs (or is feared) is a decisive shutting out of the Other, whose gaze then at once becomes, or is reminded of its, shamefaced voyeurism' (Prasad 1998).

Such a positioning seems to place the Indian viewer within a rather limited frame. Though allegedly versed enough in film language to negotiate the 'kiss', he or she is either unwilling in or incapable of acknowledging this mediation. This is due to his or her 'reverential' perspective, which is implicit in the tenets of Hinduism and which is subsequently located by Prasad within the filmic space, as a continuation of the religious experience. Yet, beyond once again committing the fallacy of equating the religious view with the filmic, such analysis denies the basic premise of Metz's entire theorization of the cinematic experience, namely, that of the 'missed encounter' between viewer and viewed object (see note 6). For Prasad's theorization to remain intact, one would have to accept as plausible the possibility of the Indian viewer watching a film without knowing what it was. Yet, as Valicha as well as Prasad have noted, this individual is clever enough to 'read' the various transfigurations of the 'kiss', whether they are more or less obfuscated (Prasad 1998; Valicha 1988). How, then, can one say this moment is 'feared' by the viewer, when it is this very figure's negotiations of the act that produce it?

Given this assessment, it might be effective at this juncture to take a detailed look at a particular song and dance sequence from a typical Bollywood film to see whether or not Prasad's 'darsanic paradigm' holds water, particularly in relation to the theorization of 'public' and 'private' realms. The song sequence I have in mind is 'Hum Tum' (You and I), a six and a half minute sequence from the Bollywood blockbuster, Bobby (dir. Raj Kapoor, 1973).[7] Before I perform a shot analysis of this sequence, it might be helpful to recount the events leading up to it, so as to better situate its subsequent negotiations. Raju (Rishi Kapoor) is trying to meet privately with the title heroine (Dimple Kapadia) but is unable to due to the latter's entourage of female friends. He sends a note with a young boy to Bobby, in which he tells her to 'dump' her friends and meet him alone at the lodge. Unfortunately, the note is intercepted (i.e., given to the wrong girl, who reads it aloud), and the entire female entourage angrily heads to the lodge where Raju is waiting, to confront him. Seeing them approaching en masse, Raju ducks, and he and Bobby manage to elude the group by hiding inside the lodge. Meanwhile, the girls outside complain to an older watchman who arrives that 'a cad has kidnapped a girl' and that they are inside the lodge. The watchman, however, replies that no one has come here, that he is on duty and, then, locking the door to the lodge, tells the girls to leave. Meanwhile, watching all this from a window inside, Bobby and Raju are at a loss, finding themselves locked in the lodge. Bobby wonders what she will do ('What will I tell my teacher?'), while Raju moves around the lodge, checking all the locks, then returns to the inner room (a bedroom) where Bobby, wearing a rather short miniskirt, is, and laughingly informs her that all the windows and doors are locked, before jumping onto the bed with a big grin on his face. As the camera tracks left to frame him and the bed in the center of the shot, Bobby, with her back to the camera, approaches him from the left, demanding to know what's so funny, and tells him to 'think of something'. As the camera closes in on Raju's image (smiling) in a medium shot, he leans forward on the bed and says, 'I *am* thinking of something'. 'What?' Bobby asks with a somewhat worried look and tone. Raju then 'says' (via playback which begins at this point):

No one can come in from outside
No one can go out from inside
Think if ever it happened like this
What would happen

Repeating the last line, he approaches her, even as she nervously, coyly turns away. Then, as he catches her arm and whirls her around to face him, he 'sings' the title phrase (now accompanied by the playback music), 'You and I ...' while Bobby breaks free of his grip to walk to the door (screen right) and close it, then turn and lean against it, looking at him. He now sings the next line ('Locked in a room ...') while 'framing' the room's outlines with his fingers and eyes. Bobby darts across the room to close the other door and, again, breathlessly leans against the now-shut door to look at Raju, who sings the next line ('And the key gets lost ...') while leaning forward and winking in the direction of the implied, off-screen Bobby, in a close-up shot. As he repeats the 'Hum Tum' (You and I) refrain, Bobby darts towards the windows where she pulls the drapes shut and then the camera cuts to a high angle shot, with both members of the couple extending their arms towards each other. She approaches him slowly with arms extended and, as they embrace and begin to turn in a circle, she 'sings'/'replies' with her arms around his neck while looking into his eyes (while the camera now frames them from the side in a medium close-up), 'Then I, too, will get lost in the charm of your eyes'. They slowly dance together, moving backwards all the while and then, falling back on the bed with her arms outstretched, Bobby begins singing the 'Hum Tum' line while the camera again cuts to a high angle (*plongée*) shot of her.[8]

As the accordion on the soundtrack swells, Raju approaches her (still framed from above) on the bed and lies down beside her. Bobby turns towards him even as the camera slowly descends focusing on the couple and, particularly, on Bobby's behind and legs (in short mini-skirt), as she stretches her arm out to touch Raju's shoulder and he runs his hand up her legs and backside. Then, even as the playback continues, there is a cut to a new scene, a dark forest or jungle-like setting. The camera is 'hidden' in a tree, framing the couple who walk towards it through the branches, descending (via crane) to frame them from ground level. Neither acknowledges its presence as the next lyrics come:

Raju: *It's pitch dark outside ...*
Bobby: *Babu, I'm getting scared!*
Raju: *Behind, some robber will rob you ...*
Bobby: *Why are you scaring me?*

After a series of romantic interactions (featuring different settings and outfits), there is a cut back to the original lodge bedroom in a match-on-action of the couple embracing as they both sing, 'Hum Tum ...' The camera now frames them in bed in a medium close-up as Bobby (again wearing her short miniskirt) turns over to Raju, providing an 'up-skirt' shot from behind as she turns and lies on him. Both repeat the 'Hum Tum' lyric ('You and I/Locked in a room ...') while embracing and, as he rises to a sitting position on the bed, the camera follows them in the same medium close-up. As they finish the lyric and Bobby starts to move her head towards Raju, there is a cut to a new scene (even as the playback continues)—they are now in a snowy mountain setting. After a few more scenes (including horses and snow), the camera again cuts back to the lodge bedroom and, as they continue to 'sing' and gaze into one another's eyes, Bobby and Raju walk out of the bedroom, arm in arm, and then, even as the watchman opens the front door, out of the lodge, leaving the watchman scratching his head as the song ends. What transpires in the preceding six and a half minutes, then, would seem to occur in what Prasad calls the 'private' realm. Rather than a tendency to 'resist the extra-communal tendency that Metz regards as constitutive of cinematic culture', or a 'tendency to frontal representation', 'Hum Tum' seems to display precisely the 'recipe' that allows for 'cinematic voyeurism' to occur (Prasad 1998: 103). While Das Gupta claims that 'all important actions and personalities must face the camera directly', and that 'the audience does not pay to see the back of the heroine's head', one might reply (to Das Gupta and Prasad) that, at least in this song, it is precisely the heroine's backside that is on display—again, not via an aesthetics of 'oppressive theatrical frontality' but, rather, from a decidedly voyeuristic perspective, i.e., in such a way that Kapadia, aka Bobby, 'lets herself be seen without presenting herself to be seen' (Das Gupta 1983: 40; Metz quoted in Prasad 1998: 102). The weaving, zooming, tilting up and down camera is constantly 'peering in' on the couple, who are 'hidden away' in the locked bedroom. Furthermore, the series of tableaux that are repeatedly cut to, along with engaging in voyeuristic cinematic techniques, become glimpses into the 'private fantasies' of the couple. That is to say, both thematically and structurally, the 'Hum Tum' song sequence becomes a representation of precisely the 'inner world' that Kakar and others claim is 'off-limits' to the darsanic camera of the Hindi cinema. Without putting too much stock into the film's subsequent success, it is safe to say that the very fact that it *was* a box office hit would seem to belie Prasad's assessment of the implied Indian viewer's (in)ability to deal with 'shamefaced voyeurism' or, more generally, with representations of the 'private realm' in the cinema.[9]

Particular attention to the specific timeframe under discussion, the 1970s, might help us understand this apparent discrepancy in Prasad's theorization, or between his theorization of the Bollywood film and the composition of the films themselves, as illustrated in this instance by *Bobby*. Prasad begins by reading Indian cinema as 'a site of ideological production' and, furthermore, 'as the (re)production of the state form' (Prasad 1998: 9). Yet, the 'Hindi feudal family romance' that he primarily associates with the mode of darsanic viewing becomes, by his own admission, 'rendered ... obsolete' during 'a moment of disaggregation' during the early 1970s (Prasad 1998: 25).[10] One might claim, then, that *Bobby* is emblematic of precisely this new politics of seeing, one adhering more to a mode of cinematic voyeurism stemming from 'the transformation of the cinematic field in the crisis of the early seventies' (Prasad 1998: 75). Yet, Prasad claims 'another deployment of the darsanic gaze can be seen in Hindi cinema of the post-1970s, especially in the Amitabh Bachchan films', and proceeds to discuss 'the most interesting example', *Main Azad Hun* (dir. Tinu Anand, 1989) (Prasad 1998: 77). In other words, though the alleged 'dominant textual form' that 'embodied the tradition of *darsana*' was 'rendered ... obsolete' by the early 1970s, Prasad rediscovers, or resurrects, the darsanic view nearly twenty years later via one film which, given that the original description of the category was 'Amitabh Bachchan films', comes rather late in Bachchan's career. Prasad proceeds to use this single 'most interesting example' to claim, 'Thus in the Hindi film the gaze is mobilized according to the rules of a hierarchical despotic public spectacle' (Prasad 1998: 25, 77–78). Thus, one might add, even after the alleged rupture caused by disaggregation and the subsequent reformist tendencies enacted by the commercial industry, one—or, Prasad, in this case—still finds Bollywood 'unfold[ing] as if under the aegis of the Symbolic' (Prasad 1998: 103).

To summarize, whereas Metz distinguishes between theatrical and cinematic voyeurism by noting the crucial *absence* of the seen object in the latter instance (thus creating the 'missed encounter' between film viewer and actor which, in turn, serves as the basis for cinematic— as opposed to theatrical—voyeurism), Prasad insists upon filling this absence via the darsanic principle which, he argues, simultaneously stems from the 'frontal' representations in popular Hindi films and the corresponding inability of the implied Indian/'Hindu' viewer to deal with a more voyeuristic presentation of the on-screen object—what Metz labels '*unauthorized* scopophilia' (Metz 1982: 63). Yet, sequences such as 'Hum Tum', with their creation of private spheres in which the Indian couple engages in discreet, erotic encounters that are framed in accordance with the logic of cinematic voyeurism, challenge Prasad's claim that such moments would be impermissible in the popular Hindi film. Additionally, the fact that *Bobby* 'spawned a whole genre of films' featuring such young lovers in such moments, further illuminates how widespread and, indeed, commonplace, such private spheres have become in Bollywood (Kazmi 1999: 19).[11]

A similar 'dressing up' of the universal medium occurs with the case of television. That is, as with the 'cultural truths' inserted within the basic cinematic experience, a notion similar to *darsana*, that of 'devotional viewing', is imposed upon the Indian television viewer. Thus, while both Ananda Mitra, an Indo-American media scholar, and Marie Gillespie, a British media ethnographer, examine the role television plays in the formation and maintenance of identity in both Indian and Indo-diasporic communities, the religious concept of *darsana* again overrides the more universal aspects of the televisual experience, buried as it is under the weight of 'cultural difference'. The concept I have in mind is that of 'flow'. This term, stemming from Raymond Williams' discussion of television, refers to the 'sequence or set of alternative sequences' which comprise the 'real programme' of a television broadcast (Williams 1975: 86–87). Such instances include not only the flow within a particular sequence of televisual programming but also the actual succession of items within and between the published sequence of events, for example, commercials and other 'interruptions' during a television broadcast (Williams 1975: 96). Thus, as Williams notes, 'a quality of the external sequence becomes a mode of definition of an internal method' (Williams 1975: 92).

Although Gillespie is more concerned with the viewing habits of Indo-diasporic viewers, and Mitra with the programming of Indian television, both primarily focus on a religious serial, *Mahabharat*. Though both distinguish, for example, between the 'social' and 'religious' programme, for Mitra, 'the primary difference between social and religious programmes is in the semantic units that make up the narrative', and for Gillespie, though 'religious belief and a religious mode of consciousness are prerequisites to devotional viewing ... the narrational strategies of the serial [*Mahabharat*] may engender devotional viewing' (Gillespie 1995a: 363, 367; Mitra 1993: 93). Thus, (again) a pre-determined religious perspective becomes the 'key with which to unlock the cultural specificity of the interpretive frameworks ... of devotional viewing' (Gillespie 1995a: 359). All interactions with the medium by Indians are filtered through the cultural suppositions which preclude the analysis, so that the televisual experience becomes, first and foremost, an articulation of the 'religious world view' that these people consciously or unconsciously manifest (Gillespie 1995a: 358).

At the same time, the underlying principle of televisual transmission, namely, flow, is used to reformulate the predominance of the particular 'religious world view ... connecting the religious and social practices in a continuous and interrelated chain' (Mitra 1993: 94).[12] Yet flow, as Raymond Williams has noted, is 'the defining characteristic of broadcasting, simultaneously as a technology and as a cultural form' (Williams 1975: 86). The pre-determined 'world view' ascribed to the Indian/Hindu disallows the effect of this phenomenon from emerging in the depiction of said subject's viewing habits—though Gillespie states that once a 'god film' has been put on, it has to be watched until the end, she makes frequent use of the pause button, which 'encouraged dialogue between ourselves and the texts', to paradoxically reaffirm the concept of 'devotional viewing' (Gillespie 1995a: 358). Similarly, though as Mitra notes, 'following 1992, there has been a rapid growth in television technology and software, with the availability of multiple channels via cable, and that the [Indian] viewer has the choice of watching a large variety of programs', an examination of how this 'external sequence' may affect the viewing of any internal unit—as well as how 'a quality of the external sequence becomes a mode of definition of an internal method' (Williams 1975: 92)—is disallowed by the scholars' limitation of their investigation to the exclusive viewing of this one show: viewing in a vacuum, so to say (Mitra 1993: 168).

These issues dealing with the televisual medium are significantly related to the delineation of the filmic context. Both Gillespie and Mitra have pointed out the thematic overlaps between 'spiritual serials' and Bollywood films ('the system of beliefs that The Mahabharata and The Ramayana propagate are to be found reinscribed and reinstated in every contemporary popular Hindi film') as well as the various structural parallels ('the use of music on Indian television is not very different from the use of music in Indian film') yet, again, these similarities are only used to uphold a 'devotional' model (Gillespie 1995a: 360; Mitra 1993: 109). Rather than seeing the gods of television shows such as Mahabharat as 'impersonations' (Chakravarty 1993), or these shows as being re-inscribed within an external flow of the televisual apparatus similar to the one that constitutes the internal experience of the Bollywood film, the devotional paradigm becomes the only one through which the viewing habits of the Indian are perused.

But a key distinction in terms of these analyses remains: namely, one between the private and public realms that Prasad sets up in relation to the cinematic, as opposed to theatrical, space. In formulating the prohibition placed upon the private, he notes, 'It goes without saying that the illusion of communal cohesion can only be maintained with the active complicity of the audience' (Prasad 1998: 104). The television and video cassette recorder, however, are simultaneously 'facilitating the increasingly central role of domestic as opposed to public worship' (Gillespie 1995a: 360). If, as Gillespie would have it, there is no difference (at least for the Indian/Hindu) between these two realms in terms of 'devotion' to the screened object, then this darsanic complex must be seen as stemming not so much from within the social space of the movie theatre, as from without it. Again, the 'Hindi–Hindu' hegemony disallows 'the Indian viewer' the possibility of ever escaping the forcing-on of this read.

Yet, as Mitra has noted, 'the distinction between education and entertainment has become increasingly fuzzy, as educational programmes have appropriated not only from the entertainment styles of Doordarshan [the Indian government-financed station], but have also relied on imported fare' (Mitra 1993: 80). Similarly, the conflation (*masala*) of various filmic codes in the Indian cinema raises questions over both its alleged proximity to 'the systems of beliefs and values that *The Mahabharata* and *The Ramayana* propagate', as well as to what extent these latter serials actually deploy 'purely religious' material (Gillespie 1995a: 360). The 1976 film, *Satyam Shivam Sundaram* (dir. Raj Kapoor), for instance, presents the voluptuous actress Zeenat Aman, with only a light white cloth over her breasts, 'praying' to a phallus-shaped stone idol of the god Shiva while lip-synching a 'devotional' tune.[13] Such conflation of religious and sexual iconography both illuminates the naïveté of the darsanic model, as well as how said model might be better grasped through the metaphor of impersonation.

The persistence of the darsanic paradigm across differing technological media also reveals a deeper ideology at play in its formulation— '*Darshana* is capable of subverting technology' (Bharucha 1990: 253). If, as Bharucha claims, 'whatever one may think … one cannot deny that' Indian religious television programming 'has been sufficiently convincing … as a source of *darshana*', then one is left with few options (Bharucha 1990). Indeed, Mitra asserts that 'the most recent appropriation by television [of *The Mahabharata*] has not necessarily changed the fundamental aspects of the story in any way', even as, in the next sentence, he mentions it being 'recoded' on television (Mitra 1993: 97).[14] Even though Mitra argues that the structural relationship between programmes is 'the key to classification and the foundation for the analysis of specific programs', that airing *The Mahabharata* on Doordarshan involves 'telling it in a style that is specific to television' and that 'all these factors [for example, television programmes' distinct signifying practices] ultimately play a role in redefining the position of the serial in the popular culture', in his estimation the serial 'retain[s] the fundamentals' and remains fundamentally unchanged (Mitra 1993: 89, 98, 101).

Perhaps most problematic in many of these theorizations of the implied Indian viewer of Indian cinema and television is the general tendency to combine Harold Garfinkel's concept of the 'cultural dope' with collectivizing pronouns, so that the cultural critic becomes both the exception to his rule and immune from critique, romantically claiming that he speaks for all his 'brethren' ('dopey' as they may be).[15] Kakar, for instance, becomes rather mystical in his delineation of 'the third eye' as the metaphor for the effective and necessary approach to take to analysing the Bollywood film (Kakar 1989: 32–33). He also seems inadvertently to describe the true function of such a 'cosmic eye', when he claims, 'Moreover, the third eye also destroys the very identities of the film's characters, replacing them with those of a child's internal family drama' (Kakar 1989). Nevertheless, by positioning themselves as 'speaking for' Indians as a constituted group of cinema and television viewers who are simultaneously shaped according to their speaker's terms, these critics take on (or give themselves) a rather disturbing religious connotation as well.[16]

Worthy of particular notice in regard to this tendency is Madan Gopal Singh's essay, 'Technique as an Ideological Weapon', in which, employing a combination of collectivizing pronouns and Althusserian-inflected Marxism, Singh attempts to describe the precise impoverishment of the Indian cinema viewer's line of vision:

> Our 'lived' experience of cinema is one of seeing ... To be sure, we see
> them [i.e., 'things'] but we do not 'sight' them. On the contrary, we
> tend to 'oversight' them more often than not. We take our seeing so
> narcissistically for granted that we rarely ever bother to find out that

the things we see have already been 'sighted' for us by the camera; that there is a mechanical instrument and, therefore, a whole lot of technical intervention in the 'reality' filtering down to us. We invariably forget—not that we remembered ever—that reality is reproduced mechanically. This is how we fall prey to an 'oversight' which is crucial for the survival of ideology ... Technique as a weapon was never so strong. (Singh 1983: 120)

Given all the talk of 'mechanical instruments' and reality being 're-produced mechanically', one would expect Singh to mention Walter Benjamin's famous essay, 'The Work of Art in the Age of Mechanical Reproduction' (1988), yet he does not. This is indeed unfortunate, as Benjamin has much to say on the matter.[17] Singh's words echo those of Prasad in his analysis of the audience of Indian cinema (from which, at this juncture, he grammatically disassociates himself)—'The consumerist audience of Indian cinema is ... condemned to live at a level of *imaginary* unity ... where everything around seems to confirm the presence of an Ultimate Subject in whose image they—the unknown citizens—are created' (Singh 1983: 125). Just as Prasad's earlier comparison of the song and dance sequence in the Bollywood film to 'a form of spectacle that belongs to the order of contracted performances like stage dances, cabarets and the striptease' is ontologically flawed, so too does Singh's conclusion regarding the aforementioned 'consumerist *symbolic*' operate 'in such a way that it restores the original unity thriving on a mythical absence'—namely, that of the work of art's 'aura', which Benjamin had first brought up in 1936 (Prasad 1998: 77; Singh 1983: 125).

'Even the most perfect reproduction of a work of art is lacking in one element: its presence in time and space, its unique existence at the place where it happens to be' (Benjamin 1988: 220). Benjamin said this missing component, 'which withers in the age of mechanical reproduction is the aura of the work of art' (Benjamin 1988: 221).[18] Film, in particular, serves as 'the most powerful agent' of these processes—i.e., of such an era's artwork substituting 'a plurality of copies for a unique existence', and its simultaneous 'tremendous shattering of tradition' (Benjamin 1988: 221). Whereas the 'original contextual integration of art ... found its expression in the cult', serving an essentially religious purpose, 'mechanical reproduction emancipates the work of art from its parasitical dependence on ritual' (Benjamin 1988: 223–24). Unfortunately, to cross-apply Benjamin's observations to the matter at hand, what seems to have taken place in the theorization of Bollywood—rather than an appreciation of how 'the quantitative shift' of mechanical reproduction has, in turn, produced 'a qualitative transformation' in the work of art's nature—is, to return to Singh's last statement, a reinsertion of that very 'parasitical dependence' (Benjamin 1988: 223-25).

In fact, one can see a synchronic correlation between the 'insensitive and forced character of early theories of the film' (stemming from a 'theatre versus film' dispute in the early decades of the twentieth century) and the body of work on Bollywood cinema, in their respective theoreticians' shared desire 'to read ritual elements into [the film]—with a striking lack of discretion' (Benjamin 1988: 227). This synchronic parallel produces additional cause for concern, given Benjamin's characterization (in 1936) of his day's 'ultrareactionary authors', who gave the film 'a similar contextual significance—if not a sacred one, then at least a supernatural one' (Benjamin 1988: 227-28). Many of the Bollywood scholars who deploy darsanic paradigms simultaneously bemoan the rise of Hindu nationalism in India without realizing how their own theorizations may inadvertently perform the 'work of the (Hindu) right'. Prasad, for instance, begins his study of Hindi film by calling attention to 'western practices of "othering"' in ethnographic studies of Indian popular culture:

> In the west such studies (of reception) are engaged in re-affirming the freedom of the 'free individual' by demonstrating the automaticity and inevitability of audience resistance to ideological interpellation. The individual subject is free because she is so constructed as to never completely fit the position that the text offers her. On the contrary, non-western subjects are distinguished by being completely at home in their ideological environment, the films they see corresponding exactly to their needs. (Prasad 1998: 15)

The very notion of 'cultural need' which Prasad critiques here, and criticizes other (Indian) scholars for reproducing, however, is also reproduced via his own theory of darsanic viewing (as something necessary not only for the Indian viewer but, indeed, to fully understand this viewer and this cinema).

To return to Singh's earlier statement regarding 'seeing' versus 'sighting', one might say (to reread his words with Benjamin's in mind) that the recognition of the loss of aura becomes the basis for the modern individual's engagement with the mechanically reproduced work of art such as the film. Indeed, it is what allows the cinematic audience 'to take the position of a critic', as this audience's primary identification is no longer with the actor but with the camera (Benjamin 1988: 228).[19] Similarly, in relation to the cameraman, Benjamin suggests the analogy of 'a surgical operation', in which, furthermore, 'the surgeon represents the opposite of the magician':

> The magician heals a sick person by the laying on of hands; the surgeon cuts into the patient's body. The magician maintains the natural distance between patient and himself ... The surgeon does exactly the reverse; he greatly diminishes the distance between himself and the patient by penetrating into the patient's body ... In short, in contrast to the magician—who is still hidden in the medical practitioner—the surgeon at the decisive moment abstains from facing the patient man to man; rather, it is through the operation that he penetrates into him. (Benjamin 1988: 233)[20]

Benjamin's passage, in turn, calls to mind a parallel analogy by Metz, describing the above 'operation' from the perspective of the cinema-goer:

> I'm at the cinema. I am present at the screening of the film. *I am present.* Like the midwife attending a birth who, simply by her presence, assists the woman in labour, I am present in a double capacity (though they are really one and the same) as witness and assistant: I watch, and I help. By watching the film I help it to be born, I help it to live, since only in me will it live, and since it is made for that purpose. (Metz 1982: 93)

It is in particular regard to this 'double capacity' that Singh's conception of 'seeing' versus 'sighting' should be (re)appraised. As Metz effectively illustrates, they are, in fact, one and the same—i.e., in 'seeing' the film's images, the viewer has already engaged in 'sighting' them or in reading the look(s) of the camera. Given that the image is thus contingent upon the viewer's mediation, the possibility of 'never remembering', of 'never sighting', becomes possible only if one considers viewers engaging in what Prasad describes darsanic devotees as doing, namely, 'clos[ing] their eyes' (Prasad 1998: 75).

In fact, it is only by conceiving of the cinematic viewer as essentially passive that one could consider the theory of darsanic viewing plausible. Yet, the film viewer, as Metz has noted, is 'constantly in a submotor and hyper-perceptive state' (Metz 1982: 96). Similarly, the cinema's ontological premise—what Benjamin describes as its destruction of aura and Metz, its 'missed encounter' (Metz 1982: 63)—disallows or actively works against this religious frame. In this vein, Metz notes that 'if the film is akin to daydream ... it is separated from it by an irreducible third trait, the materialization, lacking in the daydream and in phantasy generally, of the images and sounds' (Metz 1982: 135). If one takes the 'opiate' point of view regarding the Bollywood cinema, not only must 'the conditions of practising cinema' be seen as 'the conditions of religious art' but, furthermore, as 'the violation of the masses' (Benjamin 1988: 241; Das Gupta 1983: 41).

Such a point of view, roughly seventy years after Benjamin wrote his famous essay and over thirty years after the publication of Metz's *Imaginary Signifier*, is alive and well. Whereas today the style has been refined (so as to omit the kind of outbursts one gets early on in the writings of Sarkar and Das Gupta, for instance), one still has the essential narcotic agent lurking just beneath the refined surface of theoretically dense analysis. Three recent examples of such a trend are Ravi Vasudevan's 'The Politics of Cultural Address' (2000b), Ashish Rajadhyaksha's 'Viewership and Democracy in the Cinema' (2000) and Vijay Mishra's *Bollywood Cinema: Temples of Desire* (2002). Even as Vasudevan begins by stating, 'Especially important here is an agenda of moving beyond the deployment in Indian cinema of a rhetoric of traditional morality and identity to a focus on how cinematic address, the way spectators are positioned in terms of vision, auditory address, and narrative intelligibility, may complicate and rework the overt terms of narrative coherence', he still claims that 'the task here' is 'identifying how the "darsanic" locates characters and is responded to by them' (Vasudevan 2000b: 134, 139). Rather than 'seeing the discourse of "darsana" framing cinematic narration', Vasudevan claims, 'we need to think of "darsana" as being enframed and reconstructed by it' (Vasudevan 2000b: 140). Thus, for instance, '*if* we think of the male icon as a "traditional" marker of authority and desire which anchors the view of the female devotee ... then the scene conforms to the logic of "darsana"' (Vasudevan 2000b: 147).[21] In addition (to return to yet another favourite paradigm

of Bollywood theorists), 'the terms of cinematic narration' that Vasudevan 'sketches' are, by his account, 'rather different from the notions of spectatorship which have emerged from ... Hollywood'–'the
mixed address of the Hindi cinema', instead, 'recalls the notion of a
"cinema of attractions"' (Vasudevan 2000b: 150–51).

So, at the beginning of the twenty-first century, the model the Bollywood film recalls to a leading theorist of the Indian cinema is one
stemming from the beginning of the twentieth century. Furthermore,
he is not alone, as both Ranjani Mazumdar and Lalitha Gopalan also
invoke the 'cinema of attractions' model as relevant to an understanding of popular Hindi film (Gopalan 2002: 19, 129; Mazumdar 2007:
xxxv).[22] Nevertheless, it would be useful to examine this form of cinema
more closely to detect if, unbeknownst to the contemporary Bollywood
theoretician, there exists, even in its antediluvian connotations, an element of subversion. Tom Gunning describes the scenography of the
'cinema of attractions' as 'an exhibitionist one', and one, furthermore,
'opposed to the cinema of the unacknowledged voyeur' (Gunning
1995: 123). Yet, to return in some way to Garfinkel's analysis of the
'cultural dope' (see note 15), Gunning concludes his essay by stating
that 'cinema's first audiences [i.e., those of the "cinema of attractions"]
can no longer serve as a founding myth for the theoreticalization of
the enthralled spectator' (Gunning 1995: 129). Indeed, to do so—or,
following Vasudevan, to revitalize this myth via its cross-application to
Bollywood—would be yet again to displace onto the one 'still seated
beneath', all that the so-called 'incredulous spectator' disavows, just
as, for example, the earlier 'credulous spectators at the Grand Café
in 1895' are 'frequently and complacently evoked by the incredulous
spectators who have come *later* (and are no longer children)' (Metz
1982: 72–73).[23]

Rajadhyaksha, meanwhile, begins by making the apologist argument, claiming that what he 'wants to do here' is to develop '*a theory
of the cinema that can account for the Indian cinema*' (Rajadhyaksha 2000:
269). He then proceeds to delineate Laura Mulvey's famous argument
regarding the voyeurism of classical Hollywood cinema only as a way of
yet again describing 'the difficulty Indian (and generally non-western)
film-makers have with the concept of "story-telling" as in Hollywood
cinema' (Rajadhyaksha 2000: 276). 'Wherever it happens, and however it happens', Rajadhyaksha concludes, 'it appears to be generally

the case' that the implied viewer of Bollywood resists the 'Hollywood Mode of Production', instead becoming 'a citizen subject who fully incarnates his symbolic authority' (Rajadhyaksha 2000: 293).

The religiously inflected language deployed by Rajadhyaksha in delineating Bollywood's implied viewer is significant. Whereas he claims, contrary to earlier theorists (for example, Singh), that 'in basic technical terms, the most untutored, dunderheaded, film viewer would know that what you are seeing on screen is *not* identical to what the camera saw', his 'hazarded conjecture' regarding the 'actual' viewer parallels Prasad's thesis in its suggested 'darsanic underwriting by the Symbolic', a process which highlights this (Indian) spectator's lack of participation 'in the unfolding of the narrative', his/her lack of complicity (Prasad 1998: 103; Rajadhyaksha 2000: 287). At the same time, however, Rajadhyaksha (along with others) makes much of the 'famous "active" and vocal Indian film spectator' and argues that this characteristic is typical of '*spectators identifying themselves* through identifying the film's address' (Rajadhyaksha 2008: 33).[24] Before over-hastily assuming that such instances of 'active engagement' would effectively countermand the notion that the Indian viewer is essentially passive, however, it should be noted that 'active' participation in the cinema does not necessarily entail singing along with the songs or engaging in other forms of vocal outbursts. Active participation entails, rather, a spectator who 'is identifying only with something *seeing*: his own image does not appear on the screen' (Metz 1982: 97). The primary identification of the spectator is not, as Rajadhyakska claims, 'with *himself*' but rather 'with himself as a pure act of perception' (Metz 1982: 49; Rajadhyaksha 2008: 34). It is precisely this form of identification (contrary to that of the child in front of a mirror) that serves as 'the condition of possibility of the perceived' (Metz 1982: 49). The spectator, in other words, regardless of whether he is Indian and vocal or Indian and silent, is 'able to constitute a world of objects without having first to recognize himself within it' (Metz 1982: 46).[25]

Similarly, though Vijay Mishra states in the Preface to his recent study that 'there is no simple theory of Bombay (Bollywood) cinema', his first chapter begins by reaffirming a devotional model, one in which cinemas, as his book's subtitle suggests, are 'the temples of modern India', places where 'devotees come in huge numbers to worship, "to take *darsana*", at the shrine of the new image, the oneiric image that will

create their new gods and even their new beliefs' (Mishra 2002: xviii, 1).
In proceeding to delineate the Bombay cinema as 'a grand syntagm that
functions as one heterogeneous text under the sign of a transcendental
dharmik principle', Mishra employs theoretical film language (invoking
Metz, no less) only to reaffirm an infantilizing/devotional paradigm,
even as his 'indebtedness' to Rajadhyaksha and Prasad, as he puts it,
becomes evident (Mishra 2002: 13). As in Rajadhyaksha's case, Mishra
attempts to 'accommodate' the Indian viewer and the subsequent
'deep fantasies' belonging to or associated with him/her (Mishra 2002:
4). Again, as in the methodologies of previous Bollywood theorists,
a key binary in assessing this cinema becomes that of 'modernity/
tradition'—one, Mishra aptly notes, 'that has been detected by almost
all commentators of this form' (Mishra 2002).[26]

Thus, while current, postcolonial Indian film and theatre scholarship claims to be 'sweeping the ground anew' or employing a 'fresh'
start, a continued adherence to a devotional paradigm, stemming from
and linked to religious/theatrical models from the past, works to dele-
gitimize this claim and, rather, illuminates a consistent adherence to
a familiar pattern of 'subject–object' positioning in which the focus of
historical inquiry (popular Hindi cinema and televisual programming)
is predetermined—indeed, overdetermined—by its methodology. Such
approaches, in turn, become forms of totalizing (i.e., oversimplifying)
categorization in which neither the subject matter nor its implied
viewer is allowed to escape from the Procrustean bed of 'Indianness',
despite its often conflicting and contested nature.

Having concluded my critical overview of some of the dominant
trends and themes (and misperceptions) in the field of Bollywood
Studies, I shall now proceed to develop the first of a series of alternative readings into the dynamics that make up the Bollywood film. The
insights gleaned in this chapter, particularly regarding the cinematic
underpinnings of the implied viewer's engagement with/in Bollywood,
will continue to resonate throughout the rest of this work, serving as a
reference point and base for subsequent reframings.

NOTES

1. For a discussion of the *masala* trope, see Armes (1987), Lent et al. (1990), Chakravarty
    (1993) and Shohat and Stam (1994).

2. Kakar furthermore contrasts the 'collective fantasy' of Bollywood to 'individualized fantasy' which is 'infinitely more complex' (Kakar 1983: 89). This essay is an earlier, shorter version of Kakar's third chapter in *Intimate Relations*, 'Lovers in the Dark'.

3. Kakar goes on to note that 'psychiatric observations in India ... amply bear this out' (Kakar 1983: 91).

4. Along with Cesaire, Frantz Fanon also engages in a critique of Mannoni in *Black Skin, White Masks* (1952), particularly in Chapter 4, 'The So-Called Dependency Complex of Colonized Peoples'. Unfortunately, neither Cesaire nor Fanon comes up in Kakar's discussion.

5. The book Metz refers to is Mannoni's *L'Illusion comique ou le theatre du point de vue de l'imaginaire* (1969).

6. Metz describes the 'missed encounter' in the following manner: 'In the theatre, actors and spectators are present at the same time and in the same location, hence present one to another ... But in the cinema, the actor was present when the spectator was not (=shooting), and the spectator is present when the actor is no longer (=projection)' (Metz 1982: 63).

7. *Bobby* is mentioned by Sarkar (1975: 12, 86, 101) and by Kakar, who lists it as 'one of the biggest box office hits of the last twenty years' and one he subsequently claims to use (among others) as the basis for 'the composite love story' which he analyses in *Intimate Relations* (Kakar 1989: 30, 149, n. 6). Prasad also mentions it as one of the 'successes of the period' though, like the other two, does not discuss it in detail (Prasad 1998: 139).

8. She does not look up directly at the camera in this shot.

9. To see such song sequences as providing an 'inner' view of the 'private realm' also problematizes the notion of Bollywood as necessarily being an 'anti-psychological' cinema. For more on this latter view, see Nandy, 'An Intelligent Critic's Guide to Indian Cinema' (1995: 204-05). Furthermore, the cinematic style of 'Hum Tum' can be seen as typical of the romantic song sequence during this period (1970s). A cursory list of other Bollywood films with such sequences could include *Roti, Kapada aur Makaan* (1974), *Julie* (1975), *Kabhi Kabhie* (1976), *Satyam Shivam Sundaram* (1978), *Trishul* (1978), *Qurbani* (1980), *Silsila* (1981), *Naseeb* (1981) and *Love Story* (1981).

10. This 'disaggregation' of the Indian film industry, according to Prasad, was the result of 'a new approach to film financing by the Film Finance Corporation (FFC) in 1969', made possible by Indira Gandhi's 'interventionist policies'. Essentially, the FFC launched 'a financing policy aimed at the development of "good cinema"', i.e., not Bollywood. The resulting dissemination of funds resulted in the establishment of a parallel industry that presented potential competition to the commercial industry, particularly given that 'the new aesthetic programme was unified by an oppositional stance towards the commercial cinema'. Effects of this new approach on the latter industry included the breakdown of 'the dominant textual form's consensus-effect' and simultaneously the launching of a quest for 'new modes and targets of address' (Prasad 1998: 121-24, 138).

11. Some of the films Kazmi mentions that were 'spawned' by *Bobby* and featured similar 'young lovers' in such scenarios include *Ek Duje ke Liye* (1981), *Qayamat Se Qayamat Tak* (1988), *Maine Pyar Kiya* (1989), *Dil* (1990), *Anari* (1993) and *Dilwale Dulhaniya Le Jayenge* (1995). See also note 9. For more on the private realm in Bollywood song sequences and their creation of private selves, see Gopal and Sen (2008).

12. Though he begins his previous chapter, 'Doordarshan: A Critical Glance', with an epigraph by Raymond Williams (from *Marxism and Literature*), Mitra never mentions the latter's *Television* (1975), in which the concept of 'flow' is discussed.

13. While in Jeremy Marre's *There'll Always Be Stars in the Sky* (1983), director Kapoor states, 'The best film is a film that does not raise any controversy', in *India Today* he said, 'Let people come to see Zeenat's tits, they'll go out remembering the film' (1978).

14. Interestingly enough, Mitra states earlier in a footnote that 'television formation refers to the duality of television where it is a cultural aesthetic form by itself while it also produces or "forms" popular culture around the television texts and narratives' (Mitra 1993: 75, n. 1). Leaving aside for the moment his simultaneous omission and reformulation of Williams' concept of flow here (i.e., Mitra conceives of the two—technology and culture—as distinct forms), he does acknowledge that television is 'a cultural aesthetic form by itself'. This would, at the very least, suggest the possibility of not only a 'recoding' but also, potentially, a change in 'fundamental aspects of the [televisual] story' (Mitra 1993: 97). Bharucha meanwhile may be biased against the televisual medium in general, referring to it as 'the idiot box' (Bharucha 1990: 253). Ashish Rajadhyaksha reveals a similar bias against the flow of televisual programming in India, claiming that 'the cultural damage being done through the mass entertainment of [television] "serials" is incalculable' (Rajadhyaksha 1989: 178).

15. As Garfinkel notes:

> The misleading character of the use of the judgmental dope to portray the relationship between standardized expectancies and courses of action goes to the problem of adequate explanation as the controlling consideration in the investigator's decision to either consider or disregard the common sense rationalities when deciding the necessary relationships between courses of action, given such problematic considerations as perspectival choice, subjectivity and inner time. A favoured solution is to portray what the member's actions will have come to by using the stable structures—i.e., what they *came* to—as a point of theoretical departure from which to portray the necessary character of the pathways whereby the end result is assembled. Hierarchies of need dispositions, and common culture as enforced rules of action, are favoured devices for bringing the problem of necessary inference to terms, although at the cost of making out the person-in-society to be a judgmental dope. (1967: 68)

16. Specific critics who employ the collective pronoun include Sarkar (1975), Ray (1976), Kakar (1989), Bharucha (1990) and Singh (1983). See Philip Lutgendorf's 'Indian Theatre and Inside-Outsider' (1992), for a critique of this tendency on Bharucha's part.

17. None of the theorists discussed in this chapter mention Benjamin's 'Work of Art' in their studies.

18. Benjamin defines 'aura' as 'the unique phenomenon of a distance, however close it may be' (Benjamin 1988: 222).

19. This was the approach Benjamin referred to as 'testing'—an effective rejoinder (from the past, as it were) to Singh's 'sighting'/'oversighting' model. Furthermore, 'it is inherent in the technique of the film ... that everybody who witnesses its accomplishments is somewhat of an expert' (Benjamin 1988: 231).

20. Benjamin goes on to state, 'Magician and surgeon compare to painter and cameraman'.

21. Vasudevan makes this claim in relation to his analysis of *Devdas* (1955).

22. Gopalan begins by noting that to invoke this term, 'reminiscent of early cinema', to discuss Bollywood would be 'dismiss[ive]', yet she goes on—on the very same page—to invoke precisely this term in discussing Bollywood (Gopalan 2002: 19).

23. The one 'still seated beneath', i.e., the 'credulous spectator', being, in this case, the implied Bollywood viewer. Metz is referring here to the now (in)famous 'original' spectators of the Lumiere Bros' film featuring a train entering La Ciotat station, who 'fled their seats in terror ... because they were afraid it [the filmed train] would run them down' (Metz 1982: 72–73).

24. Other Bollywood theorists also invoke this 'vocal' Indian spectator, including Dudrah (2006: 64), Dissanayake (2003: 223) and Prasad (1998: 104).

25. The key point here is that even if the Indian viewer is vocal, this does not override the basic Metzian tenet of primary identification with the camera nor does it entail a reversal of this basic premise. As Metz notes, 'the filmic spectacle, the object seen, is more radically ignorant of its spectator, since he is not there, than the theatrical spectacle can ever be' (Metz 1982: 64). This is precisely the basis of cinema's 'missed encounter'. To say otherwise would again equate the Indian viewer with a child who is incapable of either engaging in cinematic spectatorship or, indeed, of comprehending that the film(ed) objects 'are not there'. This, unfortunately, seems to be the implication of Rajadhyaksha's attempt to 'accommodate' said '"active" and vocal' viewer (Rajadhyaksha 2008: 33). One can indeed detect parallels between Rajadhyaksha's theorization here and the previous accounts given by Kakar (1989) and Prasad (1998) of this (implied, Indian) viewer's engagement with on-screen events.

26. One may, in this instance, read 'detected' as a thinly veiled euphemism for 'imposed', in the manner that 'accommodating' (the Indian film viewer) can be seen as 'pandering' to him/her.

The Bollywood Song and Dance, or Making a Culinary Theatre from Dung-cakes and Dust*

The preceding chapter examined how an indigenous religious frame is used to (under)theorize popular Hindi cinema and its implied viewers. Another dominant paradigm, in this case stemming from the West, that is used to position the Bollywood film and its implied viewers within an antediluvian context is the musical frame, particularly as exemplified by Hollywood's 'Golden Years' of this genre, the 1930s to 1950s. In a double sense, contemporary Bollywood cinema is wedded to a pre-localized 'West' and a pre-localized (and previous) era, thus positioning its song and dance sequences as imitative (of Hollywood musicals), a framing furthered by the notion that Bollywood comes 'so far behind' Hollywood's 'Golden' era (i.e., roughly half a century later). This latter point, in turn, is seen as reflecting India's greater 'backwardness', that is, still playing the endless colonial catch-up game.

Indeed, Jane Feuer's conclusion in her work on the referenced 'Golden era', *The Hollywood Musical*, that 'the ritual marriage celebrated at the end of virtually every musical during the studio era was also a ritual celebration of a continuing marriage between Hollywood and the mass audience' (Feuer 1982: 85), is re-invoked, twenty years later, in a different context—namely, twenty-first century India—by Justine

---

* An earlier version of this chapter first appeared as an article in *Quarterly Review of Film and Video* 23 (4): 331–40.

Hardy in her book, *Bollywood Boy*, when she writes, 'In the world of Bollywood, India finds a panacea for all her ills. The poverty of life on the streets and in the rural villages is countered by the lushness of movieland sets and locations. The daily grey of arranged married life is made Technicolor by wild love stories' (Hardy 2002: 19).

Given this rather regressive state of affairs, a brief recounting of this earlier, American musical form becomes necessary, so as to define its (proto)typical characteristics, both as a genre and in its various applications within a context identified as 'modern', and simultaneously work to distinguish the contemporary Bollywood song and dance number from this outdated partner/parent. In doing so, I will reconsider several of Feuer's conclusions regarding the Brechtian capabilities of the musical as a form, as well as how the Bollywood song and dance reconfigures this older/Western form. This chapter, then, will provide an alternative reading of what has been called 'the single most enduring feature of popular Hindi cinema' (Gopal and Moorti 2008: 1). Indeed, we shall see how the Bollywood film engages in its own hyperreal, hybrid and reflexive approaches to storytelling, using song and dance sequences in ways radically differing from those entailed by either the devotional or Hollywood musical model.

In the process, this chapter will also develop further the work begun in the first chapter towards deconstructing notions of 'Indianness' as they relate to cinematic representation and representability. While the first chapter demonstrated the loopholes in the devotional model's linkage of theatrical techniques such as frontality and direct address to a religious perspective, Chapter 2 examines how the Bollywood film's use of such techniques (for example, frontality and direct address) more closely approximates a form of Brechtian distanciation.[1] Such a dual perspective—the song and dance as voyeuristic, the song and dance as Brechtian—serves as a compelling instance of Christian Metz's claim that 'the film is exhibitionist, and at the same time it is not' (Metz 1982: 93). Or at least, as he goes on to note, that 'there are several kinds of exhibitionism, and correspondingly several kinds of voyeurism, several possible ways of deploying the scopic drive, not all of which are equally reconciled' (Metz 1982: 93). This last point is particularly relevant here, as it reflects (to read along Metz's lines) the multiple frames that Bollywood films employ and thus, as this chapter will demonstrate, a rejection of monolithic interpretations of how such theatrical techniques can or, indeed, must be used in song and dance sequences. Thus, read in tandem, these opening chapters can be seen as furthering this book's larger aim, i.e., to destabilize the positioning of Bollywood within any one sphere of reference and, rather, to illuminate how several spheres of meaning are simultaneously at play within its construction.

An echo of such an approach is heard in Lalitha Gopalan's claim that 'when we turn to Indian cinema, we have to frame both theories— cinema of attractions based on spatial and temporal disjunctions, and scopophilia ... as the only satisfactory method to read its simultaneous use of both kinds of cinematic styles' (Gopalan 2002: 109). While I clearly agree that the dual or multiple frames model is the most effective approach, I question Gopalan's invocation of the 'cinema of attractions' moniker as the most appropriate to take in characterizing the (contemporary) Bollywood song and dance. As noted previously, Gopalan begins by critiquing dismissive attempts to designate such moments in films as 'sequences of attractions', arguing that 'song and dance sequences deserve another look' (Gopalan 2002: 19). However, in the very next paragraph, she goes on to employ precisely this term (which she continually invokes throughout her study) in discussing the song and dance sequence in Bollywood. At the same time, even as she references Feuer's analysis of Hollywood musicals in invoking this 'early cinema' model, Brecht goes unmentioned in her discussion of Bollywood as a 'cinema of interruptions' (Gopalan 2002: 129, 140).

Ranjani Mazumdar similarly invokes the 'cinema of attractions' model in addressing the song and dance, claiming that 'in the context of the form of popular Bombay cinema, Gunning's argument has been evocative since song sequences ... function as a landscape of "attractions"' (Mazumdar 2007: xxxvi). In this chapter, however, I will be suggesting that rather than the proto-modern 'cinema of attractions' model, it would be more effective (and timely) to see Bollywood song and dance sequences as occupying what Mazumdar calls 'the experiential realm of the postmodern' as a way of giving these sequences 'another look', particularly given the broader misconceptions that abound regarding Bollywood's irreducible 'time lag' in relation to its (always already) 'more advanced' commercial counterpart (Mazumdar 2007: 190). To invoke a term that originally applied to a form of Western cinema in the early twentieth century to characterize Bollywood nearly a century later seems to both suggest pre-determined limits to this latter cinema's innovative potentiality and serve as an echo of the primary focus in this chapter, namely, the attempt to (mis)read Bollywood songs in Hollywood musical terms.[2] Thus, rather than 'reformulat[ing]' Feuer's analysis of the musical 'for Bollywood', this chapter will demonstrate how the Bollywood song and dance reformulates Feuer's analysis (Dudrah 2006: 53–54).

In the second chapter of her book, entitled 'Spectators and Spectacles', Feuer discusses the role of direct address in the Hollywood musical stemming from the Golden Years. While pointing out that this technique 'is often cited as one of the chief means of "distanciation" in modernist theatre and film', Feuer concludes that, unlike the films of Jean-Luc Godard (1960s to 1970s) or the theatre of Bertolt Brecht (1920s to 1940s), the Hollywood musical's use of this technique ultimately entails a remystification of what, in Brecht's and Godard's cases, is essentially a technique of demystification. Furthermore, according to Feuer, 'it's absolutely essential' to see such a technique 'in this historical context', i.e., of the 'Golden Years', one in which, as she later puts it, 'the boundary between real and imaginary' was placed 'en abime' (Feuer 1982: 35, 39, 77). Unless we see the Hollywood musical in 'its proper place', concludes Feuer, 'we may mistake it for a modernist film' (Feuer 1982: 47).

The crucial distinction, in her opinion, between 'the goals of musicals and those of Godard'—which, she further argues, 'must surely be opposed'—is due, despite their 'identical methods', to 'what is being conveyed by the direct address *and the traditions behind those messages*' (Feuer 1982: 36, emphasis added). This latter appeal to tradition is constantly re-invoked by Feuer to reaffirm, each time, the pre-identified (necessary) opposition between the Brechtian/Godardian and Hollywoodian approaches, the latter being a register in which 'the potentially disorienting effects of the break in narrative are minimized' (Feuer 1982). Focussing on a particular category of musical number she calls 'the "Ode to Entertainment"', Feuer examines a series of Hollywood musicals featuring this reflexive element (Feuer 1982). In each case, Feuer first delineates the use of 'direct address' in songs in these films—for instance, Maurice Chevalier glancing at and singing to the film audience in *The Love Parade* (1929) or *Gigi* (1958)—and then points out that 'were such a device [i.e., direct address] inserted into a Godard film ... it would no doubt wrench us from our immersion in the constructed flow of the narrative' but that, in each case—whether in 1929 or 1939 or 1949 or 1953—'the tradition that evoked it [i.e., the Hollywood musical featuring direct address] cancels any critical tendencies toward that tradition' (Feuer 1982: 38–39, emphasis added). Thus, 'direct address is indeed an "alienation effect" in the Brechtian sense [in these instances] but it does not "alienate" us in the everyday sense of the term' (Feuer 1982: 41). This, again, is due to such numbers' invocation of the tradition of illusionism in which 'the demystifying shot is never used alone', but 'always cut in with shots ... which mystify the performance' (Feuer 1982: 43).

This, Feuer holds, is also true in the case of that 'seemingly even more Brechtian ... penchant the backstage [Hollywood] musical has for revealing its own inner gears', in which—unlike in 'modernist films', where 'remystification is an undesired by-product'—'a new mystification is the desired end result of demystification', and the 'split' narrative 'gets sutured back together again for the final bow' (Feuer 1982: 42–44). Even in 1954, when, as Feuer states, 'A Star is Born could ... be cynical about two of Hollywood's most cherished myths: that movies materialize out of the air, and that movie stars are just as charming and glamorous off-screen as on', mystification 'always' comes back and 'folk relations are restored' (Feuer 1982: 45). Similarly, Singin' in the Rain (1952), though engaging in the demystification of sound technology in movie musicals, 'demystifies only in order to restore illusion' (Feuer 1982: 46).

The Hollywood musical of the Golden Years, then, only appears to be 'constantly breaking through its glossy surface'; in reality, it is constantly reinscribed within—even as it reinscribes—its pre-identified 'traditions', those that 'deny technological calculation' even as they 'frequently lay bare their own' (Feuer 1982: 47). The resulting tendency is for the viewer of such fare to be (potentially) 'disoriented', only to be (ultimately) re-positioned within the illusory realm (i.e., 'assured'). Even in 'reflexive codas' that accompany the conclusions of 'wedding songs' and finales—for example, 'Be a Clown' in The Pirate (1948)—'forms of illusionism ... are replaced by theatrical illusionism', which 'liberates the dreamer [film viewer] from the constraints of day-dreaming'; 'Dorothy', in other words, 'need never return to Kansas' (Feuer 1982: 83–84). The Hollywood musical from this era, rather than allowing for a Brechtian alienation effect, or Verfremdung, 'presents its vision of the unfettered human spirit in a way that forecloses a desire to translate that vision into reality' (Feuer 1982: 84). The 'very terms it set up for itself' (or, perhaps, that Feuer sets up for it), 'however unconsciously, as an apology for mass art, prevented the musical from ever breaking out of its self-imposed hermetic universe' (Feuer 1982).

What, then, of Bollywood? Perhaps we might start by skipping twenty years ahead from the publication of Feuer's study to Hardy's *Bollywood Boy*, a book that begins by comparing Bombay (predominant site of Bollywood film production and now called Mumbai) to 'a woman's body in recline', with 'nipples of wealth' (Hardy 2002: 1). In this work, the author, like Feuer, works to situate this film industry within a particular context, namely, that of 'the oppression and omnipresent poverty of southern Asia', in which (thus) 'the current finely tuned Bollywood formula has evolved to give the audience maximum escapism and minimum reality' (Hardy 2002: 16). When the lights go down, Hardy claims, 'every member of the audience knows what they [sic] are going to get', namely, 'what they want and what they have paid to see'— dream/illusion (Hardy 2002: 17).

'These people', Hardy says (i.e., the villagers who make up, in her view, 'the core of India's filmgoers'), 'do not want realism'—'they want to be transported' (Hardy 2002: 22). As with Feuer and the Hollywood musical, a pre-located culture (and cultural desire) is summoned to position the Bollywood film within a tradition, i.e., 'its proper place', namely, among the 'smell of burning dung cakes', or rather, the romanticized 'reality' of India and Indians today (Feuer 1982: 47; Hardy 2002: 23). This sphere is similarly employed to demarcate the precise theoretical boundaries of the Bollywood film, particularly as a potential Brechtian alienation device.

Satyajit Ray once wrote, 'If I were asked to find room for six songs in a story that is not expressly a "musical", I would have to throw up my hands and give up. If I were forced, I would either revolt or go berserk' (Ray 1976: 73). Yet, as Ray notes, 'six songs per film, per *every* film, is the accepted average' (Ray 1976). Ray claims he 'would not mind the songs if they did not go against the grain of a film' and similarly calls attention to the disjuncture between singing voice (i.e., playback) and speaking voice (i.e., diegetic sound) in the Bollywood film, claiming, 'To one not familiar with the practice [i.e., of playback] the change of timbre usually comes as a jolt' (Ray 1976: 74).[3] Similarly, in discussing the choreographic patterns of these song and dance sequences,

Ray notes, 'It is not uncommon these days to have each line of a lyric sung against a different scenic background.' This is—and I am not being facetious—a daring innovation, wholly cinematic and entirely valid *if it is related in style to the rest of the film*', i.e., 'played in a style that makes for smooth transitions' to the songs (Ray 1976: 74, emphasis added).

Ray recalls reading a critique of a Hindi film in an American magazine 'which actually praised the use of songs as a sort of Brechtian alienation device, something that purposely makes the spectator aware of the artificiality of the whole thing' (Ray 1976: 73). His response? 'I do not know if the filmmakers themselves think of the songs in these terms' (Ray 1976). Thus, even though, as Feuer has pointed out, in a somewhat different context, 'in order for Godard's distancing technique to work, he has to assume that everyone is acquainted with the rules of classical Hollywood filmmaking' (Feuer 1982: 35)—an assumption Feuer makes in considering the distancing capabilities of the French *auteur*'s films—in the context of popular Hindi films, familiarity with these estranging devices is either not assumed to exist (on the filmmakers' part) or, if it does, works against the possibility of the films being seen as estranging (as in the case of mainstream audiences). The latter, according to Ray, are not jolted by the defamiliarity of the playback—'for the audiences here', the Bengali *auteur* declares, 'the jolt would probably come if they did not recognise one of their six favorites in the playback' (Ray 1976: 74).

Similarly, while the abrupt shifts of setting within these songs may be considered 'a daring innovation', it is only 'valid' if it is stylistically related to the rest of the film, as opposed to, for instance, considering this very discordance of/between elements—the abrupt rupturing of the narrative by the song(s)—as the core of its 'Brechtian' negotiation (Ray 1976: 74). Such a view, however, would imply an intentionality on the part of the filmmakers and viewers, a possibility that is once again refuted by the reinvocation of 'tradition'. Just as, within the context of Hollywood musicals in the Golden era, Feuer argued that a 'marriage' existed between studio and viewer which precluded the possibility of Brechtian demystification, so, too, in the eyes of India's most internationally recognized (though perhaps most domestically unknown) *auteur*, with the Indian viewer and Bollywood.

Perhaps unsurprisingly, the one other theorist who does bring up Brecht in relation to Bollywood, Fareed Kazmi, also opposes the dramatic conventions associated with this personage to those of the popular Hindi cinema which, in turn, he labels 'conventional' (Kazmi 1999: 56). In thus setting up Bollywood in definitional opposition to either a Brechtian approach or what he calls an 'innovative cinema', Kazmi creates a semantic impasse for Bollywood as, according to his premise, to define Bollywood as an 'innovative' cinema would indeed be a contradiction in (his) terms. Furthermore, 'even though Brecht's epic structure is theoretically the ideal democratic form' for a popular cinema, 'the chances are that it [Brecht's epic structure] will not be received by the people, especially the subalterns, since it is too intellectualized to be easily understood' (Kazmi 1999: 229).[4] To better understand, then, how contemporary Bollywood film functions, in relation to both the Hollywood musical of the previous Golden era and a Brechtian aesthetic, it is crucial to examine some actual song and dance sequences from recent Bollywood films.

Dil Se... (From the Heart, 1998) is a commercial Hindi film by Tamil director Mani Ratnam. It tells the story of Amar, a journalist played by actor Shah Rukh Khan (hereafter SRK), and Meghna, a potential suicide bomber played by Manisha Koirala, against the backdrop of military standoffs in the troubled north-eastern region. The film, at a little over two and a half hours, features five songs (i.e., one roughly every thirty minutes), which engage in a combination of strategies and diegeses, all of which can be seen as adhering to Ray's delineations of the prototypical Hindi film song. The first song, 'Chaiyya, Chaiyya', is a six and a half minute departure from the narrative proper, beginning after SRK has first glimpsed Koirala one rainy night at a train station. As her train leaves, SRK crouches under his jacket holding the two teas he had brought for him and her, even as—with the soundbridge of the rain—the music begins and the scene abruptly changes: it is now broad daylight and a(nother) woman is seductively rising from sleep on top of a moving train. She is surrounded by others—men and women, all in colourful Indian garb—and as the music gradually develops, they rise and begin dancing on top of the moving train. SRK rises, too, suddenly, amidst the bodies and as he begins lip-synching the song's title, the playback begins and all the others begin simultaneously shaking their heads to the beat, as does SRK.

This song and dance, then, featuring eighty cuts and culminating in the camera pulling up and away, even as the playback fades, into the snow-covered mountains and then descending back into the diegetic world, has no clear relationship with the film story. When we see SRK again, he is emerging from a bus and, furthermore, the woman he dances with atop the train never reappears, nor does SRK, for that matter, make any reference to the previous six and a half minutes of singing and dancing on top of a moving train. It takes place, in other words, entirely within a fantasy diegesis, one rupturing the narrative even as it is removed from it formally and aesthetically. SRK and the other dancers employ performative gestures that are highly choreographed and synchronized. Furthermore, the camera, along with making eighty cuts in six and a half minutes, pans, swoops and swirls around the dancers and the moving train, i.e., repeatedly calls attention to itself as a framing device. In other words, different and conflicting registers are evoked: though one might construe this as SRK's fantasy (i.e., from his point of view), he performs for the camera in it, thus creating the possibility that this is our (i.e., the audience's) fantasy, even as the camera's aforementioned reflexivity creates the alternate possibility that this is *its* fantasy (i.e., one constructed/assembled and 'put forth' by the cinematic apparatus).[5]

Similarly, the third song, 'Satrangi Re', takes place in a fantasy diegesis after an abrupt cut from SRK 'interrupting' Koirala while she takes a bath (featuring half a minute of shot/reverse-shot). Suddenly we are (the camera is) moving forward at a medium-fast pace through the crumbling clay ruins of some exotic landscape; the sound of the wind on the soundtrack is accentuated. The camera, after nearly another half minute of swirling through these chiaroscuro caverns giving way to immense canyons, suddenly descends to 'find' Koirala, now dressed in a rather ornate black outfit, who begins dancing just as the camera frames her (in direct address), just as the playback/rhythm begins. There will be seventy-four cuts and approximately ten scene changes in the next six minutes, featuring SRK and Koirala engaging in a series of highly choreographed articulations before abruptly shifting backdrops (for example, from the mountains to the desert to the snow to the desert, etc.) and subsequent costume changes. At one point, the camera follows Koirala walking away in a desert landscape, looking back (direct address), then descending to her reflection in a pool of water, even as direct address is maintained, turning around and pulling back to reveal Koirala in a snow-covered landscape. These formalizations of the fantasy diegesis by the cinematic apparatus work to heighten the song and dance's hyperreality as well as its detachment from the story proper. Again, the 'return' is achieved through an abrupt cut from SRK in Koirala's lap (both wearing white) in a snowy landscape, to a desert/mountain landscape (no snow) and SRK arriving at the steps of a Buddhist temple where Koirala is seated (again no recognition by either party of the previous six and a half minutes), taking her by the hand to a Buddhist priest and telling him, 'We want to get married', to which Koirala replies, 'He's crazy' and walks away.

In other words, what Peter Wollen, in reference to Godard, calls 'multiple diegesis'—i.e., multiple narrative worlds—exists in both these instances (Wollen, quoted in Feuer 1982: 68). In this vein (i.e., the Godardian context), 'multiple diegesis ... takes its meaning in antithesis to the "single diegesis" of the classic narrative cinema' (Feuer 1982). Whereas 'both the Hollywood musical and modernist cinema use dual worlds to mirror within the film the relationship of the spectator to the film', again 'the musical and Godard are worlds apart in their goals' (Feuer 1982). Whereas, in the latter's films, multiple diegesis 'may call attention to the discrepancy between fiction and reality', in the Hollywood musical, 'heterogeneous levels are created so that they may be homogenized in the end through the union of the romantic couple' (Feuer 1982: 68).

In the examples from *Dil Se...*, the 'multiple diegesis' works to *heighten* the 'discrepancy'(ies) between these registers, both through techniques of defamiliarization within these multiple diegeses (for example, their constant and inexplicable shifts) and their renunciation within/by the 'formal diegesis' of the story plot (for example, 'He's crazy'). Rather than being sandwiched between remystifying frames that 'overcome difference' and 'synthesize', these songs bifurcate the text and reveal, even as they revel in, these 'gaps'. For a demonstration of the precise difference between the Hollywood musical's negotiation of 'multiple diegesis' and that of/in Bollywood, consider (in relation to the song and dance sequences of *Dil Se...*) the dream-sequence song and dance in *Yolanda and the Thief* (1945), an 'obvious exception' to the rule of seamless transitions from 'dialogue' to 'song', or one diegesis to another (Feuer 1982: 77). In the Hollywood musical, rather than the dream sequence being placed '*en abime*', its positioning 'disorients' the spectator, who only gradually 'begins to realize' that Fred Astaire has entered a different diegesis (Feuer 1982).

Contrast, then, the 'novelty of this sequence' within its social register(s), invoking (in an 'obvious exception to the rule') 'disorientation' and 'confusion' in the spectator through its 'questioning of the boundary between dream and reality' (Feuer 1982: 79), to the prototypical nature of such shifts within the Bollywood film—in fact, so typical that, as Ray puts it, 'the jolt would probably come if they [the popular Indian film audience] did not recognize one of their six favourites [i.e., singers] in the playback' (Ray 1976: 74). In other words, despite this implied audience's 'familiarity' with the codes (which, in other contexts, is considered a prerequisite for the 'estrangement' of 'modernist art' to 'work'), despite these song and dance sequences' adherence to a Brechtian method of inserting the song in(to) the narrative—i.e., as a way of 'breaking up' the story and creating 'multiple diegesis'—despite these song sequences' 'innovative' disjunctures (e.g., of the playback, the choreography and acting styles), the possibility of seeing the Bollywood song and dance in such a reflexive vein is dismissed out of hand for lack of intentionality on the directors' parts and plausibility in terms of its implied viewers, i.e., the starving masses who (only) want 'illusionism' and who, furthermore, would be incapable of comprehending the 'intellectualized' Brechtian discourse (Hardy 2002: 17; Kazmi 1999: 229; Ray 1976: 73).

Though roughly fifty years have passed since the 'Golden Era' of Hollywood musicals, Bollywood is still seen as occupying this older space, primarily through an invocation of the cultural sphere of 'dung cakes' by media-ethnographers like Hardy who, though acknowledging the presence of other contingencies/audiences (for example, urban audiences and non-resident Indian [NRI] viewers), insist that these 'people in the dust ... make up the core of Bollywood's audience', whose implied desires (as invoked by Hardy) are used to re-situate the Bollywood film within a model of remystification (Hardy 2002: 22). Yet, Hardy concedes that 'once *Dil Se...* went on the international circuit, it became one of the most successful Hindi films to date', thereby implying that the labelling of 'illusionistic' or 'non-illusionistic' is contingent upon the implied audience and not the film itself (Hardy 2002: 23). Furthermore, invoking such a contrast reaffirms the high/low gap between, on the one hand, urban and village dwellers and, on a larger scale, resident and non-resident Indians (i.e., dung-cakes or cell phones).

Yet, though this native lumpen-proletariat allegedly lacks the discerning consciousness necessary to recognize the shifting registers of the Bollywood film's 'multiple diegesis' (and its subsequent 'modernist', i.e., 'Brechtian/Godardian', reformulations of both the work of art and the process of engaging with it), Hardy describes them as 'looking up' (from their crouched position in the dust) at the screen, 'tilt[ing] their heads to catch SRK's every pelvic thrust', and 'strain[ing] their necks' [to get a better view], i.e., engaging in (and displaying) what Christian Metz interprets 'not so much [as] a "reading competence" but rather the management of an encounter between one side, an agency that "releases" ... the film ... and on the other side, another agency that "receives" the film and "who may therefore see what the text does not want me to see"' (Hardy 2002: 22; Metz, quoted in Rajadhyaksha 2000: 270). One can thus trace the so-called familiarity with these shifts in/between 'multiple diegesis' on the part of the native (i.e., 'core') Bollywood audience along the lines of what Ray calls their 'expectation', Hardy, 'what every member of the audience knows ... they are going to get', and Feuer, in a differing context, refers to as the 'precondition' for (Godardian) distanciation to 'work' (Feuer 1982: 35; Hardy 2002: 16–17; Ray 1976: 74). In other words, the native, dust-covered viewer of popular Hindi films may be considered an 'expert' viewer, whose interest (i.e., engagement) is born from astonishment and 'who does not think unless they [sic] have a reason to' (Benjamin 1966: 4). It is precisely to such an audience that 'epic theatre addresses itself', a form(at) that 'uncover[s] conditions' through the 'process of interruption' (Benjamin 1966: 4–5). Therein, one might say, to paraphrase Benjamin, lies the formal achievement of both Brecht's and Bollywood's 'crude songs'—precisely in their ability to 'break up' the narrative proper and inject a level of 'astonishment' within the viewing process.

While Kazmi acknowledges that Brechtian devices (such as direct address) have been 'appropriated and used quite often in conventional films', he simultaneously finds it necessary to make 'a small clarification', namely, that 'it is not as if all the techniques used by innovative and modernist cinema are incorporated in conventional films. Clearly this is not possible' (Kazmi 1999: 88–89). Kazmi, perhaps keeping in mind his professed belief that Brecht's epic structure, while theoretically the 'ideal form' for a popular cinema, will not be well received by the people, suggests that filmmakers of the innovative/modernist school in India 'are getting wise to the need to appropriate elements of conventional cinema' (Kazmi 1999: 240). Yet, as *Dil Se...* demonstrates

and Creekmur and Virdi note, popular cinema has also begun 'infus-
ing elements of art cinema' into its own discourse. In other words, the
appropriators (the innovative/modernist school) are being reappropri-
ated (by the so-called conventional cinema).[6]
        The paradox that emerges is, as Ben Brantley puts it in his recent
review of *Bombay Dreams*, 'When it comes to pastiche, it helps to be
in on the joke of what is being imitated' (Brantley 2004). To claim,
in other words, that familiarity potentially *lessens* (dis)engagement (by
way of Brecht and/or Godard) is to overlook the very prerequisite for
such negotiation or 'recognition' (of intentions). The song and dance
in the popular Indian film (for example, in *Dil Se...*), unlike its Hollywood 'counterpart(s)', makes no overt attempt to 'suture' the musical
number (or its 'interruption') back within the text, nor does it work to
establish a parallel model between song and dance and film event(s).
Rather, it actively works to maintain/highlight this node's distinction
from and rupturing of the proper text, so that we are constantly shown
what the text 'tries to conceal', so that two worlds, or diegeses, are constantly on display and, rather than their compatibility, it is precisely
their distinction and incompatibility that is formally signalled (Feuer
1982: 47). Such bifurcation of the filmic text, then, allows for the Bollywood song and dance to transcend and dissolve the synthesis of the
homogenized Hollywood musical form and, in the process, consistently break out of the hermetic universe imposed on it by others, whether
so-called 'insiders' or 'outsiders'. As Hindi cinema star Hritik Roshan
replies when Hardy, finally finding her 'Bollywood Boy', compares his
dancing to Gene Kelly's, 'That's so nice but really just not true at all'
(Roshan, quoted in Hardy 2002: 258).
        A definitional shift becomes necessary at this juncture. If the musi-
cal is defined as 'a play or movie in which an often simple plot, developed by dialogue, is interspersed with songs and sometimes dances',
then 'interspersion' becomes 'interruption' via the Bollywood song
and dance (Nunberg 1996: 1190). Neither purely one form nor another (neither purely melodrama nor musical, neither burlesque nor
porn), the Bollywood song and dance comes closer to Homi Bhabha's
concept of 'stereotype-as-suture', a 'recognition of the *ambivalence* of
that authority and those orders of identification', for example, the laws
governing the ordering and separating of genres, as well as those encompassing the Bollywood song and dance in a time–space continuum

in which it is seen as perpetuating an irreducible time lag, a perpetual echo of a pre-defined order (Bhabha 1994: 80). The Bollywood song and dance, rather than 'obeying' these rules, 'problematizes the signs of racial and cultural priority, so that'—even as remystification is demystified—'the "national" is no longer naturalizable' (Bhabha 1994: 87). This 'mimicry' (of cultural and semiotic codes and conventions) 'conceals no presence or identity behind its mask: it is not what Aimé Cesaire describes as "colonization-thingification" behind which there stands the essence'[7]—rather, it is an example of what Baudrillard calls 'a hyperreal', namely, 'the generation by models of a real without origin or reality' (Baudrillard 1983: 2; Bhabha 1994: 88). In this sense, 'it is no longer a question of imitation, nor of reduplication, nor even of parody'—instead of adhering to, 'it is rather a question of substituting signs of the real for the real itself' (Baudrillard 1983: 4). A recent example of such a 'hyperreal shift(ing)' can be seen in *Aa Ab Laut Chalen* (Now Let's Return, 1999), a Bollywood film directed by Rishi Kapoor, filmed on-location and set in New York City, featuring a pair of young NRI characters, Rohan and Pooja, played by actor Akshaye Khanna (hereafter AK) and actress Aishwarya Rai (hereafter Ash).

After first picking up Ash (suitcase in hand, in colourful Indian garb, lost on a Queens Street corner) while driving a yellow cab and wearing an American-flag sweater, AK, in a later scene, protects Ash from the voyeuristic gaze of a leering young white man on a bus, by stepping between the voyeur and Ash (and thus closer to the latter). Ash then makes eyes at AK, even as romantic mood music plays. The scene abruptly cuts to the pair's two friendly uncles (bearing no actual relation) discussing the possibility of an AK–Ash relationship. The scene then cuts to Ash, in a medium close-up, looking off (but not out) by the window, while she twirls the blinds' rod in her right hand, a dreamy, desirous look in her green eyes. She then goes to lie down in bed (alone), smiling, even as saxophone-heavy mood music grows louder and then suddenly there is a cut to two figures (AK and Ash) skipping over rocks in Central Park (immediately identified as such because of the background, i.e., tall buildings), even as the playback track starts and 'Ye Kesay Mulaqat Hai' commences. In this song and dance sequence, featuring ten different locations and costume changes, and lasting roughly four and a half minutes, what we have on display (what the actor and actress engage in) is a series of 'snapshots', or what

Robert Stam would have Metz calling (in a different context, namely, the Godardian oeuvre) a 'bracket syntagma', i.e., 'a typical sample of an activity: not a couple making love, but the *idea* of a couple making love' (Stam 1985: 60).

In other words, as we see AK and Ash negotiate a series of moments (for example, 'posing' before a new car, a new house, etc., even as they lip-synch to the playback), it is the idea of these things, namely, tropes of assimilation, that are on display. Through these 'Kodak moments', then, what we may call an overtly 'commercial' aesthetic, i.e., a hyper-realist commercialism, 'impersonates' the very tropes it presents via 'a strategic confusion of the metaphoric and metonymic axes of the cultural production of meaning' (Bhabha 1994: 90).[8] These 'identity effects' produce a 'play of ... power that is elusive because it hides no essence, no "itself"'—these snapshot sequences, rather, represent (in a double sense) the 'fantasyscape' of hyperassimilation—'never that which conceals the truth' (as the ethnographer à la Hardy might have it) but rather 'the truth which conceals that there is none' (Baudrillard 1983: 1; Bhabha 1994: 90).

Through this 'generation of a real' via snapshots, 'the territory no longer precedes the map, nor survives it'—rather, 'it is the map that precedes the territory' (Baudrillard 1983: 2).[9] The song and dance ends with an abrupt cut (from the kaleidoscopic fantasyscape) to a Dunkin Donuts where Ash, now wearing a Dunkin Donuts uniform, pours coffee for a group of young white ruffians, who increasingly harass her. Again, then, she is saved by AK (now, too, a Dunkin Donuts em-ployee, though not dressed like Ash) who 'comes to her rescue'. A fight ensues, replete with 'dishoom-dishoom' fight-sequence music on the soundtrack, following which the young white ruffians (i.e., the natives) run away.

The preceding song and dance, though—and in fact, *because*—unac-knowledged within the 'formal diegesis' (i.e., Dunkin Donuts), works to '(p)re-shape' this (return to) story proper—'the problematic bound-aries of modernity are enacted in these ambivalent temporalities of the nation-space' (Bhabha 1994: 142). Either realm's disavowal of the other works to paradoxically re-suture them via this montage of shift-ing stereotypes—what Dudrah labels 'clichés'—whose conflicting views of 'assimilation', informed as they are by this literally 'commercial' aesthetic, transcend and dissolve the other's form (Dudrah 2006: 67).

These conflicting realms thus engage in an 'inversion', or 'splitting', both of and through the 'subject of identification', of Ash (whose 'fantasy' the four and a half minute song and dance sequence technically is), and the narrative (which inscribes and is ruptured by Ash), thus 'mak(ing) untenable any supremacist, or nationalist claims to cultural mastery' (Bhabha 1994: 150).[10]

Rather than functioning as an 'imagined community' as delineated by Benedict Anderson, 'the movement of meaning *between*' these two scenes/sequences/sets of representations in *Aa Ab Laut Chalen* interrupts the national narrative of the NRI experience replete with its 'sociological solidity' (Bhabha 1994: 154). In this sense, rather than what Anderson calls 'unisonance', the song and dance comes closer to representing 'the space of the nation's anomie' and thus that of the NRI, himself/herself a hybrid, introducing 'a signifying space of iteration rather than a progressive or linear seriality' (Bhabha 1994: 159). The incessant image shifts—both from one realm (Ash in bed) to another (the fantasyscape) and within this latter realm (the ten scene changes)—transform 'the "meanwhile"' (for example, of the time of Ash's implied fantasy) 'into quite another time, or ambivalent sign, of the national people' (Bhabha 1994). The 'imagined uniformity' of the filmic realm is shattered by this splitting of time and narrative, from which emerges 'a strange, empowering knowledge for the migrant that is at once schizoid and subversive' (Bhabha 1994: 168). Ash's hyperreal fantasy is literally transplanted onto the site of New York City which itself becomes the transfigured backdrop of/to her and AK's desires. In this context, 'insiders', i.e., New Yorkers, are converted into 'outsiders', i.e., 'gawking spectators' encapsulated within/by the form of the Bollywood song and dance.

In this way Ash's 're-shaping' dream can be seen as renaming the postmodern from the position of the postcolonial, 'open(ing) up the possibility for other "times" of cultural meaning and other narrative spaces', namely, what Gayatri Spivak calls 'a catachrestic space', one in which the process of reinscription and negotiation occurs in an intersubjective realm (Bhabha 1994: 175, 179, 183, 191).[11] Rather than a time lag between Bollywood song and dance and Hollywood musical, what we have is a time lag *in* representation, the crucial turning point between what Baudrillard labels the 'third' and 'fourth' phases of the image, namely, between 'mask(ing) the *absence* of a basic reality' and

'bear(ing) no relation to any reality whatsoever' (Baudrillard 1983: 11;
Bhabha 1994). Such a transition is achieved through the Bollywood
song and dance sequence's technique of incorporating, or folding, the
public sphere within its own fantasyscape, thus displacing this site's
'reality principle' with a simulation (i.e., a series of 'snapshots').

To return to Feuer via a 'postscript' to her earlier work, one might
reexamine the two 'related questions' she raises—namely, 'do new developments in musical films ... challenge ideas based on more classical
films; and ... do new developments in cultural theory challenge the
models for analysis employed in the first edition of this book'—by cross-
applying them to the Bollywood song and dance, particularly given
that Feuer replies in the negative to both questions (Feuer 1993: 123).
In answering her questions, Feuer discusses the 'emergence of the teen
musical as a "postmodern" genre' and, simultaneously, as 'an example
of the "re-construction" of the [Hollywood musical] genre' (Feuer 1993).
In the process, even as she bemoans the 'structuralist' who 'tends to
find regularity and binary thinking everywhere he looks', she creates a
binarism between the 'modernist' work of art (which provides 'decon-
structions' of 'studio-era films', 'intellectual pleasure', and whose purpose is 'critique') and the 'postmodern', which presents 'fragmented,
pastiche versions of older Hollywood genres', i.e., 'reconstructions'
(Feuer 1993: xi, 124, 128, 130). Thus, a genealogy is created in which
'instead of moving progressively from an experimental, transparent or
naïve conception ... to an increasingly more self-reflexive mode', the
'postmodern' signals a 'return' of the [American] film musical form 'to
its infancy' (Feuer 1993: 129).

Feuer's subsequent discussion of what, in her view, is the anomalous
contemporary film musical that illustrates 'the strategy of modernist
re-writing' becomes an effective entry point for a cross-analysis of the
strategies of the contemporary Bollywood film, for example, *Dil Se...*
and *Aa Ab Laut Chalen* (Feuer 1993: 126). Feuer begins her discussion
of *Pennies from Heaven* (1981) by pointing out that 'it does not take a
Screen theorist to apply this label [Brechtian] to the film', then goes
on to make her point by citing a review by Pauline Kael, in which
the latter states, 'Despite its use of Brechtian devices, *Pennies from
Heaven* doesn't allow you to distance yourself' (Kael, quoted in Feuer
1993: 126). In subsequently noting, however, that 'clearly the mass
audience which avoided this film in droves disagreed', Feuer repeats

the flawed assumption that Brechtian distanciation must, as a rule, be displeasurable. The dramaturge in question (whom Feuer goes on to quote at length), for instance, notes in the same essay cited by Feuer (the 'Notes' to one of his 'operas') that 'its content is pleasure' (Brecht 1957: 36).[12]

'The sound-image relationship in Pennies from Heaven', Feuer notes, 'exemplifies the "distancing effect" that comes from separating the elements. When, instead of singing the numbers in the film, the characters lip-synch ... we are rendered aware of the constructed nature of the text rather than "hypnotized", "intoxicated", or "fogged" out' (Feuer 1993: 127–28). Consider, then, 'this separation of the elements' in the Bollywood song and dance: as Ray noted (and the two Bollywood films discussed earlier demonstrate), these sequences 'go against the grain' of the film, particularly due to the technique of playback employed, and can be seen as 'a daring innovation', precisely because they are not 'stylistically related to the rest of the film' (Feuer 1993: 128; Ray 1976: 74). To cross-apply Feuer's analysis, one could say 'the idea that one spontaneously, naturally sings is exposed through this technique' in the Bollywood song and dance and that, furthermore, in such sequences, the 'singing' (i.e., lip-synching) actor 'undergoes a change of function' (Brecht 1957: 44; Feuer 1993: 128). Additionally, to return to the second of Feuer's initial questions in her 'Postscript', one might say that these sequences in the contemporary Bollywood film open up 'the space of cultural signification' in these very 'disjunctive' moments—moments which, even as they provide 'pleasure' (or are 'pleasurable'), engage in both a 're-writing' of the characters' identities and the very (non-interruptive) format of the film musical (Bhabha 1994: 148; Feuer 1993: 126).[13]

Is it possible, then, to theorize the Bollywood film as simultaneously engaging in 'modernist' and 'postmodernist' approaches? The crucial issue seems to be one of intentions—while Brecht's operas are theorized (by him and others) as 'pay[ing] conscious tribute to the senselessness of the operatic form', in the case of Bollywood, it is not clear whether 'the filmmakers themselves think of the songs in these terms', i.e., 'as a sort of Brechtian alienation device' (Brecht 1957: 35; Ray 1976: 73). The problem, at least on one level, seems to lie in precisely this invocation of the author's name (in this case Brecht) to perform 'a certain role with regard to narrative discourse', namely, to assure a

'classificatory function', as 'such a name [i.e., "Brecht"] permits one
to group together a certain number of texts, define them, differentiate
them from and contrast them to others' (Foucault 1998: 210). This
'author function', then, as deployed by Feuer, works to appropriate
the strategy of 'distanciation' to a distinctly 'modernist' praxis by
'discerning in the individual' the operations the text is forced to
undergo (Foucault 1998: 213). In the process, the invocation of the
author 'also serves to neutralize the contradictions that may emerge
in a series of texts', for instance, the similar deployment of strategies
that might otherwise result in mistaking the Hollywood musical for a
modernist film (Feuer 1993; Foucault 1998: 213).

Yet, to return to an earlier assumption made by Feuer in reference
to *Pennies*, even as the 'transdiscursive' Brecht claims that his 'intention was that a certain unreality, irrationality and lack of seriousness
should be introduced at the right moment [in his opera] and so strike
with a double meaning', he also crucially notes, in a footnote, that 'this
limited aim did not stop us from introducing an element of instruction' (Brecht 1957: 36). In other words, these two forms—'modernist'
and 'postmodernist'—as defined via their respective strategies, including 'alienation' for the former and 'pastiche' for the latter, may potentially overlap, particularly in the Bollywood song and dance. A classic
example of such an overlapping is in the use of non-diegetic music
(i.e., the playback) in the Bollywood sequence. While Feuer primarily
locates this 'new' convention within a postmodern frame, when it is
deployed in *Pennies*, it (and thus this film) 'exemplifies the [Brechtian]
"distancing effect"' (Feuer 1993: 127, 130). Rather than considering a
'postmodern development ... as opposed to the modernist evolution
toward deconstruction', one might point to the Bollywood song and
dance as a deconstruction of precisely such an opposition, i.e., as engaging in a form of deliberate (as opposed to 'random') pastiche (Feuer
1993: 131).[14]

It is precisely in critiquing 'from a position of complicity', for instance, that the contemporary Bollywood film 'show[s] up the commercial character both of the entertainment and of the persons en-
tertained' (Brecht 1957: 41; Feuer 1993: 137).[15] Thus, to paraphrase
Feuer, rather than asking whether or not they are really musicals (or
really serious), one might approach the Bollywood song and dance as
simultaneously 'a kind of report on life as any member of the audience

would like to see it', and 'because it took up a purely emotional attitude and spurned none of the stock narcotic attractions ... an active
collaborator in the stripping bare of the middleclass corpus of ideas'
(Brecht 1957: 43, 85–86). In this way, even as 'the gestic principle
takes over, as it were, from the principle of imitation', one might say
the hyperrealist aesthetic of the contemporary Bollywood song and
dance sequence supplants mimesis as a mode of representation, thus
both marking 'a great revolution in the art of drama' and transcending and dissolving the 'demystification/remystification dialectic' via
an aesthetic that, even though fully culinary, also deconstructs (Brecht
1957: 86, 87; Feuer 1993: 136, 137).

Like the epic drama, the Bollywood film 'is familiar with a different
kind of chain, whose course need not be a straight one but may
quite well be in curves or even in leaps' (Brecht 1957: 45). Such a
peripatetic approach is precisely what allows this cinema to engage in
a shift 'from the cultural as an epistemological object to culture as
an enactive, enunciatory site', which 'opens up possibilities for other
"times" of cultural meaning ... and other narrative spaces' (Bhabha
1994: 178). In this way, to retrace the steps of Feuer's 'Postscript' via a
postcolonial mapping, the Bollywood song and dance may be described
as embodying a 'third space', in which 'the splitting of the subject of
enunciation'—both thematically, via the departure from a certain role
or mode of acting, and structurally, via playback—'makes the structure
of meaning and reference an ambivalent process', and problematizes
neat binary divisions (Bhabha 1994: 35–37). In the process, the
'transdiscursive' function of the author is also renegotiated, so as to
allow for a destabilization of this figure's 'ideological' status as well as
for a 'reexamination' of a set of aesthetic practices and, more generally,
of film genre studies (Foucault 1998: 217–21).[16] I would argue, then,
at least within the framework Feuer sets up in relation to the musical,
i.e., the opposition of the 'modernist' and the 'postmodernist', that
such a catachrestic reading of the Bollywood song and dance, i.e., as
'Brechtian', ruptures the very theoretical underpinnings informing
such a binary and, furthermore, is slyly acknowledged by this cinema's
moniker itself.

Furthermore, in contrast to what Sumita Chakravarty calls 'the
cultural elite's traditional hostility to mass cinema' which, furthermore,
has been shared by directors associated with 'innovative' or 'modernist'

cinemas who 'often invoke the names of Walter Benjamin and Bertolt Brecht as sources of inspiration' but 'do not share these Europeans' larger social vision', to see the Bollywood film functioning in both a Brechtian vein and, crucially, as a popular cinema, dissolves and reframes Kazmi's binary of 'conventional vs. innovative' (Chakravarty 1993: 268; Kazmi 1999). Such a reframing also offers a way out of the impasse Kazmi presents, in which one must choose between an overly intellectualized innovative cinema which will not be easily understood by the people ('especially the subalterns') and a conventional cinema that, though using popular interpellations, speaks in the language of the subaltern (Kazmi 1999: 216, 229). To reframe the Bollywood film as an innovative form of popular cinema, as this chapter suggests, is to acknowledge both the effectiveness with which it combines allegedly disparate aesthetic conventions and the ability of such an approach to engage the mass audience. To better understand precisely how the Bollywood film speaks to such an audience in innovative ways, we now turn to Chapter 3.

NOTES

1. It should be noted that Brecht himself was influenced by Chinese theatre (i.e., an Eastern dramaturgical model) in the development of his theory of 'defamiliarization', or *Verfremdungseffekt*, in relation to his own (German/Western) 'epic theatre'. For further discussion of this Eastern influence on the development of Brecht's aesthetic, see his essay, 'Alienation Effects in Chinese Acting ' (1957: 91–99).

2. While one could claim that invoking Brecht in describing Bollywood amounts to the same foreclosure, I would suggest otherwise, especially given that the moniker 'Brechtian' continues to be associated with an 'innovative' approach—for example, that of Godard—and is generally contrasted with that of Bollywood which, in turn, is characterized as a 'conventional' cinema, i.e., non-Brechtian and (thus) non-innovative (Kazmi 1999). Furthermore a 'cinema of attractions' is more firmly rooted in a particular—and, crucially, earlier—temporal context than the 'Brechtian' moniker which, as I argue here, functions in a more transdiscursive fashion, freely circulating over time to apply not only to the likes of Godard (in the twentieth as well as the twenty-first century) but also to other so-called 'innovative' contemporary cinemas and *auteurs*, retaining all the while its radical, progressive connotations. It is thus in direct response (and sharp contrast) to the previous and continuing theorization of Bollywood that I invoke Brecht in discussing the Bollywood film's techniques and that doing so constitutes a radical departure from most scholarship in this field, suggesting an innovative, as opposed to antediluvian/conventional, frame for this cinema.

3. The technique of *playback* goes back to the 1930s when 'music doubling', i.e., using professional singers to perform the actual music in synchronization with the (already)

filmed actor going through the motions of singing, came into vogue. The cinema in India, however, engages in a reverse process: pre-recording the song before the film shooting. This strategy is directly linked to the popularity of both film songs and play-back singers, a handful of who perform all the songs for all the films released in the subcontinent, again, usually upwards of 800 a year (Arnold 1991: 103).

4. Kazmi simultaneously claims that conventional Indian cinema is what speaks in the language of the subalterns (Kazmi 1999: 216).

5. Patrick Colm Hogan uses this failure by characters to acknowledge the song and dance sequence as the basis for labelling the latter 'paradiegetic', i.e., '"alongside" the story without being quite part of the story' (Hogan 2008: 163). Gopalan, meanwhile, refers to this song and dance sequence as 'extra-diegetic', though still claims that 'the spatial disruption of this song infects the ensuing love story' (Gopalan 2002: 135). Corey Creekmur and Jyotika Virdi claim that 'all of *Dil Se*'s remarkable "picturizations" of songs seem to take place in Amar's imagination' (Virdi and Creekmur 2006: 143), which would technically make them 'internal diegetic', i.e., represented as stemming from the mind of a character within the story space. Although we and the character see and hear it, we assume that other characters cannot (Bordwell and Thompson 2004: 503). Apparently, there is no clear consensus here, which is largely my point.

6. Creekmur and Virdi go on to note that *Dil Se...*, which employs 'the popular form of commercial cinema', 'emphasizes the disjunction between its songs and story', and includes songs that 'are not narratively integrated' but, rather, 'in their fragmentary disruption of the storyline suggest the disintegration of "Indian" identity' (Virdi and Creekmur 2006: 143).

7. As Cesaire points out, attempts to fix the 'essence' of the Other—the process of 'thingi-fication'—belie a colonial tendency in which hybridity is seen as 'the enemy' (Cesaire 2001: 42, 63). Similarly, as Frantz Fanon has famously noted, the 'simplicity' of the Other is 'a myth created by superficial observers'; the phobic object is thus '*overdeter-mined*' (Fanon 1967: 67, 155).

8. As Sumita Chakravarty notes:

> Concentrated within this metaphor ['impersonation'] are the notions of changeability and metamorphosis, tension and contradiction, recognition and alienation, surface and depth: dualities that have long plagued the Indian psyche and constitute the self-questionings of Indian nationhood. Indian cinema, caught in the cross-currents of this national dialogue and contributing to it, has made impersonation its distinctive signature. This is more than a matter of reinforcing truisms that films impersonate life; characters impersonate real men and women; the film-viewing experience impersonates dream. Impersonation subsumes a process of externalization, the play of/on surfaces, the disavowal of fixed identity. (1993: 4)

9. It is precisely because the song and dance sequence presents a series of 'snapshots' and 'flashy montage', as Gopal and Sen claim, that it is not (as they go on to claim) 'a social realist art form' but, instead, a hyperreal pastiche, or what they somewhat oxymoroni-cally refer to as 'the realism of advertising' (Gopal and Sen 2008: 151).

10. This may be seen as precisely what Chakravarty refers to as the subsumption of 'the pro-cess of externalization', the 'play of/on surfaces', and the 'disavowal of fixed identity', by the cinematic aesthetic of Bollywood (Chakravarty 1993: 4).

11. For more on the concept of 'catachresis', see Spivak (1990b: 125).

12. Earlier in this essay, Brecht states, 'Why is Mahogany an opera? Because its basic attitude is that of an opera: that is to say, culinary. Does Mahogany adopt a hedonistic approach? It does. Is Mahogany an experience? It is an experience. For ... Mahogany is a piece of fun' (Brecht 1957: 35).

13. As Bhabha subsequently notes, 'This kind of disjunctive temporality is of the utmost importance for the politics of cultural difference' and, to continue in this catachrestic reading, in each of these 'interruptive' moments, 'there is a doubling and splitting of the temporal and spatial dimensions in the very act of signification' (Bhabha 1994: 177, 182).

14. Naturally, Feuer claims that 'random' (as opposed to 'deliberate') pastiche 'makes the film pleasurable in all the ways that Brecht would have disapproved of', thus interpolating the author, i.e., deploying the 'author function', in precisely the manner delineated by Foucault and also, in the process, 'imped[ing] the free circulation ... and recomposition' of such strategies (Foucault 1998: 92-94, 221).

15. Hardy describes this complicity as 'the current finely tuned Bollywood formula' that has 'evolved to give the audience maximum escapism and minimum reality' (Hardy 2002: 16).

16. Here I have been primarily concerned with Feuer's use of Brecht and Godard. As Foucault notes in his delineation of the 'transdiscursive':

> It is easy to see that in the sphere of discourse one can be the author of much more than a book—one can be the author of a theory, tradition, or discipline in which other books and authors will in turn find their place. (1998: 216-17)

3

Can the Bollywood Film Speak to the Subaltern?

Go and see a Hindu film ... and see ten of them while you are about it, so as to make no mistake. Here, the still water begins to move, and you will see every-thing. Henri Michaux (1986: 59)

In Chapter 2, we saw how media ethnographers such as Justine Hardy invoke 'the people in the dust' as comprising the 'core' Bollywood audience. This invocation is subsequently used to relegate the Bolly-wood film's implied viewers to an antediluvian frame and, by implica-tion, the Bollywood film itself. In this chapter, I would like to delve further into this 'locating' of the implied viewers of Bollywood within a subaltern frame as a way of both re-evaluating the cultural axiomatics of this implied subject–position and its previous and continuing theo-rization by postcolonial scholars. In this way, this chapter will continue to develop the ideas raised in the previous two chapters, concerning the theorization of the implied viewer of Bollywood as well as his/her presumed capacity to 'make meaning' of what he/she sees unfolding upon the screen.

Implicit in the identification of Bollywood's 'core' audience as 'the people in the dust' is this cinema's widespread dispersal. From its inception in 1896, as Roy Armes notes, cinema in India has been a travelling cinema—'traveling showmen established the first popular audience by taking films from place to place with their tent shows'

(Armes 1987: 106). This trend has continued to the present and, with 80 per cent of the population living in rural areas, has resulted in a 'uniquely regional' cinema further offset by, on the one hand, India's multifarious languages and regional dialects and, on the other, Indian audiences' desire for motion pictures in their own languages and dialects (Pendakur 2003: 17, 230). What is noteworthy, then, as Manjunath Pendakur points out, 'is that the Hindi-language [Bollywood] films, which make up about 20 per cent of the total production ... have captured the all-India market' (Pendakur 1990: 231). This is largely due to these films' commercial formulas, which are well known and can generally be seen as transcending the (regional) language barrier (Pendakur 1990).

This is key to note in a country where approximately 300 million are illiterate (Nayar 2004: 14). As stated in an early 1980s documentary *There'll Always Be Stars in the Sky: The Indian Film Music Phenomenon* (dir. Jeremy Marre, 1983), 'Even the remotest parts of India aren't free from Bombay's fantasy world. Travelling cinemas visit distant fairs in villages, often with illegally pirated prints'. What is interesting here is the negative stance taken towards this 'fantasy world', i.e., positioning it as a threat to Indian villagers' freedom. Such a position is compounded by opposing the cinema to the regional theatre which, 'bravely combat[s] his mechanical rival' but which 'cannot compete today with the traveling cinema'. So intones the British-accented narrator of the documentary, even as footage is presented of villagers watching a regional theatrical performance, with one Indian boy in the foreground yawning.

The cinema, then, is positioned as a threat to both the current freedom of Indians (particularly in villages) and its historical predecessor (i.e., the theatre). Indians who watch Bollywood are participating in a mass hypnosis of sorts, one that (as ethnographic documentarians such as these would have it) deprives Indians of their culture and their volition. The Indian cinema is seen as lacking maturity and, by inference, so is its audience. And yet, as the same critics will point out, 'to the vast conglomerate mass that makes up the Indian public the cinema is the only form of available inexpensive entertainment' (Ray 1976: 72). Furthermore, it is clear that 'if you think in terms of tired untutored minds with undeveloped tastes needing an occasional escape through relaxation', then 'the best prescription' becomes the Bollywood film precisely as it has been formulated, namely, as simple, escapist fare for 'tired untutored minds' (Ray 1976: 73). A rather circular form of argumentation should have become apparent by now. On the one hand, it is the Indian (village) viewer's mentality that is to blame for Bollywood; on the other, it is the industry that mass produces these 'fantasies' that 'delude' the masses.[1] Either way, it seems, the best thing to do is leave well enough alone— but not, of course, before passing judgement on both. Sheila Nayar declares, '[Bombay cinema] often has the feeling of being piecemeal and disaggregative, of being coarsely stitched together. It is pastiche—*but quite without the postmodern self-consciousness*' (Nayar 2004: 16, emphasis added). The reason for this is the aforementioned symbiosis in which viewer and film hold each other down (or are held to do so)—how can the cinema have a consciousness (let alone a 'postmodern' one) when it is made for illiterate villagers? Never mind that the structure of the films themselves seems to present an alternative possibility. It is useful to remember that when Satyajit Ray came across an American critique of Hindi films' use of songs 'as a sort of Brechtian device, something which purposely makes the spectator aware of the artificiality of the whole thing', his response was to question whether 'the film makers themselves think of the songs in these terms' (Ray 1976: 73). Needless to say, without self-consciousness, how could one think at all?

On the flipside of this discourse, one finds the serious consideration of this cinema possible but, again, only within an antediluvian frame (disaggregative but quite without the postmodern). Nayar, for instance, insists on seeing the Bollywood cinema as 'historically circumscribed by the psychodynamics of orality—that is, by the thought processes and personality structures that distinguish a non-writing mindset' (Nayar 2004: 14). Unfortunately, however, what still remains unnoticed and unconsidered are the psychodynamics of *film* literacy, particularly via the hyper-syncretic Bollywood *masala* aesthetic. Even if one does not possess what Barthes called a 'writerly' mindset, one can still know how to read a film (Barthes 1975). When the critic presents the illiterate Indian villager as 'an oral person', however, the essentializing binarism resurfaces (Nayar 2004: 15). According to Nayar, 'An oral person absorbs and organizes, and retains and recalls, information differently. For instance, he or she cannot organize thoughts with syntactical sophistication', and furthermore:

[H]is or her relationship to the world, to the group, and to the self is radically different from that of the person who can search a computer for data, or read about a character's psychological struggle, or even look up a street name on a city map. (Nayar 2004: 15)

An 'oral person', then, is 'different' from you and me. He or she has a hard time with sophisticated things. Of course, Bollywood presents no problems as (i) Indian villagers (i.e., oral people) watch it and (thus) (ii) it was always already geared towards such a mass (illiterate/oral) audience. Why, indeed, would an Indian filmmaker ever think of the songs in his film as 'Brechtian', when his audiences lack 'syntactical sophistication'? Nayar, then, employs the concept of orality to deny consciousness, or cognizance, on the Indian viewer's behalf. She does so via a series of tautologies, such as claiming that 'the analytic ... that characterizes writing arises *with writing itself*'; and by maintaining a decidedly Aristotelian conception of drama (i.e., the three unities), so that Bollywood is seen as *lacking* 'any organizing principle', and is described as 'meandering' (Nayar 2004: 16–17). Furthermore, orality is associated with 'a conservative-traditionalist' mindset (as opposed to an 'experimental' one), thus increasing the difficulty of seeing Bollywood or its implied viewers as possessing anything even remotely resembling a 'postmodern self-consciousness' (Nayar 2004: 17). In other words (or rather, in Nayar's), 'the new is invariably incorporated into the old (and in some manner, the "forever"), resulting in a kind of mythic "telescoping" of temporalities' (Nayar 2004).[2]

Given such a state of affairs, it is hardly surprising that American film criticisms describing Bollywood as a 'sort of Brechtian alienation device' are hard to come by. More to the point, once the illiterate village Indian is described as being 'an oral person', replete with all the accoutrements said status earns him or her, the critic can immediately also claim that 'Hindi films are "anti-psychological"', that 'there is no "interior" story' and that 'nothing exists within a character that is not said' (Nayar 2004: 20). Yet, upon examining even the most basic Bollywood film (or, conversely, the basic formula of the Bollywood film), one can detect several instances of 'unspokenness'. The frequent song and dance numbers, for instance, are 'unspoken' in a double sense: narratively (i.e., as departures from the realm of actual discourse) and structurally (i.e., via their use of playback). Additionally, the song and dance sequences can be seen as instances of 'interior' stories, as they reflect, often, the 'fantasies' of the characters. Furthermore, one would have to note all the shared structural aspects of cinema (cinematic literacy) that are used to convey characters' 'inner states': the point-of-view (POV) shot; mood music; plus, more generally speaking, camera movement and angles (i.e., 'framing').

Nayar, in fact, does seem to acknowledge 'the Hindi film's propensity for amplified camerawork', but, again, in her view, such technique is 'never ironic': 'Though perhaps excessive and overwrought to the literate mind, such emphatic cinematography provides cues to the [oral/illiterate] spectator that are easy to read' (Nayar 2004: 21). Yet again, this is not necessarily the case, as one can quite obviously 'misread' said style, i.e., miss its 'irony', or 'self-consciousness'. As Sara Dickey has noted in her study of popular cinema and the urban poor in south India, 'Films are not straightforward representations of either a dominant or a subordinate ideology, nor are their communicated elements absorbed without question' (Dickey 1993: 145). And yet, such a (visual/filmic) technique does, indeed, 'provide cues to the reader', only ones that are 'postmodern', in the sense that their 'readability' adheres to a logic akin to that of what Sumita Chakravarty describes as 'impersonation', for example, the play 'of/on identities', a 'disavowal of fixed identity', or of 'fixity' itself (Chakravarty 1993: 4). In other words, Nayar overlooks the transgressive, disruptive semiotics of the Bollywood film, what some have called its *masala*, and others, its bread and butter.

Nayar sees the Bollywood industry as being 'largely contoured by the particular cognitive needs of its spectators', in which the Bollywood movie's 'perceived inconsistencies and oft-cited contradictions ... make sense when examined through the prism of orality' (Nayar 2004: 21). I, on the other hand, would suggest looking at the Bollywood film's *filmic* structure itself—one which, among other things, renegotiates its alleged 'commitment to a Manichean world', as well as the overwhelmingly Manichean frame in which it is placed (Nayar 2004). In this sense, the Bollywood film may be seen as what Gayatri Spivak calls a 'supplementation', one which 'speaks in the language of the subaltern', not so that his/her 'representation can be ... assured', but rather so that these very concepts—for example, 'representation' and 'identity'/'identification'—can be reconfigured (Nayar 2004: 22; Spivak 2002).

Spivak states that 'in their current decrepitude the subaltern cultures need to be known in such a way that we can suture their re-activated cultural axiomatics into the principles of the Enlightenment' (Spivak 2002: 190). She goes on to describe the 1990s as 'a time "of the restructuring demands of globalization"', but one with a 'lack of intellectual connection between the people at work in the different spheres' (Spivak 2002). She then mentions her visit to a 'so-called biodiversity festival [in 2000] ... in a "least-developed country [LDC]"':

> (The rural and country town audience) roared its derision at biodiversity songs from two neighboring nation-states, applauding enthusiastically instead at embarrassing imitations of Bollywood (the trade-name of the hugely international Bombay film industry) 'adaptations' of moments from US MTV, unrecognizable by the audience as such, of course. (Spivak 2002: 195)

Spivak's language regarding Bollywood recalls that of Ray, who (in) famously asked in his 1948 essay, 'What is Wrong with Indian Films?', 'Or are we just plain ashamed of our films?' Ray, too, calls for 'an enlightened approach' and argues that 'there are some obstacles to this':

> [P]articularly in the representation of the contemporary scene. The influence of Western civilization has created anomalies which are apparent in almost every aspect of our life. We accept the motor car, the radio, the telephone, streamlined architecture, European costume, as functional elements of our existence. But within the limits of the cinema frame, their incongruity is sometimes exaggerated to the point of burlesque. (Ray 1976: 22)

Read in tandem, Ray's comments seem to pose questions (from the past, as it were) to Spivak's observations at the millennial bio-fest in the unnamed LDC. First, Ray's comments seem to suggest a familiarity with the West already in operation, particularly within the Bollywood frame. Simultaneously, that familiarity is recognized as being exaggerated to the point of 'making the subject appear ridiculous by treating it in an incongruous way', i.e., caricature.[3] To or for whom, then, are the imitations of Bollywood 'embarrassing'? Are they embarrassing or *the* embarrassing imitations (of Bollywood)? And why 'of course'? That is, why the assumption that the indigenous rural/country audience did not recognize the imitations as such (i.e., as 'adaptations' of US MTV)?

Given both Spivak's contextualization of the 1990s as a time of 'globalization's restructuring' and her ethnographic anecdote, I feel it would be fitting to develop these points via my own anecdotal ethnography, hopefully one that may be seen as supplementing Spivak's observations and, thus, the implied cognizance of the subaltern.[4] My father's village in northern India, Sila Kheri (population 1,200), approximately sixty miles (100 km) from Delhi, with an illiteracy rate of roughly 50 per cent, is a small farming community where about half the population subsists at the poverty level and the other half, below. Yet, over the course of the 1990s ('globalization's restructuring'), the number of households possessing television sets (TVs) dramatically increased, with the number now at about fifty. The primary (non-cable) Indian television station, Doordarshan, presents a weekly to bi-weekly fare of Bollywood films (older and more recent), which are viewed by groups of 10–20 people who gather at households with TVs. While the attendance is mixed, women and children tend to make up the majority. (Perhaps, as a side note, I could also mention my maternal uncle's village, Gogripur, about eighty miles from Delhi, with a population of 6,000, i.e., 1,200 households, and an illiteracy rate of nearly 40 per cent, where 90 per cent of households own televisions, and the usual weekly fare is Bollywood, with women and children making up the majority of the gathered audience, usually also around seven or eight per household.)[5]

Clearly, then, one might say that these villages illuminate the 'restructuring' effects of 'globalization' in the increased number of total television sets, a trend that began even earlier, in the 1980s (when 'the floodgates of the current phase of globalization ... had not yet been opened'), during which time a nation-wide delivery system was implemented (by 1985), and the total number of television sets in the country increased from half a million at the beginning of the decade to about 13 million sets by 1990 (Pendakur 1990: 245; Spivak 2002: 191). 'The process', indeed, 'had already begun', and with it, the further dissemination of Bollywood cinema to previously unreached audiences, namely, those constituting a 'subaltern' status (Spivak 2002: 191).[6] The very 'flow', in other words, that Spivak describes as 'not yet ... opened', was already present in the form of televisual broadcasting, a format(ting) itself parodying the internal structure of the Bollywood film, geared towards, for instance, a detached, or 'episodic', viewing

(Spivak 2002).[7] Even, then, as 'the general culture of Euro-US capitalism in globalization and economic restructuring ... conspicuously destroyed the possibility of capital being redistributive and socially productive in a broad-based way', the increased dissemination of Bollywood cinema via TV recirculated capitalist iconography to (re)create the possibility of an iconology of multinational/redistributive capital, one which was subsequently lampooned (or 'embarrassingly imitated') by its aesthetic reformulations, i.e., the *masala* aesthetic (Spivak 2002: 190).[8]

In such a way, then, one could argue that the 'hip global public culture story' was precisely what, via Bollywood, was becoming increasingly available to rural Indian audiences (i.e., the overwhelming majority of the population) during this time—'hip' in the sense that the 'multiculturalist cultural difference stereotypes' were themselves 'impersonated', or 'exaggerated to the point of burlesque', and thus constituted (or worked to constitute) 'a style, an idiom, a sort of iconography *of* cinema, which would be uniquely and recognisably Indian' (Ray 1976: 22, emphasis added; Spivak 2002: 192).[9] But to circle back to an earlier question or, to paraphrase it, recognizable *to whom?* It seems, in fact, as if a double recognition is in operation here: of the same set of signifiers (the 'hip stories and stereotypes') but from differing vantage points. Even as one of the vantage points (that of the cultural anthropologist or, in this case, anecdotalist) attempts to speak for, or in the name of, the other, the latter, too, replies via a reappropriation of its speaker's terms and languages. This doubling, then, can be seen in the larger institution of cinema, the same that first appeared in India in 1896 and continues to be both spoken of and for by distinct yet overlapping fields of knowledge-production.

Such an approach (question-and-answer-ing) would seem to 're-awaken' some assumptions first laid aside, namely, that 'the permeability of global culture must be seen as restricted' (Spivak 2002: 194). The 'hugely international' approach of Bollywood (in terms of both its internal composition and external dissemination) allows for/creates a permeability in(to) not only regions untouched by its implied other (i.e., Hollywood) but those 'metropolitan countries' whose borders and frontiers were seemingly so well policed (i.e., Europe/US) as well (Spivak 2002). In other words, to mix metaphors, the dissemination of information technology in the form of television allows for 'channels of interpenetration' with(in) which 'subaltern cultures' can play a 'generative public role' (Spivak 2002: 194–95). The irony here is that such 'cultural formation' is achieved via the filmic and televisual mediums' literalization of Spivak's 'concept-metaphor' of 'suturing' (Spivak 2002: 199). Via its tropes of contamination, hybridization and reformulation, the Bollywood film works to achieve a 'recoding' of a 'delegitimized cultural formation', both that of itself and that of its (implied, native, illiterate) viewer (Spivak 2002: 199). An interesting meta-reflection on the compartmentalization of the humanities is that while both Spivak and Homi Bhabha employ the concept of 'suture' in one or more uses (but both, primarily, as metaphors, or 'concept-metaphors'), neither makes any reference to the term's meaning within the realm of film studies. If to 'suture', in this latter context, can be seen as describing the process whereby the apparatus of the cinema interpellates the viewer into its fold (i.e., its mimetic, or 'diegetic', world), then the Bollywood cinema can be said to 'tear' this fabric (i.e., the process) via its 'numerous sidetracks', 'digressions' (which 'may be fun, funny, maudlin, titillating', but are not 'narratively instrumental'), 'deviations', 'narrative blind alley(s)' and 'willingness to digress', all of which, of course, are 'reflected in the obligatory song and dance numbers that punctuate, sometimes puncture, virtually every conventional Bollywood movie' (Nayar 2004: 17). But how, via 'this lack of any organizing principle, this constant detouring and often lengthy meandering', is such a 'tearing' of the fabric of the concept-metaphor of 'suture' attained (Nayar 2004)? And, more importantly, what implications does it have for the implied (native/ illiterate) viewer, to say nothing of this viewer's theorist?

To start with the last point, so long as the telos of said suturing is constructed as '(into) the principles of the Enlightenment', and so long as 'the Hindi film is ... derided by film scholars and critics for its stringy and episodic nature, for its lack of organic consistency', Bollywood remains conceptualized within a wholly Aristotelian (i.e., Western) frame, for example, that from which it derives its name/is named (Nayar 2004: 17; Spivak 2002: 190). Similarly, so long as viewers are assumed to be 'socially excluded from the media experience', and/ or unable to recognize cross-cultural references, recent increases in the dissemination of information technologies at the rural/village level (i.e., post-'restructuring of globalization') are not allowed to factor into the overall categorization of the subaltern as such (Nayar 2004: 14;

Spivak 2002: 195).[10] Furthermore, a fusion of these two lines is also
disallowed, thereby relegating the 'native' viewer of Bollywood to 'an
oral mindset', one 'quite without ... postmodern self-consciousness'
(Nayar 2004: 16).

To suture the competing senses of suture itself, then, would be to
allow for the possibility of (i) cinema/media as supplementation, (ii)
Bollywood as that particular form of supplementation, in which non-
Aristotelian methodologies predominate and yet (iii) empowerment,
or rather, 'an *uncoercive* rearrangement of desires' occurring at the
lowest level (Spivak 2002: 173). Cinema/media as supplementation
becomes a 'new kind of education' in which the cinematic interaction
(i.e., reading of the filmic language) becomes a way of reconfiguring
both the previously limited/limiting positioning of the subaltern and
'the built-in limitation of the intellectual community, with its critical
imprimatur derived exclusively from *literate* thought and perception'
(Nayar 2004: 22). Only, rather than seeing Bollywood as speaking *for*
the subaltern and remaining within the 'orality' model (as Nayar would
have it), one might argue (via playback) that Bollywood has not been
'speaking' (for the audience or the actors) and that this has been known
all along. That is, rather than offering up 'authentic or valid—or even
real—representation', Bollywood presents impersonations that become
forms of subaltern self-questioning (Nayar 2004). Such a process
functions on the utilization of cinematic principles to disrupt and/or
disable the functioning of these principles. However, this process can
only work, can only be achieved via, paradoxically, an apprehension
of those very principles, both for the screen(ed) image (no longer
there, but signifying its absence) and the screening spectator (present
and 'reading' the coded language through his/her eyes, scanning the
images for those very traces which are re-presented).[11]

The exhibition of Bollywood by either travelling cinema or television
in the rural Indian village setting becomes (i.e., can be seen as), to
paraphrase Spivak, a post-modernizing instrument for teaching, much
like a primer's use of images, only, in this case, a kinetic and flagrantly
non-Aristotelian primer (Spivak 2002: 210–11). Similarly, the viewing
of Bollywood (in either of the above technological formats) becomes 'an
exercise in ... text-ing' through 'the closest general educational facility
to which the teachers ... and the students might have access' (Spivak
2002: 219, 221).[12] Before performing a close reading of a Bollywood

film in order to see how such 'text-ing' is precisely achieved, it is necessary to consider briefly two larger issues framing this discussion, namely, the 'problem of subaltern consciousness' and the formulation of a 'Third Cinema'.

Midway through her introduction to the work of the Subaltern Studies collective, Spivak states:

> Once again, in the work of this group, what had seemed the historical predicament of the colonial subaltern can be made to become the allegory of the predicament of all thought, all deliberative consciousness, though the elite profess otherwise. This might seem preposterous at first glance. A double take is in order. (Spivak 1988b: 12)

Spivak proceeds to elaborate such a 'double take' by reading the 'retrieval of subaltern consciousness' as 'the charting of what in post-structuralist language would be called the subaltern subject-effect' (Spivak 1988b: 12). Such a 'subject-effect' may be seen as 'part of an immense discontinuous network ("text" in the general sense) of strands that may be termed politics, ideology, economics, history, sexuality, language, and so on' (Spivak 1988b: 12-13). It is thus 'different knottings and configurations of these strands' that 'produce the effect of an operating subject' (Spivak 1988b: 13). The 'subject', then, is summoned post hoc and becomes 'the effect of an effect', or a metalepsis, i.e., 'the substitution of an effect for a cause' (Spivak 1988b: 13). In such a way, Spivak reads the project 'to retrieve the subaltern consciousness' (as initiated by the subaltern studies collective) as 'a *strategic* use of positivist essentialism in a scrupulously political interest' (Spivak 1988b). Such a 'reading strategy', furthermore, becomes most useful when the term 'consciousness' is deployed in 'the narrow sense', i.e. as '*self*-consciousness' (Spivak 1988b: 14). Indeed, Spivak goes on to note that 'confusion arises because of the use of the word "consciousness"' and that she is not trying to 'clear the confusion' but is instead intent on reading the project of the subalternists 'against the grain'—what she calls a 'transactional reading'—i.e., as '*strategically* adhering to the essentialist notion of consciousness' which, in turn, would 'fall prey to an anti-humanist critique' (Spivak 1988b: 15).[13]

Keeping in mind this formulation of the subaltern 'subject position', let us turn to the second paradigm framing this discussion, the formulation of a 'Third Cinema' praxis. In Teshome Gabriel's seminal study stemming from the Third Cinema conference in Edinburgh in 1988, he positions film as an ideological tool and proceeds to enumerate, under the aegis of the age-old binarism of Western/non-Western, the 'essential elements' of a Third (World) Cinema (Gabriel 1989a: 44). Creating a table of 'Comparisons of Filmic Conventions' (which, he notes, 'are tendencies, not absolutes') with 'Western Dominant Conventions' occupying the left-hand column and 'Non-Western Use of Conventions', the right, Gabriel considers several aspects of film composition. These include Camera Angle (only the West employs angle shots primarily for aesthetic look); Camera Placement (while emotions are portrayed in close-up by the West, there is 'minimal use of the convention' in the non-Western—'This is perhaps due to lack of emphasis on psychological realism'); Parallel Montage (in the non-Western usage, 'cross-cutting serves an ideological purpose and denotes ironical contrast and class distinction'); and POV ('It is not uncommon to see a look directed at the camera, hence a direct address to the audience' in the non-Western context) (Gabriel 1989a: 46–47).

'The sum total of what is listed above', Gabriel concludes, 'as technique or elements of the film-making process is what expresses ideology'. Furthermore, those (Western) films 'that hide the marks of production are associated with the ideology of presenting "film as reality"', whereas those exhibiting marks of production are associated with 'the ideology of presenting "film as message"'. The ideology of the Third World film thus generically defined, the film employing 'non-Western conventions', or 'tendencies', is said to announce itself as 'a polemic comment on the way things are in their "natural" reflection'. A 'logical consequence' of this is the differing use by Western and non-Western films of the conventions of time and space in cinema (Gabriel 1989a: 46–47).

Consider, then, the case of 'a paradigmatic instance of the theme of impersonation' in popular Hindi cinema, Vijay Anand's 1965 film, Guide (Chakravarty 1993: 46). 'Enormously popular, imbued with high production values, drawing upon literary material, having an acclaimed musical score and choreography, Guide,' according to Chakravarty, 'represents a checklist of the Bombay cinema's "success formula"' (Chakravarty 1993: 46). Rather than taking an approach that may be considered '"allegorical" in the most ordinary sense ... or semiotic in the most formulaic way', however, it is crucial for my intentions in this chapter to examine this film from a filmic perspective, for example, paying close attention to its *découpage* (Spivak 1996: 244).[14] *Guide* tells the story of Rosy (Waheeda Rehman) and Raju (Dev Anand). The latter is a famous guide in the historic city of Udaipur (Rajasthan) whose services are enlisted by Rosy's husband, Marco. The latter, an archaeologist, has 'saved' Rosy, daughter of a *devadasi*, from the 'ignominy' associated with this profession by marrying her.[15] Marco forbids Rosy from dancing and generally shows more interest in the local caves than in his bride.

Unhappy over her marriage, Rosy tries to kill herself by taking poison. She is discovered by Raju, who cares for her while the oblivious Marco continues his archaeological dig. Later, after discovering what has happened and accusing Rosy of merely trying to attract attention, Marco sends a letter saying (via voice-over as Rosy 'reads'), 'If you want to leave, leave. Here's 1,000 rupees'. Passing the letter absent-mindedly to Raju, Rosy walks off, idly leafing through the folded bills. Suddenly, she hears the rustle of anklets and impetuously turns to ask Raju where she might purchase some. Having made her purchase, Rosy asks Raju how far Chittor is. They then hitch a ride on the back of a hay-filled truck and, as they pass a woman carrying a clay urn, Rosy reaches out to snatch it off the bewildered woman's head. Laughing, she places the urn on her head and turns to Raju, saying, 'What kind of a guide are you that you say nothing?' Raju replies:

I don't understand. Till yesterday you looked like a forty-year-old woman who had lost all her happiness, desires and hopes on the middle of some road. And today you look like a sixteen-year-old girl, innocent, ignorant, full of childhood mischief.

'Do you know why?' asks Rosy. 'Why?' replies Raju. Then, following an abrupt cut, Rosy 'replies' via playback—the song, 'Aaj Phir Jeene Ki Ta Manna Hai' (Today again I have a desire to live), suddenly begins:

I pulled my sari wrap from the thorns
Broke my relationship, put on anklets
No one should stop my heart's flight

Then, as the camera tracks her movement, Rosy tosses the urn—the camera tilting down to follow its trajectory—as she 'sings', 'There goes the heart ...' and the urn smashes against the pavement. Rosy is now framed from above (i.e., a high angle), lying back on the moving truck as she sings the melody's title refrain: 'Today again I have a desire to live ... Today again I've decided to die (for love)'.

After the stanza is 'sung' a second time, a brief musical interlude ensues, during which we see the truck stopping. A shot of a man on a camel follows, in which first Rosy's hand and then Rosy enters from screen-right, handing a bill to the man. The camera cuts to a close-up shot of Raju's face, watching in anticipation and then shrugging, even as the musical interlude concludes and Rosy 'sings' the next stanza while riding on a camel:

> I'm not in my own control
> My heart is somewhere then I'm somewhere else

The camera pans right to show a line of camels with riders, then tracks alongside them up to Rosy, singing. There is a cut to a medium shot of Rosy on the camel with the camel guide in the foreground (screen-left), leading the camel and smiling. A medium close-up of Rosy follows, while she 'sings' the next stanza:

> I don't know what my life found
> Laughing I say, ha, ha, ha ...

As the camera tracks right, pulling back as the camel procession advances, another camel-rider enters the frame: a woman whose head and face are completely covered by her veil. As Rosy repeats the song's title refrain, she playfully pulls her own veil over her face and head while the other woman pulls her veil up to first gawk and then laugh at this mimicry. From the following shot of Raju seated on a camel more concerned with eating leaves off a tree, there is an abrupt scene change: with the Chittor tower looming in the background (screen-left), Rosy runs forward along a raised walkway (screen-right), dancing (i.e., making hand and arm gestures) as the camera continues pulling back to track her from below (i.e., a low angle). As she continues coming forward (and the camera, pulling backward), more and more of the tower becomes visible/enters the frame and, finally, Rosy runs out of the shot (screen-right). The following shot shows her running (a match-on-action) towards a statue, grabbing its pillars and throwing back her head as she 'sings' the next verse:

Either I'm pent up or a storm
Someone say where I am.

Rosy continues running from building to building in the ancient Chittor fort, singing, dancing and 'posing'. While the playback continues, the camera cuts to Raju picking up her shoe and trying to catch up with her. In the following shot, Rosy is framed walking along a precipice in the foreground with the city below and behind her as she continues to 'sing' ('Fearing that on my life's journey somewhere I don't get lost'), nearly losing her balance ('A new route') at times. The following over-the-shoulder shot frames Rosy from Raju's POV, standing below and looking up (with his back to the camera). After additional shots of Rosy dancing with intricate hand gestures before the landscape of the fort, a cut takes us to Raju in silhouette in an archway. The camera then tilts up to a mirror in which the figure of Rosy, in blue *sari*, is visible, then pans right to another mirror in which Raju appears, then again pans right and down to frame him (from behind) looking out a window. The camera now moves forward, out the window (over Raju's shoulder), to frame Rosy, below, on the steps of another building, with Raju in close-up/profile on screen-left (again mimicking his POV).

As Rosy continues singing ('Having come out of yesterday's darkness/I have seen with rubbed eyes'), the camera cuts to a close-up of her in profile, as she turns to face the camera and 'sing', in direct address, 'I have decided', before repeating the title stanza for the last time as the camera engages in a series of shot-reverse shots, or eyeline matches, parodying Raju's and Rosy's gazes at one another from different vantage points in the fort. A sudden cut then takes us from Rosy 'singing' to Rosy dancing (with now only her jingling anklets again on the soundtrack) back in her hotel room, while Raju watches her, then complements her dancing as she comes to a stop.

What should be immediately clear from this song sequence is that the Bollywood film transcends and dissolves Gabriel's 'Western/non-Western' division and, in fact, often employs techniques associated

with the former to achieve ends associated with the latter. In particular, camera angles and placement associated with 'Western' convention
(for example, rapid and frequent cuts, close-ups) are used to create
the kind of 'parallel montage' Gabriel associates with 'non-Western'
conventions. The form of the Bollywood film, as exemplified by this
sequence from *Guide*, is hybrid and thus problematizes 'the fundamental basis of difference between Western and Third World discourses'
(Gabriel 1989b: 60). The language of the Bollywood film, particularly
in the frequent song sequences, 'opens up a space of "translation"':

> [A] place of hybridity, figuratively speaking, where the construction of
> a political object that is new, *neither the one nor the Other*, properly alien
> ates our political expectations, and changes, as it must, the very forms of
> our recognition of the 'moment' of politics. (Bhabha 1989: 117)

Such a space of 'translation' also summons Dickey's description,
building on the writing of Christine Gledhill, of film watching as 'a
process of negotiation' which 'opens possibilities for a fuller appreciation of the meaning of cinema, allowing as it does "space to the subjectivities, identities and pleasures of audiences"' (Gledhill, quoted in
Dickey 1993: 14).

Marco is in the cave and there are prisoners in the cave. Recalling
one of the oldest allegories of the visual experience—and one that is,
furthermore, all too often and too easily applied to the experience
of viewing a film[16]—one might say that Rosy, in leaving her husband,
has left the cave (the allegorical setting in which he remains chained
and which made Rosy a prisoner, too). Consider, then, 'what a release
from [her] chains it would be, and what a healing for [her] deluded
mind' (Chappell 1996: 230–31).[17] Beyond an echo of this sentiment in
the lyrics of the song ('Broke my relationships, put on anklets'; 'Having come out of yesterday's darkness'), one can trace this 'unchaining'
at the formal level of the film: this is precisely the moment the film
'breaks free' of its narrative proper, departs one world, replete with its
signifiers and conditions, and abruptly enters another. The *découpage*
is literally sped up, developing new juxtapositions.

Marco is in the cave and Rosy now claims to be 'seeing more
truly'—as she sings, 'I have seen with rubbed eyes' (Chappell 1996:
232). Having left her archaeologist husband behind in his cave, she
has 'come out of yesterday's darkness', and the operation of her eyes

(thus, following the Socratic allegory, her consciousness) has experienced a 'disturbance', paradoxically 'arriv[ing] at a clearer understanding' (Chappell 1996: 235). Yet, all of this is doubled by the formal structuring (and rupturing) of the narrative proper, which similarly experiences a 'disturbance', with incessant cuts from one setting to the next, one shot composition to another. Furthermore, as it is not Rosy (Waheeda Rehman) who technically sings these lines, one has another instance of that Platonic 'thrusting out' at the formal level, as Rosy/Rehman is 'cut' and replaced with Rosy/Lata Mangeshkar.[18] It is precisely in these ways that 'familiar themes ... are reworked, "estranged", and explored in philosophic-aesthetic terms' (Chakravarty 1993: 49). Yet, this line of analysis can, and must, be developed further.

To return to Gabriel's observations regarding the consequences of ideology, one might say that the result of the Bollywood film's 'different use of the conventions of time and space' is precisely to place emphasis on the representation of the political, to reconfigure ideology, so that the viewer's 'impression of reality' is restructured, or reformulated. Simultaneously, in doing so (i.e., in restructuring/reformulating, or 'negotiating' the language of the Bollywood song sequence), the viewer functions as the enunciating agency of this discourse. In the words of Christian Metz:

> I'm at the cinema. I am present at the screening of the film.
> I am present. Like the midwife attending the birth who, simply
> by her presence, assists the woman in labour, I am present for
> the film in a double capacity (though they are really one and
> the same) as witness and as assistant: I watch, I help. By watching
> the film I help it to be born, I help it to live, since only in me
> will it live, and it is made for that purpose: to be watched, in
> other words to be brought into being by nothing other than
> the look. (1982: 93)[19]

Even before the spectator's identification with a particular character or characters (for example, Rosy or Raju), there is the 'preliminary identification with the (invisible) seeing agency of the film itself as discourse, as the agency which puts forward the story' (Metz 1982: 96). Yet, whereas in the film adhering primarily to 'Western conventions', all traces of enunciation are abolished (in conformity with the ideology of presenting 'film as reality') and the viewer is made to believe that 'he is himself that subject' (i.e., putting forth the story), in the case of the Bollywood film—one in which the marks of production are rather flagrantly exhibited—the viewer is reminded precisely of the constructed nature of what he or she sees, and thus, through this realization on the viewer's part, this film (style) works to announce itself 'as a polemic comment on the way things are in their "natural" reflection' (Gabriel 1989a: 47).[20]

The implied viewer of the Bollywood film is thus thrice removed—or, rather, the film is: first, at the level of the 'missed encounter' between film and viewer, i.e., the physical absence of the already screened actor(s) at the time of screening;[21] second, via the actors' 'departure' within the diegesis from the narrative proper into an interstitial 'fantasy' time and space in which the diegetic order is indefinitely paused or temporarily discarded; and finally, in an echo of the first remove, the separation of voice and image via the technique of playback. Yet paradoxically, it is 'in the viewer'—through him or her—that these isolated components are conjoined, for whom, one might say, 'Rosy sings'. It is the implied viewer who, by recognizing ('reading') these disjunctions, synthesizes them into what may simultaneously be called 'story' and 'flight from story'—a cinematic interruption via the very suturing effect of the cinematic experience.

This is to say the implied viewer 'grasps' the film, and at a very basic level. As Metz puts it, 'In the cinema the *subject's knowledge* takes a very precise form without which no film would be possible' (Metz 1982: 48). Here, one can chart another 'limit'—that of the 'irreducibility' of experience itself when mediated by film (i.e., 'mediatized').[22] To return to a point made in the first chapter, either one views a film (i.e., understands that what he or she is viewing is a 'film', thus having met the requisite conditions, for example, suspension of disbelief, awareness of the 'missed encounter', or what one might call 'cinematic engagement') or one does not. In fact, the very reflexive play that the Bollywood film engages in via the song sequence (replete with playback and incessant shifts in time and space) becomes premised on this very 'knowingness', this awareness of distances and separations, for its cinematic pleasure. This is what is unique about the paradigmatic Bollywood film such as *Guide*: its engagement with the viewer via so many disruptions.[23]

Additionally, when these 'disruptions' are formally signalled, i.e., coincide with thematic elements and narrative motivations (as with

'Aaj Phir Jeene Ki ...'), one can trace a further development of the effectivity-via-distancing trope, i.e., the song sequence's formal effect on the narrative itself (recalling here the previously mentioned 'second remove'). The fact that Rosy has this 'experience' (i.e., that of the song sequence) and that it is 'removed', or distanced, from the diegetic world (her world at the level of story; our world—i.e., the viewers'—at the level of discourse), creates a montage of form and content: her 'fantasy' does not exist or, more precisely, it is a 'fantasy' that the viewer helps shape. In this sense, song sequences such as 'Aaj Phir Jeene Ki ...' serve as 'a persistent parabasis to the development of any continuous ethnocultural narrative or of a continuous re-inscription' (Spivak 1990a: 231).[24] The Bollywood film, then, can be described as 'revamping schemas' (the 'bare-bone, routinized devices that solve perennial problems') to 'suit new purposes', a process of revision Noel Carroll calls 'amplification', in which cinematic innovations are devised by 'synthesizing familiar schemas in fresh ways' (Carroll, quoted in Bordwell 1997: 152–53). If, to return to Gabriel's formulation of Third World cinema, 'there cannot be mediation without ideology', then one may describe the ideology of the Bollywood film, via the sequence in *Guide*, as reflexive framing that produces, through the viewer ('sutured' into the film and thus 'making [its] meaning'), abstract ideas not present in any one image (Gabriel 1989b: 61).[25]

It might be useful at this juncture to reconsider the previously delineated 'limit' of subaltern consciousness by engaging in a 'transactional reading' of Spivak's theorization via a consideration of the underlying concept of intentionality. To paraphrase Spivak, this discussion will move by a necessarily circuitous route in its effort to problematize her theorization of the subject. That is to say, by reconfiguring John Searle's paradigm of Intentionality within a specifically cinematic context, I hope to simultaneously destabilize Spivak's conception of (the limitations of) subaltern consciousness and show how the film viewer actively engages in (re)shaping the cinematic discourse. In his essay of the same name, Searle describes Intentionality as 'that property of many mental states and events by which they are directed at or about or of objects and states of affairs in the world' (Searle 1983: 1). Furthermore, he insists, 'Intentionality is not the same as consciousness' (Searle 1983: 2). While attempts may be made to conflate the two terms on the basis that 'all consciousness is consciousness *of*', Searle posits a crucial distinction, namely, between the two senses of 'of': whereas certain experiences (for example, of anxiety) are identical with the state of which they are an experience, intentionality is distinct from that (object/state) of which it is an experience (Searle 1983).

Such a theory becomes particularly relevant to the purposes of this chapter when applied to 'the problem of perception' (Searle 1983: 37). Searle makes a point 'that has often been ignored in discussions of the philosophy of perception', namely, that 'visual ... experiences have Intentionality' (Searle 1983: 39).[26] In proceeding to delineate the intentionality of visual perception, Searle argues for 'a version of "naïve" (direct, common sense) realism', in which three elements are involved: 'the perceiver, the visual experience, and the object (more strictly, the state of affairs) perceived' (Searle 1983: 57). Searle represents his account of visual perception in the following manner:

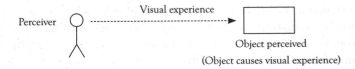

Searle argues that the use of an arrow in his diagram is 'meant to indicate that the visual experience has Intentional content, it is directed at the Intentional object, whose existence is part of its conditions of satisfaction' (Searle 1983: 57).[27] At the same time, in the case of what he labels 'visual hallucination', Searle claims 'the perceiver has the same visual experience but no Intentional object is present' (Searle 1983: 57–58). Such a scenario is represented in the following manner:

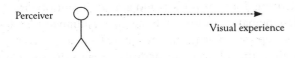

To perform a transactional reading of Searle's argument (as a subset of the transactional reading of Spivak), i.e., if the object perceived is a film (either projected on a screen or transmitted via television), we might proceed in the following fashion:

1. the experience of a film (or of watching a film) is not itself the film;

2. the 'of' in this experience is Intentional;
3. the subject of a film experience is the perceiver;
4. the visual experience of a film has conditions of satisfaction;
5. the notion of perception involves the notion of succeeding;
6. to say the film is perceived implies that its content is satisfied;
7. but the Intentional object (the state of affairs depicted on-screen) is both present and absent,[28]
8. therefore, two distinct forms of visual experience are combined from the perceiver's POV[29] and
9. this combining of two distinct forms of visual experience is what constitutes the satisfaction of the film's content.

To say I have a visual experience that there is a film playing there (i.e., before me) is just to specify the Intentional content; to say I *perceive* a film implies that the content of the film is satisfied. And in this transactional reading, 'satisfying the content' of the film, i.e., 'succeeding', entails precisely an awareness or conflating of the above-mentioned two levels of 'visual experience'—what Metz calls 'story' and 'discourse' (Metz 1982).[30]

While Searle also makes note of 'the Network' in his delineation of Intentionality, it is key to note that, rather than equating the subject with these 'different knottings and configurations of ... strands', so as to produce the 'effect' of a subject (i.e., a metalepsis), this latter concept remains distinct from the 'network' of signifiers Spivak describes (Spivak 1988b: 13). Indeed, while acknowledging that 'Intentional contents do not determine their conditions of satisfaction in isolation', Searle also points out that the subject is aware of this network and, in fact, from this subject's POV (for example, the perceiver in a visual experience), this is his or her network, i.e., 'agents stand in indexical relations to their own Intentional states, their own Networks, and their own Backgrounds' (Searle 1983: 65-66).

It is precisely in this way that one might read Spivak's description of Bollywood films and their song and dance sequences, and *Guide's* in particular, i.e., as 'actively transforming the filmic conventions of the Hollywood musical and recoding the myth of India in the process' (Spivak 1996: 258). The subject of the film—i.e., the film viewer, or 'perceiver'—rather than being 'the effect of an effect', serves as the 'operating subject' who produces the resulting cinematic effects, for example, of the song sequence such as 'Aaj Phir Jeene Ki ...' (Spivak 1988b: 13). Here, we can chart the 'limit' of the 'irreducibility' of subaltern consciousness via what Metz calls the 'double movement' of 'all vision': 'projective (the "sweeping" searchlight) and introjective: consciousness as a sensitive recording surface (as a screen)' (Metz 1982: 50). It is in such a manner that one might say the Bollywood film 'speaks to *and* from the "people" as it constitutes itself for representation' (Spivak 1996: 257). If *Guide* is, as Spivak would have it, 'an indigenous translation' of the novel it was based on and 'thus speaks *for* India', such a 'transaction' could only occur via an 'actively transforming' viewer. In other words, as Kazmi notes, 'a film not only immerses and absorbs an audience into its world, there is also a countercurrent where the spectator immerses the film into his (psychic) world, brought to the threshold of consciousness by the energy emanating from the viewing situation itself' (Kazmi 1999: 230).

Whereas 'post-structuralist theories of consciousness and language suggest that all possibility of expression, spoken or written, shares a common distancing from a self so that meaning can arise', it is crucial to note—even as the film can be said to engage in such a 'distancing' via the 'missed encounter'—that the film experience (i.e., experience of viewing, or 'perceiving', a film) is contingent upon the direct participation of the viewing self (Spivak 1987: 212). While the viewer, too, may be said to 'distance him or herself' via identification with one or more of the characters on-screen, or even via identification with the camera/cinematic apparatus, it is important to remember that the spectator '*identifies with himself*', i.e., as 'a pure act of perception', indeed, as the very 'condition of possibility of the perceived' and thus 'as a kind of transcendental subject, which comes before every *there is*' (Metz 1982: 49). This is what Searle refers to as the 'arrow' in his diagram of the visual experience, i.e., the directedness, or Intentionality, of perception (Searle 1983).

Spivak has claimed to 'have no problem' with either Bollywood or the 'poor benighted folks' she describes in 'Righting Wrongs', 'know[ing] about' and wanting to watch it. Yet, she simultaneously claims that it is 'the abundantly permeating ... idiom of Hindi Cinema, which wasn't allowing them [the poor benighted folks] to see'.[31] One can detect a similar contradiction between her theorization of the problem of 'sub-altern consciousness' (i.e., its irreducibility) and her subsequent claim that 'Bombay musicals' such as *Guide* can engage in 'active transformations of filmic conventions' (Spivak 1996: 258). Due to her '*découpage* for the sake of the [literary] discipline', what Spivak's approach to the question of subaltern consciousness 'disenables', specifically in relation to the perception of the Bollywood film, is the filmic resonance of this term and its requisite contingencies (Spivak 1996: 244). Rather than occluding the self and/or its 'recoverability' (what Spivak refers to as 'a matter of "negative consciousness"'), meaning in the cinematic frame is activated (i.e., made 'comprehensible') by the visual experience of a subject who resides in what Metz refers to as 'a sub-motor and hyper-perceptive state' (Metz 1982: 49; Spivak 1988b: 11).

Furthermore, it is precisely because the Bollywood film such as *Guide* is 'contaminated by song', because 'there is ... lipsynching here', that the 'connection' to consciousness 'remains intact' (Spivak 1996: 261). Rather than considering these elements (i.e., song sequences) as 'distractions' that help to 'diffuse the potentially shocking impact of having a defiant and courageous woman at the heart of the narrative', one might see them engineering just such an impact and in the process performing in precisely the manner accorded to the literary version of *Guide*, i.e., 'ironizing the early metanarratives' and 'carving open domains of self' (Kabir 2001: 70; Mishra 2002: 44–45). Of course, in order to do so, one must see the film as engaging in precisely what such critics claim the cinematic version is incapable of doing, namely, 'transcend[ing] its own specific mode' (Mishra 2002: 47).

Even as Spivak has previously claimed she 'do[esn't] know how to talk about films', this has not stopped her from making the occasional attempt to do so with, as I hope to illuminate, rather surprising results, given her previously reached conclusions regarding the (irretrievable) figure of the subaltern and his or her attendant—and equally irretrievable—consciousness (Spivak 1993: 243). In an essay based on an address made at a conference on cultural value and in a self-claimed 'deconstructive' spirit, Spivak engages in a reading of an Indian film, *Genesis* (1986), by Mrinal Sen (Spivak 1990a). In attempting to understand this film, Spivak posits a variety of viewers or viewer 'types': (*i*) 'the ethnographically savvy viewer'; (*ii*) 'the savvy diasporic'; (*iii*) 'the metropolitan third worldist'; (*iv*) 'the non-theoretical metropolitan third worldist'; and (*v*) 'the appropriate, indeed felicitous, viewer' (Spivak 1990a: 230).[32]

While acknowledging that this is 'a crude taxonomy', Spivak argues that it is still 'slightly more complex than first world/third world, Eurocentric/marginal' (Spivak 1990a: 230). She then proceeds to discuss these hypothetical viewers' engagements with this film, beginning with the title 'flash[ing] on the screen: GENESIS', claiming (in a rather problematic interpellation of these latter 'figures') that 'as the opening credits unroll, we notice that it is Sen's first collaborative film, with French and Belgian support' (Spivak 1990a: 230). A preliminary point regarding Spivak's attempt to speak for 'the viewers' of this film: she assumes they are literate, i.e., can in fact read both the film's title and the opening credits. In her accompanying delineations of the film's 'bold strokes' (which require 'no knowledge of Indic aesthetics or ethnics ... to flesh out'), Spivak focusses on a sequence in which the actress in the film sings, 'without subtitles':

> Here, framed in the film, is a parody of culturalist art, inaccessible ex-
> cept to the authentic native; the audience of postcoloniality has no ac-
> cess to the authentic text. The song is in a Rajasthani dialect, ironically
> the only verbal marker that this is 'Rajasthan'. It is, however, the most
> stunningly double-edged moment in the film. For it is also a negotiation
> of a banality belonging to the internationally accessible idiom of a gen-
> eral 'Indian' mass culture of long standing—the Bombay film industry:
> the woman breaks into a folk song. (Spivak 1990a: 235–36)

Again, we have a problematic configuration: on the one hand, 'no knowledge of Indic aesthetics or ethnics is required'; on the other hand, the song sequence in the film—a 'parody of culturalist art'—is 'inaccessible except to the authentic native'; yet, simultaneously it allegedly belongs to an 'internationally accessible idiom', i.e., that of Bollywood.[33]

Given that Spivak has claimed that 'the historical predicament of the colonial subaltern can be made to become the allegory of the predicament of *all* thought, *all* deliberative consciousness', one might add to her 'crude taxonomy' of viewing positions the claim that *all* viewers, if indeed cognizant of the fact that what they are viewing is a film, engage in a basic form of 'identification', without which 'the film would become incomprehensible' (Metz 1982: 46; Spivak 1988b: 12). It is, indeed, 'not surprising' from precisely this (filmic) perspective that 'it is within the most touristic footage in the film' that the 'emergence of the autonomous aesthetic moment' occurs (Spivak 1990a: 235).

Without paying close attention to *this* disciplinary *découpage*, one may not see that 'the commodification of woman's body ... in the commercial cinema' is fundamentally 'different in kind' from its 'commodification in the commercial temple' (Spivak 1996: 254). As Walter Benjamin has noted and, indeed, Spivak attests, filmic representations are 'distanced by the work of the screen' (Spivak 1996: 260). This distancing, or 'missed encounter', is what, in turn, creates the space for the implied viewer's interpellation.

But what happens to this 'missed encounter' of the cinema when transposed to television? It is, after all, via this latter medium that Bollywood films are increasingly viewed in India, particularly in rural/village areas (Pendakur 1990, 2003; Singhal and Rogers 2001). Doordarshan (the Indian government-financed television station), on average, broadcasts two Bollywood films a week, one shown over the course of three consecutive days, with commercial breaks every fifteen minutes; the other shown on one night, usually on the weekend, also with periodic commercials. To better grasp both the transposition of film to the televisual medium and, particularly, the Bollywood film in such a transposition (within a 'Third World' milieu), it is necessary to turn to Marshal McLuhan's study, *Understanding Media: The Extensions of Man*, first published in 1964. In his section on movies ('The Reel World'), McLuhan formulates the literary bias (to be picked up forty years later by Nayar), claiming that 'movies assume a high level of literacy in their users and prove baffling to the nonliterate' (McLuhan 1964: 285). This statement is immediately followed by an example featuring confused Africans, whose culture McLuhan goes on to call 'backward or oral' (McLuhan 1964: 287):[34]

> Again, it has been found that nonliterates do not know how to fix their eyes, as Westerners do, a few feet in front of the movie screen, or some distance in front of a photo. The result is that they move their eyes over photo or screen as they might their hands. It is this same habit of using the eyes as hands that makes European men so 'sexy' to American women. Only an extremely literate and abstract society learns to fix their eyes, as we must learn to do in reading the printed page. For those who thus fix their eyes, perspective results. (McLuhan 1964: 287–88)

Along with again invoking, on the one hand, the 'Western'/'non-Western' binary, McLuhan further conflates the latter of said binary with 'nonliterates' who naturally, following his literary analogy, lack 'perspective'; this, again, because only a society 'extremely literate and abstract' can learn to 'fix their [sic] eyes'. Yet, when he turns to TV ('The Timid Giant'), he claims:

> Yet it is hard for literate people, with their habit of fixed points of view and three-dimensional vision, to understand the properties of two-dimensional vision. If it had been easy for them, they would have had no difficulties with abstract art. (McLuhan 1964: 313–14)

Here, it would seem, a contradiction arises: on the one hand, only 'literate *and* abstract societies' (the counter equivalent to 'oral and backward'?) can 'learn to fix their eyes', and thus develop 'perspective'; on the other, 'literate people' have (had) 'difficulties with abstract art'. What is it about this medium that 'fosters many preferences that are quite at variance with literate uniformity and repeatability'? And what does all this yield for the view of the illiterate Indian villager who watches Bollywood on Doordarshan TV?

According to McLuhan, 'the old literate habit ... yielded suddenly to depth reading'; the 'mosaic form of the TV image ... commands immediate participation in *depth*' (McLuhan 1964: 325). Yet, 'putting movies on TV', McLuhan feels, would result in 'a hybrid that is neither' (McLuhan 1964: 332). One might, at this moment, recall Bhabha's space of 'translation', and consider that the Bollywood film is particularly well suited to this format(ting) of TV, given its already episodic and hybrid composition (Bhabha 1989: 117). To return to an earlier point, it is precisely in concordance with what Raymond Williams calls 'the central television experience', namely, 'the fact of flow', that one sees the particularly well-suited 'hybridity' of the Bollywood film for the televisual medium (Williams 1975: 95). For just as there is a televisual flow which is 'centrally important in our experience of television', there exists a similarly crucial 'flow' within the Bollywood film. These are both flows of 'otherwise diverse or at best loosely related items', i.e., on the one hand, the sequence of units constituting the television programming and, on the other, the Bollywood film narrative (Williams 1975: 96).

Because, as in the case of *Guide*, there are typically half a dozen song and dance sequences in the typically three hour long Bollywood film, one could say the narrative is frequently interrupted (on average, every thirty minutes though, naturally, never so systematically, i.e., 'on time'). When this film, with its built-in 'interruptions', is transposed to TV, with its own programmed 'interruptions' (i.e., commercial breaks), the result, or resulting fracture, rather than diminishing the film's flow, works with it.[35] Furthermore, this 'aesthetic of interruptions', as I have argued elsewhere, allows for the creation of a context within which viewers:

> are allowed to transfigure a basic level of cinematic engagement, i.e., the suspension of disbelief, into an experience saturated with their own critical responses. Whether or not it is supplemented with ... reading materials, the first half of the film is mulled over, discarded, recollected, and/or forgotten by viewers, so that the next day, a new perspective becomes possible, thanks to the rupturing of the cinematic experience. (Gehlawat 2004: 105)

These fissures, both within the Bollywood film and via its televisual transmission, work paradoxically to infuse the viewing experience, so that, again, an opportunity to engage in 'texting', even without books or the ability (literally) to read, becomes possible.

Recalling my earlier catachrestic reading of Plato's cave allegory ('catachrestic' in relation to its typical application to the film experience), one could describe the Bollywood film and the televisual apparatus broadcasting it as 'a teaching machine', i.e., a device creating 'contingencies of reinforcement' that can simultaneously be described as 'an *uncoercive* rearrangement of desires' (Skinner 1968: 65; Spivak 2002: 173).[36] In this way, the cinematic experience—in which, for instance, 'the spectator is not amazed when the image "rotates" (=a pan)' and yet is aware of not turning his or her head (Metz 1982: 50)—can paradoxically be seen as allowing for precisely that form of 'reorientation' in which the film viewer engages in the skill of 'scene-shifting' (Chappell 1996: 236).[37] Where one goes from here remains an open question, but the transmission of Bollywood film does, at the very least, provide a way of experiencing what Brecht called an 'A-effect' through a 'B-grade' approach, or the beginning of 'the undoing of centuries of oppression', via 'a suturing education' (Spivak 2002: 197). While cinema '*may* aid [subaltern] viewers in resisting or subverting those elements of upper class judgments that they find oppressive' and while Bollywood may focus 'on the concerns and world-view of the dominated', the more important preliminary point here is that

Bollywood films, in their widespread and increasing circulation, *can* serve as a supplement to the enlightenment of subaltern viewers (Dickey 1993: 144; Kazmi 1999: 216). It is precisely in this way that Bollywood can and does function as an innovative form of popular cinema.

NOTES

1. A similar tautological form of reasoning is observed by Sara Dickey, when she notes that 'the common image of cinema participation, accepted and promulgated at all social levels, is one of the poor watching and even demanding the unsavory, low-brow material of films' (Dickey 1993: 6). In other words, the poor demand lowbrow cinema, which is why the cinema (primarily patronized by the poor) is lowbrow. For further discussion of such a paradigm, see Chapter 1.

2. For more of this notion of Bollywood engaging in 'mythic telescoping', see Nandy (1981: 91).

3. This is the definition of 'burlesque' from the *American Heritage Dictionary*, 3rd edition (1996). The second definition of the term goes on to state: 'A ludicrous or mocking imitation; a travesty'; and the third definition: 'a variety show characterized by broad ribald comedy, dancing, and striptease'.

4. As Spivak has noted, 'Although a single example does not prove a case, a single counterexample makes human generalizations imperfect' (Spivak 1996: 251). It is precisely in this latter sense that I wish to supplement Spivak's anecdote.

5. My thanks to Sarla Mann for her assistance in procuring this data.

6. At this point, one might argue that, given the TV sets, the villagers are no longer 'subalterns'. However, I would dispute such a claim, arguing rather that, as said status has historically been, even as it continues to be, associated with illiteracy, which has remained steady during this same time, it would be rather inconsistent to eliminate the subaltern status immediately after the arrival of a medium that has simultaneously been theorized as 'non-literate', or oral (Nayar 2004).

7. That is, the 'flow for information technology' (Spivak 2002). I would argue that this, instead, should be read as the flow *of* said technology. The paradigm of 'episodic viewing' (via television) that I have sketched here relates to what Raymond Williams calls the 'flow' of televisual sequencing (Williams 1975). See Chapter 1 for an extended discussion of this.

8. As Spivak describes it, 'In the strictest sense of commodity (a product produced for exchange), the three classical dance traditions of India and multiple folk forms are put into a hopper and swirled around with free-form musical structuring to produce a "global" India' (Spivak 1996: 258). The specific film Spivak is discussing here, *Guide* (1965), will be taken up in the following pages.

9. The point here being that Bollywood becomes a meta-textual reflection *on/of* cinema, as institution and storytelling device.

10. As Arvind Singhal and Everett M. Rogers note:

> Prior to 1983, television access in India was limited to 28 percent of the nation's population. Only 30 million Indians (less than 5 percent of the population),

mostly located in metropolitan cities, regularly watched television. Five years later, in 1988, 62 percent of the population could access television signals, and over 100 million Indians regularly watched television. In 2000, some 90 percent of India's population could access television signals, and over 500 million (50 percent of the population) regularly watched television. (2001: 85)

Singhal and Rogers define 'people who have access to television' as 'those who live in a geographical area where a television signal can be received' (Singhal and Rogers 2001: 87). Furthermore, they note that 'Doordarshan's programmes, relative to previous decades, increasingly reach rural, poor, and female audiences' (Singhal and Rogers 2001: 105, n. 14). See also Pendakur (2003: 46–51).

11. In this sense, this process comes closer to Spivak's definition of 'just "reading"', i.e., 'suspending oneself into the text of the other' (Spivak 2002: 181).

12. 'Text-ing', as Spivak defines it, i.e., *texere*, is to weave, to fabricate, i.e., to interweave or combine (elements) into a complex whole; to contrive (something complex or elaborate) in this way (Nunberg 1996: 1857, 2023). One might also compare the concept of 'suture' deployed here to such this notion of 'text-ing'.

13. In this sense—and with no small irony—Spivak may be seen as 'speaking for' the Subalternists, i.e., positioning them in relation to her own 'transactional' reading, something she claims they [the Subaltern theorists] 'oblige' her to do and something that 'would get the group off the dangerous hook of claiming to establish the truth-knowledge of the subaltern and his consciousness' (Spivak 1988b: 4, 26).

14. Spivak claims to undertake such an 'ordinary', 'formulaic' approach towards *Guide* in order, paradoxically, to make 'the literary critic ... helpful for the study of culture'. Such an approach, she claims, becomes 'an enabling limitation, a *découpage* for the sake of the [literary] discipline' (Spivak 1996). It is precisely the filmic connotation of this latter term—i.e., the dividing of action into shots—that I will be interested in examining and applying in the following discussion.

15. The 'temple dancer' is paradoxically associated with prostitution. As Chakravarty notes, this profession is 'ambivalently located between spirituality or art and carnality or prostitution' (Chakravarty 1993: 50).

16. The allegory I have in mind, and that this sequence recalls, is Plato's 'Allegory of the Cave'. For a classic instance of the application of this allegory to the film-viewing experience, see Jean-Louis Baudry, 'The Apparatus: Metapsychological Approaches to the Impression of Reality in Cinema' (1992: 690–707).

17. Indeed, one can trace an inverse parallel between the allegorical function of the anklets in this sequence and the unshackling of the chains that bind the prisoner's legs in the Socratic dialogue.

18. Mangeshkar, the playback singer for this sequence, is listed in the *Guinness Book of World Records* as having recorded the most number of songs ever. It should also be noted that all Bollywood film songs employ the technique of playback, in which actor and actress lip-synch to the pre-recorded song. Usually, it is the same singer, or singers, providing the voice(s) for almost all the films, for example, Lata Mangeshkar. This fact is known by Indian audiences, whether they be in the city or in the village. The film songs also play frequently on Indian radio. For more on playback singing and sound, see Arnold (1991).

19. Interestingly enough, to continue the Platonic parallel, the famous Socratic method is referred to in the *Theaetetus* as 'the art of midwifery or maieutic', which Aristotle was referencing in calling Socrates the 'inventor of the method of induction' (Skinner 1968: 108, n. 2).

20. It is precisely in this sense that my reading here deviates from what I consider the 'normative' (mis)application of Plato's cave allegory to the realm of cinema: whereas the typical approach, for example, that of Baudry, likens film viewers to the chained prisoners *in* the cave—and thus the film, as shadow, to 'delusion'—I am attempting to liken the Bollywood film experience to the prisoner who is thrust *out* of the cave, thus making the Bollywood film integral to the process of 'reorientation', or 'scene-shifting', leading to 'enlightenment' (Chappell 1996: 236).

21. 'In the theatre, actors and spectators are present at the same time and in the same location, hence present one to another ... But in the cinema, the actor was present when the spectator was not (=shooting), and the spectator is present when the actor is no longer (=projection)' (Metz 1982: 63).

22. That is, as a supplement to Spivak's establishment of a 'limit' with regard to both the 'failure' of cognitive thought and the recoverability of subaltern consciousness (Spivak 1988b: 5-7, 11).

23. It is in this manner that *Guide* functions 'as an allegory of the cinema and of the life of the performer in general' and, as Chakravarty goes on to note, 'both exploits and undercuts the seductive power and the fragility of roles and the expectations they arouse' (Chakravarty 1993: 52). It is perhaps for these reasons that she subsequently claims, '*Guide* may well serve as Bombay cinema's ideal-typical scenario of self-reflexive desire' (Chakravarty 1993: 52).

24. As Spivak notes, 'The *OED* defines "parabasis" as "going aside", "address to the audience in the poet's name, unconnected with the action of the drama"' (Spivak 1990a: 243, n. 38).

25. This is precisely how the Bollywood film can be said to function more as an 'innovative' cinema than as a 'conventional' one or, indeed, how an apparently conventional cinema (such as Bollywood) can be innovative. See Chapter 2 and also Kazmi (1999).

26. In short, 'the "of" of "experience of" is ... the "of" of Intentionality' (Searle 1983: 39).

27. As Searle notes in an accompanying parenthetical, such a delineation is not meant to imply that the visual experience exists in the physical space between the perceiver and the object (Searle 1983: 57).

28. That is to say, following Metz's description of the 'missed encounter', the places and people depicted on screen are no longer physically present when the film is screened; rather, it is their images, or shadows, that appear, signifying their physical absence (Metz 1982: 63).

29. Namely, the two forms delineated above—one in which there is an actual 'object perceived' (which is causing the 'visual experience') and one in which no Intentional object is present (what Searle calls 'visual hallucination').

30. Metz claims that while the viewer is aware of the film's 'construction' (i.e., its discourse) and, in fact, needs to be aware of this in order to successfully follow or read the 'coding' of the film (i.e., its filmic language, the way its meaning is assembled), he or she also 'doesn't want to know' this or, rather, 'suspends' this knowledge so as to experience the film as 'story' (Metz 1982: 91-97).

31. Written response to the author, 22 July 2005.

32. Along with the problematic positing of these essentialized types, it is interesting to note that Spivak entirely elides the subaltern viewer as 'category'/'type' in her analysis of what is ostensibly the space of marginality.

33. Furthermore, this invocation (of the so-called 'authentic native') is itself a problematic construction, given Spivak's earlier remarks regarding the 'inaccessibility' of such a figure.

34. Infact, McLuhan generally equates the two, i.e., 'oral' as 'backward'.

35. Whereas 'Western' films (i.e., following Gabriel, those adhering to 'Western conventions') 'were not made to be "interrupted" in this way' (Williams 1975: 92), I would argue that such interruption is precisely what constitutes the essence of the Bollywood film, i.e., its paradoxical, or hybrid, flow. For more on the concept of 'flow', see Chapter 1; for a further discussion of the interruption(s) of the Bollywood film, see Chapter 2.

36. As Metz notes, 'When I say that "I see" the film, I mean thereby a unique mixture of two contrary currents: the film is what I receive, and it is also what I release, since it does not pre-exist my entering the auditorium and I only need close my eyes to suppress it' (1982: 51).

37. Underscoring the catachrestic nature of this interpretation, the film viewer, rather than turning 'the whole body', is in a 'sub-motor and hyper-perceptive state' (Chappell 1996; Metz 1982: 49). Furthermore, he or she, rather than turning *away* from the 'shadow-play', focusses his or her eyes *upon* it, i.e., 'apprehends' it. Here, then, one sees the 'limit' of the Socratic allegory—or, for that matter, the non-(medium)-specific 'allegorical' reading, for example, Spivak's 'literary *découpage*'—as a 'method of considering this *instrumentality*' of the film experience (Spivak 1996: 244, emphasis added).

Ho Naa Ho: The Emergence of a Homosexual Subtext in Bollywood

In this chapter, I take as my starting point the conclusion reached in the previous chapter—that Bollywood can and does function as an innovative form of popular cinema—as a way of coming to terms with the recent 'emergence' of a homosexual subtext in popular Hindi cinema. As several theorists (and even more viewers) have recently noted, the 'secret politics' of homosexuality in Bollywood have become less and less secretive, with blatantly 'gay' characters and subtexts emerging in mainstream films which have gone on to become box-office successes. Without reading too deeply into such outward successes, I would like to examine what the emergence of this homosexual subtext suggests for the shifting dynamics of the Bollywood film and its onscreen representations of homo/heterosexuality and whether, as Rajinder Dudrah has asked, 'there are genuine queer possibilities opening up here, or if they are simply being subsumed within the dominant heteronormative workings of Bollywood cinema' (Dudrah 2006: 139).[1]

In Hindi, *ho naa ho* literally means 'happens or does not happen', though in terms of usage it can be translated as, 'Whether or not it happens'. The phrase is taken from the title of one of the films to be discussed in this chapter, *Kal Ho Naa Ho* (Tomorrow Happens or Doesn't Happen, dir. Nikhil Advani, 2003). In this chapter, I will be building on the reorienting possibilities of the Bollywood film highlighted in the previous chapters to reframe representations of (homo)sexuality and reformulate the subsequent theories that have emerged to 'explain' these (homo)sexual representations. Simultaneously, my exploration of homosexual subtexts in Bollywood films will work to address Dudrah's question and serve as a litmus test of sorts for this cinema's capacity to innovatively deviate from an ostensibly heteronormative frame. My analysis of the Bollywood film's alleged commitment to heterosexuality proceeds in four parts: (*i*) an overview of certain binarisms that have been and continue to be invoked in the theorization of (homo) sexuality, particularly with regard to 'Eastern' or, in this case, 'Indian' culture; (*ii*) a case study of the recent Bollywood blockbuster, *Kal Ho Naa Ho*, including a close reading of this film's final wedding number and its reformulations of the previously delineated binarisms; (*iii*) a case study of the even more recent Bollywood blockbuster, *Dostana* (dir. Tarun Mansukhani, 2008), including close readings of several of its particularly 'gay' sequences and (*iv*) a reconsideration of earlier, less blatantly 'queer'—though arguably more homoerotic—moments in Bollywood films in light of recent developments. The title of the first section of this chapter is a direct reference to the title of the first chapter of Eve Kosofsky Sedgwick's *Epistemology of the Closet* (1990), a text whose own implicit binarisms I intend to excavate in the following pages, even as I assemble what might be called an epistemology of the homosexual subtext in Bollywood. The referencing of Sedgwick at the outset is thus meant to signal the meta-critical stance I intend to take in this section, re-examining these binarisms in order to more fully appreciate the Bollywood film's problematic relationship with and, indeed, reformulation *of* them.

SOME BINARISMS

The study of sexuality and, more particularly, homosexuality in the Bollywood film has, in recent years, seen an upsurge in interest from critical theorists, particularly those aiming to link the latest on-screen (homo)sexual innovations to a South Asian diaspora or, more precisely, to 'South Asian queer diasporic spectatorship' (Gopinath 2005: 99). In order to perform simultaneously a reading of the homosexual subtext in the Bollywood film and of its contemporary theorization, it is necessary to first take a few steps back and re-examine the formation of a discourse concerning 'Eastern' sexuality. In the third part of the first volume of *The History of Sexuality*, Michel Foucault claims that 'historically, there have been two great procedures for producing the truth of sex', namely, an *ars erotica* and a *scientia sexualis* (Foucault 1990). Along with other 'Eastern civilizations', Foucault includes India in the societies 'which endowed themselves with an *ars erotica*', which he then goes on to describe in detail:

> In the erotic art, truth is drawn from pleasure itself, understood as a practice and accumulated as experience; pleasure is not considered in relation to an absolute law of the permitted and the forbidden, nor by a reference to a criterion of utility, but first and foremost in relation to itself; it is experienced as pleasure, evaluated in terms of its intensity, its specific quality, its duration, its reverberations in the body and the soul. (Foucault 1990: 57)

'On the face of it', Foucault declares, 'our [Western] civilization possesses no *ars erotica*', but rather a *scientia sexualis* in which 'procedures for telling the truth of sex ... are geared to a form of knowledge-power strictly opposed to the [*ars erotica*]' (Foucault 1990: 58). In particular, Foucault has in mind the confession as emblematic of this latter form of sexuality—'a form that is far removed from the one governing the "erotic art"' (Foucault 1990: 62).[2]

In describing the 'making of a complex machinery for producing the true discourses on sex', then, Foucault clings to this binarism of 'Eastern' and 'Western' sexualities. Though he questions whether 'the *scientia sexualis* ... has not functioned, at least to a certain extent, as an *ars erotica*', he concludes (as he begins) by saying, '*Scientia sexualis* versus *ars erotica*, no doubt' (Foucault 1990: 70–71). Similarly, though he posits the possibility of the former functioning as the latter, or rather the latter as not 'disappear[ing] altogether from Western civilization', nowhere does he consider the inverse possibility, namely, of a so-called (i.e., so-labelled) *ars erotica* functioning in, or masquerading as, the form of a *scientia sexualis* (Foucault 1990: 70). To paraphrase Foucault, then, such mechanisms need to be taken seriously and require a reversal in the direction of analysis: rather than concluding that *scientia sexualis* 'is but an extraordinarily subtle form of *ars erotica*', we must question whether, in the Bollywood film, the so-called *ars erotica* subtly (or not so subtly) functions in the capacity of its alleged other (Foucault 1990: 71, 73).

One may begin such an endeavour by paraphrasing Eve Kosofsky Sedgwick (even as such an act 'might require revisions or rupturings') and proposing that a dominant discourse of Bollywood is structured, or 'fractured', by the endemic crisis of homo/heterosexual definition (Sedgwick 1990: 1, 14).[3] In other words, the presentation of homosexual and heterosexual as binary opposites belies a more dynamic, unsettled and tacit relation between the two (Sedgwick 1990: 9–10). To invoke Sedgwick's definitional crisis in the context of Bollywood, however, requires an immediate intervention into her epistemology, as she begins by considering Michel Foucault's genealogy of sexuality to be 'axiomatic' and maintains a rather Foucauldian (i.e., Western-based) focus throughout her study of the 'closeted' space(s) of homosexuality. Though Sedgwick asserts that her approach is 'deconstructive' and goes on to list a number of binary oppositions that her analysis seeks to deconstruct, nowhere is the 'East/West' binarism underlying all of this mentioned among the twenty-two binarisms she claims have ineffaceably marked 'our culture' (Sedgwick 1990: 11).[4] For me to make such an intervention (into Sedgwick's epistemology of the closet), then, requires an examination of how the Bollywood film (re)configures allegedly distinct forms of sexuality and how these reformulations in turn negotiate the above-mentioned crisis of homo/heterosexual definition. Before doing so, I would like to first review recent theorizations of homosexuality in the Bollywood film, so as to more effectively delineate the state of the field and anticipate my own intervention.

Gayatri Gopinath, one of the leading queer theorists to focus specifically on Bollywood, begins her analysis of homosexuality in the Bollywood film by making a general point: despite the 'groundbreaking' studies in recent years that have paid careful attention to aspects of production, narrative and genre in the Indian popular cinema, less attention has been given to how 'spectatorial strategies may at least temporarily displace or destabilize its [the Bollywood film's] ideological project' (Gopinath 2005: 97).[5] Gopinath goes on to say she is particularly concerned with the potential destabilization caused by queer readings of the Bollywood film, which she immediately associates with 'queer audiences' and 'diasporic audiences' and, indeed, 'queer diasporic audiences' (Gopinath 2005: 95). These audiences, in Gopinath's view, are the generators of such a queer reading and all its possible 'interpretive interventions and appropriations' (Traub,

quoted in Gopinath 2005: 95). All of these (queer/diasporic) spectators, real and/or potential, collectively 'reimagine their relation to an
"originary" past national location', even as 'cinematic images which
in their "originary" contexts simply reiterate conventional nationalist
and gender ideologies may, through queer reading practices, be refash-
ioned' (Gopinath 2005: 97, 99).

While temporarily suspending the question of whether there ever
is an 'originary' in Bollywood, one might begin by asking whether the
constitution of a queer subjectivity is contingent upon a queer diaspora
and, simultaneously, if the Bollywood *film* (and not just its queer
diasporic spectators) can engage in such 'queering'. While Gopinath
asserts that queer themes in Bollywood films remain 'nontransgressive
in their native Indian context', and that she 'certainly do[es] not want
to replicate the notion that queer diasporic spectators are somehow
automatically or inevitably resistant readers', she does remain
primarily—in fact, exclusively—concerned with how '*these* spectators
[queer/diasporic] ... may enact particular viewing strategies' in order
to 'remake' the Bollywood film (Gopinath 2000: 283; Gopinath 2005:
98, emphasis added). Thus, even as she posits, for instance, the song
and dance sequence in these films as 'a peculiarly *queer* form', and
one 'particularly available for queer viewing strategies', Gopinath
also asserts that it is 'the differently subjective lens of transnational
spectatorship' that is responsible for 'de-coding', or 're-coding', these
elements and the film as a whole (as 'queer') (Gopinath 2000: 283).[6]

Another theorist of queerness in Bollywood, Thomas Waugh, even
as he cites ethnographer Lawrence Cohen's warning against reducing
analysis 'to a set of categories ... all too easily grounded in a globalizing
heterosexual/homosexual opposition', retains Gopinath's 'home and
the world' binary and, in fact, further articulates the construct, impli-
cating in many ways what was implicit yet never directly stated in Gopinath's original formulation: class division (Cohen, quoted in Waugh
2001: 283). Again invoking Cohen's caution, Waugh links queerness
in Bollywood films to what Cohen calls 'middle-class metropolitan
movements and identities', which Waugh subsequently shortens to
'MMMIs' (Waugh 2001: 284). It is the 'MMMI dynamic, the incredibly
lively diasporic queer movement', that 'inventories and dissects, interpellates and reclaims ... that which is unspoken back home' (Waugh
2001).[7] At the same time, Waugh notes, 'it would be absurd to dismiss

the core of subaltern agency in the Hindophone audienc[e]' (Waugh 2001: 283).

Despite this latter crucial point, however, Waugh's (re)formulation of the MMMI paradigm can be seen as further embellishing Gopinath's 'native/diasporic' binary via a 'lower/middle', or, indeed, sub-proletarian/bourgeois dichotomy. Only MMMIs (or those with access to 'the differently subjective lens of transnational spectatorship') can read (or 're-code' or 'de-code') queerness in the Bollywood film, as these latter moments are incapable of being realized 'back home' (despite the absurdity of dismissing subaltern agency). Yet, as Waugh simultaneously notes, 'One must not go so far as to assume the mythical purity of sexual cultures hermetically sealed from all external interaction', and indeed, 'who can say where the imported MMMIs end and the indigenous authentic begins?' (Waugh 2001: 285). To overlook what Margaret Jolly and Lenore Manderson call 'cross-cultural *exchanges* in sexualities' would be to reinvoke the Foucauldian paradigm of *ars erotica* versus *scientia sexualis*, no doubt, positing sexuality as neatly configured along (alleged, essential) cultural divides (Foucault 1990; Jolly and Manderson, quoted in Waugh 2001: 285).

As a way of avoiding the pitfalls of such facile dichotomies (East/ West, heterosexual/homosexual, etc.), one might instead, along with R. Raj Rao, see 'how homosexuality thrives in covert yet recognized places in Indian culture', and, indeed, 'how ... forms of homosexuality are actually engendered under the auspices of normative patriarchal culture', particularly in and by the Bollywood film (Rao 2000: 299).[8] In this sense, it becomes particularly useful to detach the concept of 'queer readings' from a necessary, pre-located queer audience and, in fact, (re)consider it within more aesthetic terms. As Alexander Doty notes:

> My use of the terms 'queer readings', 'queer discourses', and 'queer po-
> sitions', then, are attempts to account for the existence and expression
> of places within culture, cultural production, and cultural reception
> that are 'queer' or 'different' and which can't fully, clearly, or accurately
> be articulated through heterosexual positions and discourses. (Doty,
> quoted in Feuer 1993: 139)[9]

Crucial to such a formulation is the recognition of the possibil- ity that 'various and fluctuating (queer) positions might be occupied whenever *anyone* produces or responds to culture' (Feuer 1993). In this sense, to return to Gopinath's delineation of the song and dance sequence as a 'particularly queer' element, a 'queer reading' would 'shift emphasis from narrative resolution as heterosexual coupling ... and toward readings based on non-narrative, performative and spectacular elements (an emphasis on the numbers)' (Feuer 1993: 141). It is particularly with such a paradigm in mind that I would like to make my intervention and read the emergence of a homosexual subtext in a contemporary Bollywood film. In doing so, I will be drawing directly on my own experience watching the recent blockbuster, *Kal Ho Naa Ho* (hereafter *KHNH*), with a predominantly South Asian-diasporic audience at the packed Eagle Theatre in Jackson Heights, Queens, on the opening weekend on the film's release.[10]

KAL HO NAA HO: A CASE STUDY

The storyline is simple (for a typical Bollywood film): girl likes boy, boy likes girl, girl falls in love with other boy, other boy helps first boy make girl fall in love with him (Boy 1). Of course, in the process, it becomes clear that Boy 2, too, has feelings for the girl, making his ultimate sacrifice (because he has a heart condition and only a little time left to live) perhaps all the more tragic, were it not for the saccharine tone of the Bollywood film. This latter tone, depending on one's religious bent (or lack thereof), could be attributed either to Bollywood's impersonating style or to its implied viewers' inclination to see things in relation to *dharma*—i.e., a cosmic moral law.[11] The fact that the overwhelming majority of the theatre audience (of which I was a part) did not remain to watch the film's conclusion, however, seems to put into question such a *dharmic* reading. What does become immediately clear is *KHNH's* use of the 'erotic triangle' trope described, in a different context, by Sedgwick, in which 'the bond that links the two rivals is as intense and potent as the bond that links either of the rivals to the beloved' (Sedgwick 1985: 21).[12] Via this bond, *KHNH* can be said to enact a shift in register from 'dostana', or male friendship, to 'yaari', a relationship entailing 'much more than a friend' (Rao 2000: 304–05).[13]

Indeed, beyond the film's most obvious subtext—the assimilation of young, bourgeois Indians into 'globalized' American culture (i.e., post-9/11 New York City)—resides a more dangerous subtext, one that literally seeps into the text and threatens to overturn its heterosexual logic. I am referring, of course, to the homosexual subtext that is consistently brought to the surface—and exploited for crude laughs (which it received in my experience)—between the two male leads, Bollywood heartthrobs Shah Rukh Khan and Saif Ali Khan. To paraphrase Chris Straayer, my intention here is to view this homosexual subtext as an instance of *hypothetical* queerness, i.e., neither character's homosexuality is an obvious fact of the film (Straayer 1995). Furthermore, this 'axis of erotic play' between the two male leads is situated within a predominantly heterosexual framework (Waugh 2001: 292). As Shah Rukh (Aman) helps Saif Ali (Rohit) lure the girl in question (Preity Zinta) with his 'six-day strategy' (first ignoring and then overwhelming Preity's character, Naina), the two male leads are constantly thrust into ambiguous spheres of sexual meaning. At one point, Aman is coaching Rohit on how to seduce Naina. Suddenly, an older female Indian character, Kanta-ben, arrives on the scene. As she witnesses this 'courtship rehearsal' with an expression of horror and disbelief, the breakfast tray she is holding begins to shake—Kanta-ben has mistaken this courtship rehearsal for a homosexual encounter.

In this character's facial and bodily gestures, then, the double meaning of these scenes' sexuality is confirmed, as well as by the audience's laughter. One can see 'the bond between rivals ... as being even stronger, more heavily determinant of actions and choices, than anything in the bond between either of the lovers and the beloved' (Girard, quoted in Sedgwick 1985: 21). However, what is interesting to note is the accompanying relief that was audible in the noisy theatre at the presence of Kanta-ben (the surrogate authority figure) and her subsequent shock at witnessing this act. As the director, Nikhil Advani, notes, 'You had already seen her once, so you were waiting for her. The minute you ... saw Aman and Rohit were embracing each other, were talking about love, you knew she was going to come. It was fantastic. The reaction in the [movie] house was exactly what we wanted'.[14] The reactions of the Jackson Heights audience in my experience, then, seem to confirm the intended 'reading' of this character even as they illuminate the instability of this character's function: Kanta-ben's presence figuratively confirms and nominally repudiates the homosexual subtext. I would thus argue that it is the dual function of this presence that renders it problematic (at the level of discourse) and, thus, pleasurable (at the level of story).

While such sexual comedies of error are hardly new, the Bollywood version works to reveal and simultaneously destabilize the larger ambivalence existing within Indian culture—on the one hand, its infusion with and recognition of 'homosexual' elements (most typically, *hijras*, or male cross-dressers) and, at the same time, its overt rejection of homosexuality.[15] Though such a collusion of cultural elements may hardly be unique to India or to popular Hindi cinema, its particular reworking in Bollywood allows it to transcend its closeted position and, in the process, transform the entire story. This is made possible, in part, through the particular aesthetic employed by Bollywood, a systematic reformulation of tropes often referred to as 'impersonation'. As Sumita Chakravarty notes:

> Concentrated within this metaphor are the notions of changeability and metamorphosis, tension and contradiction, recognition and alienation, surface and depth: dualities that have long plagued the Indian psyche and constitute the self-questionings of Indian nationhood. Indian cinema, caught in the cross-currents of this national dialogue and contributing to it, has made impersonation its distinctive signature. This is more than a matter of reinforcing truisms that films impersonate life; characters impersonate real men and women; the film-viewing experience impersonates dream. Impersonation subsumes a process of externalization, the play of/on surfaces, the disavowal of fixed identity. (Chakravarty 1993: 4)

Through such a trope, 'Indianness' becomes defined through the absence of any such structured essence—'the dialectics of juxtaposition and contamination thus inform this notion' (Chakravarty 1993: 4). Such an aesthetic lampoons its own ideology, in this case, the heterosexuality of the film (and culture at large), culminating in the sought after (heterosexual) marriage.

These frequent scenes of sexual 'misunderstanding' between the two male characters point to the emergence of a decidedly non-*dharmic* explanation for characters and their actions: namely, that Aman and Rohit are more interested in each other than in Naina, who seems to be the convenient cover for their closeted relationship, serving as 'the object of exchange between two men', and a 'bonding device that serves to cement male friendship' (Gopinath 2000: 291). If Aman and Rohit really do have sexual feelings for one another, then Aman's sacrifice is not a heterosexual one (giving up the Girl to the other Boy) but rather, a homosexual one (giving up the *Boy* to the Girl). This sacrifice is made for (and in the face of) the dominant heterosexual order, one reinforced by the concept of the arranged marriage. And it is precisely in its diasporic state that this order reasserts itself so vigorously. Indeed, the quivering Kanta-ben ultimately feels compelled to try physically to prevent Aman from meeting Rohit, as she believes their 'union' will prevent Rohit from successfully wooing Naina and attaining the validating (heterosexual) marriage.

The irony (only one of many) is that it is precisely in order to *ensure* this marriage that Aman is looking for Rohit. Yet, Kanta-ben's misunderstanding illuminates the close relationship the two male characters share, one in which they engage in more intimate acts with each other than either ever does onscreen with Naina. To see Aman, then, as the 'queer friend' works in two ways: on the one hand, he is the selfless heterosexual providing the girl he loves with a surrogate lover. However, the very sacrifice involved in this relationship opens up the possibility that Aman, in fact, means it when he tells Naina repeatedly, 'I don't love you'. Aman's tears, in other words, are shed not for his inability to consummate the heterosexual union but rather because the homosexual relationship that culminated in the process must come to an end once the former union is finalized.

The audience and I, while watching the film, continually laughed at this homosexual subtext, climaxing when Rohit's father takes him to a strip club in an effort to fix what he thinks is his son's 'problem'—'a scene', as the director notes, 'between a father who suspects his son of being gay and a son who has no idea why he's being brought to the strip bar ... a first time for Indian cinema'.[16] Again, in a gesture—what Advani refers to as 'the unsaid'—meaning is conveyed. When Rohit tells his father, even as he keeps his back to the scantily-clad Western women dancers, that there is 'no problem with girls', his father thrusts his clenched fist out repeatedly, as if to say (which he then does), 'So you are a *real* (i.e., heterosexual) man!' Thus, even the formal resolution of this subtext is enacted in silence. It does not need to be said—it is supposedly understood by both father and son, as well as the (laughing) audience.

Yet, what precisely is understood? That Rohit is not gay and will (thus) marry Naina? Or that he, like Aman before him, realizes a homosexual relationship cannot be officially sanctioned by his/their diasporic culture? It is key to note that this type of self-sacrifice is itself destabilizing, as it is employed on both hetero- and homosexual levels, by both male characters. Regardless of the level on which one chooses to read the film, the fact remains that the resolution is built upon this sacrifice. Even, and especially, if one applies a 'straight' read, one must concede that this heterosexual union is rather hollow and asexual, as neither Naina nor Rohit truly loves the other. Rather, it represents a sacrifice and is thus more a matter of appearances or, rather, an 'impersonation'.

No wonder, then, that during the tagged-on finale, which features Naina and Rohit, twenty years later, reflecting back on Aman (who has presumably died since then), the theatre lights came up and the audience began walking out. This premature departure comes precisely because this scene, confirming Naina and Rohit's enduring heterosexual union, was of secondary importance. The primary issue was Aman's sacrifice, as well as Rohit's consenting to go along with this sacrifice, out of the love the men felt for each other. This love is nowhere more on display than in the penultimate and protracted parting scene, in which Rohit sits weeping by Aman's bedside and intermittently holding his hand, while Naina can only stand outside, watching. And so, if the subsequent heterosexual resolution is so crucial to retaining and reaffirming the 'dharmic' order, it is rather odd that by the time it comes, half the audience is already walking away.[17]

If 'the motif of male bonding ... serves as the metonym of national unity and amity', then KHNH's homosexual subtext—its shift from the register of 'dostana' to 'yaari'—works to enact a 'gaze-in-crisis', one exemplified by Kanta-ben's shocked reaction to the sight of Aman and Rohit's 'impersonation', that is 'neither simply male nor female' but 'a differential gaze that the cinematic image simultaneously destabilizes and appropriates' (Chakravarty 1993: 214–15). Chakravarty is right to suggest that such a mode of parody works to 'problematize difference' and 'charts new territory in notions of the gaze'—in fact, becoming a 'transsexual' gaze (even as the male star becomes 'a collective creation' and the object of said gaze)—yet 'certain questions', which 'may be posed to tease out the implications for spectatorship of this generic cross', remain unaddressed in her study (Chakravarty 1993: 215, 220, 233). Though she devotes an entire chapter to 'Masculinity and Masquerade', beginning with an epigraph by Judith Butler and concluding by positing a set of binaries that are displaced via Bollywood's 'impersonating' style, nowhere is the 'endemic crisis of homo/heterosexual definition' mentioned or discussed (Chakravarty 1993).[18]

To better grasp the implications of this 'gaze-in-crisis' stemming from a shift in homosocial registers, a closer examination of the performative nature of the Bollywood film is required, i.e., how the concepts of gender and sexual identity it purports to express are, in Butler's terms, 'manufactured and sustained through corporeal signs and other discursive means' (Butler 1990: 173). Using Butler's notion of 'gender parody', I will attempt to engage in such a reading, focussing specifically on a song and dance sequence from *KHNH*, in order to tease out the underlying queer dynamics at play. As Gopinath has noted, queer desire tends to emerge precisely in such (song and dance) sequences and a 'queer reading' of these musical moments (constituting forty per cent of the average popular Indian film) would engage in precisely the kind of shifting previously delineated by Feuer, i.e., from an emphasis on narrative resolution to the numbers (Feuer 1993: 141; Gopinath 2000: 285).

KHNH's penultimate song and dance sequence, 'Maahi Ve', ostensibly celebrating Rohit and Naina's engagement, is preceded by a shot of Kanta-ben giving Rohit *ashirwad*, or religious blessing, while Naina, in a voiceover, says, 'God listened to Kanta-ben. Rohit's marriage was with a girl'. Even as she speaks, we see the queer Indian wedding planner, Jean le Bon, flitting about in the background. Approaching the soon-to-be groom with a big smile while fluttering his lashes and playing with a garland, this figurative *hijra* character, replete with beret, puts his arm around Rohit even as he rather limp-wristedly raises one hand to his chin and says, 'Good!'. Almost simultaneously, Kanta-ben, in the middle of giving Rohit her blessing, angrily pushes Le Bon away, and the two men briefly wave goodbye to each other.[19]

A fade takes us to the next shot—a descending tilt framing the entrance to the ceremony hall, lined on either side by scores of festooned attendees, waiting to give their blessings. As the camera continues to descend, Le Bon appears in the immediate foreground, filling up the frame as he stretches his arms upwards, striking a pose and saying, 'This is the

bam [sic]'.[20] He then claps his hands as he says, 'Voila!' and whisks away
(off-camera), revealing Rohit, whose father lovingly clutches him from
behind, clinging to his shoulders with eyes closed, his lips murmuring
inaudibly even as his son embarrassingly gestures (and mouths), 'Dad!'.
His father finally releases him and they make their way into the hall,
where the song and dance sequence will commence.

The engagement party, then, is literally framed by the queer wedding
planner. The combination of Naina's comment (on the soundtrack),
Le Bon's queer presence and mannerisms, and Kanta-ben's by now
formulaic reaction, infuses the allegedly heterosexual context with
a decidedly homosexual tint—to the point that even Rohit's father
embracing him from the rear takes on homosocial overtones. With
the awkward embrace of father and son positioned directly behind
Le Bon, his departure from the frame paradoxically becomes/enacts a
form of revelation—father and son now seem caught, in flagrante delicto,
in a queer pose. The entire heterosexual wedding, then, becomes
foregrounded as a 'queer construction' via Le Bon's presence, and
the parodic atmosphere and, in the process, heterosexuality itself are
framed as a masquerades, as the various elements of this sequence
(visual and aural), in Butler's phrase, 'disrupt the regulatory fiction of
heterosexual coherence' (Butler 1990: 173).

In the following five minutes (and sixty-two shots) of the actual song
and dance sequence, over twenty separate formulations of motifs—what
in cinematic terms could be considered 'bracket syntagms', or a series
of tableaux vivants—are vividly enacted and blended, thus working to
create a series of images that function as 'parodic displacements' of
both sex and gender norms. The song kicks off with Aman dancing
with a row of background female dancers, employing classical Indian
head and hand gestures (themselves derivations/parodies of ancient
forms set forth by the Natyasastra). From this the camera cuts to Rohit's
family on the side, following along tentatively, swivelling their necks in
unison to the bhangra beat. Following this the camera cuts to Rohit
and Aman dancing together, even as they then begin parodying the
icon of the Hindu deity Krishna by dancing with legs crossed while
simulating flute-playing. The camera then cuts to Rohit and Naina
waltzing (even as the bhangra briefly adopts a faux-classical melody),
only to have Rohit twirl out of Naina's arms and into Aman's (as Naina
twirls away/off-camera).

Pausing in their embrace to simultaneously look at the camera/ implied audience, the two male leads shrug their shoulders and resume waltzing, even as Le Bon enthusiastically claps from the sidelines. When he is immediately pushed aside by Kanta-ben, Le Bon seamlessly transforms this shove (into Rohit's father) into an artful pose in which he stands on one leg, leaning against Rohit's dad, eagerly and rather limp-wristedly waving to Rohit and Aman, while Kanta-ben holds her head off to the side.

The camera cuts to Naina, holding various multicoloured swaths of silk cloth and, in a high angle shot (and homage to Busby Berkeley), looking up in direct address, even as she twirls (or, is twirled) while holding the multicoloured swaths which are pulled out in a circle around her. The *découpage* in this sequence tends to vary in accordance with the music, for example, when the latter approximates a classical waltz refrain, the tempo of the cinematography makes subsequent shifts, so as to 'mirror' the soundtrack. Similarly, the rate of cutting alternates between fast-paced (primarily for the dancing scenes) and stop-still for particularly significant moments, for example, Rohit and Aman pausing to look at the camera while dancing together, or Le Bon posing against Rohit's dad. In other words, the cinematographic pacing works to underscore this sequence's parodic aesthetic, in which, for instance, scenes of homosocial ambiguity serve as 'pauses' in the generally fast-paced editing, caesuras that, through their very brevity, further enhance the sequence's contrived nature.

From here the camera cuts to the first of two cameos in the number (both of which were greeted with audible recognition by the Jackson Heights audience), featuring the popular Bollywood actress Rani Mukherjee, who 'steals' Rohit and Aman from Naina's side and engages in a Punjabi-style dance with them. The camera then cuts to curtains parting and Aman 'directing' the older Indian women (with baton in hand) as they 'hum' the playback behind individual microphones. Following this is a tableau vivant of a little girl walking behind a cardboard cut-out wedding carriage and waving to Naina (to whom the camera cuts, creating an eyeline match), in whose eyes tears form right on time.

Without missing a beat, the camera again cuts to Rohit and Aman dancing together (facing each other), only to again be interrupted (literally, physically separated) by another older female Indian character who glares at them as she stands between them. Rohit and Aman again face the camera and begin sheepishly feigning similar, separate, and thus 'safe' dance moves. Then the second cameo arrives, Rani Mukherjee's cousin and fellow Bollywood star, Kajol, who has, in particular, appeared in numerous previous films with Shah Rukh, a fact referenced by the cameo (Shah Rukh/Aman taps Kajol's shoulder even as she dances and she turns to smile at him even as she continues dancing) and acknowledged by audience members with exclamations of recognition.

The camera again cuts to more group dancing, then features a sped-up interlude (comprised of fifty-three shots in forty seconds), the incessant cuts arriving with (and matched to) tabla drums on the soundtrack and repeated shouts of 'Hey, hey!' from the dancers. As the camera cuts and the bhangra beats quickly become a techno-fest, everyone starts dancing ecstatically—there are even two brief shots of Jean le Bon and Kanta-ben dancing together. In the fifty-third shot, then, Aman suddenly begins falling in slow-motion, even as the others continue dancing around him and, as he completes a series of 360-degree spins, the images of the dancers' bodies in their multicolour garb are superimposed over his, even as the music continues. A cut to Aman's point-of-view follows, and the image of the dancers shifts from colour to black-and-white, moving in and out of focus. A final cut takes us (and Aman, on a gurney) from the carnival of 'Maahi Ve', to the hospital, mirroring and setting up the protracted parting scene between the two male leads.

In this sequence, then, parody becomes pastiche, as a series of juxtapositions are enacted with cinematic and bodily precision. Binaries become blurred (East/West, hetero/homosexual) even as the 'endemic crisis of homo/heterosexual definition' is highlighted and simultaneously destabilizes the heteronormative trappings of the ostensible event that encompasses (i.e., defines) it. The queer posturings of Rohit and Aman work to transcend and dissolve both static conceptions of gender and sexuality, as well as their alleged (hetero)sexual identities, via a series of 'dissonances' in which:

[T]he giddiness of performance is in the recognition of a radical contingency in the relation between sex and gender in the face of cultural configurations of causal unities that are regularly assumed to be natural and necessary. In the place of the law of heterosexual coherence, we see

sex and gender denaturalized by means of a performance which avows
their distinctness and dramatizes the cultural mechanism of their fabri-
cated unity. (Butler 1990: 175)

The audience's reaction to this sequence, which can be described
as 'parodic laughter', illuminates their 'recognition' of this radical contingency and, in fact, their willingness to 'play' with it. Contrary to
Fredric Jameson's notion of pastiche as humorless, the 'parodic displacements' on display in 'Maahi Ve' can be said effectively to enact
inversions of alleged opposites in which the audience's laughter and
exclamations of 'recognition' are precisely the outcome of a 'context
and reception in which subversive confusions can be fostered' (Butler
1990: 177; Jameson 1988).

The buoyancy of 'Maahi Ve' stands in stark contrast to the following and final song sequence of the film, a 'sad' rendition of the title
track depicting the actual (heterosexual) marriage. Such a contrast further highlights the film's homosexual subtext (the homosocial bond
underlying the erotic triangle of Naina, Rohit and Aman), as the film
shifts emphasis from 'narrative resolution as heterosexual coupling',
to an emphasis on the numbers (Feuer 1993: 141). As David Savran
says of Hollywood films in a comparable genre, the plot, 'propelled
by the machinations of a closeted gay man, ends in a literal or symbolic death' (Savran 2003: 182). The pathos (or, perhaps, bathos) of
KHNH, however, rests predominantly on the very loss of this symbolic
(queer) subject, played by a superstar who increasingly appears in the
role of the 'doomed lover'. But whereas male Bollywood icons previously appeared as either 'Manjun-lovers' (passive, poetic and child-
like) or 'Krishna-lovers' (phallus incarnate), the character of Aman is
a mixture of types and, in that vein, even more 'queer' (Chakravarty
1993: 205). If this lover (awarded 'Best Supporting Actor' for his performance) and, more precisely, the form of male bonding on display
in the film, is seen or serves as 'the metonym of national unity and
amity', then one may paradoxically describe the ensuing 'gaze-in-crisis',
coming after the laughter of 'Maahi Ve', as a tacit recognition of the
hollowness of the arranged (heterosexual) marriage and the passion of
the homosocial bond underlying it, even if it can only be laughed at
(Chakravarty 1993: 214–15).

To return to the earlier notion of 'queer reading'—one, for instance,
'stress[ing] the wild exaggeration of the *mise-en-scène*' that 'might even

ignore the ending'[21]—the experience described here of viewing *KHNH* at the Eagle Theatre may be seen as adhering to just such a read. Yet would this not merely validate Gopinath's and Waugh's earlier binarism, in which it is precisely the queer/diasporic audience that becomes associated with 'queer viewing strategies'? Temporarily setting aside *KHNH*'s aesthetic 'queerness' (i.e., the film's own 'queer strategies'), one might focus solely on the issue of spectatorship to address this question. Gopinath, in her Epilogue, describes the 'near vertiginous experience' of watching *KHNH* in Chennai (Madras), as she was nearing completion of her book (Gopinath 2005: 187). 'Watching the film in Chennai', she concludes, 'crystallized many of the questions I have tried to grapple with in this book' (Gopinath 2005: 188). While she notes that it 'was a major hit both in India and in the South Asian diaspora', Gopinath simultaneously claims that 'the reconfiguration of the relation between diaspora and nation through a consolidation of heteronormativity is particularly evident in *Kal Ho Naa Ho*' (Gopinath 2005: 188–89). What is particularly startling to Gopinath is the way in which 'representations of (male) homosexuality [in *KHNH*] are folded into, and indeed buttress ... patriarchal authority' (Gopinath 2005: 190).

Though she notes the previously mentioned 'queer elements', including the misunderstandings of Kanta-ben ('apparent misrecognition that is predictably played for laughs'), Gopinath claims:

> The film predictably reasserts the dominance of heteronormative familial and romantic arrangements: Aman conveniently dies of a tragic heart condition, exiting the homosocial triangle and paving the way for marriage and child-bearing as his male buddy declares his love for the film's female love interest. (2005: 190)

And the audience walks out. That is to say, it is precisely the 'predictable', all-too-convenient nature of the (heterosexual) resolution that opens it up to a queer reading—or, rather than 'a film like *Kal Ho Naa Ho*' revealing how 'conventional' (i.e., heteronormative, patriarchal) discourses are 'able to absorb and neutralize the challenge posed by queer male desire', one might question, given both the ending of *KHNH* and the audience reaction at the Eagle Theatre, whether this patriarchal, heteronormative logic is not itself 'neutralized' (Gopinath 2005: 191). Gopinath herself raises precisely such a possibility earlier on in her book when she describes a 'queer reading' as 'allow[ing] for the possibility of triangulated desire that does not solidify' into homosexual or heterosexual, but rather 'opens up a third space where both hetero and homoerotic relations coexist simultaneously' (Gopinath 2005: 105).[22] Given 'the remarkable latitude within public spaces [in India] for male friendships that can easily tip into homoeroticism'— what Rao calls 'an ambivalent greyness'—and the utilization in Bollywood films such as *KHNH* of an aesthetic of 'impersonation', it becomes possible to argue that, rather than there being an 'originary' context (in which queer themes remain 'nontransgressive'), the parody in *KHNH* 'is of the very notion of an original', i.e. (as with 'Maahi Ve'), a 'perpetual displacement' and 'parodic proliferation' that, in Butler's words, 'deprives hegemonic culture and its critics of the claim to naturalized or essentialist' notions of sexuality and/or gender roles (Butler 1990: 175–76; Gopinath 2000: 283, 291; Gopinath 2005: 97, 99; Rao 2000: 303).[23]

Rather than remaining 'unspoken back home', one might conclude, particularly given Gopinath's description of the Chennai audience's excited responses to *KHNH* and the fact that it was a blockbuster in India as well as across the diaspora, that the homosexual subtext of this film, rather than being accessible to only a select few (MMMIs, nonresident Indians [NRIs] or otherwise), is 'readable' by all its audiences, wherever it may be screened (Gopinath 2005: 187–88; Waugh 2001: 284).[24] As a way of concluding this part of my discussion, I would like to draw attention to a poster for *KHNH* (see Figure 4.1).[25]

Here, one sees precisely the 'triangle' informing the filmic plot: Rohit in the foreground with Aman behind him and Naina behind Aman. Yet, upon closer examination (see Figure 4.2), one detects a detail through the bar of the title: Aman's hand, precariously near Rohit's right nipple, the 'Naa' (No) of the title superimposed over this space. This poster conveys the film's precise 'crisis of homo/heterosexual definition', even as its structure evokes a 'confessional' moment, a homosocial detail adhering to 'a law of the permitted and the forbidden', which, nonetheless, seeps through its literal interdiction and imbues the overall 'promotional image' with a trace of its very deviation (Foucault 1990: 57).[26] In this detail resides what Manfred Pfister might term a 'discrepant awareness', both of the underlying homosocial bond between the two male characters, as well as the 'procedure for producing the truth of sex' (Foucault 1990: 57; Pfister

Figure 4.1: A poster advertising *KHNH* (dir. Nikhil Advani, 2003)
(personal photograph)

1988). What the movie image 'confesses' to us, then, is simultaneously its 'queer desire' and its superficial covering over of this desire, itself 'experienced as pleasure' (Foucault 1990: 57).[27] *Ars erotica* as *scientia sexualis*, no doubt.

FROM SUBTEXT TO HYPERTEXT: THE CASE OF *DOSTANA* (2008)

While *KHNH* takes great pains (and pleasure) to superficially cover over its homosexual subtext, *Dostana*, coming five years later, does away

Figure 4.2: A close-up of 'the forbidden' in *KHNH*
(personal photograph)

with such superficial disavowals, coming out of the closet and celebrating its so-called 'queerness' in a much more blatant fashion. At the same time, the allegedly 'gay' union that this film celebrates is, at least on the surface, an impersonation. *Dostana* (in Hindi, 'a friendship') tells the story of Sameer/'Sam' (Abhishek Bachchan) and Kunal (John Abraham), two Indian immigrants in Miami who pretend to be gay (and in a gay relationship) in order to live in an apartment occupied by an Indo-American woman, Neha, where no (straight) men are allowed. When Sam's mother inadvertently (and, indeed, mistakenly) discovers that her son is 'gay', she is at first shocked but then comes to accept her son's homosexual identity as well as his (false) relationship

with Kunal. The film culminates with Sam and Kunal attaining their
joint residency permit (as a gay couple) and simultaneously revealing
to Neha that they are, indeed, not 'really gay', and proceeding to move
out of her apartment, even as she embarks on a relationship with another (straight) Indian man, Abhi (Bobby Deol).

Thus, while *Dostana* is not about a 'really gay' couple, it is rife
with 'queer moments' that further illustrate Butler's notion of 'gender parody'. Sam and Kunal's relationship becomes a performance
in which 'the essence or identity that they ... purport to express' is a
'fabrication' that is 'manufactured and sustained through corporeal
signs and other discursive means' (Butler 1990: 173). The epistemological uncertainties set into motion by this impersonation are fully
revealed at a dinner party that Neha throws one evening. Neha's gay
boss, 'M', is in attendance, as is the apparently gay immigration officer assigned Sam and Kunal's file. Sam and Kunal ham it up in full
'gay' mode, not only to convince Neha and her gay boss that they
are indeed gay, but also to placate the gay immigration officer, Javier,
who arrives unexpectedly, informing them that, as many people pretend to be gay in order to attain residency, he is here to check up on
them. It is precisely at this moment, then, as M and Sam and Officer
Javier and Kunal are all dancing together in a blatantly homoerotic
way that Sam's mother (Kiron Kher) arrives at the door. This sudden
arrival functions in a manner similar to that Walter Benjamin describes in characterizing the estranging effect of Brecht's epic theatre:
'the stranger' (in this case, Sam's mom) who appears at the door is
'suddenly confronted with certain conditions', namely, the apparent
homosexuality of her son (Benjamin 1966: 5). This 'interruption' of
Sam and Kunal's homosexual impersonation works to 'uncover the
conditions' upon which it is premised (the performative gestures associated with gender and sexual 'norms'), even as it (thus) makes them
strange (Benjamin 1966: 18). The tableau of her son dancing with another man, 'caught' unawares in a homoerotic moment, causes Sam's
mom, in turn, to pass out.

The following song sequence, 'Maa da Laadla', featuring Sam's
mom constantly 'misperceiving' so-called 'straight' moments for queer
ones, provides a classic instance of Butler's claim that 'the naturalized
effects of heterosexualized genders are produced through imitative
strategies' (Butler 2004: 127). The sequence begins with Sam's mom

(who remains unnamed in the film) sobbing in bed and looking at a photo of Sam and Kunal (in men's clothing). Suddenly, as she looks, the photo changes: first Sam and then Kunal is suddenly wearing a *sari*. As she continues gazing, horrified, at the shifting photo image, the playback begins, with a voice singing, 'Your son rides the bride's palanquin'. The song sequence features Sam's mom walking around in public places where, in a series of 'double takes', she (mis)perceives Sam and Kunal's behaviour as manifestations of a 'queer' identity. The 'real' (straight) image—for instance, Sam and Kunal playing football on the beach—suddenly transforms in Sam's mom's eyes to a 'misperceived' moment—Sam and Kunal playfully tussling in the sand together—which then shifts to an imagined (queer) moment: Sam and Kunal still on the beach but now in Indian wedding clothes, with her son again wearing a *sari* (and a beard).

Each 'mistaken' moment is followed by the sudden appearance of a group of dancers dressed in day-glo orange and yellow costumes with bright yellow turbans and orange plumes, who dance around Sam's (increasingly confused) mom. Yet this latter figure, again in a nod to Butler's point regarding the essentially *performative* nature of identity, goes through the motions of being distraught in syncopation with the rhythm of the sequence and the dancers, performing her 'disapproving' gestures (for example, hitting her head, shaking her head, wagging her finger) as a choreographed sequence that is also enacted by the grinning, festooned dancers who suddenly appear and disappear around her. Wherever Sam's mom goes in this song sequence, she suddenly 'sees' her son and Kunal enacting their 'gay' identity: as babies in strollers, being pushed side by side with pacifiers in their mouths; as a couple walking by arm in arm; as businessmen in suits; as old men in wheelchairs; indeed, as a series of shifting 'impersonations'. The sequence concludes, then, with Sam's mom yet again passing out. When she 'comes to', however, an interesting development occurs. In a scene, the director describes as 'not a funny scene' but, indeed, 'an emotional chord to be touched', Neha confronts Sam's mother about her son's (closeted) identity:

> For the past three years, your son hid the biggest truth of his life from you because he knew that you wouldn't be pleased. You'll be happy, but Sam? If he can lie for your happiness, then can't you accept the truth for his happiness? Whatever God does is for the best. Right, Auntie?

Sam's mom listens carefully to Neha and, though still sad, nods her head slowly. Following a short sequence featuring Neha at her job, Kunal arrives home where Sam's mom greets him at the door with a *pooja* tray (i.e., one for worship or prayer) and, while the theme song from another Bollywood film (*Kabhi Khushi, Kabhie Gham*) plays, Sam's mom bids Kunal welcome and embraces him. She then goes on to tell her son that she accepts him for what he 'is' and offers her blessing to Sam and Kunal:

> Sam's mom (hereafter 'SM'): Son, *forgive me. I couldn't understand your love.*
> Sam: Mom, *I need to tell you something.*
> SM: Son, *what kind of a mother am I? I prayed for my own son's sorrows. Sorry.* [to Kunal] *I had bought these [removing her gold bracelets] for my daughter-in-law.*
> Sam: Oh, *come on! Are you really serious, Mom?*
> SM [to Kunal]: *I don't know whether you're my daughter-in-law or my son-in-law. But whatever you are, accept it as a gift from me [hands Kunal her bracelets]. And do observe a fast on Karva Chauth for my son's long life.*
> Sam: Mom!
> SM [to Kunal]: *I'll send you the offerings. I'm leaving him in your care.*

Here, we see the multiple layers of impersonation in *Dostana's* constructions of sexual identity, with Sam rebelling against his mother's acceptance of his (alleged) homosexuality, even as he ostensibly maintains this role. The comment made by the director, Tarun Mansukhani, regarding this scene is particularly key to note:

> Definitely a statement I wanted to make with this film was that, as a parent, you must accept your child's preferences and choices because it's theirs and not for you to decide for them. However, to bring across a message like that, I knew I had to do it in a humorous way, in a way that would make it appealing for an entire audience, rather than just a select few.[28]

In other words, even though Sam and Kunal are not actually gay, Sam's mom learns to accept her son as gay. Thus, even though or, indeed, because Sam and Kunal's 'gay' relationship is an impersonation, the overall thrust of the film is a progressive one, featuring a mother who overcomes her own initial homophobia to embrace her son and his 'partner' and bless their 'queer' relationship.

Furthermore, this negotiation of homosexuality demonstrates how a popular cinema such as Bollywood can innovatively deviate from and, in the process, question the underpinnings of an ostensibly heteronormative frame. *Dostana* cleverly illuminates the Butlerian thesis that sexualized genders are products of imitative strategies and that, furthermore, 'the reality' of heterosexual identities is 'performatively constituted' (Butler 2004: 128). What is also key to note, however, is how the film utilizes certain Bollywood techniques typically associated with heteronormative storylines in doing this. In the process, as Mansukhani notes, *Dostana* creates a seeming paradox, namely, a mainstream gay movie. While one could rightly question whether, indeed, such is the case, given that the male leads are merely pretending to be gay, I would suggest that to focus on this particular detail—and on these two characters' 'actual' sexuality—is to miss the point and, indeed, how the film 'queers' the ostensibly heteronormative framework it operates within. Thus, while *Dostana*'s homosexuality is neither subtextual nor actual, by 'outing' this subtext, the film simultaneously works to undermine the ostensibly heterosexual narrative of the film, drawing attention to what had previously only been alluded to and, in the process, illuminating the ease with which allegedly distinct forms of sexual identity can be traversed and/or misread.

Given the enormous success of this film and, indeed, the claims being made about it (for example, the first 'gay' Bollywood movie), one might all too quickly assume that, prior to 2008 (or 2003), there were no 'gay themes', subtextual or otherwise, in Bollywood. However, this is clearly not the case. What I would like to do in the final section of this chapter, then, is re-examine some of the earlier instances of what might be called 'homoerotic' play or, to paraphrase Sedgwick, male homosocial desire, in Bollywood films, leading up to and in light of the more recent (and overt) displays of male homoeroticism (Sedgwick 1985: 2).

BETWEEN *DOSTS*

The title of this section again references Sedgwick (*dosts* being 'male friends' in Hindi) and it is only fitting to thus begin (again) with a reference to her earlier theorization of male homosocial bonds. Two important and in many ways interrelated concepts informing Sedgick's first book, *Between Men* (1985), are those of male homosocial desire and the erotic triangle. As noted in the earlier discussion of *KHNH*, in this latter schemá, 'the bond that links the two rivals is as intense and potent as the bond that links either of the rivals to the beloved' (Sedgwick 1985: 21). We see precisely such a bond develop between Rohit and Aman in *KHNH*, a bond which, indeed, unbalances and threatens to overturn the heterosexual plot. Yet in many ways, it is precisely because the film is set in the 'West', that many, if not most, of this male duo's 'bonding moments' are (mis)perceived as signifying 'homosexuality'—note, for instance, the use of the (English) word 'gay' to identify homosexuality in recent Hindi films.[29] However in the Indian, rather than NRI, context, we see some deviation from the 'diacritical opposition between the "homosocial" and the "homosexual"' that Sedgwick argues exists disproportionately for men in Western society (Sedgwick 1990: 2). Rao and Ashok Kavi have pointed to the existence of a 'same sex closeness', or homosociality, in 'every walk of Indian life', in which what might immediately be seen as 'gay' in a Western context thrives precisely because it remains unnamed or, indeed, is given another name—that of 'dosti', a friendship that, as Rao has noted, can easily shift registers to 'yaari', entailing something 'much more than a friend' (Kavi 2000; Rao 2000: 304–05).

This 'same-sex closeness', or the imperceptible shift/s from 'dosti' to 'yaari', is precisely what we see between male characters in earlier Bollywood films. One could begin by pointing to the films of one of the biggest stars of popular Hindi cinema and the real-life father of Sam in *Dostana*, Amitabh Bachchan. In the 1980 version of *Dostana* (dir. Raj Khosla), Bachchan and Shatruganh Sinha co-star as Vijay and Ravi, boyhood friends who have grown up to become successful in their own occasionally conflicting walks of life (Vijay is a police officer, Ravi an attorney). An erotic triangle is formed when Vijay and Ravi both fall in love with the same woman, Sheetal (Zeenat Aman), yet, as an example of the male bond's predominance, the two remain 'the best of friends'. While this is not the same storyline as the 2008 version of *Dostana*, the two films do share a similar (triangular) structure in which the male bond arguably becomes just as intense and potent as that linking either to the woman.

However, this is where the parallels end. For whereas the more recent *Dostana* features many overtly eroticized and/or blatantly 'gay' moments (for example, all the frequent misperceptions by Sam's mom of her son's physical interactions with Kunal), nowhere—not in a single song—do we see the kind of tenderness that is on display in the first song of the original *Dostana*, in which Vijay and Ravi sing to one other, and to their friendship, on stage in their old high school before a packed audience.[30] First Ravi, then Vijay, sing the same line to each other: 'Whatever enemies we make in the world, let our friendship flourish!' As Ravi then goes on to sing the next line, about 'those days of childhood, those days of dreams', Vijay smiles at Ravi and Ravi coyly smiles back at Vijay. Ravi then sings the next line, 'We spent many years together and became men together. Our childhood was interesting. Long live our friendship!' The two then repeat the opening line in unison and, during the ensuing musical interlude, stand beside each other, looking out at the audience and then turning to one other and smiling.

One never gets the level of intimacy on display in this (opening) sequence in the new *Dostana*—gone is the physical proximity between the two men as they sing to one another; gone is the twinkle, in close-up reaction shots, in Shatruganh Sinha's eye.[31] As Rao notes, numerous other examples of such 'dosti' (slipping into 'yaari') can be given, including many, if not most, of the films starring Amitabh Bachchan in the 1970s. In *Zanjeer* (dir. Prakash Mehra, 1973), the actor Pran sings a similarly endearing song to Bachchan and, of course, there is the 'famous' example (also cited by Sam in the new *Dostana*) of *Sholay* (dir. Ramesh Sippy, 1975), in which Bachchan and fellow actor Dharmendra are best friends who sing to each other of their friendship ('Ye Dosti, Hum Nahi Toden Gai'/This Friendship, We Will Not Break) as they take turns driving their motorcycle. Similarly, there is *Namak Haram* (dir. Hrishikesh Mukherjee, 1973), in which Rajesh Khanna sings what Rao characterizes as a 'love song' to Bachchan, plus *Anand* (1971), also directed by Mukherjee, in which Bachchan evokes 'a silent, quiet, brooding sexuality', as Kavi puts it, in playing a doctor looking after a dying cancer patient, played by Khanna (Kavi 2000: 310; Rao 2000: 302). And then there is the (in)famous shower scene in *Silsila* (dir. Yash Chopra, 1981), featuring Bachchan and Shashi Kapoor.

In this scene, Bachchan and Kapoor, who play brothers, are showering together (and are shown naked, in a medium shot, from the waist up). Shekhar casually tosses the soap, then says, 'I'm having fun', followed by a request to Amit to pick up the soap. Amit begins to bend over to pick up the soap while Shekhar, standing behind him, pretends to keep nonchalantly scrubbing himself, all the while looking up innocuously. Then, in mid-bend, Amit stops and stands back up, turning around to face Shekhar as he says, 'Hey brother, I don't want to pick up the soap!' Both men begin laughing uproariously, then continue showering and engaging in conversation. Again, while not overtly homosexual, this type of homoerotic space is no longer present in recent (and more blatantly 'gay') films such as *KHNH* and the new *Dostana*. In those films, most if not all of the allegedly 'homosexual' moments are those that are perceived by other characters (hence their designation as 'gay'), whereas in the scenes from these earlier films, the moments of homosocial bonding—both more prevalent and intimate in their encoding than that of recent fare—are almost always private. Even when Vijay and Ravi sing on stage at the beginning of the original *Dostana*, they are singing to one another (and spend at least half the time looking at each other as they sing), whereas in more recent films such as *KHNH* and the new *Dostana*, the male leads no longer sing to one another, much less shower with one another.[32]

If, as Kavi has stated, a 'percolating gay culture has been trying to break free' beneath the surface of the Bollywood film, 'waiting for the moment to emerge from subtext into text', then one *might* point to the *Dostana* of 2008 as being that moment, particularly as, some six months after the film was released, New Delhi's highest court decriminalized homosexuality, overturning the longstanding Section 377 of the Indian Penal Code which, among other things, prohibited homosexual intercourse (Kavi 2000: 307; Timmons and Kumar 2009). While the film was not directly involved in the Delhi court's decision, it is immediately invoked in discussing this decision, as an instance of how there has been an increased acceptance of 'homosexuality' in India (Timmons and Kumar 2009). However, it might be noted that, even as 'homosexuality' becomes 'accepted' (both by the Delhi High Court and Sam's mom in *Dostana*), it comes with the disappearance of earlier forms of homoerotic 'male bonding'.

The emergence of the homosexual subtext, then, in mainstream Bollywood cinema seems to simultaneously signal the innovativeness of this cinema and, paradoxically, a curtailment of 'the possibilities of playful impersonation ... that are available to men' (Chakravarty 1993: 305). Homoerotic play (such as that on display in the earlier films mentioned here) has paradoxically become less subversive now that it has been 'outed'. While *Dostana*'s director, Tarun Mansukhani, claims that 'strangely', what he will always be proudest of is that his film features 'the first time one has seen two men kissing ... in any Indian film', he also goes on to add, 'And just for the record, no, they did not actually kiss' (see note 27). Even as this long-awaited 'kiss' emerges on the Bollywood screen, then, it is absent or, indeed, in plain sight and simultaneously hidden from view.[33] To return to Gopinath's attempt to trace the trajectory of queer desire along diasporic lines and link its emergence (or readability) to the 'queer diaspora', such a 'disappearance' (of earlier, subtler forms of male homoeroticism on screen) undermines attempts to fashion a narrative in which queer desire becomes more prevalent as its distance from the 'homeland' grows. While Bollywood has explicitly signalled that 'it's okay to be gay' (even if you actually are not), one could argue that such acceptance comes with a trade-off (no, they did not actually kiss; no, they are not actually gay) and that equally if not more homoerotic instances of male bonding were already on display even before they became so (openly) acceptable.

NOTES

1. In this chapter, I will specifically be focussing on instances of male homosocial desire in Bollywood. For a discussion of female homosocial desire in Hindi cinema, see Gayatri Gopinath's *Impossible Desires* (2005).

2. Foucault describes the confession as 'a ritual of discourse in which the speaking subject is also the subject of the statement', one in which 'the truth is corroborated by the obstacles and resistances it has had to surmount in order to be formulated' (Foucault 1990: 61–62).

3. Sedgwick, naturally, is discussing twentieth-century Western culture.

4. To her credit, Sedgwick does state that 'the scope of the kind of hypothesis I want to pose does seem to require a drastic reductiveness, at least in its initial formulation' (Sedgwick 1990: 11, n. 19). It should also be noted here that, while Foucault's notion of discourse largely informs one of the 'core' texts of postcolonial studies, in Edward Said's *Orientalism* (1978), there is—perhaps because of the near simultaneity of the two books' publication—no mention of this particular aspect of Foucault, i.e., his *History of Sexuality*, in *Orientalism*. Thus, even as a Foucauldian framework is employed to challenge the East/West binarism, Foucault's own Orientalizing discourse goes unmentioned by Said.

5. Thomas Waugh amplifies this point in a subsequent essay, noting:

> In this task [of tracing queerness in Bollywood] I have found little help in postcolonial theory, which I find all too often constrained by frameworks of race, class and gender which cannot account fully for sex, indispensable as they are. Much

of the theoretical attention to postcolonial culture and politics I find still squea-
mish by and large about same-sex practice or identities, and much of the recent
proliferation of breakthrough scholarship on Indian popular cinemas hardly less
so. (Waugh 2001: 282)

6. Gopinath labels the song and dance sequence 'one of the key components of Bolly-
    wood cinema' (Gopinath 2005: 100).
7. At this point in his essay, Waugh naturally cites Gopinath's work.
8. While Gopinath's and Waugh's discussions—which may be characterized as an 'initial
    queering' of Bollywood—are constructive, they need to be further elaborated, particu-
    larly with regard to the problematic nexus of (queer) aesthetics and (diasporic) specta-
    torship implicit in their work.
9. This description of his 'queer' terms subsequently appears in Doty's Making Things Per-
    fectly Queer (1993: 1–3) as well as in his essay, 'There's Something Queer Here' (1995:
    72–73).
10. Kal Ho Naa Ho (hereafter KHNH) was released globally in November 2003 and opened
    to full houses in New York, Fremont, Los Angeles and Houston, and fifty-two other
    theatres across the United States. It was one of the biggest Bollywood successes of the
    year at the box-office in India, the United States and the United Kingdom. Addition-
    ally, it went on to win top prizes in an assortment of categories at the 2004 Bollywood/
    Filmfare Awards, including Best Supporting Actor, Best Lyrics, Best Music Director
    and Best Playback. While my experience is just one of many, I want to position it in
    direct relation to both the film's global box-office success and Gopinath's own experi-
    ence of watching the film in India. Thus, it is my intention to treat the reactions of this
    audience as a representative sampling though, naturally, everyone may not have had the
    same reaction to the film.
11. Such a religious paradigm for the viewer of Hindi films bases itself upon the 'Hindi/
    Hindu' equivocation, in which Indians are characterized as 'Hindu', and their subse-
    quent viewing habits (as well as, thus, the composition of on-screen events) are delin-
    eated via the Hindu concept of 'darsana', or reverential gazing. See, for example, Prasad
    (1998) and Mishra (2002). For an extended critique of this paradigm, see Chapter 1.
12. One can trace this 'triangular' structure—and subsequent male bond—in Bollywood
    films dating back to Sangam (dir. Raj Kapoor, 1964) and in films such as Muqaddar
    ka Sikandar (dir. Prakash Mehra, 1978), Qurbani (dir. Feroz Khan, 1980), Dostana (dir.
    Raj Khosla, 1980), Silsila (dir. Yash Chopra, 1981) and Naseeb (dir. Manmohan Desai,
    1981), to name but a few. See Gopinath (2000), Rao (2000) and Waugh (2001) for
    discussions of some of these earlier instances. Waugh claims that homosocial trian-
    gulation is 'a narrative structure that is arguably more prevalent in Bollywood than in
    Hollywood, Howard Hawks notwithstanding' (Waugh 2001: 291, n. 18).
13. While 'dostana' refers to a 'male friendship', Rao's and Raj Ayyar's definitions of yaari,
    derived from yaar, or friend, entail 'much more than a friend', even as yaari 'goes far be-
    yond the Western notion of Platonic friendship, which, above all, is non-sexual': 'A yaar
    is an individual with whom one feels a deep, almost intangible connection. Definitions
    of this term have varied through time, sometimes denoting a lover, at other times a
    friend' (Rao 2000: 304–05; Thomas 1995: 165). I would also add that the sexual ambi-
    guity of the term 'Platonic', with regard to its specific historical connotations regarding
    (male) 'friendship', further destabilizes both the 'East/West' and 'sexual/non-sexual'
    divides, as posited by Rao.

14. Director's Commentary Track on the DVD of the film *Kal Ho Na Ho* (dir. Advani, 2008).

15. As Gopinath notes, 'Hijras, who may be cross-dressed biological men, eunuchs, or hermaphrodites, form communities that have a ritualized, historically rooted role in Indian society' (Gopinath 2000: 294). A derivation of such a figure appears late in the film in the character of the wedding planner, 'Jean le Bon', a (presumably) gay Indian man replete with striped sailor's shirt, tight-fitting pants and a beret. India maintains an official ban on homosexuality, although the High Court in Delhi recently overturned this ban. As Suparna Bhaskaran notes, 'The Indian Law Commission, presided over by Lord Macaulay, introduced the colonial antisodomy statute, Section 377, into the Indian Penal Code on October 6, 1860, in British India' (Bhaskaran 2002: 15). The July 2009 overturning of this ban by the Delhi High Court, while a landmark ruling, applies only to the territory of India's capital, though lawyers and advocates note that 'it is likely to force India's government either to appeal the decision to the Supreme Court, or change the law nationwide' (Timmons and Kumar 2009).

16. While this particular set-up may be 'a first', it should be noted that such 'queer moments', or scenes of sexual misunderstanding, have often appeared in earlier Bollywood films. Some of these have been discussed in this book (see note 14).

17. I do not intend this 'premature departure' to be seen as axiomatic, but rather as indicative of both the superficiality of the heterosexual conclusion of the film—approximately one minute long—and the audience's recognition of its irrelevance. The scene's extreme brevity seems to also provide a formal acknowldgment of its unimportance, particularly coming after the protracted parting scene between the two male leads.

18. Though Chakravarty begins with a quote from Butler's 'Sex and Gender in Simone de Beauvoir's Second Sex' (1986), that is the last time she mentions Butler—the latter's perspective on these issues literally remains suspended above the chapter without ever being brought into its discussion.

19. This pushing away of the 'suspect' queer character becomes an iconic gesture for Kantaben.

20. This is perhaps a queer enunciation of 'the bomb', i.e., the place to be.

21. See Feuer 1993: 142.

22. Gopinath makes no reference to Homi Bhabha's deployment of 'a third space' in his piece of the same name, though such a parallel does, at the very least, seem to nominally counter Waugh's previous assertion concerning the lack of potential dialogue between queer and postcolonial approaches to the subject matter. See Bhabha (1990b).

23. Gopinath, coincidentally, while citing both Chakravarty and Butler, never mentions either the former's concept of 'impersonation' or the latter's concept of 'gender parody', in her discussions of queerness in Bollywood.

24. Indeed, Gopinath's 'vertiginous experience' of watching *KHNH* in India may very well have been due to this realization, though whether it factored into her subsequent 'crystallization' is another issue. Waugh, in many ways, opens himself up to a similar critique in his assessment of an earlier Bollywood film, *Main Khiladi, Tu Anari* (I'm the Player, You're the Naïve One, dir. Sameer Malkan, 1994) which, he simultaneously claims, 'has been widely recognized as the most vivid site of big things happening [re: queer subtexts] by the Mumbai gay circle ... and by local and foreign queer academics', and 'was so successful [in India] that it led to the sequel, *Tu Chor Main Sipahi* (You're the Thief, I'm the Officer, 1998)' (Waugh 2001: 288). What, then, of the general (native)

audience, i.e., the one responsible for making it a (domestic) hit? Did it not 'recognize' what the Mumbai gay circle and global queer academics did?

25. I wish to emphasize that this is a promotional image, i.e., it does not appear in the film but, rather, has been produced post hoc as a way of selling the film. While there are multiple images from the film that depict the homosexual subtext (for example, the scenes previously discussed), I am concerned here not with any particular image *from* the film but rather with the one *of* the film used for promotional purposes. While there are multiple movie posters for *KHNH*, nearly all accentuate in their composition the triangular relationship at the heart of the story. This particular image is a photograph I have taken of one of the posters on display at the Eagle Theatre and originally produced by Dharma Productions.

26. This trace only becomes fully legible after screening the film. Thus, to invert the familiar adage, it is a case of re-judging the cover (image) by the film.

27. It is precisely in this way that the masquerade of (hetero)sexuality in *KHNH* seeks to 'approximate the ideal of a substantial ground of identity', even as, in its occasional discontinuities, the 'groundlessness of this "ground"' is revealed and, indeed, revelled in (Butler 1990: 179).

28. Director's Commentary Track on the DVD of the film *Dostana* (2008).

29. *Dostana* provides examples of this, both when Kunal explains to Neha's aunt that 'Hum gay hai' (We are gay), and in the end credits sequence, when a 'God' figure (sporting dark sunglasses and a ridiculously large staff) proclaims, 'Ye such hai, key apke beta gay hai!' (It is true, that your son is gay!)

30. Sam and Kunal, for that matter, never sing a song together throughout the film, either to one other or with one another. Even in the ostensibly 'gay' song sequence in the film, 'Maa da Laadla', they do not sing and, in the remixed version of this song that appears during the end credits, they sing separately, i.e., lip-synch the lyrics in separate frames, and not to one another. Similarly, in *KHNH*, while Rohit and Aman occasionally dance with one another in the 'Maahi Ve' sequence and sing together, they never sing *to* one another.

31. Indeed, the twinkle has been replaced with the wink in recent 'homosocial' sequences in Bollywood films, for example, the several that Sam and Kunal give to the camera— i.e., the audience—in the end credits version of 'Maa da Laadla'.

32. Bachchan and Kapoor also sing to one other in *Trishul* (1978), Vinod Khanna and Bachchan in *Parvarish* (1977), Bachchan to Amjad Khan in *Yaarana* (1981) and also to Sanjeev Kumar in *Silsila* (1981).

33. In this sequence, Kunal grabs Sam in an embrace and 'kisses' him, i.e., we see the back of Kunal's head juxtaposed with the lower side of Sam's face, then a close-up of Sam's startled eyes (though his lips are, again, hidden from view by Kunal's neck), followed by a close-up of Kunal's face (with eyes squinting shut) 'kissing' Sam (though his lips are again hidden, this time by Sam's neck and shirt collar).

Usage Problem: Simulation and Hyper-assimilation in the (Crossover) Bollywood Film

In the preceding chapter, the various strategies of *Kal Ho Naa Ho* and *Dostana* were examined in relation to contemporary theoretical paradigms of cultural identity and representation in Bollywood. In many ways, these films can be seen as embodying the central tenets of contemporary Bollywood cinema, engaging in 'play', even as they seriously reformulate—one might even say, undermine—previous notions of 'Indianness'. In keeping with this line of inquiry, it is my intention in this final chapter to examine the postmodern strategies of the twenty-first century Bollywood film in relation to contemporary films stemming from the West that attempt to approximate or, in some cases, appropriate, the Bollywood style. I will be concerned in this chapter, then, with understanding how the representational strategies utilized by these different films attempt to rework broader conceptions of both Bollywood and a so-called 'Indian' cultural identity in an increasingly transnational context. It is thus necessary to begin by engaging in a series of re-readings: of Fredric Jameson's theorization of the postmodern; of Aijaz Ahmad's critique of Jameson's notion of a 'cognitive aesthetics' as it relates to 'Third World' texts; and of Arjun Appadurai's further development of a Jamesonian praxis with regard to electronic media. In the process of rereading (and reconfiguring) these theorists' paradigms, I hope to more effectively prepare the ground for my subsequent discussion of the Bollywood film within a transnational, postmodern frame.

COGNITIVE MAPPING

In his now famous essay, 'Postmodernism, or The Cultural Logic of Late Capitalism', Fredric Jameson charts the emergence of a new 'postmodern hyperspace', as well as a 'new radical cultural politics' through which this hyperspace may be read (Jameson 1991: 44, 50). Jameson labels this new radical practice an aesthetic of *cognitive mapping* and proceeds to delineate how such a reading practice may serve as an enabling function, one that 'seeks to endow the individual subject with some new heightened sense of ... place in the global system' (Jameson 1991: 54). Thus, 'the problem of postmodernism—how its fundamental characteristics are to be described, whether it even exists in the first place, whether the very *concept* is of any use', is simultaneously presented as an aesthetic and a political one (Jameson 1991: 55). The cognitive map, Jameson informs us, is 'not exactly mimetic in that older sense' but, rather, via the theoretical issues it poses, 'allow[s] us to renew the analysis of representation on a higher and much more complex level' (Jameson 1991: 51).

When Jameson's discussion of postmodernity shifts to the 'Third World' context, however, the level of complexity diminishes somewhat (Jameson 1986). As Aijaz Ahmad has noted, along with Jameson's problematic assertion that 'all third world texts are necessarily ... to be read as ... national allegories', his theorization of 'the Third World' is an essentialized one, inextricably wed to the concept of nationalism (Jameson, quoted in Ahmad 1992: 98). Thus framed, the only choice for 'the Third World' lies between a nationalist identity and a 'global American postmodernist culture' (Ahmad 1992: 101). Such a premise— of First World/Third World and nationalism/postmodernism—could indeed, to paraphrase Ahmad, be radically reformulated by considering that we live in one world and not three; 'not in terms of a binary opposition but as a contradictory unity', replete with differences as well as 'profound overlaps' (Ahmad 1992: 103).

In the process of 'un-freezing' Jameson's theorization of global space in an era of multinational capital, the epistemological uncertainty of the 'Third World' as a category becomes evident, as does the non-specificity of allegory to the so-called Third World.[1] Indeed, it is precisely in considering the possibility of a 'third space', one located in between Jameson's choices, that a shift from literature to film as the focus of discursive analysis works as an additional corrective to the theorization of the so-called Third World.[2] For whereas Ahmad rightly questions the configuration of a Third World text as essentially one thing or another (as well as questioning the equally dubious definition of postmodernism along such dichotomized lines), he also notes that:

> [T]hose who live [in the so-called Third World] within the consequences of that 'long past', good and bad, and in places where a majority of the population has been denied access to such benefits of 'modernity' as hospitals or better health insurance or even basic literacy; can hardly afford the terms of such [postmodern] thought. (Ahmad 1992: 68–69)

By shifting the terms of the debate from 'basic literacy' to a basic *film* literacy, one can simultaneously avoid denying the (real and imagined) inhabitants of the so-called Third World both knowledge of and access to a 'cognitive mapping' of postmodern aesthetics.

Implicit in such a shift, as Arjun Appadurai has noted, is a theory of rupture in which electronic media (for example, film and television) 'transform the field of mass mediation' by working to 'interrogate, subvert, and transform other contextual literacies' (Appadurai 1996: 3). Furthermore, such a 'break' is 'explicitly transnational' and thus allows for a more nuanced picture of 'the new global culture economy' to emerge—namely, as 'a complex, overlapping, disjunctive order that cannot any longer be understood in terms of existing center-periphery models' (Appadurai 1996: 9, 32). Appadurai shifts the grounds of the debate to incorporate what he labels 'an elementary framework for exploring such disjunctures', namely, his delineation of the five 'dimensions of global cultural flows'—ethnoscapes, mediascapes, technoscapes, financescapes and ideoscapes (Appadurai 1996: 33–36).[3] It is in relation to these dimensions and what Appadurai, 'in traditional anthropological terms', refers to as 'the problem of enculturation', that I would like to situate my discussion of the transnational and postmodern strategies of the contemporary Bollywood film (Appadurai 1996: 43). Particularly, I would like to reconfigure Appadurai's 'problem of reproduction in a deterritorialized context' via a consideration of the contemporary

Bollywood film's formation of 'zones of transculturation': rather than 'media-' and 'ideoscapes' based on 'ethnoscapes', I would like to view the Bollywood film as 'fantasyscape', i.e., as a series of seamless simulations that simultaneously, paradoxically 'fracture and fragment' media- and ideoscapes of national identity, the nation and, indeed, the alleged divide between a so-called Third World aesthetic of national allegory and a global postmodern praxis (Appadurai 1996: 37).[4]

BOLLYWOOD ETYMOLOGY

Consider the name(ing) of this cinema itself: an implied Other that, in turn, implies an (earlier) Other. So that each time it is literally and aesthetically invoked, it invokes its Other, recalls it so that it is seen always as the Other of this Other, an illegitimate brother who will never be that basic, posited reality, nor mask and pervert it, nor signify its absence, except in relation to it, and that, always already, too, as essentially an inferior. So that it is always already defeated, is always already incapable of redeploying itself, doubly wedded as it is to this inferiority complex—the mere substitution of a letter, a B-rate version of a model of reality itself already distorted/distorting, and absent.[5]

In viewing Bollywood within its predefined boundaries and simultaneously as a hyperreal cinema, one must take into account the concept of assimilation, particularly if one is to claim that it becomes a defining element of a cinema so named (i.e., pre-constituted). Bollywood implies a 'B-ing' of Hollywood, a necessitated degradation—its own 'masking and perversion' which is, allegedly, not so much its own but only a 'B-rate' version of another's, thus a double degradation or, conversely, doubly degraded (Baudrillard 1983). Simultaneously, one may say (as an inverse proof of the aforementioned status) that it perpetually seeks access to this denied status—what else, indeed, would an inferior so defined desire?[6]

The concept of assimilation becomes particularly crucial in coming to terms with (i.e., defining) Bollywood in an era of so-called globalism, both aesthetically and in terms of production, distribution and exhibition. But, as one may posit such a milieu as always already existing, it is not essential, i.e., one could easily claim that Bollywood, for instance, was reflecting such structural and aesthetic aspects as those associated with the era of globalism even before this latter era came to be. Again, then, paradoxically, what is at stake here is an essential(ist) question, one of definitions and terminology, as well as, almost more importantly, usage. What one might note and deem more important to this question, particularly in terms of usage, is the shifting/-ed demographic base (i.e., the posited basic reality) in the West, for example, the UK and US where non-resident Indians, or 'NRIs', now make up one of the fastest growing, and wealthiest, immigrant populations. Their status, both as represented Others (essentialist) and consumers (more recent), cannot be underestimated. But what is the context in which the Bollywood film's deployment of insider/outsider strategies takes place? How could one describe this setting or, more precisely, how is it presented?

In a recent Bollywood blockbuster, *Kabhi Khushi, Kabhie Gham* (Sometimes Happiness, Sometimes Sorrow, dir. Karan Johar, 2001), a musical interlude entitled 'Vande Mataram' (Hail Mother India) introduces the viewer to London via the arrival of one of the Indian protagonists, Bollywood superstar Hrithik Roshan, in this new land. The sequence, lasting approximately two minutes, begins with seven aerial shots of famous sites (for example, Big Ben, the Thames) while the voice on the playback sings 'Vande Mataram', thus creating an aural montage, reconfiguring these sites as 'Indian' or, indeed, this setting itself as 'Indian'. In the eighth shot of the sequence, a group of white women (and one light-skinned Indian woman) wearing Indian clothes turn to face the camera as they lip-synch the 'Mataram' refrain, further defamiliarizing this landscape and these bodies. This is followed by a rapid-fire series of images (consisting of roughly forty-one shots in less than thirty seconds) of 'London sites', including Virgin Records, Starbucks, Coffee Republic, Caffe Nero, Dolce et Gabbana, Versace, Armani, Yves Saint-Laurent and Max Mara. This montage illustrates the changed nature of London itself, having become supplanted by multinational capital and now itself becoming merely the setting for such companies—or, rather, becoming wholly comprised of these international stores. The 'London' on display, then, is a global amalgam of products and chains—the real has been substituted with its commercial equivalent.[7]

Following this sequence and thematically furthering it, Hrithik is seen dancing with Indian-garbed women in classical Indian style in the middle of London, even as Western/British insiders—now having become displaced outsiders, or bystanders—stand watching in the background. Following a cut, we see Hrithik walking towards the camera with the troupe of previously seen Western/white women, now wearing tight, short orange and green dresses, thus further jumbling the concepts of autonomous/distinct cultures via the blending of colours (Indian tricolour) and bodies (white). Hrithik is then seen making classical Indian dance gestures with his hands with a group of Western/white women (and one Indian) seated along the Thames riverbank, again wearing Indian dress. The 'idea' of London here is one of 'a cultural mishmash', in which there no longer exists a 'real' (re: basic reality), but rather a site which foreign elements have supplanted/co-opted (i.e., made their own). In a similar vein, 'the "other" (à la Hrithik) is never outside or beyond' but rather 'emerges most forcefully, within' said simulacrum (Bhabha 1990a: 4, emphasis added).[8]

If assimilation is defined as (i) the act or process of assimilating and/or (ii) the state of being assimilated, then Bollywood cinema, i.e., one which engages in/reproduces such hyperreal sequences, may be said to equate 'b' with 'a', so that the state itself (static) becomes an act or process (kinetic). Similarly, to recall Aimé Cesaire's Discourse on Colonialism (1955), one may say, if assimilation is specifically defined as the process by which a minority group gradually adopts the customs and attitudes of a/the prevailing culture, such a process becomes reciprocal, two way, a basic reality being posited/positing itself through its simultaneous positing of its Other. And again the posited basic reality is destabilized, thus problematizing the base of the image transformation superstructure, as well as (thus) the ability to say definitively what constitutes, or can constitute, a hyperrealist aesthetic.

For the purposes of this chapter, let us say (to paraphrase Baudrillard) that hyper-assimilation is entirely in simulation. Its hyper-accelerated performance and its hyper-inversions of tropes and signifiers produce the simultaneous transcendence and dissolution of the process of assimilation (Baudrillard 1983). If, as Trinh recalls Deleuze remarking, our civilization is not one of the image but, rather, a civilization of the cliché, then one might say that it is the clichéd image that dominates the Bollywood film scene (Trinh 1991). How, then, by 're-circulating a limited number of propositions and rehashing stereotypes', can the Bollywood film scene be seen as 'criticizing stereotype' and be constituted as 'a powerful practice' (Trinh 1991: 190)? And, to come approximately full circle, could one call such a practice 'hyperreal'?

Consider the title of one of the more recent 'crossover' films, *Bollywood/Hollywood* (dir. Deepa Mehta, 2002), a film that its director says, 'really *is* a Bollywood/Hollywood movie'.[9] How would one define such a film? Perhaps, more than either term (Bollywood or Hollywood) the crucial concept, or defining element, is the slash, or virgule, separating/connecting the two. This diagonal mark, as the dictionary defines it, is used especially to separate alternatives, as in 'and/or', but also to represent the word 'per'. The usage note for this latter term becomes crucial as, in fact, it constitutes a *usage problem*: 'Per is appropriately used in a description of ratios. In its more general use to mean "according to" it is best reserved for business and legal communications, unless the writer seeks a tone of jocular formality' (Nunberg 1996: 1342).

What if one read the title in this way: 'Bollywood according to Hollywood'? What would this mean, or entail? Hollywood itself has various meanings, both metonymic and metaphoric. Beyond being the name of both a district of Los Angeles and a city in south-east Florida, it is used to refer metonymically to the US film industry (noun proper) as well as adjectivally, as in (*i*) of or relating to this industry and (*ii*) flashy and vulgar (after 'Hollywood' in the first sense, i.e., as the district of California). And what then would be the implication of its reverse/ion, i.e., 'Hollywood/Bollywood'? Could there be such an equivalence? Using a series of recent Hollywood, Bollywood and 'Bollywood/Hollywood', or so-called 'crossover' films, and employing/deploying concepts from Baudrillard, Bhabha and Trinh, this chapter will address the usage problem of simulation and hyper-assimilation in the (Crossover) Bollywood film. In doing so, I hope to formulate/differentiate the praxis of the contemporary Bollywood film (using the films somewhat archetypically) within the hegemony of the pre-posited order from which Bollywood derives its name. In other words, to paraphrase Bhabha, this chapter sets out to explore the Janus-faced ambivalence of film language in the construction of the Janus-faced discourse of the nation—in this case, one that is, as Spivak has pointed out, more of a political construct than a place, particularly in the so-called era of the 'non-resident Indian', or NRI (Bhabha 1990a; Spivak 1990b: 78, 87). But first, in order to understand the potential ramifications of these films' deployments of signifiers and tropes, it is necessary to familiarize ourselves with Baudrillard's discussion of the simulacrum and the hyperreal.

BAUDRILLARD, BOLLYWOOD AND THE HYPERREAL

Baudrillard begins his essay on 'The Precession of Simulacra' by stating, 'It is no longer a question of imitation, nor of reduplication, nor even of parody. It is rather a question of substituting signs of the real for the real itself' (Baudrillard 1983: 4). Whereas 'feigning or dissimulating leaves the reality principle intact ... simulation threatens the difference between "true" and "false", between "real" and "imaginary"' (Baudrillard 1983: 5). The key, initial distinction, according to Baudrillard, is between 'representation' and 'simulation'—whereas the former 'starts from the principle that the sign and the real are equivalent', the latter starts 'from the *utopia* of this principle', i.e., 'envelop(ing) the whole edifice of representation as itself a simulacrum', enacting 'reversion ... of every reference' (Baudrillard 1983: 11). The transition from representation to simulation, Baudrillard goes on to say, 'marks the decisive turning point' (Baudrillard 1983: 12). Whereas, with the former, the notion of ideology is retained, with the latter, there is no 'last judgment to separate truth from false, the real from its artificial resurrection' (Baudrillard 1983: 12).

Consider, then, the case of Bollywood or, more particularly, the case of the highest grossing film in Indian history, the aforementioned *Kabhi Khushi, Kabhie Gham* (K3G). Coming in at over three hours (at 209 minutes, more nearly four) and containing seven songs whose settings serendipitously span India, the UK and Egypt, K3G may be described as the archetypal contemporary Hindi film, both in its number and use of song and dances and in their internal logic (for example, 'jumping' from location to location with no regard for narrative or formal logic; also 'jumping' temporally, i.e., into and out of the song and dance sequence; and additionally—structurally—in the use of playback). The film tells the story of the Raichand family, whose eldest son elopes to London with the woman he loves after failing to receive his father's approval for marriage. Soon after, the younger son also journeys to London in an attempt to find his brother and reunite the family. For the purposes of this chapter, i.e., the interrelationships of the hyperreal and hyper-assimilation, it is crucial to examine one particular song and dance, 'Deewana Hai Dekho' (aka, Who Are You?), the reason being that, in this story of NRIs travelling from India (Delhi) to the UK (London), it is this song and dance sequence, the fourth in the film and following the 'Vande Mataram' interlude, that addresses the issues of (hyper) assimilation and hyperrealism most vividly.

The song and dance, featuring Bollywood. superstars Kareena Kapoor (K-Ko) and Hrithik Roshan, as well as scores of background dancers straight out of a United Colors of Benetton commercial, employs various famous sites in the UK as backdrops—a sort of *National Geographic* aesthetic in reverse, i.e., the UK as the exotic place on display, associated (metonymically/metaphorically) with representative sites. In this sense, i.e., in the slippage between metonym and metaphor, the substitution of one for the other—enhanced, perhaps, by its sped-up pace, i.e., five and a half minutes, featuring eighty cuts, or an average shot length of four seconds—the song and dance sequence may be described as adhering to Baudrillard's third level of the image, i.e., as masking the *absence* of a basic reality (Baudrillard 1983: 11). In this sequence, a hyper-saccharine aesthetic is employed, featuring, along with the rapid cutting, bright, gaudy colours and similar smiles. Here we already see evidence of the utopia of equivalence—and reversion of reference—that distinguishes simulation from representation.

Yet upon closer examination of these actual sites, an interesting development unfolds. While ostensibly (i.e., on the narrative level), these sites include a university, a rugby stadium, a museum, and a shopping mall, and while the 'jumps' from one site to the next may, to some extent, be described as adhering to an internal narrative logic, these are, in fact, sites dispersed across the UK. When one checks the credits, one discovers that, while the university where the song and dance begins is supposed to be in London (identified as 'King's College' by an off-screen campus radio deejay), it is in fact the Stowe School in Buckingham. Similarly, the rugby stadium that K-Ko and Hrithik 'jump' to from said (London) school is the Millennium Stadium in Cardiff, Wales. The museum that immediately follows is the British Museum in Bloomsbury, and the next site they jump to is the Bluewater Shopping Complex in Kent (not to be confused with the next site, the Bicester Shopping Centre in Oxfordshire). All of this in five and a half minutes. Yet, none of this (i.e., the actual geographical disparities between sites) is noticeable—i.e., on the surface, the sequence literally bears no relation to any reality whatsoever: it is a pastiche of places, seamlessly cut and pasted together. Yet, this seamlessness is the key, for it creates a Turing Test of sorts for the image sequence: if one cannot tell whether the reality is real, i.e., that the places represented are actually where they are supposed to be (London), does it matter? In other words, the sequence's ability to be taken for a (displaced) basic reality paradoxically distinguishes its status as hyperreal.

Even to one 'familiar' with these aforementioned places and locations, it may be plausible that, given the pacing, such a one (i.e., the 'cultural insider') may not recognize the difference between the real and the simulated. One viewer from Kent might recognize the first shopping centre as being (from/in) Bluewater; another, from Wales, may recognize the Millennium Stadium. Yet, neither necessarily can infer within five and a half minutes that the assemblage of images, or sites, just seen in succession was not, ostensibly, there (i.e., where the sites were presumed to be—or, to paraphrase Metz, were put forth by the story as being). The only way of actually knowing is post hoc, via a search on the Internet Movie Database (and that, too, requires some searching). The real has been supplanted by signs of the real; the song and dance sequence becomes (is) a 'generation by models of a real without … reality' (Baudrillard 1983: 2). How, then, does the sequence translate in terms of identity and assimilation? For this, we must turn to K-Ko and Trinh (1991).

K-Ko and *K3G*

K-Ko's name in *K3G*, 'Pooja', is itself crucial. Shortened upon arrival to London to 'Poo', one may see her name as an example of hyper-assimilation at the nominal level, i.e., a nominal assimilation made hyperreal. Along with shortened name, Poo's clothes are decidedly shorter (halter tops and micro-miniskirts) and her most typical response becomes a laconic 'Whatever', delivered in an Indian-accented Mae West drawl. This latter term, indeed, can be associated with her shortened name (Poo), just as her former name (Pooja) could be seen as typifying an opposite sentiment (i.e., *pooja*, or prayer). Thus, Pooja's voyage from Indian to NRI, i.e., from 'Pooja' to 'Poo', can be seen as a transition from metaphoric injunction to metonymic function, thus illustrating the 'politically contaminated and ambivalent function of the non-resident Indian' (Spivak 1990b: 67).

Just as Poo(ja) was previously the Chandni Chowk insider, she is now equally 'at home' in London—in fact, the process of assimilation is non-existent, or seamless.[10] The sequence leading up to the 'Who Are You' song and dance provides a demonstration of such hyper-assimilation. As Poo and her two female friends drive into the college, the aforementioned radio announcer proclaims, 'This is King's College radio. It's 9:45 and Poo's just entered the college'. Similarly, wherever Poo and her friends go, the focus is on Poo. When she passes a young Indian (i.e., NRI) clad stylishly in black leather jacket and sunglasses on his motorcycle, who blows a kiss while chatting with his entourage and says, 'Hey, Poo', she merely replies, 'Whatever'. When this young man, Ravi, then asks, 'Movie tonight?' she replies, 'Tell me how it waa-aas', to much laughter, even as she and her friends saunter off.

It is with the arrival of Hrithik in a red Lamborghini (invoking a synchronized, lip-synched exclamation of 'Oh-my-gosh!' from a group of nearby blondes) that Poo's status as campus idol is challenged. The blondes, as well as the other students, all gather around Hrithik as he emerges from his sports car in a sleeveless leather top and sunglasses, flexing his muscles as he picks up a guitar and begins playing right on the beat of the playback, which has already begun, even as the others begin swaying and clapping along. The song consists of K-Ko and the others pursuing Hrithik, asking/singing, 'Who are you?' even as Hrithik plays out one stereotypical fantasy after another, from playing guitar on the college quad to scoring the winning point at the rugby match. The blondes, meanwhile, having now become cheerleaders (replete with instantaneous costume change, another staple of the Bollywood song and dance), sing, 'We're cool like that/We're hip like that/Groove like that/We'll win like that', then burst into giggles (again via playback) while primping with their pompoms. Hrithik turns to blow them a kiss, the sweat visibly flying off him. As the camera cuts in an eyeline match to the cheerleaders, giggling behind their pompoms, K-Ko 'walks on' to the screen (in the foreground), looking first at the cheerleaders (behind her), then turning to look directly at the camera, even as it tracks her walking past them, rolling her eyes, turning fully forward and, with both hands slightly raised, delivering her metonymic line, 'Whatever'.

It is with this word, this gesture, this movement that K-Ko, 'Poo', comes closest to—in fact, personifies (as metonymic/metaphoric function)—the 'unoccupied space' Trinh speaks of, in which 'accepting negativity (otherness defined by the master) has led to a new positivity (identity as reclaimed by the other), which in turn opens to a set of new negativities and positivities (the questioning and renaming of otherness, through the unnaming of both the master and his other)' (Trinh 1991: 187). As K-Ko walks across the scene, thus 'flattening' it, she makes it, too, a background to her, so that when she 'returns' to the song and dance (i.e., her voice disappears, the playback resumes, and she returns to her previous performative role), this rupture makes her ensuing dramatic persona/performance even more of an impersonation, both of generic (meta) tropes and performative (micro) mode, particularly as she repeats this gesture, this slippage out of one role and into another, 'tak(ing) pleasure in making abrupt turns and repeated detours, so as to outplay her own game, rendering impotent the master's world of refined distinctions and classifications' (Trinh 1991: 188).[11]

'Walking on beaten paths' (or across the cliché-ridden screen/scene), K-Ko/Poo 'may laugh, and laugh at herself for she may realize she must and she can, at any moment, stray from the itinerary chosen' (Trinh 1991: 188). Rather than, on the one hand, the nation (as personified by K-Ko/Poo in her metonymic/metaphoric function, i.e., the NRI) being 'a soul, a spiritual principle', and rather than 'Bombay cinema ... often hav(ing) the feeling of being piecemeal and disaggregative (i.e., pastiche) ... but quite without the postmodern self-consciousness', this cinema, as personified by K-Ko in K3G, displays both a strategy stemming back to Sanskrit theatre (i.e., stepping out of character to also become the narrator and 'know[ing] [s]he is playing only a part'), as well as (thus) what DuBois called a 'double consciousness', a soul contaminated by the politics of deracination, that 'defies the normality of all binary oppositions' (DuBois 1989: 5; Nayar 2004: 16; Renan 1990: 19; Shekar and Sahai 2004: 19).[12]

Pooja is 'Poo', and all gestures have become bracketed by her 'Whatever'. But what is bracketed is itself a simulation—and so 'she un-builds; she builds and builds up to no total. No total she can possess while carrying out the ceaseless work of dispossessing—herself and the possessors' (Trinh 1991: 188). The song title's question—'Who Are You?'

(which she merely lip-synchs though, again, this is indiscernible)—goes unanswered. Or rather, it is unanswered by Hrithik (to whom the question is ostensibly directed), yet is answered by she who poses the question (or, is posed by this question). The answer, to paraphrase Trinh, is in the joyful negation of the very notions of identity and ethnicity (Trinh 1991: 187). It is precisely with such a (re)framing of 'Indianness' in mind that we now turn to examine how 'Bollywood' itself circulates as a cinematic signifier in a series of recent films by Hollywood and South Asian diasporic directors.

BOLLYWOOD/HOLLYWOOD

'The film, Bollywood/Hollywood', its DVD tag reads, 'is a madcap lovesong to both East and West with Bollywood music, Hollywood choreography, North American locations. And the actors? Bollywood's best!' (Cinebella 2002). To begin with the last claim, neither of the film's two leads, Rahul Khanna (Rahul) or Lisa Ray (Sue/Sunita), has had a significant career in Bollywood. In fact, the primary link to Bollywood is via Khanna's younger brother, Akshaye, who makes a cameo appearance in one of the song and dance sequences. This primarily English-language film by Deepa Mehta, a director born and raised in India and now based in Canada, tells the story of Rahul, a second-generation Indo-Canadian living in Toronto who, upon being pressured by his family to get married to an Indian girl, proposes to Sue/Sunita, a young woman whose ethnicity is unclear, that she pretend to be his Indian fiancée in return for payment, not realizing that she actually is Indian. The film's songs (a total of four in less than two hours) are introduced with superscripts that run across the screen à la Brecht, for example, 'Rahul's Song', 'Sue's Song', 'Romantic couple song', etc. In these sequences, though (Hindi) playback is employed, the performances are generally either purely dramatic or performative.

Take, for example, the third song ('Sue's Song'), in which Akshaye Khanna (Bollywood icon) makes a cameo appearance, arriving just before Sue breaks out in (Hindi) song at a large Indian gathering. Akshaye's presence could have been hyperreal-inducing had he appeared in (the middle of) the song, i.e., 'in medias res', and not, as he does, before it begins, as the 'celebrity brother' of Rahul, thus pre-defined and serving as, rather than severing, the bridge to that 'basic reality' the film attempts to lampoon, or imitate. In what sense, then, did director Deepa Mehta mean that the film 'really is a Bollywood/Hollywood movie'? Is it, to return to an earlier question, to imply a 'Bollywood according to Hollywood'?

The referentiality of the film ultimately remains encapsulated by/ within its Hollywood choreography, i.e., its overt style (for example, the Brechtian superscripts). This only serves to distinguish the film's reality from fantasy, with performances, similarly, that remain static, failing to explore or display the 'Janus-faced discourse' where 'meanings may be partial because they are in medias res', i.e., 'caught, uncertainly, in the act of "composing"' (Bhabha 1990a: 3). Though similar to K3G thematically (i.e., in dealing with NRIs), Bollywood/Hollywood only lives up to its name, structurally speaking: rather than 'disturbing the comfort and security of stable meaning' (thus leading to 'a different conception of montage', for example, the K-Ko 'flattening' effect), Mehta's 'madcap love-song to both East and West' simply 'parod[ies] the cliché' (i.e., East and West), thus failing to restore to the images all that one does not see in them (Trinh 1991: 110-11).

In another recent film, Daisy von Scherler Mayer's The Guru (2002), one finds an even more interesting case of appropriation, in this case, by Hollywood of the Bollywood form. This English-language film tells the story of Ramu (Jimi Mistry), an NRI living in New York who becomes attracted to Sharonna (Heather Graham), a porn movie actress, and goes on to play the role of an Indian 'sex guru'. Director von Scherler Mayer creates a two minute song and dance sequence in the film which is, in her words, 'a recreation of an old-fashioned Bollywood movie'.[13] This sequence, like those in Bollywood/Hollywood, is formally bracketed as fantasy (thus, again, revivifying its dichotomy with the real): Ramu, while watching an 'old-fashioned Bollywood movie' on his TV (featuring dancers in old-fashioned Indian costumes yet shot in colour), 'enters' the song and dance sequence after first 'seeing' Sharonna, his love interest, suddenly appear in the role of the lead female performer, 'singing' in Hindi (i.e., lip-synching) and dancing (i.e., imitating classical Indian dance gestures). The camera, simulating Ramu's point-of-view, closes in on the TV screen, until the latter's frame has become the former's: Ramu is now in von Scherler Mayer's (colourized) 'recreation' of 'Kya Mil Gaya', an 'old-fashioned Bollywood movie' song and dance, featuring scores of dancers alongside Sharonna and Ramu in 'colorful Indian garb' ('You have to have big groups', the director intones on the commentary track. 'In a real Bollywood movie, there'd probably be fifty more dancers').

The choice of adverb on the director's part in this last parenthetical is illuminating, as when one watches the original sequence for the song (from 'an old-fashioned Bollywood movie', *Sasural*, directed by T. Prakash Rao and released in 1961), one finds a five minute sequence in black and white, featuring merely the actor and actress in both Western and Indian attire. Furthermore, as the total time of the sequence illuminates, von Scherler Mayer shortens (by over half) the duration of the original version of the song. Also, *Sasural* is not listed in the credits for *The Guru*, which only list the playback performers (Lata Mangeshkar and Mohammed Rafi). On the other hand, the other song included in this sequence, the one 'Kya Mil Gaya' segues into ('You're The One That I Want'), is associated with the movie it was originally featured in (*Grease*, directed by Randal Kleiser and released in 1978) in the credits, thus further highlighting the absence of the other.

Given the director's comments and the film's (lack of) credits, one may conclude that von Scherler Mayer may not have actually watched *Sasural*. Yet, it hardly matters, since, even in colour, the 'recreated sequence' Mistry watches on TV will appear to be—or, appears to be—the 'actual' Bollywood film sequence. Again, as with the (actually) diverse locations for the *K3G* song, the images can be successfully mistaken as being 'real'. Even if one listened to the DVD commentary track (already quite conceivably a select audience), unless one had previously seen *Sasural* and remembered it, one would still be lead to believe that von Scherler Mayer's 'recreation' was, in fact, sincere, especially given the abundance of 'cultural insider' comments she makes on the commentary track, for example, 'If this were a real Bollywood movie ...', as well as her failing to mention *Sasural* by name. And having thus 'successfully impersonated' (i.e., created) the 'Bollywood element', the director can quite sincerely assert that *The Guru* was about 'incorporating Bollywood elements' and 'trying to recreate that [Bollywood] look'.

Yet ultimately she is mistaken. *Sasural*, the film from which 'Kya Mil Gaya' was taken, was released in 1961 (the same year as Godard's musical, *Une Femme est Une Femme*). Hardly, an 'old-fashioned movie' (though, like many of Godard's films, it *is* in black and white), the original sequence in *Sasural* features a panoply of formal techniques, including wipes, dissolves, abrupt cuts, close-ups, eyeline matches and, of course, playback. Furthermore, unlike the 'recreated' sequence in *The Guru* (though like the typical Bollywood fare), the original sequence features nearly half a dozen (abrupt) scene changes, as well as attendant costume changes. In other words, the original's format works to transcend its content—in one dissolve, for example, a giant black X is superimposed over glimpses of water in bull's-eye rings which grow larger and larger, until they 'become' the river of the next scene—all this, of course, in a matter of seconds.

The irony here is that, were von Scherler Mayer truly faithful to the original, the majority of *The Guru*'s Western audiences might have found the 'Kya Mil Gaya' sequence either 'inauthentic' or, perhaps, more overtly a 'recreation', i.e., a re-interpretation. What passes as simulation, then, is in fact representation along Baudrillard's third level of the image, namely, the masking of the *absence* of a basic reality (Baudrillard 1983: 11). Simultaneously, what is referred to as 'old-fashioned' (i.e., the so-called 'original' Mistry first watches on his TV) actually only '*plays at being*' so, and thus 'is of the order of sorcery' (Baudrillard 1983: 12). Yet, it is in this sorcery that Orientalism's seeds lie, as an essentialized Other is 'reproduced' and passed off as a reflection of 'a basic reality' (Baudrillard 1983: 11).

Here, then, the flexibility of the hyperreal praxis becomes apparent: it can be effectively utilized towards opposing ends. In this sense, its contextualization becomes doubly relevant. Whereas the deployment of hyperrealism within the K3G sequence works to enhance the destabilization of tropes and signifiers, in the case of *The Guru*, a similar technique is used to *deny* (by paradoxically recreating) cultural distinction, ensconcing itself within complacent platitudes about 'old-fashioned' Bollywood.[14] In moving beyond the frames of these latter worlds, both structurally and aesthetically, the Bollywood film world (re)creates a world view that works not only to draw awareness to all those elements lacking from the former 'basic reality' but to offer, in its stead, an 'impersonation' that transcends and dissolves the very notion of otherness. Replying, as it were, to its own status as 'illegitimate', Bollywood finds itself 'B-coming' in a way that makes difficult the all-too-easy divisions imposed by colonizing systems in which the 'other' can only develop an inferiority or a dependency complex (Fanon 1967).

The Bollywood style, as exemplified by *K3G* and in contrast to that of *The Guru* (i.e., the Hollywood style), intervenes precisely 'at the moment at which pastiche appears' or, conversely, its intervention is precisely the appearance of this moment (Jameson 1988: 16). Rather than parody becoming impossible, however, and/or pastiche becoming 'parody that has lost its sense of humor', the Bollywood pastiche retains its distinctive latter sense and uses it to perform a hyper-mimicry of tropes associated with the process/state of assimilation (Jameson 1988).[15] By supplanting any 'normal' sense of such a process through its own hyper-contextualization, it posits a way of resisting the logos of Orientalism—not by avoiding the signifiers associated with these sign systems but, paradoxically, by reproducing them via a thoroughly 'commercialized' aesthetic. Before considering contemporary critics' theorization of this 'commercial' aesthetic (and its subsequent effects on representations of the nation and national identity), I briefly want to examine one final film that further develops both the conception and reception of a 'crossover Bollywood' aesthetic. The film I have in mind is British-based Indo-diasporic director Gurinder Chadha's *Bride and Prejudice* (2004).

From Amritsar to L.A.

Bride and Prejudice (hereafter *B&P*) engages in multiple adaptations—of Jane Austen's famous novel, of Hollywood musicals, and of Bollywood conventions. For the purposes of this chapter, however, I am primarily concerned with the latter form of adaptation. Coming in at just under two hours, *B&P* contains five musical numbers, some—such as the third song, 'No Life without Wife'—predominantly drawing upon previous Hollywood sources (for example, *Grease* and *West Side Story*), others—such as the second song, 'India's the Place to Be', featuring pop star Ashanti 'singing' in Hindi while accompanied by half a dozen bare-chested male dancers and numerous pyrotechnics—engaging in more of an MTV aesthetic. However, I would like to focus on the final song, 'Show Me the Way to Love', which is the most blatantly 'Bollywoodesque' song sequence in the film.[16]

'Show Me the Way to Love' begins in a Mexican restaurant in L.A., where Darcy (Martin Henderson) has taken the visiting Lalitha (the novel's Lizzy), played by Bollywood superstar Aishwarya Rai, for dinner.[17] Darcy and Lalitha converse (in English) over margaritas and tortilla chips while a mariachi band plays in the background. As the couple stare into each other's eyes, momentarily at a loss for words, the playback music begins, even as first the mariachi band members and then the two bartenders begin shaking, respectively, their maracas and drink makers to the beat. An abrupt cut takes us to Lalitha and Darcy running, in slow motion, through a series of shooting fountain jets at night and then dancing with each other as the playback singing commences.[18]

Another abrupt cut takes us to Darcy driving Lalitha through the palm tree-lined streets of L.A. in a convertible, then walking through the Disney Concert Hall, stopping occasionally to admire its architecture, even as the playback singing continues (though they still refrain from lip-synching). From here another cut takes us to a night scene with Lalitha, now alone, 'singing' (i.e., lip-synching the English lyrics) and dancing outside her relative's house. The camera cuts from Lalitha to Darcy, now also alone, walking along the pool in his backyard and, seeing her image in the pool briefly, smiling to himself. From here the sequence moves to Lalitha and Darcy running to board a helicopter and going for a ride over the Grand Canyon. After a series of panoramic shots, a cut takes us to the duo atop a misty mountain.

In this most Bollywood of song settings, Darcy and Lalitha engage in a brief embrace and, without lip-synching, stare out at the (implied) beautiful vista while smoke and clouds pass by in abundance. Another abrupt cut takes us to the couple walking, arm in arm, on a Santa Monica beach while a gospel choir sings in the background (on the beach).[19] As the camera tracks left to follow the couple, the length of the gospel choir, standing on an apparently unending bleacher, keeps increasing even as its members, all black and in full choir dress, continue to provide an emotional rendering of the song's chorus, with an occasional member breaking out in a 'spontaneous' refrain (for example, 'Show them the way!') as Lalitha and Darcy continue walking, oblivious to the choir's presence. On two occasions, additional onlookers—in the first instance, a row of surfers emerging from the waves and, in the second, two lifeguards descending the stairs of their station—'spontaneously' lip-synch the song's Indian-inflected harmony. Finally, all of these onlookers—the entire choir, the surfers and the lifeguards—form a

circle around Lalitha and Darcy and then disappear as the couple embraces, looking at the sunset as the song trails off with a single guitar
echoing the melody.

Beyond its own rather convoluted elements, what makes this sequence particularly interesting is its alternate version. Chadha made
two versions of this film—one, *B&P*, in English, primarily intended for
global distribution, and the other, *Balle Balle! Amritsar to L.A.*, dubbed
in Hindi and geared for release in India.[20] In the Indian version of
'Show Me to Love' (entitled 'Tum Se Kahen' and primarily sung in
Hindi, unlike its counterpart), the ordering of events changes, cutting
straight from the fountain jets to the scenes at night featuring Lalitha
and Darcy separately fantasizing about each other. Moreover, in the
Indian version, Darcy 'sings'—in Hindi.[21] Additionally, the most 'Bollywoodesque' moment in the song—atop the misty mountain—is also
extended and features both Darcy and Lalitha 'singing' to each other
in Hindi, as opposed to merely gazing mutely at the apparently breath-
taking sunset, as they do in *B&P*.

While Berges notes that 'we wanted it [*B&P*] to be very playful, and
have fun with Bollywood, but we never wanted to parody it', the tendency among Western critics of the film was either to see *B&P* as a Bollywood film or, at the very least, as deliberately imitating one.[22] This
assessment is simultaneously used to position the film as essentially a
'trivial' work of 'low art'—'a travesty, of course', featuring 'clumsy song-
and-dance numbers', and a 'Bollywood formula' that the film 'hews
to' (Denby 2005; Dargis 2005; Mathews 2005). Yet, the dual versions
of the film—and their differences, particularly in relation to the treatment of the song sequences (for example, 'Show Me to Love'/'Tum Se
Kahen')—seem to underscore Chadha's assertion that 'what I wanted
to do was make a film that used a different film language, an Indian
film language, and make that film language accessible to people who
live in suburbs of cities all over the world'.[23]

In other words, *B&P*, rather than adhering to what may be called a
'Bollywood aesthetic' (for example, that of *K3G*), utilizes various elements of this film form in order to create a work that may more accurately be described as having a 'crossover' aesthetic, one which, for
instance, considers Darcy singing in Hindi as being 'too much' and
'too different'.[24] Even as Chadha professes her desire to 'just go Bollywood' with/in the final song sequence, one can trace more of a parallel

to *Bollywood/Hollywood* in *B&P*'s overt attempts to call attention to its Bollywoodesque song sequence's extreme unreality (what Chadha calls 'the *Blazing Saddles* moments'), rather than, as with the 'Who Are You' sequence in *K3G*, blurring the line separating reality and unreality and engaging in a hyperreal praxis.[25]

RESHAPING THE SCAPE

I would like to conclude this chapter by examining the theorization of this 'commercialized' aesthetic in the contemporary Bollywood film—one largely based on the aforementioned hyperreal praxis—as well as what its subsequent effects on formulations of the nation and national identity might be. As a backdrop to this discussion, it will be useful to keep in mind E. Ann Kaplan's delineation of what she calls a 'commercial or co-opted postmodernism', particularly in relation (or in contrast) to what she labels a 'utopian postmodernism' (Kaplan 1988: 4).[26] This is not to suggest that this dichotomy is necessarily tenable but, rather, that it potentially provides a useful way of gauging the Bollywood film's particular strategies that, in turn, may rework such dichotomies of postmodernity.

The contemporary theorization of Bollywood appears to take a rather straightforward approach to this 'commercial' aesthetic. Lalitha Gopalan, for instance, in discussing what she calls the 'sequences of attractions' comprising many song and dance numbers, claims that 'the object-laden *mise en scène* endorses consumerism' (Gopalan 2002: 19). Similarly, Shohini Chaudhuri finds that consumerism is 'given a blessing in Bollywood narratives', furthermore noting that 'this is in stark contrast to earlier films, where NRIs never figured' and the West was seen as dangerous, i.e., in terms of its corrupting influences (Chaudhuri 2005: 157). Today's Bollywood films, in Chaudhuri's view, 'reconcil[e] global consumer lifestyle with traditional "Indian" values' and, in a near paraphrase of Gopalan's assessment, 'endorse global consumerism' (Chaudhuri 2005: 156–57, 161).[27] David Martin-Jones has taken this position to its logical extreme, arguing that 'films like *K3G*' which 'celebrate the wealth that market capitalism can create', in turn increase the desirability of the foreign settings featured in such films as tourist destinations for Indians (Martin-Jones 2006: 53). Martin-Jones further develops this symbiosis between filmic representations and the tourist industry in his attempts to show 'how the flows of international trade and tourism' between India and Scotland have affected the aesthetics of popular Indian films (Martin-Jones 2006).

To reinvoke Appadurai's terminology mentioned at the outset of this chapter, one might say that, in these critics' theorizations, financescapes are being used to shape mediascapes and, furthermore, such foreign locales in Bollywood films—rather than illuminating the 'problem of reproduction in a deterritorialized context'—are used to provide 'geographic specificity' and correspond 'precisely to the "real" experience of the tourist' (Appadurai 1996: 37; Martin-Jones 2006: 54). It will be useful at this juncture to recall Dean MacCannell's discussion of the tourist experience here, particularly given that Martin-Jones insists on the 'definite recognizability' of these foreign locales (Martin-Jones 2006: 54). MacCannell describes the experience of the tourist as one engaging in 'sight ⟶ marker ⟶ sight transformations' and, furthermore, that these transformations 'are not merely something that may occur in the act of sightseeing' but, rather, 'are an essential element of the act' (MacCannell 1976: 121). In this process, tourists replace recognition of a sight—London, for instance—with recognition of a symbolic marker, for example, Big Ben. Thus, in these instances, sightseers do not in any empirical sense see London but rather its symbolic markers (MacCannell 1976: 121, 111). The 'tourist experience' is thus one that has, at its very basis, a semiotic substitution. Therefore, in Martin-Jones' terms, the so-called 'precisely "real" experience' of 'geographical specificity' can more accurately be described, particularly in sequences such as 'Vande Mataram' and 'Who Are You?' in K3G, as the simulation of a basic reality. In this sense, the viewing of such sequences, rather than affording any 'real' experience of specific places, envelops representation itself as a simulation (Baudrillard 1983).

To claim, then, that such a hyperreal experience results in a straightforward 'endorsement' of consumerism becomes problematic. Such sequences in contemporary Bollywood films, rather, seem to lead to the disappearance of geographic specificity (what Jameson has called a 'postmodern hyperspace') and, thus, to what MacCannell labels 'sight obliteration' (Jameson 1991: 44; MacCannell 1976: 126). If, to juxtapose Martin-Jones' and MacCannell's discourses, one labels such sequences in Bollywood films as 'promotional advertisements' for specific tourist destinations, then one might argue that the advertisements are supplanted by their own representational strategies. This, in turn, would put into question the 'reconciliation' of global consumerism with 'traditional' Indian values and, indeed, suggest a recontextualization of each (Chaudhuri 2005: 156-57).

The shifting terrain of cultural identity in an era of transnationalism is vividly captured in the seamless yet unfixed surfaces of the Bollywood film. The presentation of fantasyscapes that fail to correspond to any social reality, seems to suggest a deconstruction of both essentialized notions of 'Indianness' (whether invoked culturally or aesthetically) and, in the process, problematizes Kaplan's previously noted distinction between two strains of postmodernism. Indeed, one might say that the contemporary Bollywood film such as *K3G* presents a 'commercial postmodernism' that works to move beyond 'oppressive binary categories' (Kaplan 1988: 4). Furthermore, such strategies work to counter the conception of a Third Worldist aesthetic of national allegory, offering a postmodern impersonation in the place of an antiquated sense of national identity. Rather than reinvoking 'India' as the hegemonic center of all discourse, Bollywood presents *itself* as the 'fount of all identities', thus invoking a crucial shift: from the so-called 'real' to a simulation (Kaur 2005: 326).

NOTES

1. Though Jameson claims to use the term 'third world' in 'an essentially descriptive sense', it nevertheless functions as the necessary oppositional force in his self-described 'First-world/Third-world dialectic', without which his entire methodology—and its contingencies of difference—would collapse. Rather than seeing the Third World (text) as 'locked in a life-and-death struggle with first-world cultural imperialism', one might indeed frame this (inter)relationship in less agonistic terms, particularly given that the medium under discussion here is film and not literature (Jameson 1986: 67-68). For additional discussion of this issue, see Lazarus (2004a).

2. Jameson unfortunately maintains this essentialized difference even in the realm of film, noting 'the radical dissymmetry' between the two [First and Third world cinemas] and insisting that they can have 'nothing whatsoever in common, formally or epistemologically' and, furthermore, that the Third World film requires 'the enlightening First-World co-ordinate'—in this case, Godard—in order to be critically reformulated (Jameson 1992: 199, 196).

3. (i)   Ethnoscapes: the landscape of persons who constitute the shifting world in which people live.

    (ii) Technoscapes: the global configuration of technologies moving at high speeds across previously impermeable borders.

    (iii) Financescapes: the global grid of currency speculation and capital transfer.

(iv) Mediascapes: the distribution of the capabilities to produce and disseminate information and the large complex repertoire of images and narratives generated by these capabilities.

(v)   Ideoscapes: ideologies of state and counter-ideologies of movements, around which nation-states have organized their political cultures (Appadurai 1996).

4. I derive the term 'transculturation' from Mary L. Pratt, who describes it as being used by ethnographers 'to describe how subordinated or marginal groups select and invent from materials transmitted to them by a dominant or metropolitan culture'. According to Pratt, the term was coined in the 1940s by Cuban sociologist Fernando Ortiz who 'proposed the term to replace the paired concepts of acculturation and deculturation that described the transference of culture in reductive fashion imagined from within the interests of the metropolis' (Pratt 1992: 5, 229, n. 4). For more on Bollywood as 'fantasyscape', see Chapter 2.

5. The phrase 'always already', originally employed by Althusser, is invoked in Baudrillard's definition of the (hyper)real, namely, 'that which is always already reproduced' (Baudrillard 1983: 146).

6. For more on the formation/projection of such an 'inferiority complex', see Frantz Fanon, Black Skin, White Masks (1967), particularly Chapter Four, 'The So-Called Dependency Complex of Colonized Peoples' (pp. 83–108).

7. Interspersed within this rapid-fire sequence are shots of women running by in Indian tricolour dress, i.e., white Indian suits with orange and green shawls. Ranjani Mazumdar claims that the 'nationalist refrain of the sound track seems rather ridiculous', while Patrick Hogan describes this sequence as 'both highly suggestive and highly ironic', claiming that 'hearing this nationalist mantra sung over a montage of the main sights of London is, for me, laugh-out-loud funny' (Mazumdar 2007: 140; Hogan 2008: 179).

8. Again, Hogan claims this interlude 'suggests a radical criticism of categorical identity … of tying one culture to a person as his or her essence' (Hogan 2008: 179).

9. Director's Commentary Track on the DVD of the film Bollywood/Hollywood (dir. Deepa Mehta, 2002).

10. Chandni Chowk is the famous market of Old Delhi.

11. For further discussion of the concept of 'impersonation' as it applies to Bollywood, see Chakravarty (1993).

12. DuBois describes double consciousness as 'a peculiar sensation … this sense of always looking at one's self through the eyes of others' (DuBois 1989: 5). DuBois' concept of 'twoness', discussed in the same passage, is also relevant to this idea.

13. Director's Commentary Track on the DVD of the film The Guru (dir. Daisy von Scherler Mayer, 2002).

14. A pernicious additional result of this sequence in The Guru is that, upon reviewing the original, one expects the singers/actors to break into 'You're The One That I Want' (in the voices of Olivia Newton-John and John Travolta) halfway through. Then again, as it is only plausibly true Bollywood fans who would have seen both versions, it is safe to assume that such a result would be met with no small humor on the viewer's part.

15. Jameson, in this essay, furthermore, defines pastiche as 'blank parody', a 'neutral practice … without parody's ulterior motive, without the satirical impulse, without laughter, without that still latent feeling that there exists something normal compared to which what is being imitated is rather comic' (Jameson 1988: 16).

16. In the Director's Commentary Track on the DVD of the film Bride and Prejudice (dir. Gurinder Chadha, 2004), Gurinder Chadha notes, 'I shot it [B&P] all in a very

Bollywood style and I realized, in the cutting, I was trying to make it more Western, and the two were fighting each other. So in the end, with this song ["Show Me to Love"], I said, "You know what? To hell with it, let's just go Bollywood with it"'.

17. Though allegedly a Mexican restaurant in L.A., the scene was actually shot in a Spanish restaurant in South London that was subsequently 'Mexicanized', according to Chadha's husband and co-writer, Paul Mayeda Berges.

18. At this point–and for most of the song–neither Darcy nor Lalitha engages in lip-synching.

19. Chadha calls this 'the *Blazing Saddles* moment'.

20. Co-writer Berges notes that the film, in its two versions, simultaneously opened at No. 1 in the UK and India, a feat he calls 'unprecedented'. It might also be noted here that the Indian version, while available on DVD, only comes with the (rather poorly) dubbed Hindi language track and no subtitles. At the same time, the Indian DVD features a song menu, noticeably absent on the *B&P* DVD.

21. Chadha and Berges note that Darcy breaking into song (in Hindi) was 'too much' (Berges) and 'too different' (Chadha) and, furthermore, as the director states, that it made the song too long. One assumes, given that these changes (re: Darcy singing) were made for the non-Indian release, the implied audience (for whom Darcy singing would have been 'too much' and 'too different') was a non-Indian one. Though Chadha mentions that she thinks the Indian version is also included on the (American) DVD, she is mistaken, as it is not. As noted previously, the dubbing quality, both in this sequence and throughout all of the songs, is rather poor, i.e., it is rather clear that Darcy is not actually singing, though the effect is indeed rather bizarre. The gospel choir, meanwhile, sings in English in both versions.

22. Some sample reviews reflecting this view include David Denby's synopsis in *The New Yorker* (2005); Karen Durbin, Polly Shulman and Manohla Dargis's reviews in the *New York Times* (2004–05); as well as Jack Mathews' review in the *New York Daily News* (2005). Also, interestingly, at least two of the listed critics–Durbin and Mathews–assume Aishwarya Rai is actually singing in the film (Durbin 2004; Mathews 2005).

23. Director's Commentary Track on the DVD of the film *Bride and Prejudice* (dir. Gurinder Chadha, 2004).

24. Director's Commentary Track on the DVD of the film *Bride and Prejudice* (dir. Gurinder Chadha, 2004).

25. While one could claim that the illusion of the sequence in *K3G* is also broken via K-Ko's 'flattening effect', the radical changes of setting are not directly referenced and so the 'hyperspace' of this sequence–ostensibly 'London'–remains seamless. Conversely, one could say that, in the *B&P* song sequence, one is also given more of 'an idea' of the place–L.A.–than the (actual) place itself, though the sequence's frequent '*Blazing Saddles* moments' do seem to highlight this collusion of metaphor and metonymy.

26. 'A "utopian" postmodernism involves a movement of culture and texts beyond oppressive binary categories', whereas a '"commercial" or co-opted postmodernism ... is described as radically transforming the subject through its blanketing of culture' (Kaplan 1988: 4).

27. Chaudhuri goes on to note that 'after all, Hindus worship a god of business success–Ganesh–and a goddess of wealth–Lakshmi' (Chaudhuri 2005: 161).

Conclusion: Travelling Bollywood

Bollywood and the corpus dedicated to its study have continued to make great strides in the twenty-first century. Even as Bollywood continues to be one of the most prolific cinemas in the world, critical texts examining this cinema are on the rise (Pendakur 2003; Kavoori and Punathambekar 2008). While Bollywood's influence increases globally, however, a persistent streak remains in its study, namely, an adherence to the concept of the nation-state, whose underpinnings are used to frame the subsequent discussion of Bollywood. This tendency ensues despite an acknowledgment of Bollywood's increasingly global span as well as its increasingly transnational composition.

To paraphrase Peter Hitchcock, one could say the idea of the nation continues to serve as the predominant means of identifying Bollywood as a cinema (Hitchcock 2003: 4). Likewise, an approach highlighting the transnational features of the Bollywood film/industry presents not only a 'formidable challenge to this orthodoxy' but, indeed, works to reconfigure transnationalism as 'a condition of possibility in the analysis of global difference' (Hitchcock 2003: 5). As a way of concluding, then, I would like to examine some of the recent works of Bollywood theorists in specific regard to the concept of the nation and the attendant formatting of the Bollywood film.

In one of the recent studies of Bollywood, Jyotika Virdi begins by acknowledging that 'to say that Hindi cinema is a national cinema at once begs several questions', including, 'What is a nation?' and 'What are the criteria by which we designate a cinema "national"?' (Virdi 2003: 26). Yet, framing the study of Bollywood in this way is itself begging the question, making 'the Nation' the concept around which all discussions regarding Bollywood take place, what Virdi

labels 'the national imaginary' (Virdi 2003: 27-28).[1] Thus, even as
she acknowledges that 'the Indian nation is a political entity' and that
'Nations, therefore, are nothing more than the fictional fancies of their
creators', Virdi finds Bollywood to be 'one of the constitutive forces in
popularizing the national' (Virdi 2003: 28, 29, 31). Defining the scope
of a 'national cinema' includes 'where the films are made, by whom,
and under whose ownership' (Virdi 2003: 31). It is paradoxically, then,
by addressing these components of Virdi's criteria for a national cinema
that I intend to delineate the Bollywood film/industry's transnational
structure and dissemination.

Though Virdi herself acknowledges that 'global reconfiguration
... demands a new understanding of cultural politics', she describes
'Indian identity' as being 'under siege in the era of globalization' and
claims 'the [Indian] nation' has now been 'penetrated by transnational
forces' (Virdi 2003: xi, 197, 202). Her choice of words in delineating (the
relationship between) the transnational and the national is suggestive
of her generally antagonistic structuring of these concepts, though
Virdi defers credit for this to the Bollywood film itself. Thus, it is (in
Virdi's view) Bollywood cinema that engages in 'binary oppositions',
that 'pits the national against the transnational', so that 'the nation'
in Bollywood is constantly reimagined and resecured (Virdi 2003:
202-03, 205).

Indeed, this predilection for the nation-state can, in many ways, be
mapped onto Virdi's study itself, as a reflection of her own 'cinematic
imagination': the still gracing her book's original cover from the 1955
film song sequence, 'Mera Joota Hai Japani', whose sentiment continues, in the twenty-first century, to capture the thrust of Bollywood
Studies (and whose lyrics, more often than not, serve as an epigraph to
these contemporary studies).[2] Indeed, Tejaswini Ganti's essay derives
its title from this song's lyrics, even as its author asserts that 'Indianization [in Bollywood] is a practice of constituting difference—between
India and the West' (Ganti 2002: 283).[3] Like Virdi, then, Ganti employs this trope to center her discussion of Bollywood cinema around
the [Indian] nation. Furthermore, though she acknowledges the 'cos-
mopolitan nature of the Bombay film industry', Ganti ultimately finds
'Indianization' to be 'a conservative process that precludes innovation
in narrative and generic practices'.[4]

It is particularly in relation to this latter concept that we might consider Virdi's earlier classification of a 'national cinema' in regards to

ownership (Virdi 2003: 31). The question we might pose—or, to follow the contemporary trend, see Bollywood cinema as itself posing—is, in what sense? That is to say, who 'owns' the circulating film? By examining the actual distribution of the Bollywood film (to begin with a latter point, so as to work our way backwards to Virdi's question concerning production and simultaneously to anticipate the question of exhibition), one could say that this tendency towards a conservative process might itself be precluded by seeing the process in a transnational, rather than national, frame.[5] 'What is noteworthy', as Majunath Pendakur, among others, has pointed out, 'is that Hindi language films [i.e., Bollywood] have captured the all-India market *and* have reached out to Indians settled in Africa, [the] Middle East, South East Asia, North America, and Australia' (Pendakur 2003: 27, emphasis added). One could also add to this the observation Raminder Kaur and Ajay Sinha make in the introduction to their edited anthology on Bollywood, namely, that 'it is well known that non-Indian populations in numerous other parts of the world, extending from Latin America to Africa and the Middle East, the former USSR and even China, also cheered and applauded popular Indian cinema throughout the twentieth century' (Kaur and Sinha 2005: 20). Indeed, one can add to this latter point, 'and into the twenty-first'.[6]

Yet, for all of Kaur and Sinha's titular claims to transnationality, their introduction, too, begins by citing the *Shri 420* lyrics regarding Japanese shoes and an essentially Indian heart (Kaur and Sinha 2005: 11). Though noting the 'globalized cultural economy of Indian film', and Bollywood's introduction of a 'fragmentary process' (where Hollywood, in their view, 'pushes world cultures towards homogenization') and, indeed, 'in its very (sometimes) contentious name ... the crossing of borders', Kaur concludes by claiming that 'in Hindi cinema, India is reinscribed as a hegemonic centre', even as one is literally 'led back to India as the fount of all identities' (Kaur and Sinha 2005: 15, 16, 21; Kaur 2005: 326). This fixation with 'Indianness', however, comes at the same time as Kaur and Sinha and, indeed, most contemporary theorists of Bollywood acknowledge the increasing role of the NRI (non-resident Indian) in the formation of an 'Indian identity' in Bollywood films.[7] Yet rather than seeing this latter figure as potentially reformulating the very notion of an essentialized 'Indianness', Kaur depicts the diasporic subject as 'central not just to economic targets but also to the making of a national, Bollywood cinema' (Kaur 2005: 311).

The theorization of the NRI by Indian and Indo-diasporic scholars, then, in many ways echoes that of 'the Bantu' or 'the Madagascan', by European colonial ethnographers (for example, Mannoni), in which Bollywood becomes 'the umbilical cord that anchors them [NRIs] to their past', even as the NRI paradoxically revivifies the Nation-State or, in this parlance, 'the mother country' (Rao 2001: 159).[8] The NRI, in other words, 'even though born abroad', remains 'essentially an Indian' (Kaur 2005: 323). This is precisely the sentiment behind the oft-quoted lyrics from 'Mera Joota Hai Japani', as well as their consistent quotation by studies of Bollywood. Yet, as these very same critics note, much has changed since 1955. It is not merely that Bollywood films travel around the globe (a phenomenon that, in many ways, was already noticed in the mid-1950s) but how their formatting increasingly displays, like a well-marked passport, imprints of these journeys, that marks this cinema as increasingly transnational, particularly in the so-called digital era.

Pendakur has noted the rise of digital video disc (DVD) technology in the mid-1990s, as well as how this affected the distribution of Bollywood films, claiming that between 1998 and 2001, 'the demand for DVDs of Indian movies grew rapidly and Indian distributors expanded their inventory from 15–20 titles to 15,000 titles' (Pendakur 2003: 45). Though he rightly observes that this new format allowed for 'inclusion of additional information', nowhere is what is perhaps the most crucial feature of this format—by way of underscoring Bollywood's transnationality—mentioned (Pendakur 2003: 46). The feature I have in mind is alternate language tracks. The typical contemporary Bollywood DVD comes formatted with multiple subtitling and audio options. Furthermore, based on a random sampling of recent Bollywood films released on DVD, this opportunity to 'take advantage of the capacity of the medium and to use it in as inventive a way as possible' continues to grow, particularly when compared to other globally disseminated cinemas (Becker, quoted in Crowdus 1999).[9]

In 2003, *Kal Ho Naa Ho* (discussed in Chapter 4) was released on DVD by Yash Raj Productions (itself now a transnational entity with distribution centers around the globe, including in the US), featuring optional subtitles in English, Dutch and Arabic. The following year, *Veer-Zaara* (dir. Yash Chopra, 2004) was released, both theatrically and on DVD (also by Yash Raj Productions), with the latter format featuring optional subtitles in Gujrati, Bengali, English, Spanish, Dutch, Arabic, Tamil, Telugu, Kannada, Malayalam and Hebrew. The following year, the DVD release of the blockbuster, *Bunty aur Babli* (dir. Shaad Ali Sahgal, 2005), also by Yash Raj Productions, featured optional subtitles in all the languages featured on the *Veer-Zaara* disc, save Hebrew but with the addition of French. In two years, in other words, the number of subtitling options saw nearly a fourfold increase. This, combined with Bollywood DVDs' multizone formatting, allows for a greater dissemination and accessing than any other global cinema in circulation today and, furthermore, reveals how the DVD format, as utilized by Bollywood distribution outlets, works to transcend the 'shield-like' regionalism of language,[10] taking full advantage of 'the capacity of the [digital] medium' (Becker, quoted in Crowdus 1999).

In this way, DVD (as utilized by Bollywood) serves as an effective metonym for globalization. This is not simply due to its intrinsically transnational infrastructure but, more precisely, because of how Bollywood has taken advantage of this infrastructure, making Bollywood films literally accessible to multiple audiences around the world. This contemporary element of the Bollywood film underscores its previously noted transnational appeal and also, to return to another earlier point, how 'ownership' of the Bollywood film is made flexible, literally allowing multiple channels of access to its hybrid form.

As for where the films are made, one can see an even earlier indication of Bollywood's inherent transnationality. For whereas Virdi notes that 'transnational locations were not uncommon' in Bollywood films of the 1960s, one can also consistently point to such locations in Bollywood throughout the 1970s, 1980s, 1990s and, indeed, up to the present day (Virdi 2003).[11] It is in relation to the song and dance sequence, too, that another salient point arises, namely, that there are at least two ways of looking at these films: as complete narratives, with a beginning, middle and end (in that order), or as a series of episodes, an ordering further enhanced by the DVD format (which normally 'chapters' a film so as to allow for one to immediately 'jump' to a particular scene in the film).[12] This latter way of receiving the film, even as it offers up a postmodern reworking of the first scenario's rather Aristotelian set-up, is additionally reinforced by the 'onset of cable and satellite television in 1991', through which 'song sequences start airing on the numerous film-based programs on television or appear as commercials between other programs' (Ganti 2002: 295–96). Furthermore, as Anustup Basu has recently noted, due to their independent travel along 'video, cable, and [DVD] circuits', these song sequences 'often seem

to detach themselves from relations of fidelity to the filmic whole',
following what he describes as the '"indifferent" logic of "geotelevisual"
production and dissemination' (Basu 2008: 156).[13] Such an 'altered
media landscape', with its frequent—one might even say, typical—
fragmentation of the Bollywood film, works to rupture the normative
paradigm through which Bollywood cinema continues to be read,
even as it simultaneously works to throw into question who 'owns' the
Bollywood film and how it is literally viewed, particularly since 1991.

A final example of Bollywood's increasingly global reach can be
found in its influence on the aesthetic composition of other contemporary cinemas. Along with the recent instances of a 'Crossover Bollywood' phenomenon stemming from North America and the UK
(discussed in Chapter 5), one can see traces of Bollywood in cinemas
coming from China, Taiwan, Korea, Hong Kong, Egypt, and even in
less ostensibly 'crossover' features from the US.[14] Bollywood, in other
words, rather than encompassing a nation, might more effectively be
seen as possessing a particular aesthetic, one which is essentially hybrid
and transnational, mixing and re-appropriating elements from multiple
sources and redeploying them in a global context, via global media.

While contemporary theorization of this film style continues to
cling to the rather archaic notion of the nation-state as a guide to
meaning, the Bollywood film continues to chart new trajectories and,
in the process, continually re-questions the very concept of 'a national
cinema proper', or of adapting 'appropriately' (and the attendant 'hegemonic authorization of what it means to be a "proper Indian"'), via
a thoroughly improper aesthetic that Sumita Chakravarty has called
'impersonation' (Chakravarty 1993: 4; Ganti 2002: 290; Kaur 2005:
315; Virdi 2003: 7). Yet, as an 'imaginary state'—in a double sense, i.e.,
as a film (and thus 'imaginary' in Metz's sense of the term) and as a national construct—Bollywood, rather than fuelling (let alone fulfilling)
a 'desire for origins', functions as a challenge to this latter construct's
very cognitive rationale (Chakravarty 1993: 3; Hitchcock 2003: 11). It
is precisely in this sense that the emergence of the NRI as a constitutive figure in the theorization of Bollywood 'begs the question' of the
nation-state hegemony, giving, rather than a sating of 'deep roots' that
paradoxically surface through distance, the lie to the very construct
being used to identify Bollywood as a 'national cinema', what Patricia
Uberoi calls 'the caricature of the nostalgic NRI' (Uberoi 1998: 328).

It is indeed 'too glib' to assume that Bollywood enacts a 'religious-like nostalgia for people of the Indian diaspora', just as it is equally dubious to assume that the films making up this corpus provide '"a shared culture" that links everyone who is ethnically Indian' (Kaur 2005: 313–14). Yet, it is equally problematic to continually insert 'the Nation' into the space of the discussion concerning Bollywood, as if the former were an inescapable point of entry for the latter. Just as there are 'qualitatively different levels of engagement' with film (as a discourse), one can argue that the Bollywood film's formatting con-taminates the narrative proper with its own hybridity (Kaur 2005: 321). Or, paradoxically, the perpetual referencing by Bollywood films, particularly in song and dance sequences, of reference-less (because over-referenced) moments and spaces—what one could call the 'music video-ization' of the film form—works to reformulate attendant con-ceptions of national identity rooted in a telos that, in practical terms, may very well be severed from its allegedly internal components when circulated transnationally.

Rather than clinging to the half-century-old notion of Raj Kapoor in Japanese shoes with an Indian soul, one can reassess the 'dil' of Bollywood by closely examining not only its structure but how it is transmitted—in other words, 'how cultural expression and commodity circulation can share the rubric of cultural transnationalism within the same cognitive space' (Hitchcock 2003: 25). Reframing Bollywood in this manner allows precisely for the possibility that the very shifting terrain of identity formation as a form of cultural expression can no longer be projected onto the cinema (as national formation) but rather implies a reversal: from making Bollywood the convenient scapegoat for reactionary nationalist strains, to seeing it as the vanguard of a transnational approach to popular cinema.

NOTES

1. This national imaginary, Virdi contends, 'is sustained in no small part by ... Hindi cinema' (Virdi 2003: 28).
2. The film is Raj Kapoor's *Shri 420* (Mr. 420) and the lyrics from the song, 'Mera Joota Hai Japani', are, 'Mera joota hai japani, ye patloon englishstani, Sar pe lal topi russi, phir bhi dil hai Hindustani' (My shoes are Japanese, these pants are English, On my head, a red Russian hat, and yet my heart is still Indian).

3. Just a few lines further, Ganti claims her goal is 'to bypass the dichotomies that have characterized the study of Hindi cinema' (Ganti 2002).

4. See Ganti (2002, 298, n. 1).

5. As Ganti notes, 'Audiences are portrayed as monolithic only in the case of Indianization' (Ganti 2002: 299, n. 17).

6. As Yves Thoraval notes: 'Commercial Indian cinema has had a marked influence on Egyptian cinema', as well as in places 'as diverse as Iran, the Maghreb, Indonesia, Salalah in Oman, or Mukalla in South Yemen ... or Kassala in Sudan, Asmara in Eritrea, Uzbekistan, Cambodia, or Syria' (Thoraval 2000: ix). Brian Larkin (1997) has also noted Bollywood's popularity in Nigeria, while Narmala Halstead (2005) has noted its popularity in Guyana; Thomas Blom Hansen (2005), its popularity in South Africa; and Christiane Brosius (2005), its reception in Germany. Furthermore, Pendakur has noted the number of Bollywood films distributed outside of India, including in the Arabian Gulf, Sri Lanka, Burma, the UK and Ireland, the Fiji Islands, Singapore, Mauritius, Tanzania, the Maldives, Kenya, Malaysia, Djibouti, Sanna, the West Indies, Gambia and Liberia (Pendakur 2003: 23).

7. Kaur notes, 'Venturing into the third millennium, the overseas market [for Bollywood] is less of an afterthought for it has the potential to bring in substantial earnings to filmmakers and distributors' (Kaur 2005: 310).

8. One crucial difference between the likes of Mannoni and the current theorists of Bollywood is that, in the latter instance, we have a rather stark case of self-orientalizing by critics whose very critical distance from their so-called subjects belies the uniform notion of 'Indianness'.

9. It should also be noted that Bollywood DVDs are multizone, i.e., come formatted to play in all regions. They, thus, have a Code '0', for universal play, as opposed to Hollywood (American) DVDs and, for that matter, European DVDs, which normally come specifically formatted for operation in only one zone, namely, their own. Thus, at the literal (or digital) level of formatting, Bollywood DVDs are transnational. Bollywood DVDs also tend to be released, or become available, almost immediately after the film's theatrical release.

10. See Pendakur 2003: 25.

11. The most typical instances of such a transnational aesthetic are in the song and dance numbers, which may typically 'jump' from one location to another with no diegetic logic or even a semblance of explanation. For more on this, see Chapter 2. Ganti also notes that 'many Hindi films have song sequences shot in Europe, North America, or Australia' (Ganti 2002: 298, n. 9).

12. Bollywood DVDs also typically come formatted with song menus, further enhancing this form of episodic viewing.

13. Basu describes 'geotelevisuality' as 'the projection and reception of images, sounds, and words through worldwide distances, across territorial, cultural, linguistic, and religious frontiers' (Basu 2008: 157).

14. Some recent examples of films displaying such traces include *The World* (2004), *The Wayward Cloud* (2005), *Inside Man* (2006) and *Slumdog Millionaire* (2008).

Bibliography

Ahmad, A. 1992. *In Theory: Classes, Nations, Literatures*. London: Verso.

Appadurai, A. 1996. *Modernity at Large: Cultural Dimensions of Globalization*. Minneapolis: University of Minnesota Press.

———. (ed.). 2001. *Globalization*. Durham: Duke University Press.

Appadurai, A. and C. Breckenridge. 1991. 'Marriage, Migration and Money: Mira Nair's Cinema of Displacement', *Visual Anthropology* 4(1): 95–102.

Armes, R. 1987. *Third World Filmmaking and the West*. Berkeley: University of California Press.

Arnold, A. 1991. *Hindi Film Git: On the History of Commercial Indian Popular Music*. Ann Arbor: UMI Press.

Bad Object-Choices (ed.). 1991. *How Do I Look?: Queer Film and Video*. Seattle: Bay Press.

Barnouw, E. and S. Krishnaswamy. 1980. *Indian Film*. New York: Oxford University Press.

Barthes, R. 1975. *The Pleasure of the Text*. New York: Farrar, Straus & Giroux.

Basu, A. 2008. 'The Music of Intolerable Love: Political Conjugality in Mani Ratnam's *Dil Se*', in S. Gopal and S. Moorti (eds), *Global Bollywood: Travels of Hindi Song and Dance*, pp. 153–76. Minneapolis: University of Minnesota Press.

Baudrillard, J. 1983. *Simulations*. New York: Semiotext(e).

———. 1987. *Forget Foucault*. New York: Semiotext(e).

Baudry, J.-L. 1992. 'The Apparatus: Metapsychological Approaches to the Impression of Reality in Cinema', in G. Mast, M. Cohen and L. Braudy (eds), *Film Theory and Criticism: Introductory Readings*, pp. 690–707. New York: Oxford University Press.

Benjamin, W. 1966. *Understanding Brecht*. London: Verso Editions.

———. 1988. 'The Work of Art in the Age of Mechanical Reproduction', in H. Arendt (ed.), *Illuminations*, pp. 217–52. New York: Schocken Books.

Bhabha, H. 1989. 'The Commitment to Theory', in J. Pine and P. Willemen (eds), *Questions of Third Cinema*, pp. 111–32. London: BFI.

———. 1990a. 'Introduction: Narrating the Nation', in H. Bhabha (ed.), *Nation and Narration*, pp. 1–7. New York: Routledge Press.

———. 1990b. 'The Third Space', in J. Rutherford (ed.), *Identity, Community, Culture, Difference*, pp. 207–21. London: Lawrence & Wishart.

———. 1994. *The Location of Culture*. New York: Routledge Press.

Bharucha, R. 1990. *Theatre and the World: Performance and the Politics of Culture*. New York: Routledge Press.

148   Reframing Bollywood

Bharucha, R. 2000. *The Politics of Cultural Practice: Thinking through Theatre in an Age of Globalization*. Hanover, NH: Wesleyan University Press.

Bhaskaran, S. 2002. 'The Politics of Penetration: Section 377 of the Indian Penal Code', in R. Vanita (ed.), *Queering India: Same-Sex Love and Eroticism in Indian Culture and Society*, pp. 15–29. New York: Routledge.

Bordwell, D. 1997. *On the History of Film Style*. Cambridge, MA: Harvard University Press.

Bordwell, D. and K. Thompson. 2004. *Film Art: An Introduction*. New York: McGraw-Hill.

Bose, D. 2006. *Brand Bollywood: A New Global Entertainment Order*. New Delhi: Sage Publications.

Bourdieu, P. 1991. *Language and Symbolic Power*. Cambridge: Harvard University Press.

Brantley, B. 2004. 'Coloring by the Numbers', *New York Times*, 30 April.

Brecht, B. 1957. *Brecht on Theatre*. London: Methuen.

Breckenridge, C. and P. van der Veer (eds). 1993. *Orientalism and the Postcolonial Predicament: Perspectives on South Asia*. Philadelphia: University of Pennsylvania Press.

Brosius, C. 2005. 'The Scattered Homelands of the Migrant: Bollyworld through the Diasporic Lens', in R. Kaur and A. Sinha (eds), *Bollyworld: Popular Indian Cinema through a Transnational Lens*, pp. 207–38. New Delhi: Sage Publications.

Butler, J. 1986. 'Sex and Gender in Simone de Beauvoir's Second Sex', *Yale French Studies* 72(3): 35–49.

———. 1990. *Gender Trouble: Feminism and the Subversion of Identity*. New York: Routledge.

———. 1993. *Bodies That Matter: On the Discursive Limits of 'Sex'*. New York: Routledge.

———. 2004. 'Imitation and Gender Insubordination', in S. Salih and J. Butler (eds), *The Judith Butler Reader*, pp. 119–37. Malden, MA: Blackwell Publishing.

Cesaire, A. 1955. *Discourse on Colonialism*. New York: Monthly Review Press.

Chakravarty, S. 1993. *National Identity in Indian Popular Cinema, 1947–1987*. Austin: University of Texas Press.

———. 1999. 'Can the Subaltern Weep? Mourning as Metaphor in *Rudaali* (The Crier)', in D. Robin and I. Jaffe (eds), *Redirecting the Gaze: Gender, Theory, and Cinema in the Third World*, pp. 283–306. Albany: State University of New York Press.

Chappell, T.D.J. (ed.). 1996. *The Plato Reader*. Edinburgh: Edinburgh University Press.

Chaudhuri, S. 2005. *Contemporary World Cinema: Europe, the Middle East, East Asia and South Asia*. Edinburgh: Edinburgh University Press.

Creekmur, C. 2001. 'Picturizing American Cinema: Hindi Film Songs and the Last Days of Genre', in P. Wojcik and A. Knight (eds), *Soundtrack Available: Essays on Film and Popular Music*, pp. 375–406. Durham: Duke University Press.

———. 2006. 'Popular Hindi Cinema and the Film Song', in L. Badley, R. Palmer and S. Schneider (eds), *Traditions in World Cinema*, pp. 193–202. New Brunswick, NJ: Rutgers University Press.

Crowdus, G. 1999. 'Providing a Film Archive for the Home Viewer: An Interview with Peter Becker of the Criterion Collection', *Cineaste* 25(1): 47–50.

Dargis, M. 2005. 'Mr. Darcy and Lalita, Singing and Dancing', *New York Times*, 11 February.

Das Gupta, C. 1981. *Talking about Films*. New Delhi: Orient Longman.

———. 1983. 'The "New" Cinema: A Wave or a Future?', in A. Vasudev and P. Lenglet (eds), *Indian Cinema Superbazaar*, pp. 39–49. New Delhi: Vikas.

Denby, D. 2005. 'The Film File: Bride and Prejudice', *The New Yorker*, 81(3), 7 March.

Desai, J. and R. Dudrah. 2008. 'The Essential Bollywood', in R. Dudrah and J. Desai (eds), *The Bollywood Reader*, pp. 1–17. New York: McGraw-Hill.

Devy, G.N., G.V. Davis and K.K. Chakravarty (eds). 2010. *Ethnographies*. New Delhi: Orient Blackswan.

Dick, P. 1969. *Do Androids Dream of Electric Sheep?* New York: Signet.

Dickey, S. 1993. *Cinema and the Urban Poor in South India*. New York: Cambridge University Press.

Dissanayake, W. 2003. 'Rethinking Indian Popular Cinema: Towards Newer Frames of Understanding', in A. Guneratne and W. Dissanayake (eds), *Rethinking Third Cinema*, pp. 202–25. New York: Routledge.

Dissanayake, W. and K.M. Gokulsing. 1998. *Indian Popular Cinema: A Narrative of Cultural Change*. Stoke on Trent: Trentham Books.

Doty, Alexander. 1993. *Making Things Perfectly Queer: Interpreting Mass Culture*. Minneapolis: University of Minnesota Press.

———. 1995. 'There's Something Queer Here', in C. Creekmur and A. Doty (eds), *Out in Culture: Gay, Lesbian, and Queer Essays on Popular Culture*, pp. 71–90. Durham: Duke University Press.

DuBois, W.E.B. 1989. *The Souls of Black Folk*. New York: Bantam.

Dudrah, R. 2006. *Bollywood: Sociology Goes to the Movies*. New Delhi: Sage Publications.

Durbin, K. 2004. 'The Class Acts', *New York Times*, 4 November.

Dwyer, R. 2000. *All You Want Is Money, All You Need Is Love: Sexuality and Romance in Modern India*. London: Cassell.

Dwyer, R. and C. Pinney (eds). 2001. *Pleasure and the Nation: The History, Politics and Consumption of Public Culture in India*. New Delhi: Oxford University Press.

Dwyer, R. and D. Patel. 2002. *Cinema India: The Visual Culture of Hindi Film*. New Brunswick: Rutgers University Press.

Eck, D. 1998. *Darsan: Seeing the Divine Image in India*. New York: Columbia University Press.

Elsaesser, T. and A. Barker. 1990. *Early Cinema: Space-Frame-Narrative*. London: BFI.

Eng, D. and A. Hom (eds). 1998. *Q & A: Queer in Asian America*. Philadelphia: Temple University Press.

Fanon, F. 1952. *Black Skin, White Masks*. New York: Grove Weidenfeld.

———. 1965. *A Dying Colonialism*. New York: Grove.

Feuer, J. 1982. *The Hollywood Musical*. Bloomington: Indiana University Press.

———. 1993. *The Hollywood Musical*, 2nd edn. Bloomington: Indiana University Press.

Foucault, M. 1990. *The History of Sexuality, Volume 1: An Introduction*. New York: Vintage.

———. 1998. 'What Is an Author?', in J. Faubion (ed.), *Essential Works of Foucault, 1954–1984*, Vol. 2, pp. 205–22. New York: The New Press.

Gabriel, T. 1989a. 'Towards a Critical Theory of Third World Films', in J. Pine and P. Willemen (eds), *Questions of Third Cinema*, pp. 30–52. London: BFI.

———. 1989b. 'Third Cinema as Guardian of Popular Memory: Towards a Third Aesthetics', in J. Pine and P. Willemen (eds), *Questions of Third Cinema*, pp. 53–64. London: BFI.

Ganti, T. 2002. '"And Yet My Heart Is Still Indian": The Bombay Film Industry and the (H) Indianization of Hollywood', in F. Ginsburg, L. Abu-Lughod and B. Larkin (eds), *Media Worlds: Anthropology on New Terrain*, pp. 281–300. Berkeley: University of California Press.

Garfinkel, H. 1967. *Studies in Ethnomethodology*. Englewood, NJ: Prentice-Hall.

Gehlawat, A. 2004. 'Pressing Buttons: The Use of Media in the Classroom', *Community Review* 18(1): 105–07.

Geraghty, C. 2006. 'Jane Austen Meets Gurinder Chadha: Hybridity and Intertexuality in *Bride and Prejudice*', *South Asian Popular Culture* 4(2): 163–68.

Gillespie, M. 1995a. 'Sacred Serials, Devotional Viewing, and Domestic Worship: A Case-study in the Interpretation of Two TV Versions of *The Mahabharata* in a Hindu Family in West London', in R. Allen (ed.), *To be continued ... Soap Operas around the World*, pp. 354–80. London: Routledge.

———. 1995b. *Television, Ethnicity and Cultural Change*. New York: Routledge.

Girard, R. 1972. *Deceit, Desire, and the Novel: Self and Others in Literary Structure*. Baltimore: Johns Hopkins University Press.

Gopal, S. and B. Sen. 2008. 'Inside and Out: Song and Dance in Bollywood Cinema', in R. Dudrah and J. Desai (eds), *The Bollywood Reader*, pp. 147–57. New York: McGraw-Hill.

Gopal, S. and S. Moorti (eds). 2008. *Global Bollywood: Travels of Hindi Song and Dance*. Minneapolis: University of Minnesota Press.

Gopalan, L. 2002. *Cinema of Interruptions: Action Genres in Contemporary Indian Cinema*. London: BFI.

Gopinath, G. 2000. 'Queering Bollywood: Alternative Sexualities in Popular Indian Cinema', in A. Grossman (ed.), *Queer Asian Cinema: Shadows in the Shade*, pp. 283–97. Binghamton, NY: Harrington Park Press.

———. 2005. *Impossible Desires: Queer Diasporas and South Asian Public Cultures*. Durham: Duke University Press.

Gunning, T. 1995. 'An Aesthetic of Astonishment: Early Film and the (In)Credulous Spectator', in L. Williams (ed.), *Viewing Positions: Ways of Seeing Film*, pp. 114–33. New Brunswick, NJ: Rutgers University Press.

Halstead, N. 2005. 'Belonging and Respect Notions vis-à-vis Modern East Indians: Hindi Movies in the Guyanese East Indian Diaspora', in R. Kaur and A. Sinha (eds), *Bollyworld: Popular Indian Cinema through a Transnational Lens*, pp. 3261–83. New Delhi: Sage Publications.

Hansen, K. 1992. *Grounds for Play: The Nautanki Theatre of North India*. Berkeley: University of California Press.

Hansen, T. 2005. 'In Search of the Diasporic Self: Bollywood in South Africa', in R. Kaur and A. Sinha (eds), *Bollyworld: Popular Indian Cinema through a Transnational Lens*, pp. 239–60. New Delhi: Sage Publications.

Hanson, E. (ed.). 1999. *Out Takes: Essays on Queer Theory and Film*. Durham: Duke University Press.

Hardy, J. 2002. *Bollywood Boy*. London: John Murray Publishers.

Hawley, J. and S. Goswami. 1981. *At Play with Krishna: Pilgrimage Dramas from Brindavan*. Princeton: Princeton University Press.

Hitchcock, P. 2003. *Imaginary States: Studies in Cultural Transnationalism*. Urbana: University of Illinois Press.

———. 2007. 'Niche Cinema, or *Kill Bill* with *Shaolin Soccer*', in G. Marchetti and T. Kam (eds), *Hong Kong Film, Hollywood and New Global Cinema: No Film is an Island*, pp. 219–32. New York: Routledge.

Hogan, P. 2008. *Understanding Indian Movies: Culture, Cognition, and Cinematic Imagination*. Austin: University of Texas Press.

Jaikumar, P. 2003. 'Bollywood Spectaculars', *World Literature Today* 77(3/4): 24–29.

Jameson, F. 1986. 'Third World Literature in an Era of Multinational Capitalism', *Social Text* 15: 65–88.

———. 1988. 'Postmodernism and Consumer Society', in E. Kaplan (ed.), *Postmodernism and Its Discontents: Theories, Practices*, pp. 13–29. New York: Verso.

Jameson, F. 1991. *Postmodernism, or the Cultural Logic of Late Capitalism*. Durham: Duke University Press.

——. 1992. *The Geopolitical Aesthetic: Cinema and Space in the World System*. Bloomington: Indiana University Press.

Jameson, F. and M. Miyoshi (eds). 1998. *The Cultures of Globalization*. Durham: Duke University Press.

John, M. and J. Nair (eds). 2000. *A Question of Silence: The Sexual Economies of Modern India*. New York: St. Martin's Press.

Kabir, N. 2001. *Bollywood: The Indian Cinema Story*. London: Channel 4 Books.

Kakar, S. 1983. 'The Cinema as Collective Fantasy', in A. Vasudev and P. Lenglet (eds), *Indian Cinema Superbazaar*, pp. 88–97. New Delhi: Vikas.

——. 1989. *Intimate Relations: Exploring Indian Sexuality*. Chicago: University of Chicago Press.

Kaplan, E. (ed.). 1988. *Postmodernism and Its Discontents: Theories, Practices*. New York: Verso.

Kapoor, R. 1978. 'Let People Come to See Zeenat's Tits', *India Today*. Available at http://www.indiatoday.com/itoday/20070702/60-78to82.html (accessed on 18 March 2010).

Kaur, R. 2005. 'Cruising on the *Vilayeti* Bandwagon: Diasporic Representations and Reception of Popular Indian Movies', in R. Kaur and A. Sinha (eds), *Bollyworld: Popular Indian Cinema through a Transnational Lens*, pp. 309–28. New Delhi: Sage Publications.

Kaur, R. and A. Sinha. 2005. 'Bollyworld: An Introduction to Popular Indian Cinema through a Transnational Lens', in R. Kaur and A. Sinha (eds), *Bollyworld: Popular Indian Cinema through a Transnational Lens*, pp. 11–32. New Delhi: Sage Publications.

Kavi, A. 2000. 'The Changing Image of the Hero in Hindi Films', in A. Grossman (ed.), *Queer Asian Cinema*, pp. 307–12. Binghamton, NY: Harrington Park Press.

Kavoori, A. and A. Punathambekar (eds). 2008. *Global Bollywood*. New York: New York University Press.

Kazmi, F. 1999. *The Politics of India's Conventional Cinema: Imaging a Universe, Subverting a Multiverse*. New Delhi: Sage Publications.

Keith, A. 1924. *The Sanskrit Drama in Its Origins, Development, Theory and Practices*. Oxford: Clarendon Press.

Khilnani, S. 1998. *The Idea of India*. New York: Farrar, Straus, Giroux.

La Bruce, B. 1995. 'Pee Wee Herman: The Homosexual Subtext', in C. Creekmur and A. Doty (eds), *Out in Culture: Gay, Lesbian, and Queer Essays on Popular Culture*, pp. 382–88. Durham: Duke University Press.

Larkin, B. 1997. 'Indian Films and Nigerian Lovers: Media and the Creation of Parallel Modernities', *Africa* 67(3): 406–40.

Lazarus, N. 2004a. 'Fredric Jameson on "Third-World Literature": A Qualified Defence', in D. Kellner and S. Homer (eds), *Fredric Jameson: A Critical Reader*, pp. 42–61. New York: Palgrave Macmillan.

——. (ed.). 2004b. *The Cambridge Companion to Postcolonial Literary Studies*. Cambridge: Cambridge University Press.

Lent, J. et al. (eds). 1990. *The Asian Film Industry*. Austin: University of Texas Press.

Lutgendorf, P. 1992. 'Indian Theatre and Inside-Outsider', *The Drama Review* 36(4): 162–171.

Lutze, L. 1985. 'From Bharata to Bombay: Change in Continuity in Hindi Film Aesthetics', in L. Lutze and B. Pfleiderer (eds), *The Hindi Film: Agent and Re-agent of Cultural Change*, pp. 3–15. New Delhi: Manohar.

MacCannell, D. 1976. *The Tourist: A New Theory of the Leisure Class*. New York: Schocken Books.

Martin-Jones, D. 2006. 'Kabhi India Kabhie Scotland: Recent Indian Films Shot on Location in Scotland', *South Asian Popular Culture* 4(1): 49–60.

Mathews, J. 2005. 'A Beautiful Bride', *New York Daily News*, 10 February.

Mazumdar, R. 2007. *Bombay Cinema: An Archive of the City*. Minneapolis: University of Minnesota Press.

McLuhan, M. 1964. *Understanding Media: The Extensions of Man*. New York: McGraw-Hill.

Metz, C. 1982. *The Imaginary Signifier: Psychoanalysis and the Cinema*. Bloomington: Indiana University Press.

Michaux, H. 1986. *A Barbarian in Asia*. New York: New Directions.

Miller, T. 2005. 'Introduction to Part IV: Media Production and Consumption', in A. Abbas and J. Erni (eds), *Internationalizing Cultural Studies: An Anthology*, pp. 227–31. Oxford: Blackwell Publishing.

Mishra, V. 2002. *Bollywood Cinema: Temples of Desire*. New York: Routledge.

Mitra, A. 1993. *Television and Popular Culture in India: A Study of the Mahabharat*. New Delhi: Sage Publications.

Mulvey, L. 1975. 'Visual Pleasure and Narrative Cinema', *Screen* 16(3): 6–18.

Nandy, A. 1981. 'The Popular Hindi Film: Ideology and First Principles', *India International Centre Quarterly* 8(1): 89–96.

——. 1995. *The Savage Freud and Other Essays on Possible and Retrievable Selves*. New Delhi: Oxford University Press.

——. (ed.). 1998. *The Secret Politics of Our Desires: Innocence, Culpability, and Indian Popular Cinema*. New York: St. Martin's Press.

Nayar, S. 2004. 'Invisible Representation: The Oral Contours of a National Popular Cinema', *Film Quarterly* 57(3): 13–23.

Nunberg, G. (ed.). 1996. *The American Heritage Dictionary of the English Language*, 3rd edn. Boston: Houghton Mifflin Company.

Pendakur, M. 1990. 'India', in J. Lent, G. Semsel, K. McDonald, M. Pendakur (eds), *The Asian Film Industry*, pp. 229–52. Austin: University of Texas Press.

——. 2003. *Indian Popular Cinema: Industry, Ideology and Consciousness*. Cresskill, NJ: Hampton Press.

Pfister, M. 1988. *The Theory and Analysis of Drama*. Cambridge: Cambridge University Press.

Pines, J. and P. Willemen (eds). 1989. *Questions of Third Cinema*. London: BFI.

Prakash, S. 1983. 'Music, Dance and the Popular Films: Indian Fantasies, Indian Repressions', in A. Vasudev and P. Lenglet (eds), *Indian Cinema Superbazaar*, pp. 114–18. New Delhi: Vikas.

Prasad, M. 1998. *Ideology of the Hindi Film: A Historical Construction*. New York: Oxford University Press.

——. 2003. 'This Thing Called Bollywood'. Available at www.india-seminar.com/2003/525/525%20madhava%20prasad.htm (accessed on 31 March 2004).

——. 2008. 'Surviving Bollywood', in A. Kavoori and A. Punathambekar (eds), *Global Bollywood*, pp. 41–51. New York: New York University Press.

Pratt, M. 1992. *Imperial Eyes: Travel Writing and Transculturation*. New York: Routledge.

Rajadhyaksha, A. 1989. 'Debating the Third Cinema', in J. Pines and P. Willemen (eds), *Questions of Third Cinema*, pp. 170–78. London: BFI.

——. 2000. 'Viewership and Democracy in the Cinema', in R. Vasudevan (ed.), *Making Meaning in Indian Cinema*, pp. 267–96. New Delhi: Oxford University Press.

Rajadhyaksha, A. 2008. 'The "Bollywoodization" of the Indian Cinema: Cultural Nationalism in a Global Arena', in A. Kavoori and A. Punathambekar (eds), *Global Bollywood*, pp.
17–40. New York: New York University Press.

Rajadhyaksha, A. and P. Willemen (eds). 1999. *Encyclopaedia of Indian Cinema*. London:
BFI.

Rao, M. 2001. 'Heart of the Movie', in L. Joshi (ed.), *Bollywood: Popular Indian Cinema*, pp.
137–69. London: Dakini.

Rao, R. 2000. 'Memories Pierce the Heart: Homoeroticism, Bollywood-Style', in A. Grossman
(ed.), *Queer Asian Cinema*, pp. 299–306. Binghamton, NY: Harrington Park Press.

Ray, S. 1976. *Our Films, Their Films*. New Delhi: Orient Longman.

Renan, E. 1990. 'What is a Nation?', in H. Bhabha (ed.), *Nation and Narration*, pp. 8–22.
New York: Routledge.

Richmond, F., D. Swann and P. Zarrilli (eds). 1990. *Indian Theatre: Traditions of Performance*.
Honolulu: University of Hawaii Press.

Saari, A. 1985. 'Concepts of Aesthetics and Anti-aesthetics in the Contemporary Hindi
Film', in L. Lutze and B. Pfleiderer (eds), *The Hindi Film: Agent and Re-agent of Cultural
Change*, pp. 16–28. New Delhi: Manohar.

Said, E. 1978. *Orientalism*. New York: Vintage.

Sarkar, K. 1975. *Indian Cinema Today: An Analysis*. New Delhi: Sterling.

Sarkar, S. 2002. *Beyond Nationalist Frames: Postmodernism, Hindu Fundamentalism, History*. New
Delhi: Permanent Black.

Savran, D. 2003. *A Queer Sort of Materialism: Recontextualizing American Theater*. Ann Arbor:
University of Michigan.

Searle, J. 1983. *Intentionality: An Essay in the Philosophy of Mind*. Cambridge: Cambridge University Press.

Sedgwick, E. 1985. *Between Men: English Literature and Male Homosocial Desire*. New York:
Columbia University Press.

———. 1990. *Epistemology of the Closet*. Berkeley: University of California Press.

Shekar, R. and K. Sahai. 2004. 'Koodiyattam', *Housecalls* 5–6(1): 19.

Shohat, E. and R. Stam. 1994. *Unthinking Eurocentrism: Multiculturalism and the Media*. New
York: Vintage.

Shulman, P. 2004. 'Dear Reader, Elizabeth Has Returned. And She's Wearing a Sari', *New
York Times*, 7 November.

Singh, M. 1983. 'Technique as an Ideological Weapon', in A. Vasudev and P. Lenglet (eds),
Indian Cinema Superbazaar, pp. 119–25. New Delhi: Vikas.

Singhal, A. and E. Rogers. 2001. *India's Communication Revolution: From Bullock Carts to Cyber
Marts*. New Delhi: Sage Publications.

Skinner, B. 1968. *The Technology of Teaching*. New York: Meredith Corporation.

Spivak, G. 1987. *In Other Worlds: Essays in Cultural Politics*, p. 152. New York: Methuen.

———. 1988a. 'Can the Subaltern Speak?', in L. Grossberg and C. Nelson (eds), *Marxism and
the Interpretation of Culture*, pp. 271–313. Urbana: University of Illinois Press.

———. 1988b. 'Subaltern Studies: Deconstructing Historiography', in R. Guha and Spivak
(eds), *Selected Subaltern Studies*, pp. 3–32. New York: Oxford University Press.

———. 1990a. 'Poststructuralism, Marginality, Postcoloniality and Value', in P. Collier and
H. Geyer-Ryan (eds), *Literary Theory Today*, pp. 219–44. Ithaca, NY: Cornell University
Press.

Spivak, G. 1990b. *The Post-colonial Critic: Interviews, Strategies, Dialogues*, ed. S. Harasym. New York: Routledge.

——. 1993. *Outside in the Teaching Machine*. New York: Routledge Press.

——. 1996. 'How to Teach a "Culturally Different" Book', in D. Landry and G. MacLean (eds), *The Spivak Reader*, pp. 238–66. New York: Routledge.

——. 1999. *A Critique of Postcolonial Reason: Toward a History of the Vanishing Present*. Cambridge, MA: Harvard University Press.

——. 2002. 'Righting Wrongs', in N. Owens (ed.), *Human Rights, Human Wrongs*, pp. 164–227. Oxford: Oxford University Press.

Stam, R. 1985. *Reflexivity in Film and Literature: From Don Quixote to Jean-Luc Godard*. Ann Arbor: UMI Research Press.

——. 1989. *Subversive Pleasures: Bakhtin, Cultural Criticism, and Film*. Baltimore: Johns Hopkins University Press.

Straayer, C. 1995. 'The Hypothetical Lesbian Heroine in Narrative Feature Film', in C. Creekmur and A. Doty (eds), *Out in Culture: Gay, Lesbian, and Queer Essays on Popular Culture*, pp. 44–59. Durham: Duke University Press.

——. 1996. *Deviant Eyes, Deviant Bodies: Sexual Re-orientation in Film and Video*. New York: Columbia University Press.

Thomas, R. 1995. 'Melodrama and the Negotiation of Morality in Mainstream Hindi Film', in C. Breckenridge (ed.), *Consuming Modernity: Public Culture in a South Asian World*, pp. 157–82. Minneapolis: University of Minnesota Press.

Thoraval, Y. 2000. *The Cinemas of India, 1896–2000*. New Delhi: Macmillan.

Tillis, S. 1999. *Rethinking Folk Drama*. Westport, CT: Greenwood Press.

Timmons, H. and H. Kumar. 2009. 'India Court Overturns Gay Sex Ban', *New York Times*, 2 July.

Trinh, T. 1989. *Woman, Native, Other*. Bloomington: Indiana University Press.

——. 1991. *When the Moon Waxes Red: Representation, Gender, and Cultural Politics*. New York: Routledge.

Trivedi, H. 2008. 'From Bollywood to Hollywood: The Globalization of Hindi Cinema', in R. Krishnaswamy and J. Hawley (eds), *The Postcolonial and the Global*, pp. 200–210. Minneapolis: University of Minnesota Press.

Uberoi, P. 1998. 'The Diaspora Comes Home: Disciplining Desire in *DDLJ*', *Contributions to Indian Sociology* 32(2): 305–36.

Valicha, K. 1988. *The Moving Image: A Study of Indian Cinema*. Bombay: Orient Longman.

Vanita, R. (ed.). 2002. *Queering India: Same-Sex Love and Eroticism in Indian Culture and Society*. New York: Routledge.

Vasudev, A. and P. Lenglet (eds). 1983. *Indian Cinema Superbazaar*. New Delhi: Vikas.

Vasudevan, R. (ed.). 2000a. *Making Meaning in Indian Cinema*. New Delhi: Oxford University Press.

——. 2000b. 'The Politics of Cultural Address in a "Transitional" Cinema', in C. Gledhill and L. Williams (eds), *Reinventing Film Studies*, pp. 130–64. New York: Oxford University Press.

Virdi, J. 2003. *The Cinematic ImagiNation: Indian Popular Films as Social History*. New Delhi: Permanent Black.

Virdi, J. and C. Creekmur. 2006. 'India: Bollywood's Global Coming of Age', in A. Ciecko (ed.), *Contemporary Asian Cinema: Popular Culture in a Global Frame*, pp. 133–43. New York: Berg.

Waugh, T. 2001. 'Queer Bollywood, or "I'm the Player, You're the Naïve One"', in M. Tinkcom and A. Villarejo (eds), *Keyframes: Popular Cinema and Cultural Studies*, pp. 280-97. London: Routledge.

Williams, L. 1989. *Hard Core: Power, Pleasure and the 'Frenzy of the Visible'*. Berkeley: University of California Press.

——. (ed.). 1995. *Viewing Positions: Ways of Seeing Film*. New Brunswick: Rutgers University Press.

Williams, R. 1975. *Television: Technology and Cultural Form*. New York: Schocken Books.

——. 1977. *Marxism and Literature*. Oxford: Oxford University Press.

Willis, A. 2003. 'Locating Bollywood: Notes on the Hindi Blockbuster, 1975 to the Present', in J. Stringer (ed.), *Movie Blockbusters*, pp. 255-68. London: Routledge.

Filmography

A Star is Born. Dir. George Cukor. Perf. Judy Garland, James Mason, Jack Carson. Warner Bros., 1954.

Aa Ab Laut Chalen. Dir. Rishi Kapoor. Perf. Aishwarya Rai and Akshay Khanna. Eros Entertainment, 1999.

Anand. Dir. Hrishikesh Mukherjee. Perf. Rajesh Khanna and Amitabh Bachchan. Digital Entertainment Inc. (DEI), 1971.

Anari. Dir. K. Muralimohana Rao. Perf. Karisma Kapoor and Venkatesh. Spark Worldwide, 1993.

Balle Balle! Amritsar to L.A. Dir. Gurinder Chadha. Perf. Aishwarya Rai and Martin Henderson. Sony BMG, 2004.

Bobby. Dir. Raj Kapoor. Perf. Dimple Kapadia and Rishi Kapoor. Yash Raj Films, 1973.

Bollywood/Hollywood. Dir. Deepa Mehta. Perf. Rahul Khanna and Lisa Ray. Cinebella, 2002.

Bride and Prejudice. Dir. Gurinder Chadha. Perf. Aishwarya Rai and Martin Henderson. Miramax, 2004.

Bunty aur Babli. Dir. Shaad Ali Sahgal. Perf. Abhishek Bachchan, Rani Mukherjee, Amitabh Bachchan.Yash Raj Films, 2005.

Devdas. Dir. Bimal Roy. Perf. Dilip Kumar, Vyjayanthimala, Suchitra Sen. Mohan Films, 1955.

Dil. Dir. Indra Kumar. Perf. Aamir Khan and Madhuri Dixit. Maruti International, 1990.

Dil Se... Dir. Mani Ratnam. Perf. Shah Rukh Khan, Manisha Koirala, Preity Zinta. India Talkies, 1998.

Dilwale Dulhania Le Jayenge. Dir. Aditya Chopra. Perf. Shah Rukh Khan and Kajol. Yash Raj Films, 1995.

Dostana. Dir. Raj Khosla. Perf. Amitabh Bachchan and Shatrughan Sinha. Dharma Productions, 1980.

Dostana. Dir. Tarun Mansukhani. Perf. Abhishek Bachchan and John Abraham. Yash Raj Films, 2008.

Ek Duje ke Liye. Dir. K. Balachander. Perf. Kamal Hassan and Rati Agnihotri. Prasad Productions, 1981.

Genesis. Dir. Mrinal Sen. Perf. Shabana Azmi, Naseeruddin Shah, Om Puri. International Film Circuit, 1986.

Gigi. Dir. Vincente Minnelli. Perf. Leslie Caron and Maurice Chevalier. MGM, 1958.

Grease. Dir. Randal Kleiser. Perf. Olivia Newton-John and John Travolta. Paramount Pictures, 1978.

Guide. Dir. Vijay Anand. Perf. Dev Anand and Waheeda Rehman. Eros, 1965.

Inside Man. Dir. Spike Lee. Perf. Denzel Washington, Clive Owen, Jodie Foster. Universal, 2006.

Julie. Dir. K.S. Sethumadhavan. Perf. Lakshmi Narayan and Vikram. DEI, 1975.

Kabhi Kabhie. Dir. Yash Chopra. Perf. Amitabh Bachchan, Rakhee. Yash Raj Films, 1976.

Kabhi Khushi, Kabhie Gham. Dir. Karan Johar. Perf. Shah Rukh Khan, Kajol, Hrithik Roshan, Kareena Kapoor. Yash Raj Films, 2001.

Kal Ho Naa Ho. Dir. Nikhil Advani. Perf. Shah Rukh Khan, Saif Ali Khan, Preity Zinta. Dharma Productions, 2003.

Love Story. Dir. Rajendra Kumar. Perf. Kumar Gaurav and Vijayata Pandit. Bombino Video Pvt. Ltd., 1981.

Main Azad Hun. Dir. Tinu Anand. Perf. Amitabh Bachchan and Shabana Azmi. Apollo Video, 1989.

Main Khiladi Tu Anari. Dir. Sameer Malkan. Perf. Saif Ali Khan and Akshay Kumar. Eros, 1994.

Maine Pyar Kiya. Dir. Sooraj Barjatya. Perf. Salman Khan and Bhagyashree. DEI, 1989.

Muqaddar ka Sikandar. Dir. Prakash Mehra. Perf. Amitabh Bachchan, Vinod Khanna, Rakhee, Rekha. Eros, 1978.

Namak Haram. Dir. Hrishikesh Mukherjee. Perf. Amitabh Bachchan and Rajesh Khanna. Worldwide Entertainment Group (WEG), 1973.

Naseeb. Dir. Manmohan Desai. Perf. Amitabh Bachchan and Hema Malini. Aasia Films Pvt. Ltd., 1981.

Parvarish. Dir. Manmohan Desai. Perf. Amitabh Bachchan and Vinod Khanna. Eros, 1977.

Pennies from Heaven. Dir. Herbert Ross. Perf. Steve Martin and Bernadette Peters. MGM, 1981.

Qayamat Se Qayamat Tak. Dir. Mansoor Khan. Perf. Aamir Khan and Juhi Chawla. Eros, 1988.

Qurbani. Dir. Feroz Khan. Perf. Feroz Khan, Vinod Khanna, Zeenat Aman. Eros, 1980.

Roti, Kapada aur Makaan. Dir. Manoj Kumar. Perf. Manoj Kumar and Zeenat Aman. DEI, 1974.

Sangam. Dir. Raj Kapoor. Perf. Raj Kapoor, Rajendra Kumar, Vyjayanthimala. R.K. Films Ltd., 1964.

Sasural. Dir. T. Prakash Rao. Perf. Rajendra Kumar and Saroja Devi. Yash Raj Films, 1961.

Satyam Shivam Sundaram. Dir. Raj Kapoor. Perf. Zeenat Aman and Shashi Kapoor. R.K. Films Ltd., 1978.

Sholay. Dir. Ramesh Sippy. Perf. Dharmendra and Amitabh Bachchan. Eros International, 1975.

Shri 420. Dir. Raj Kapoor. Perf. Nargis and Raj Kapoor. R.K. Films Ltd., 1955.

Singin' in the Rain. Dir. Stanley Donen and Gene Kelly. Perf. Gene Kelly and Debbie Reynolds. MGM, 1952.

Silsila. Dir. Yash Chopra. Perf. Amitabh Bachchan, Rekha, Shashi Kapoor. Yash Raj Films, 1981.

Slumdog Millionaire. Dir. Danny Boyle. Perf. Dev Patel and Freida Pinto. Fox Searchlight Pictures, 2008.

The Guru. Dir. Daisy von Scherler Mayer. Perf. Jimi Mistry and Heather Graham. Universal, 2002.

The Love Parade. Dir. Ernst Lubitsch. Perf. Maurice Chevalier and Jeanette MacDonald. Paramount, 1929.

The Pirate. Dir. Vincente Minnelli. Perf. Judy Garland and Gene Kelly. MGM, 1948.

The Wayward Cloud. Dir. Tsai Ming-liang. Perf. Kang-sheng Lee and Shiang-chyi Chen. Deltamac Co. Ltd., 2005.

The World. Dir. Jia Zhangke. Perf. Tao Zhao, Taisheng Chen, Jue Jing. Zeitgeist Films, 2004.

There'll Always Be Stars in the Sky: The Indian Film Music Phenomenon. Dir. Jeremy Marre. Channel 4 Productions, 1983.

Trishul. Dir. Yash Chopra. Perf. Amitabh Bachchan, Shashi Kapoor, Poonam Dhillon. Trimurti Films, 1978.

Tu Chor Main Sipahi. Dir. Guddu Dhanoa. Perf. Akshay Kumar and Saif Ali Khan. Eros, 1996.

Une Femme est Une Femme. Dir. Jean-Luc Godard. Perf. Anna Karina, Jean-Claude Brialy, Jean-Paul Belmondo. Pathé, 1961.

Veer-Zaara. Dir. Yash Chopra. Perf. Shah Rukh Khan, Preity Zinta, Rani Mukherjee. Yash Raj Films, 2004.

West Side Story. Dir. Jerome Robbins and Robert Wise. Perf. Natalie Wood and Richard Beymer. MGM, 1961.

Yaarana. Dir. Rakesh Kumar. Perf. Amitabh Bachchan and Amjad Khan. AK Movies, 1981.

Yolanda and the Thief. Dir. Vincente Minnelli. Perf. Fred Astaire and Lucille Bremer. MGM, 1945.

Zanjeer. Dir. Prakash Mehra. Perf. Amitabh Bachchan and Pran. DEI, 1973.

Index

About the Author

Ajay Gehlawat is Assistant Professor of Theatre and Film in the Hutchins School of Liberal Studies at Sonoma State University, the US. Previously, he also taught at the City University of New York and at Pratt Institute, New York, the US. He is the author of numerous articles on contemporary issues in film studies, postcolonial theory and popular culture.